# Skip·Beat!☆

Shojo Beat

# Skip·Beat!

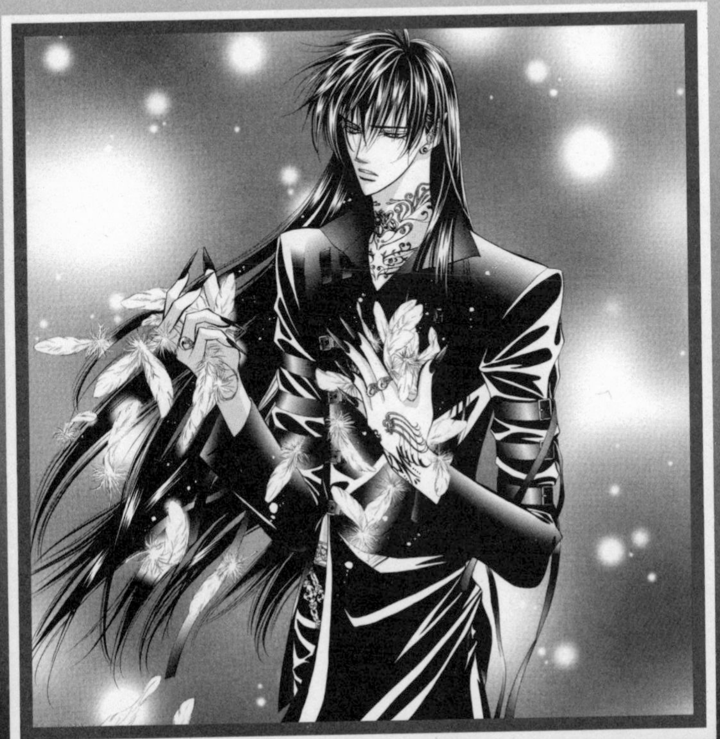

8

Story & Art by Yoshiki Nakamura

# Skip·Beat!

**Volume 8**

## CONTENTS

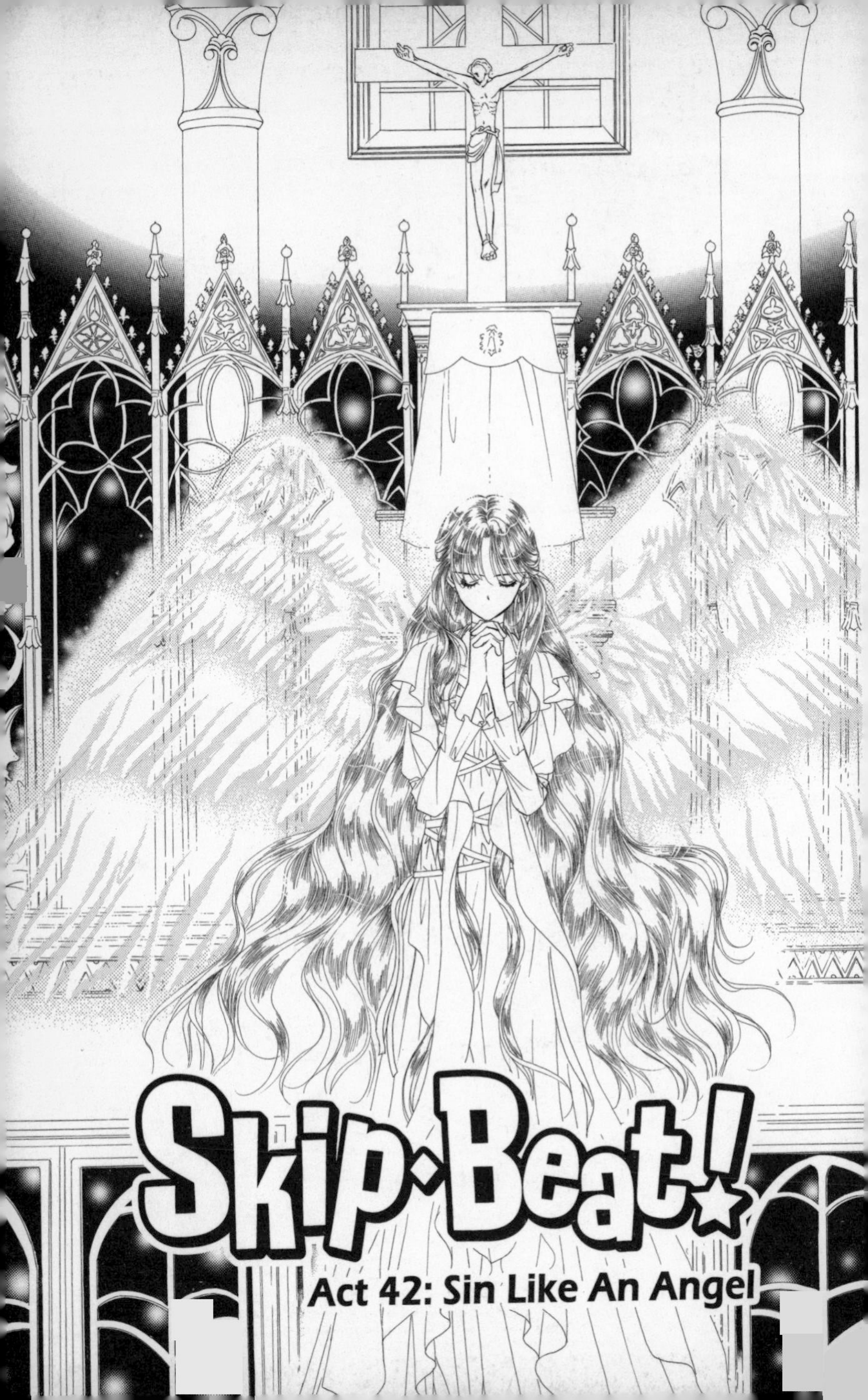
Skip·Beat!
Act 42: Sin Like An Angel

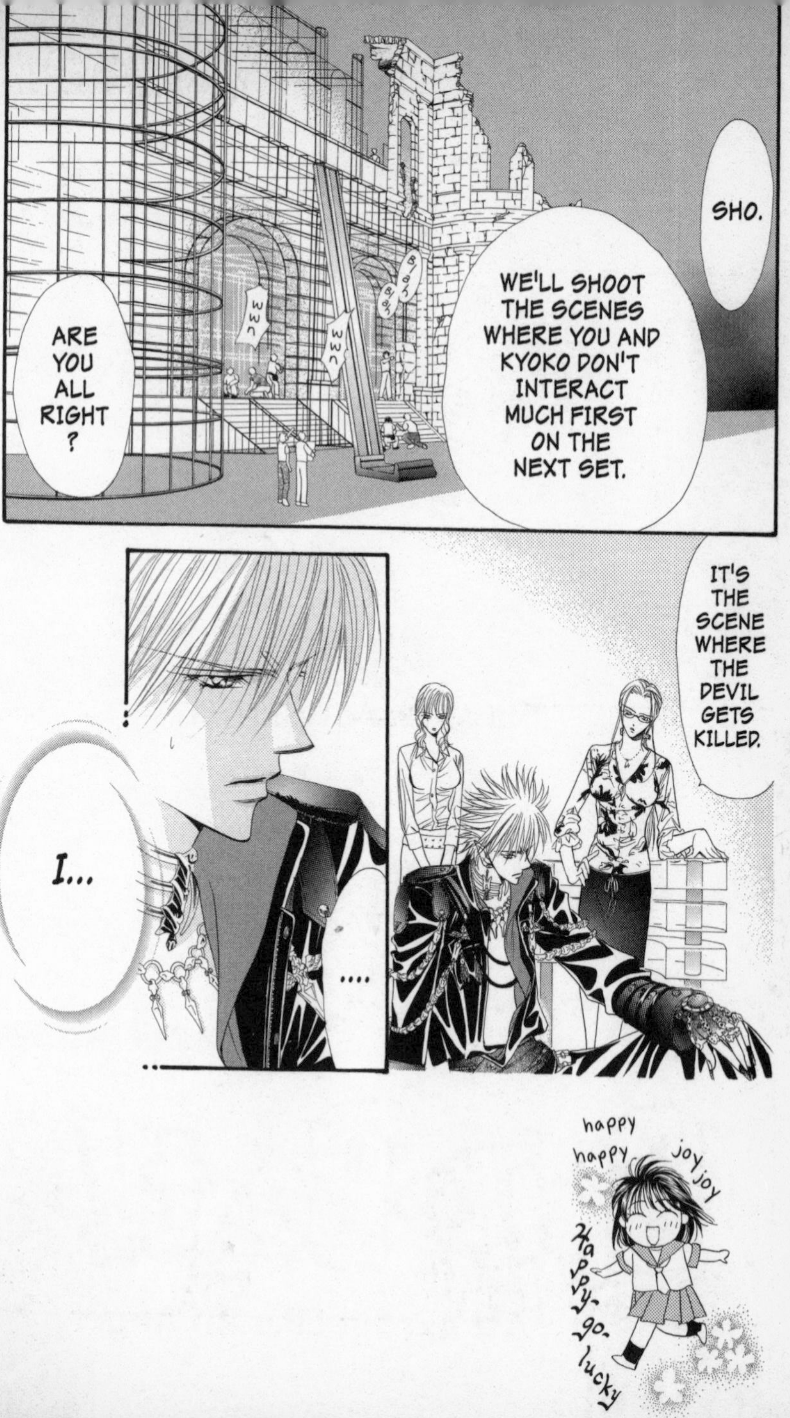
SHO.
WE'LL SHOOT THE SCENES WHERE YOU AND KYOKO DON'T INTERACT MUCH FIRST ON THE NEXT SET.
Blah Blah
ARE YOU ALL RIGHT?
IT'S THE SCENE WHERE THE DEVIL GETS KILLED.
....
I...
happy happy joy joy
Happy-go-lucky

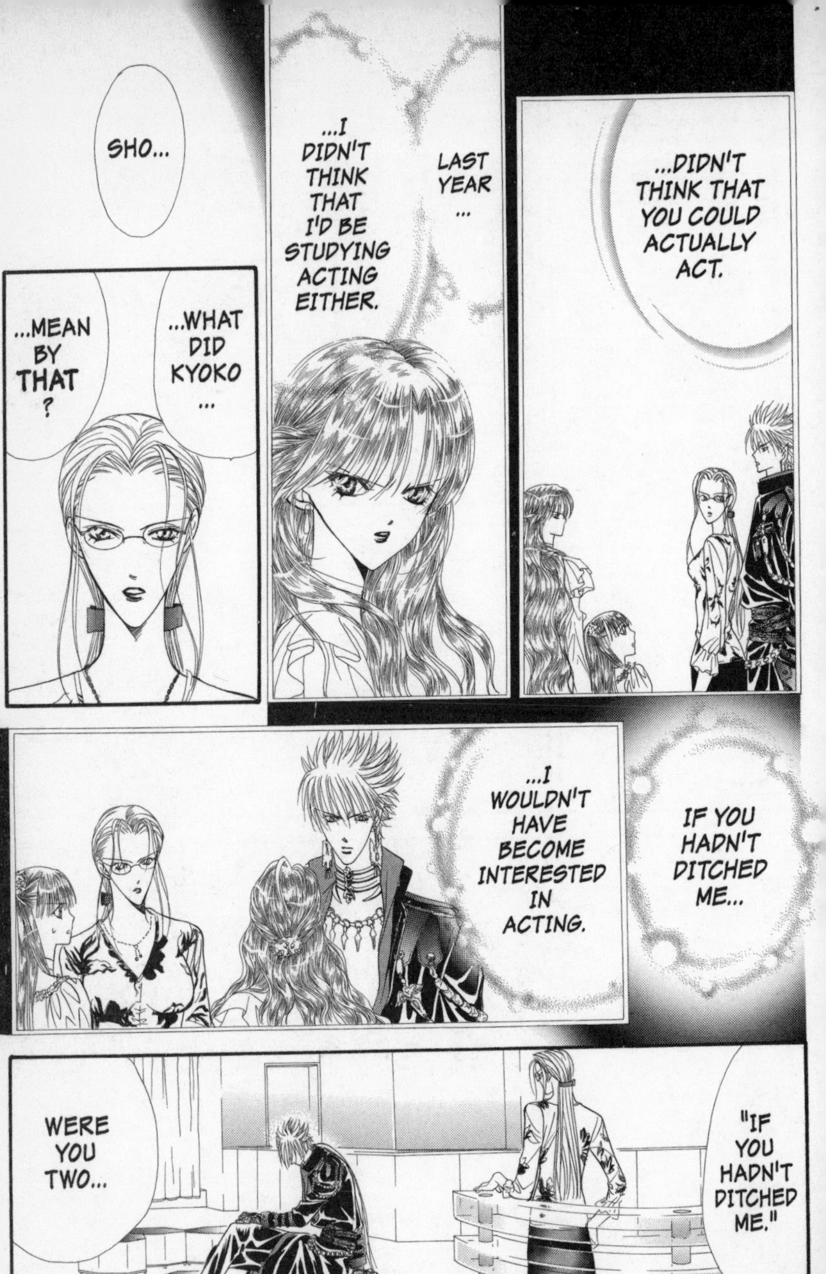
...DIDN'T THINK THAT YOU COULD ACTUALLY ACT.
LAST YEAR...
...I DIDN'T THINK THAT I'D BE STUDYING ACTING EITHER.
SHO...
...WHAT DID KYOKO...
...MEAN BY THAT?
IF YOU HADN'T DITCHED ME...
...I WOULDN'T HAVE BECOME INTERESTED IN ACTING.
"IF YOU HADN'T DITCHED ME."
WERE YOU TWO...

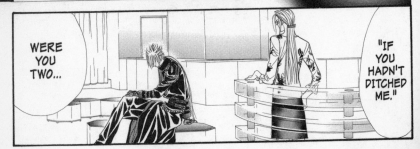

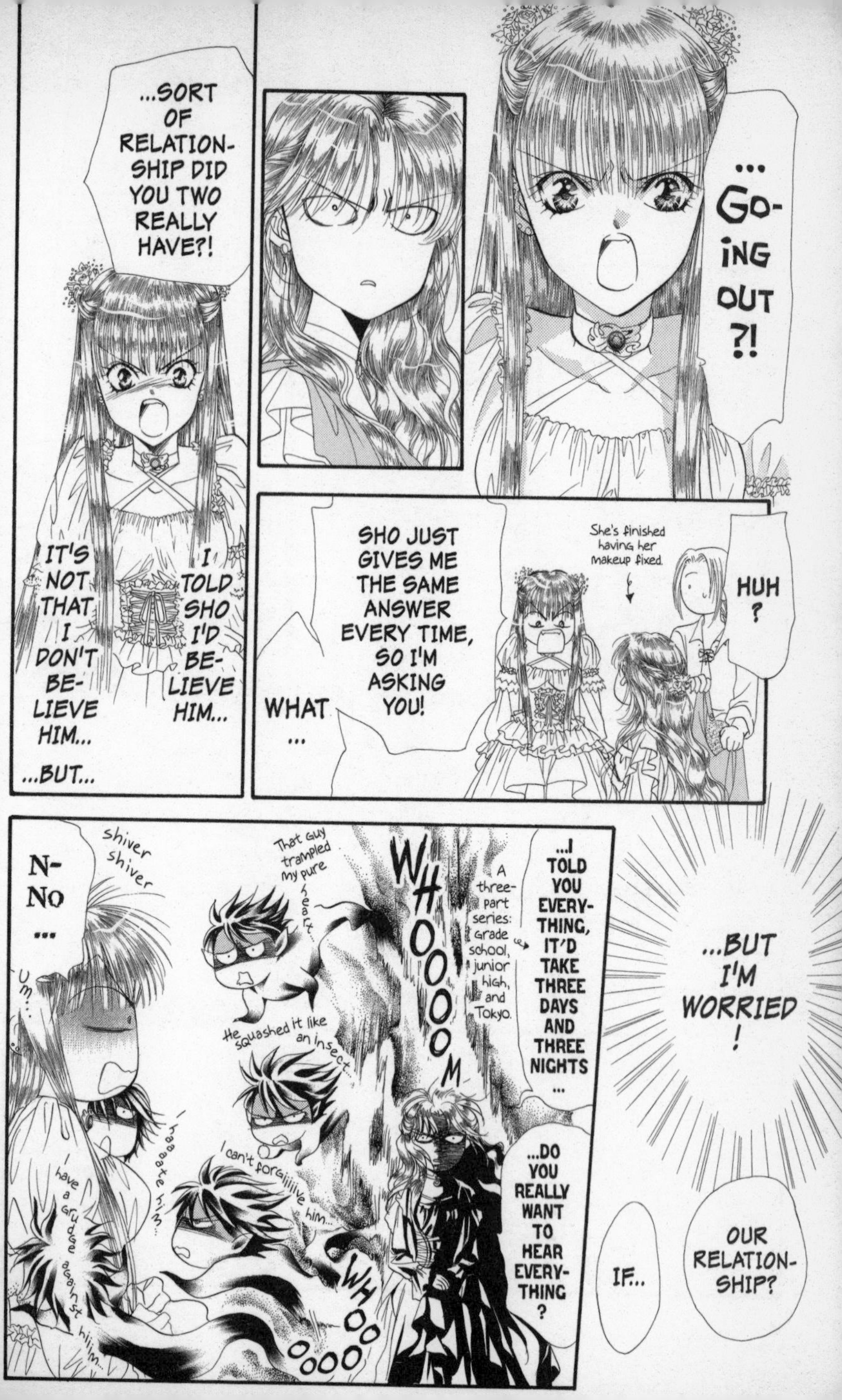
...GO-ING OUT?!
HUH?
She's finished having her makeup fixed.
SHO JUST GIVES ME THE SAME ANSWER EVERY TIME, SO I'M ASKING YOU!
WHAT...
...SORT OF RELATION-SHIP DID YOU TWO REALLY HAVE?!
I TOLD SHO I'D BE-LIEVE HIM...
IT'S NOT THAT I DON'T BE-LIEVE HIM...
...BUT...
...BUT I'M WORRIED!
OUR RELATION-SHIP?
IF...
...I TOLD YOU EVERY-THING, IT'D TAKE THREE DAYS AND THREE NIGHTS...
A three-part series: Grade school, junior high, and Tokyo.
...DO YOU REALLY WANT TO HEAR EVERY-THING?
WHOOOOOM
WHOOOOOO
That guy trampled my pure heart...
He squashed it like an insect...
I can't forgiiiiive him...
I haaaate him...
I have a grudge against hiiim...
shiver shiver
N-No...
Um...

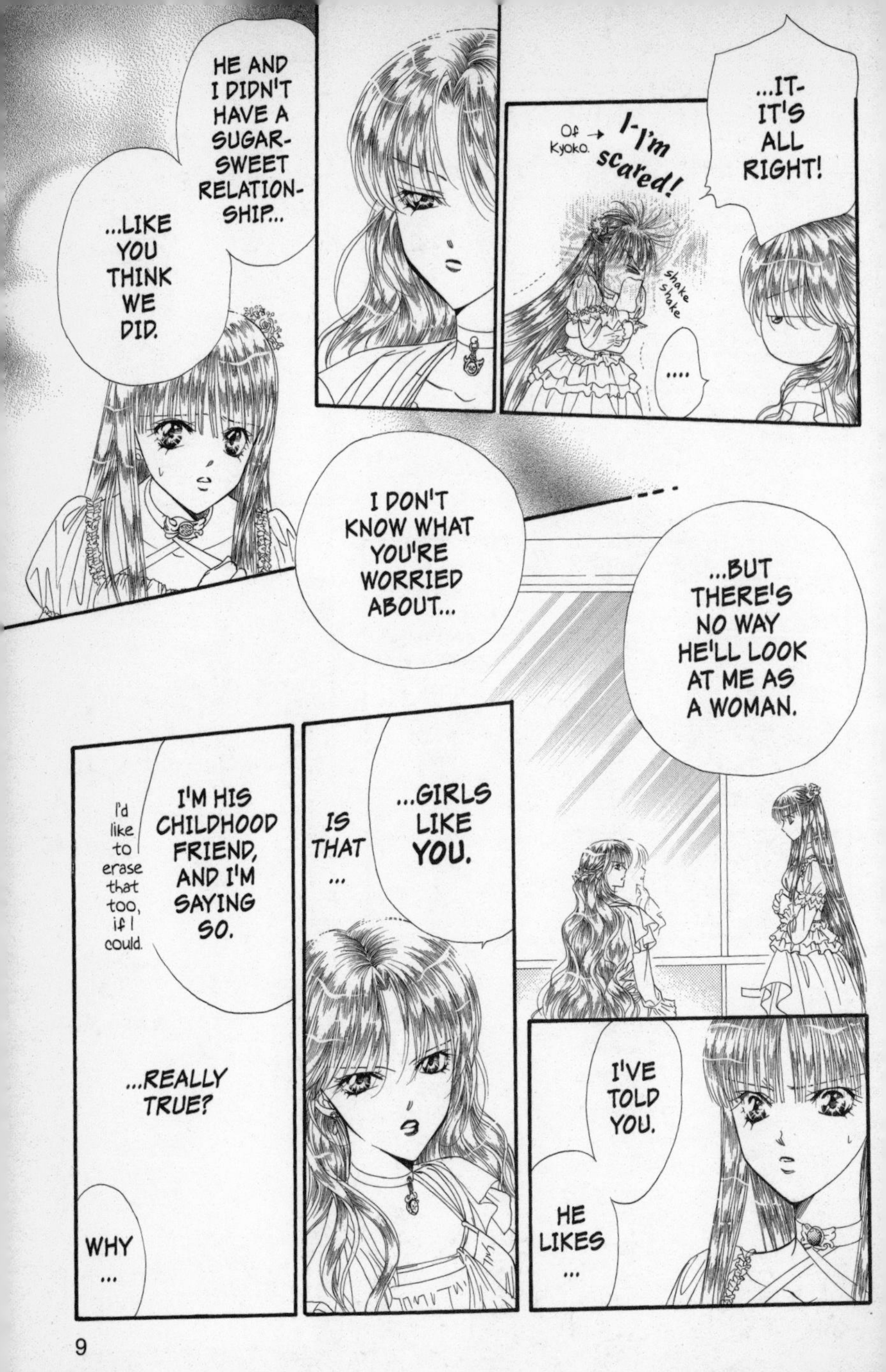
...IT- IT'S ALL RIGHT!
I-I'm scared!
Of Kyoko.
shake shake
....
HE AND I DIDN'T HAVE A SUGAR-SWEET RELATIONSHIP...
...LIKE YOU THINK WE DID.
I DON'T KNOW WHAT YOU'RE WORRIED ABOUT...
...BUT THERE'S NO WAY HE'LL LOOK AT ME AS A WOMAN.
I'VE TOLD YOU.
HE LIKES ...
...GIRLS LIKE YOU.
IS THAT ...
I'M HIS CHILDHOOD FRIEND, AND I'M SAYING SO.
I'd like to erase that too, if I could.
...REALLY TRUE?
WHY ...

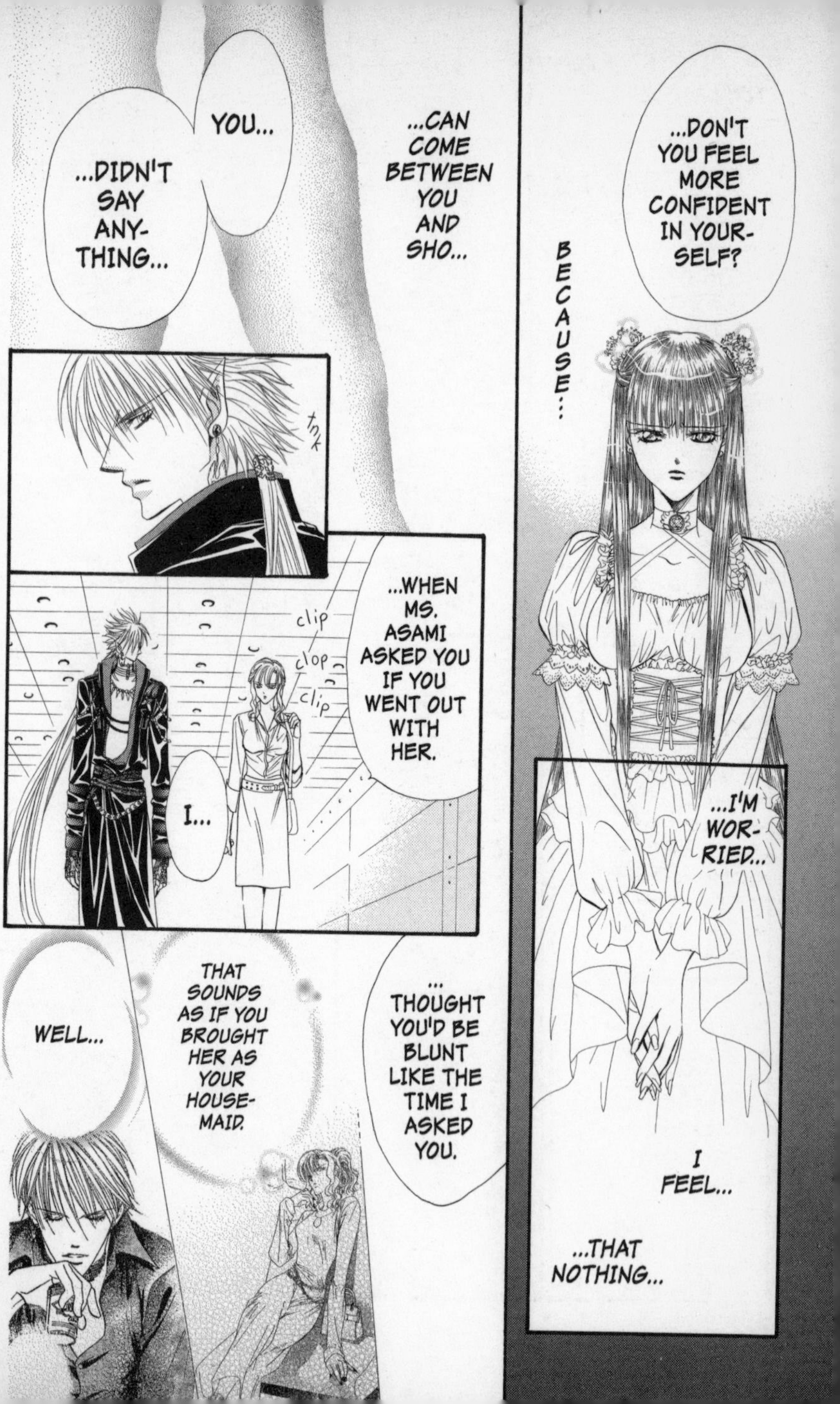
...DON'T YOU FEEL MORE CONFIDENT IN YOUR-SELF?
BECAUSE...
...I'M WOR-RIED...
I FEEL...
...THAT NOTHING...
...CAN COME BETWEEN YOU AND SHO...
YOU...
...DIDN'T SAY ANY-THING...
tnk
...WHEN MS. ASAMI ASKED YOU IF YOU WENT OUT WITH HER.
clip
clop
clip
I...
...THOUGHT YOU'D BE BLUNT LIKE THE TIME I ASKED YOU.
THAT SOUNDS AS IF YOU BROUGHT HER AS YOUR HOUSE-MAID.
WELL...

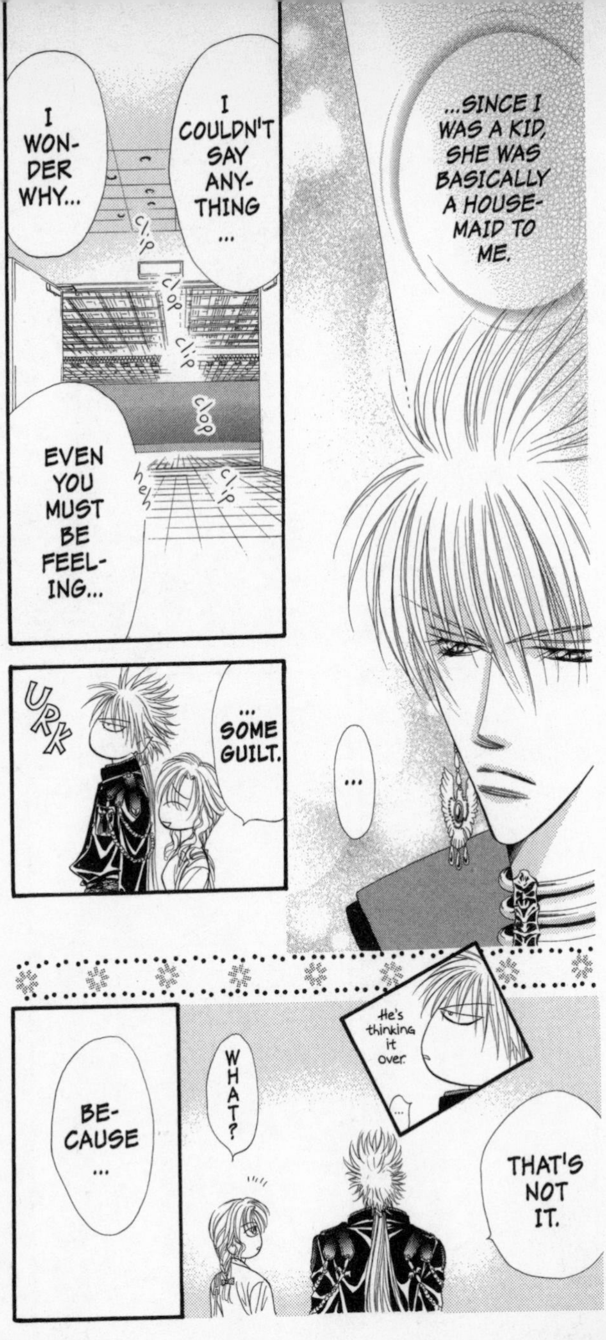
...SINCE I WAS A KID, SHE WAS BASICALLY A HOUSE-MAID TO ME.
...
I COULDN'T SAY ANY-THING ...
I WON-DER WHY...
clip clop clip clop clip
heh
EVEN YOU MUST BE FEEL-ING...
... SOME GUILT.
URK
He's thinking it over.
...
THAT'S NOT IT.
WHAT?
BE-CAUSE ...

## Greetings

Hello. I'm Nakamura. In Volume 7, the sad result was that the only new illustration was the one on the title page. I'm really sorry... ...But this time, my schedule is really tight too (It's my fault. I take too much time doing my storyboards, penciling, and inking ) I believe that my editor would like me not to draw that much new stuff for Volume 8 too, if possible... ...therefore...I won't try to fill all the blank spaces like always...I'll just draw stuff that comes out naturally... Yes...the title page illustration. That was supposed to be included last time. I'd done the penciling, but didn't time to finish it. While I was drawing it, I thought that it looks like a character from a shonen manga that was really popular once... (No...I've never read the manga or watched the anime...)

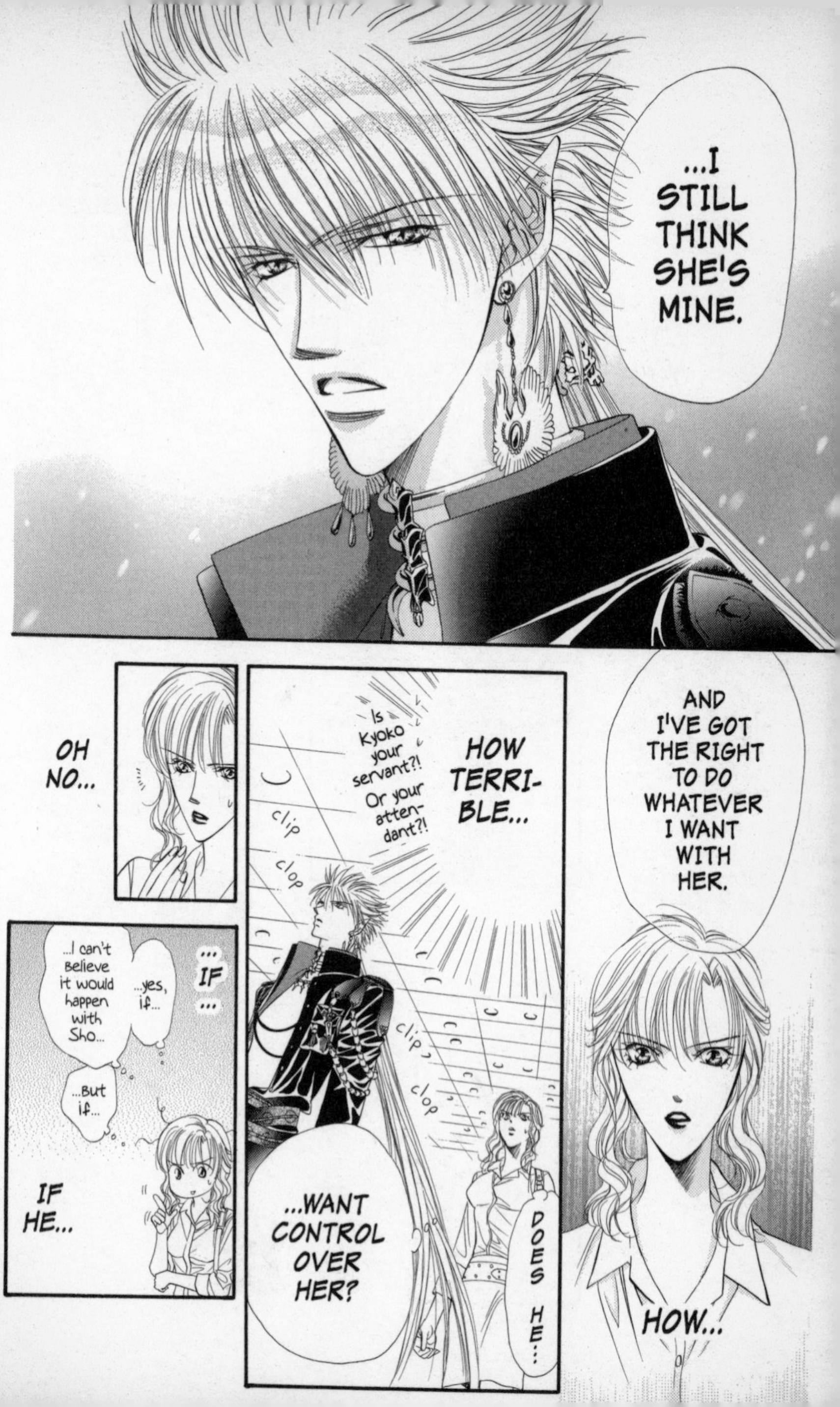
...I STILL THINK SHE'S MINE.
AND I'VE GOT THE RIGHT TO DO WHATEVER I WANT WITH HER.
HOW...
HOW TERRIBLE...
Is Kyoko your servant?! Or your attendant?!
clip
clop
clip
clop
DOES HE...
...WANT CONTROL OVER HER?
OH NO...
...IF...
...yes, if...
...I can't believe it would happen with Sho...
...but if...
IF HE...

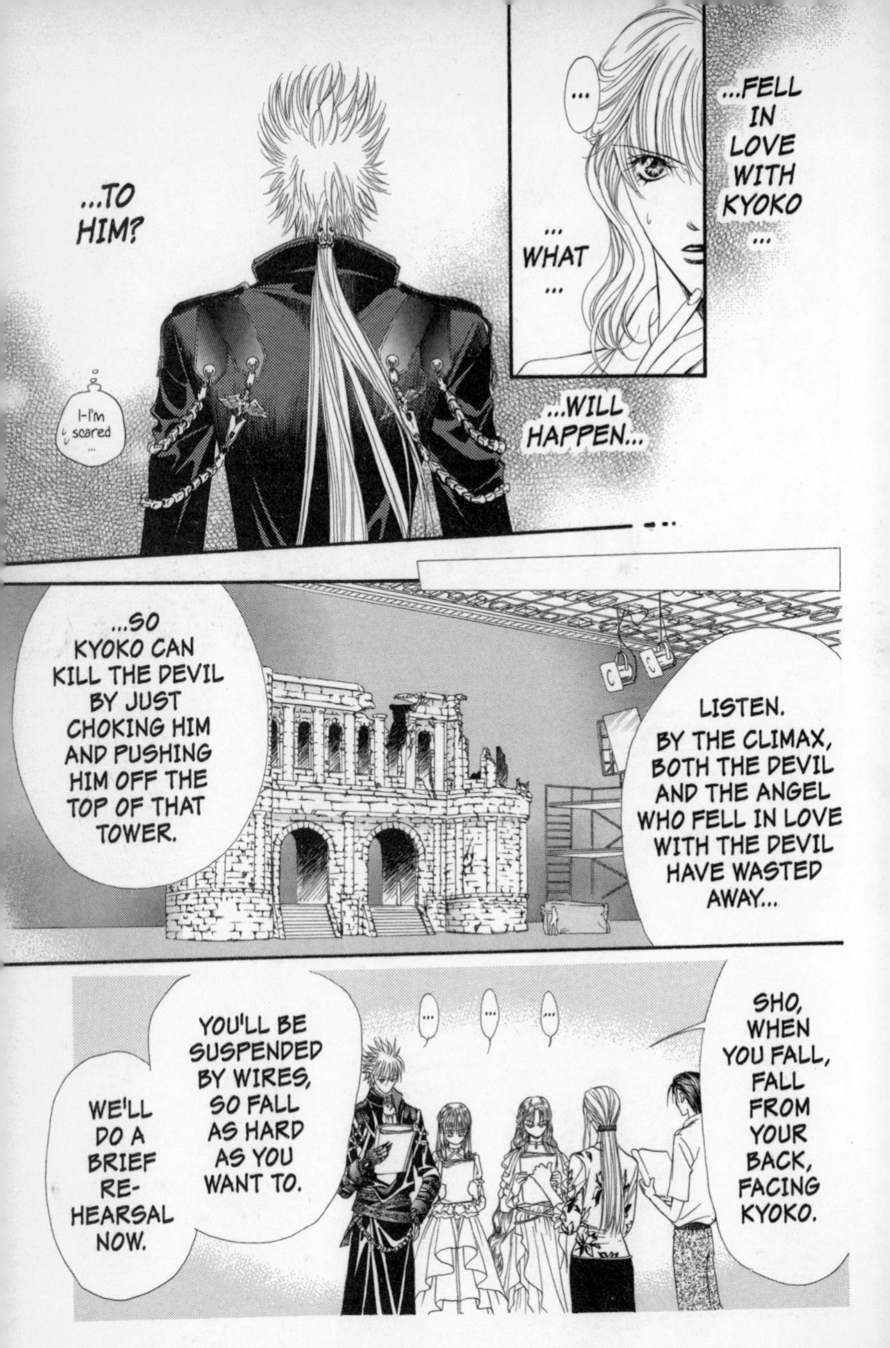
...
...FELL IN LOVE WITH KYOKO ...
... WHAT ...
...WILL HAPPEN...
...TO HIM?
I-I'm scared ...
LISTEN. BY THE CLIMAX, BOTH THE DEVIL AND THE ANGEL WHO FELL IN LOVE WITH THE DEVIL HAVE WASTED AWAY...
...SO KYOKO CAN KILL THE DEVIL BY JUST CHOKING HIM AND PUSHING HIM OFF THE TOP OF THAT TOWER.
SHO, WHEN YOU FALL, FALL FROM YOUR BACK, FACING KYOKO.
...
...
...
YOU'LL BE SUSPENDED BY WIRES, SO FALL AS HARD AS YOU WANT TO.
WE'LL DO A BRIEF RE-HEARSAL NOW.

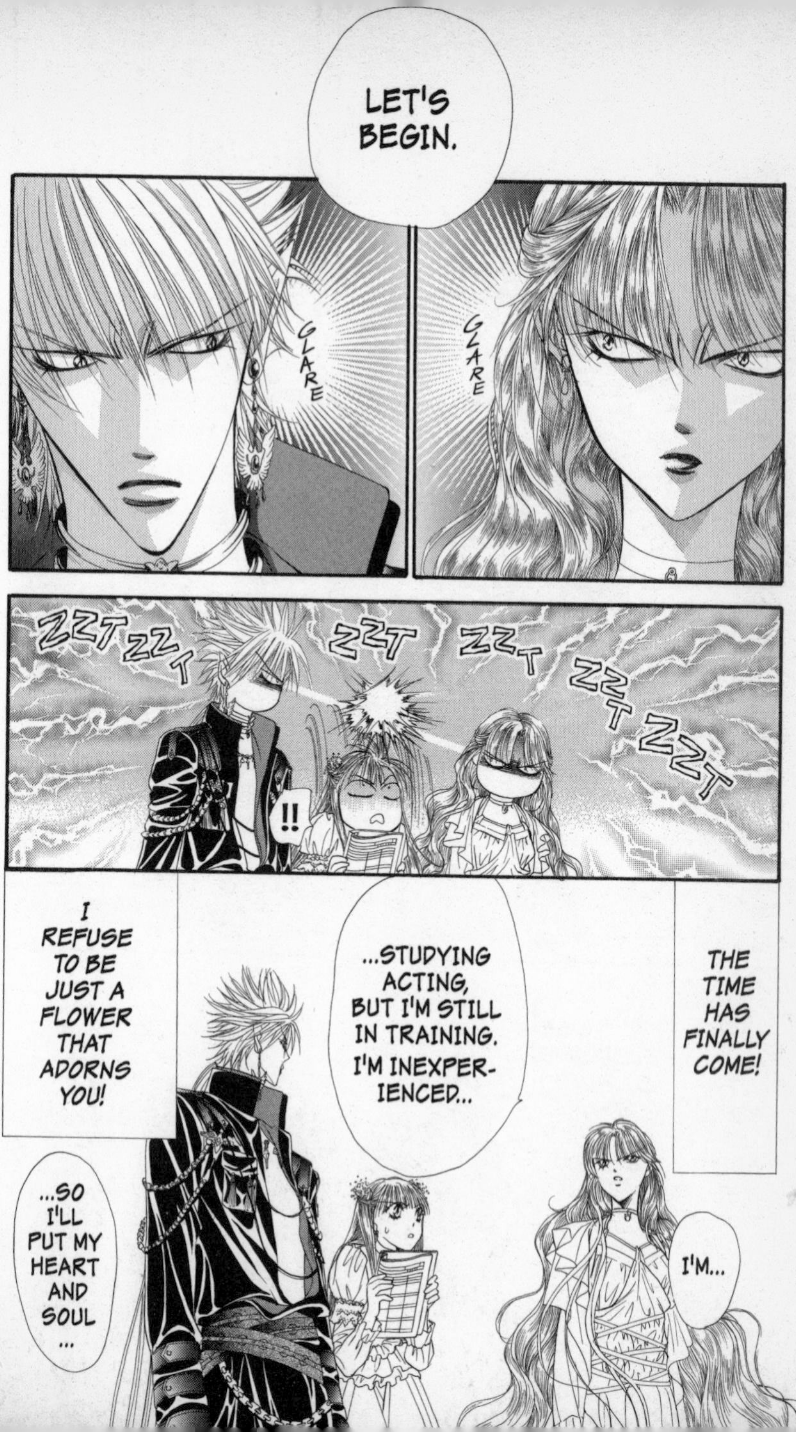
LET'S BEGIN.
GLARE
GLARE
ZZT
ZZT
ZZT
ZZT
ZZT
ZZT
!!
THE TIME HAS FINALLY COME!
I'M...
...STUDYING ACTING, BUT I'M STILL IN TRAINING. I'M INEXPERIENCED...
I REFUSE TO BE JUST A FLOWER THAT ADORNS YOU!
...SO I'LL PUT MY HEART AND SOUL ...

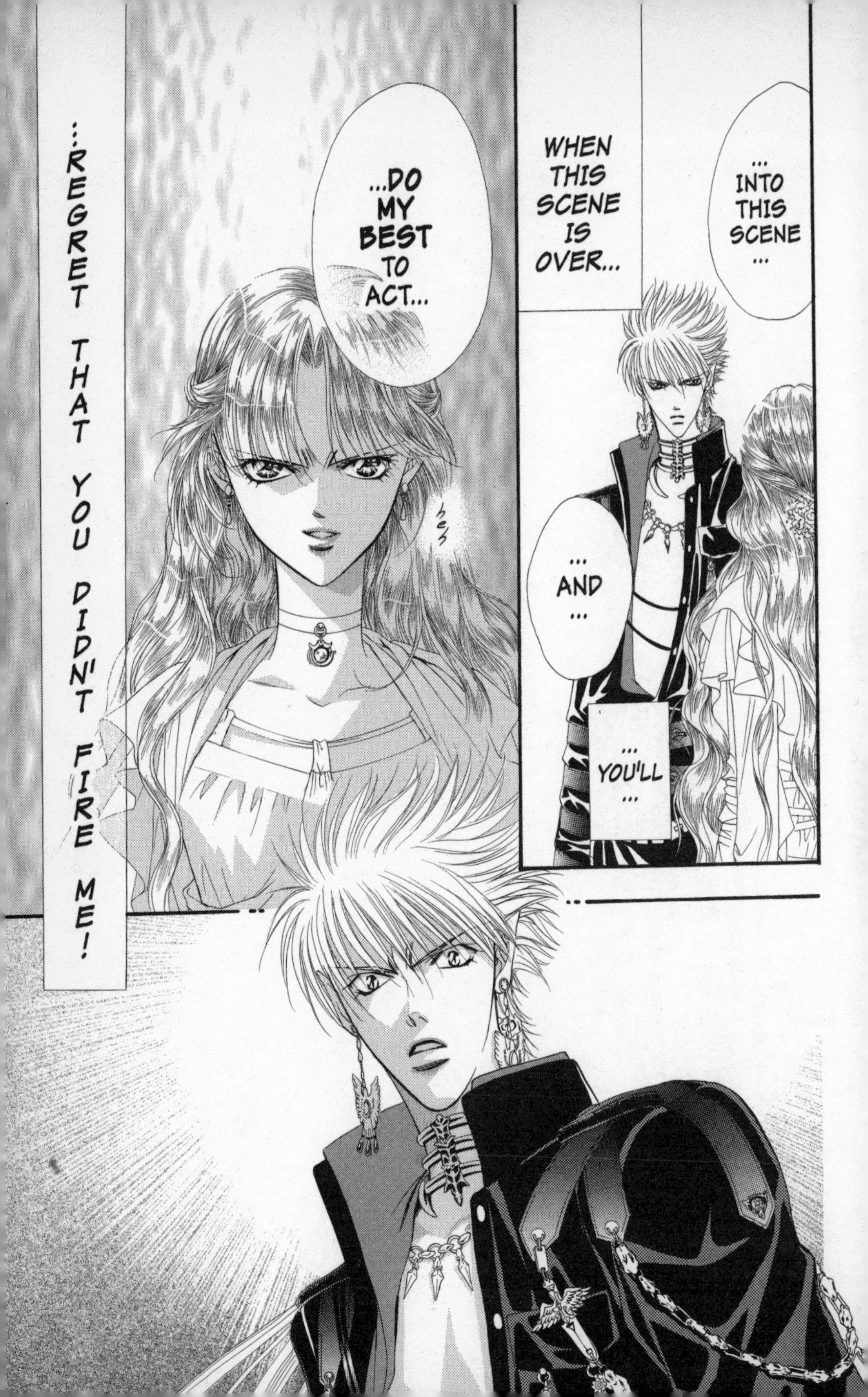

...INTO THIS SCENE...
WHEN THIS SCENE IS OVER...
...AND...
...YOU'LL...
...DO MY BEST TO ACT...
...REGRET THAT YOU DIDN'T FIRE ME!

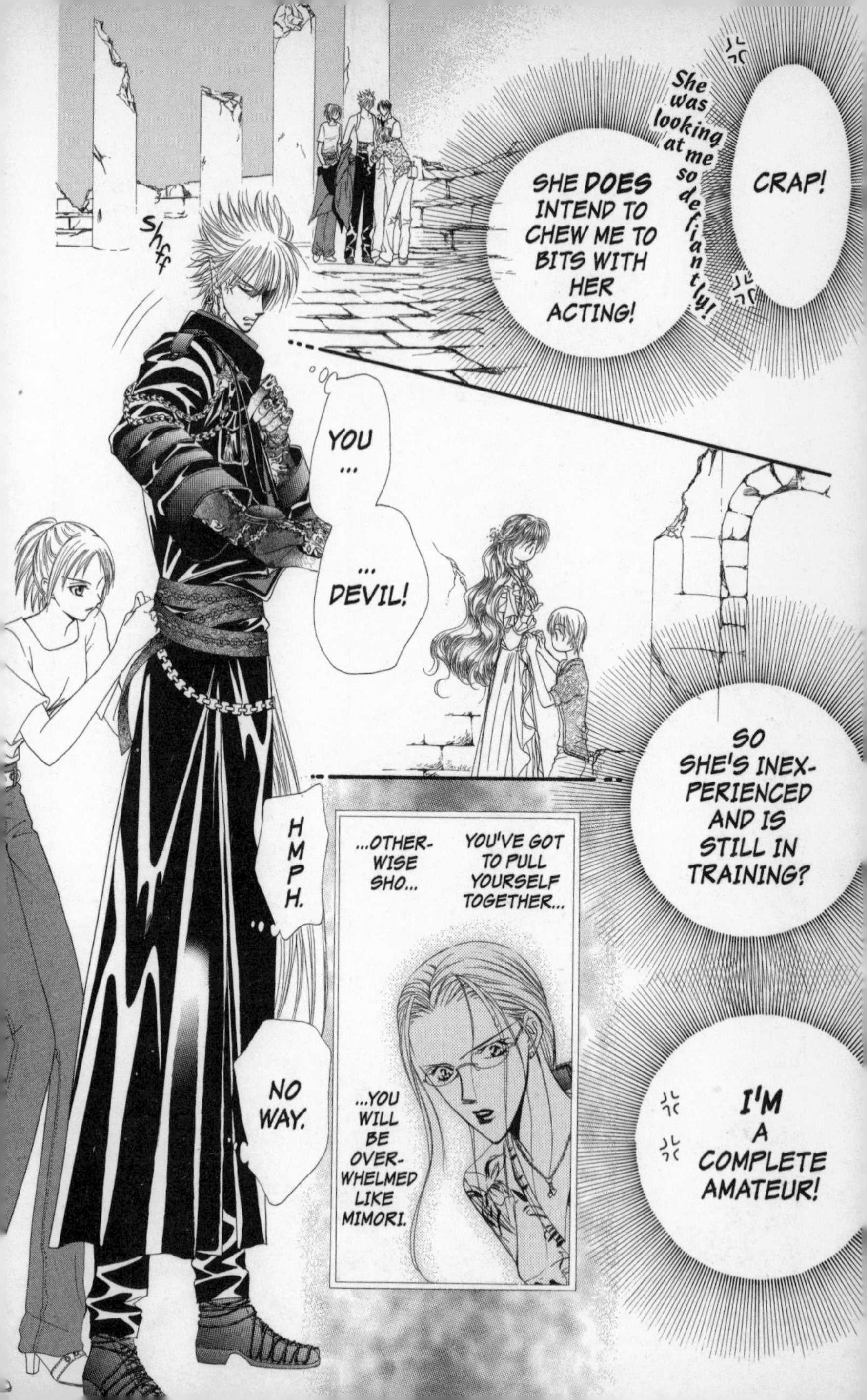
CRAP!
She was looking at me so defiantly!
SHE DOES INTEND TO CHEW ME TO BITS WITH HER ACTING!
Shff
YOU ...
... DEVIL!
SO SHE'S INEXPERIENCED AND IS STILL IN TRAINING?
I'M A COMPLETE AMATEUR!
YOU'VE GOT TO PULL YOURSELF TOGETHER...
...OTHERWISE SHO...
...YOU WILL BE OVERWHELMED LIKE MIMORI.
HMPH.
NO WAY.

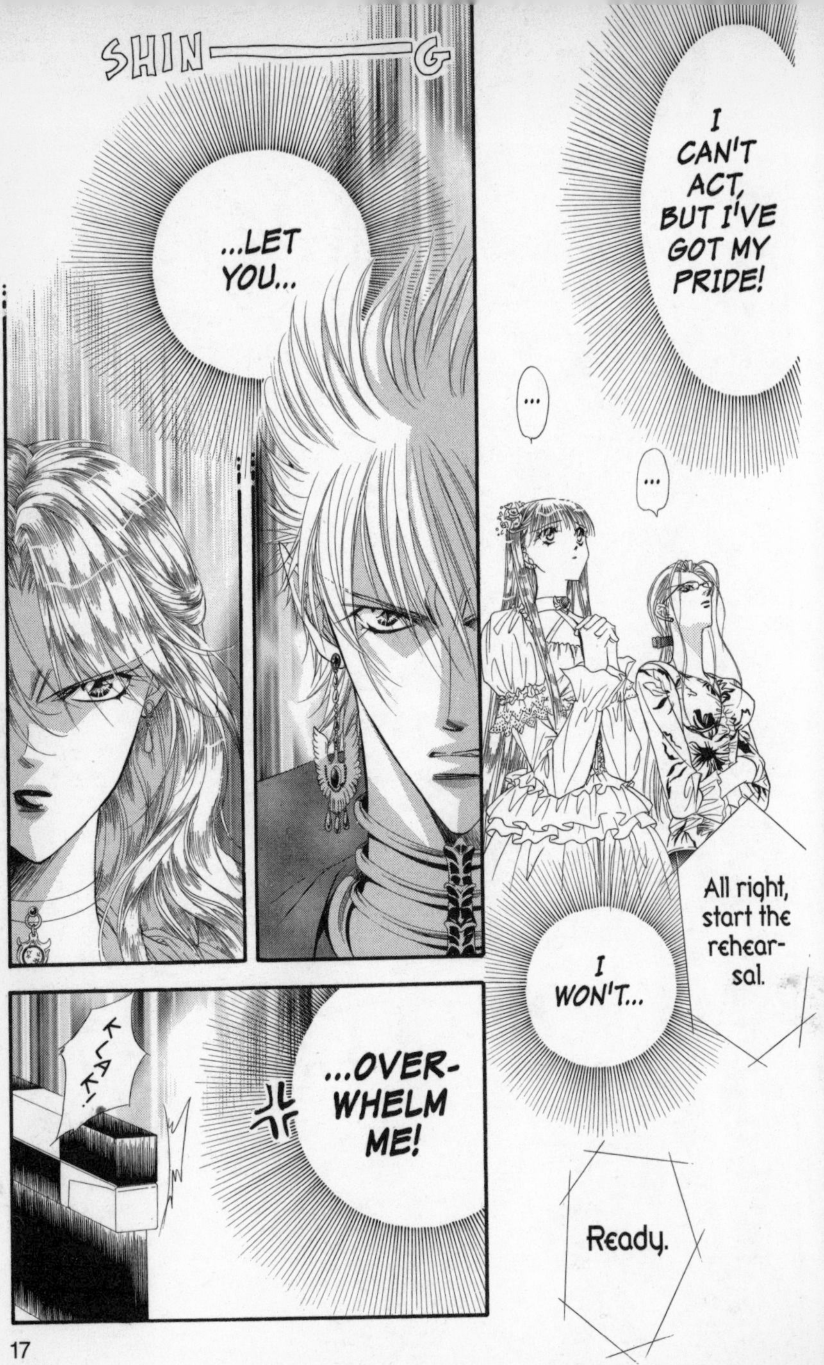
I CAN'T ACT, BUT I'VE GOT MY PRIDE!
...
...
All right, start the rehearsal.
Ready.
I WON'T...
SHIN—G
...LET YOU...
...OVERWHELM ME!
KLAK!

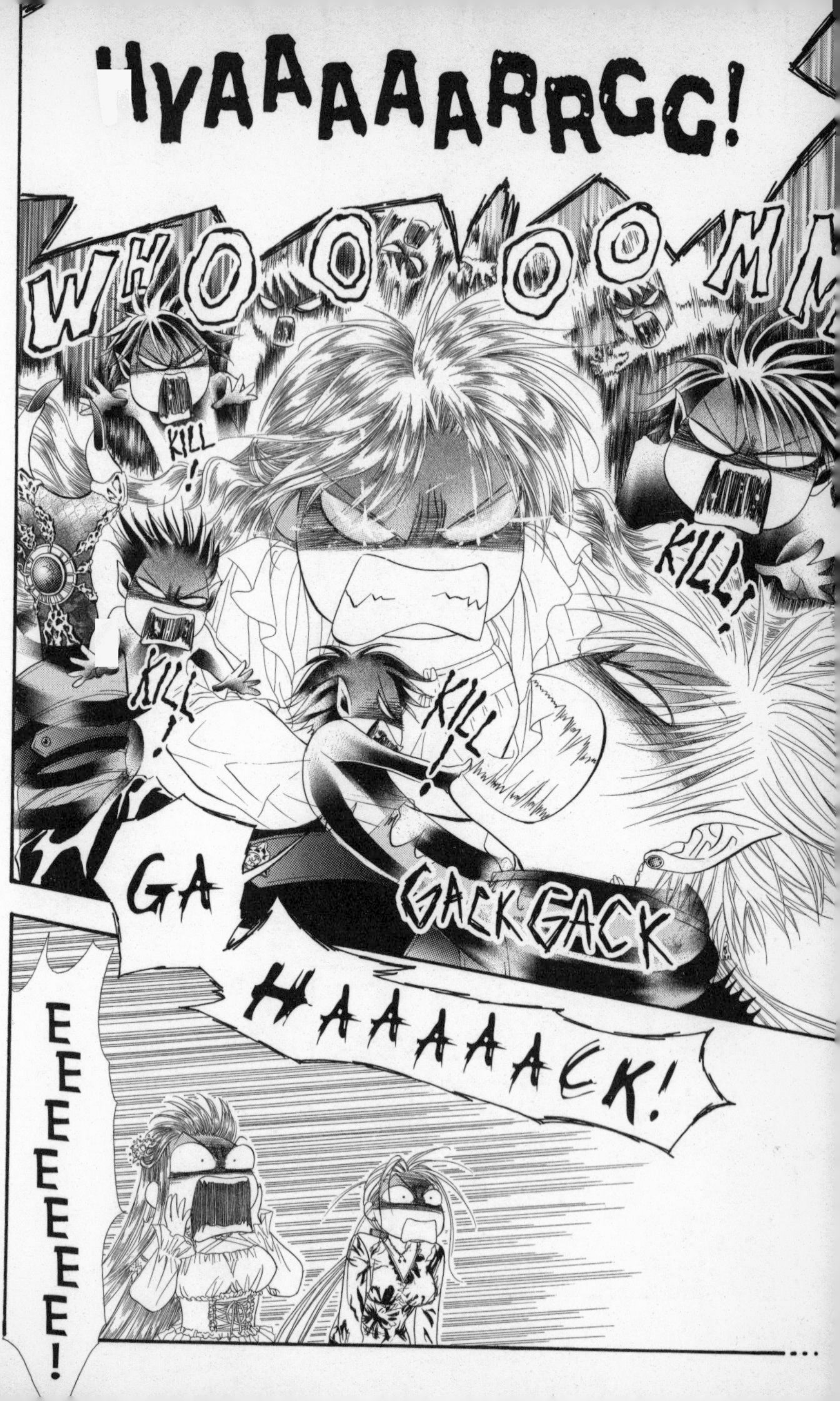
HYAAAAARRGG!
WHO-O-WOO-OM
KILL!
KILL!
KILL!
KILL!
GACK GACK
GA
HAAAAAACK!
EEEEEEEE!
...

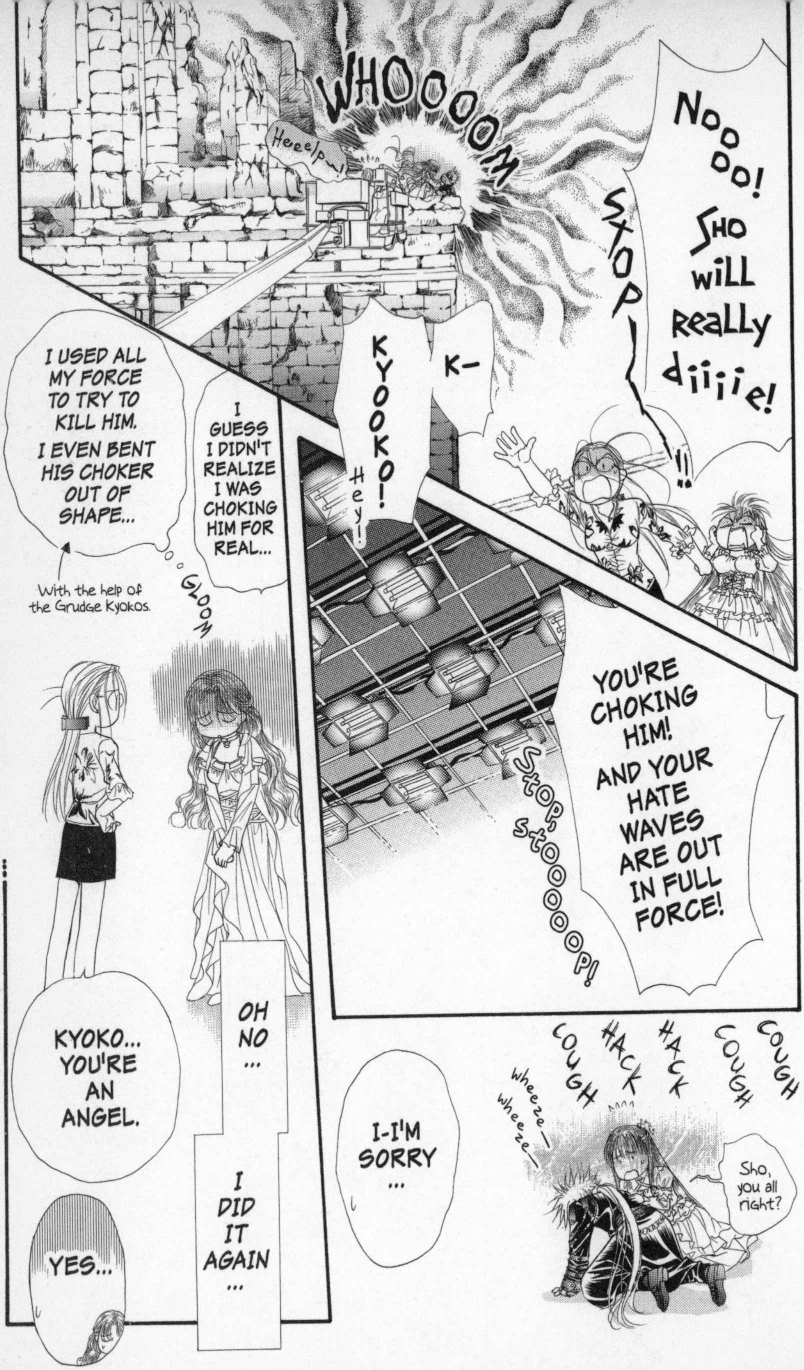

Noooooo! Sho will really diiiie!
STOP—!!
WHOOOOM
Heeelp~!
K—
KYOOKO!
Hey!
YOU'RE CHOKING HIM! AND YOUR HATE WAVES ARE OUT IN FULL FORCE!
Stop, stoooooop!
I GUESS I DIDN'T REALIZE I WAS CHOKING HIM FOR REAL...
I USED ALL MY FORCE TO TRY TO KILL HIM. I EVEN BENT HIS CHOKER OUT OF SHAPE...
With the help of the Grudge Kyokos.
GLOOM
COUGH
COUGH
HACK
HACK
COUGH
wheeze— wheeze—
Sho, you all right?
I-I'M SORRY...
OH NO...
I DID IT AGAIN...
KYOKO... YOU'RE AN ANGEL.
YES...

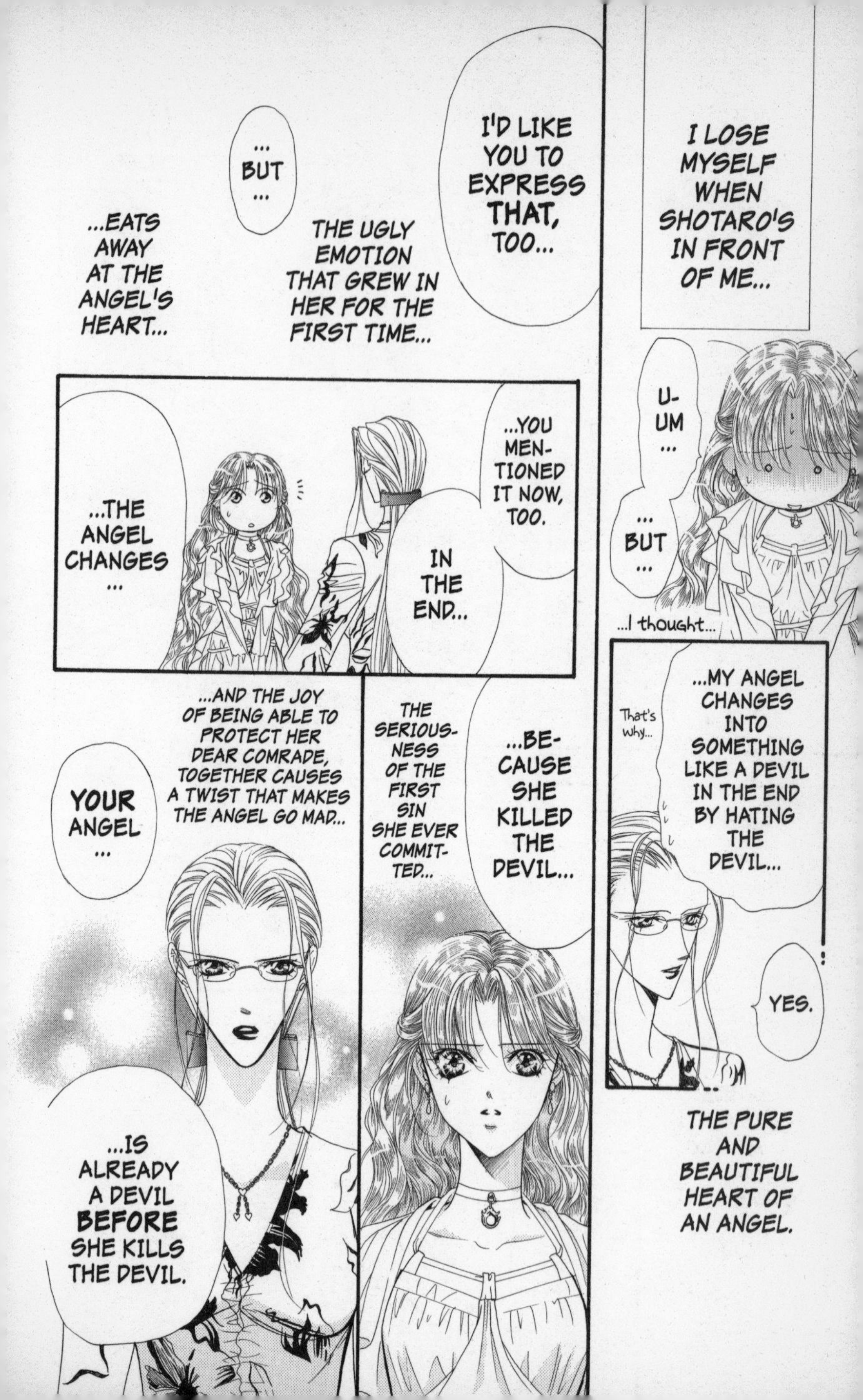
I LOSE MYSELF WHEN SHOTARO'S IN FRONT OF ME...
U-UM...
...BUT...
...I thought...
...MY ANGEL CHANGES INTO SOMETHING LIKE A DEVIL IN THE END BY HATING THE DEVIL...
That's why...
YES.
THE PURE AND BEAUTIFUL HEART OF AN ANGEL.
I'D LIKE YOU TO EXPRESS THAT, TOO...
...BUT...
THE UGLY EMOTION THAT GREW IN HER FOR THE FIRST TIME...
...EATS AWAY AT THE ANGEL'S HEART...
...YOU MENTIONED IT NOW, TOO.
IN THE END...
...THE ANGEL CHANGES...
...BECAUSE SHE KILLED THE DEVIL...
THE SERIOUSNESS OF THE FIRST SIN SHE EVER COMMITTED...
...AND THE JOY OF BEING ABLE TO PROTECT HER DEAR COMRADE, TOGETHER CAUSES A TWIST THAT MAKES THE ANGEL GO MAD...
YOUR ANGEL...
...IS ALREADY A DEVIL BEFORE SHE KILLS THE DEVIL.

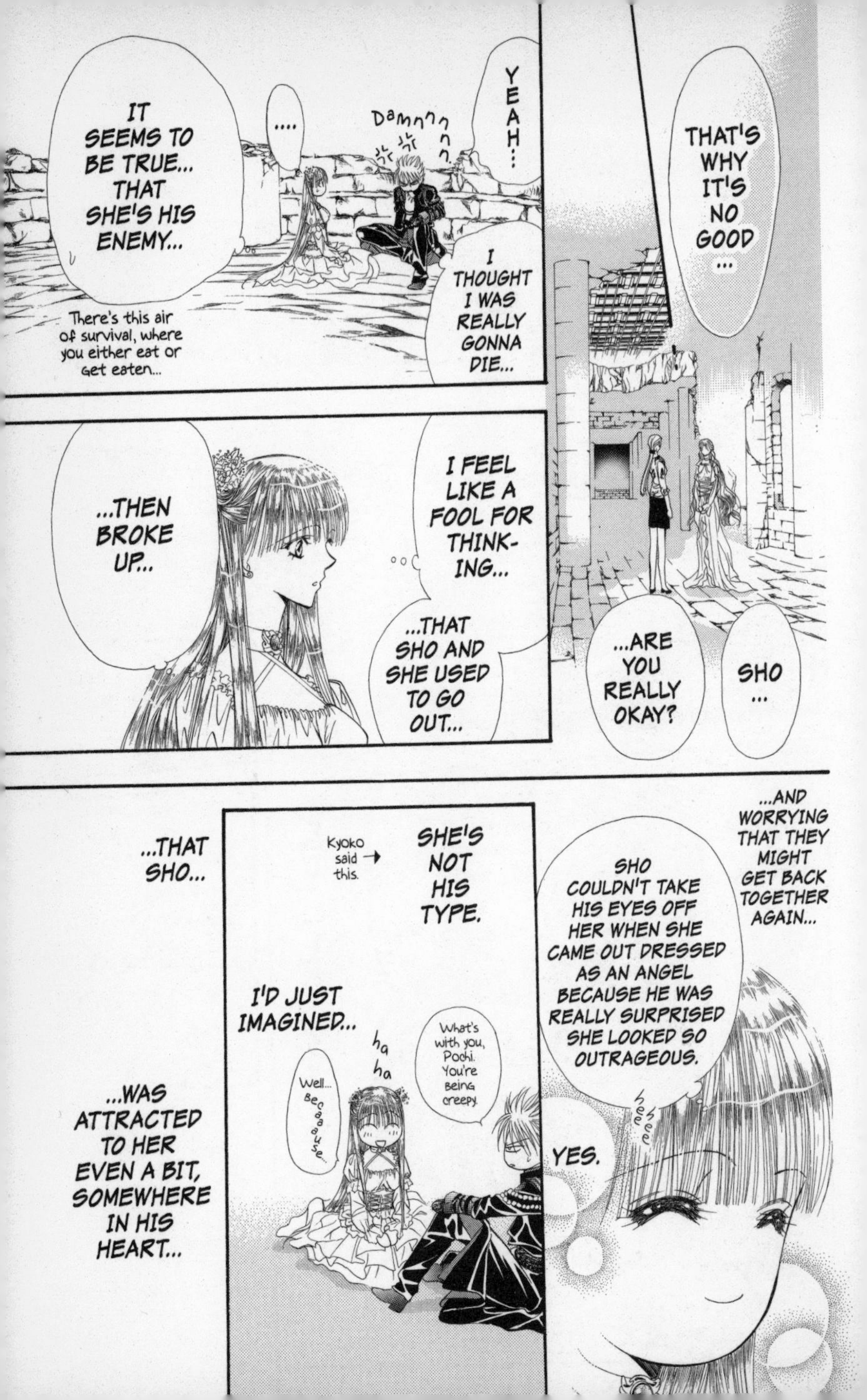
THAT'S WHY IT'S NO GOOD...
SHO...
...ARE YOU REALLY OKAY?
YEAH...
Damnnnnnn
I THOUGHT I WAS REALLY GONNA DIE...
....
IT SEEMS TO BE TRUE... THAT SHE'S HIS ENEMY...
There's this air of survival, where you either eat or get eaten...
I FEEL LIKE A FOOL FOR THINKING...
...THAT SHO AND SHE USED TO GO OUT...
...THEN BROKE UP...
...AND WORRYING THAT THEY MIGHT GET BACK TOGETHER AGAIN...
SHO COULDN'T TAKE HIS EYES OFF HER WHEN SHE CAME OUT DRESSED AS AN ANGEL BECAUSE HE WAS REALLY SURPRISED SHE LOOKED SO OUTRAGEOUS.
hee hee
YES.
SHE'S NOT HIS TYPE.
Kyoko said this.
I'D JUST IMAGINED...
What's with you, Pochi. You're being creepy.
ha ha
Well... Becaaause...
...THAT SHO...
...WAS ATTRACTED TO HER EVEN A BIT, SOMEWHERE IN HIS HEART...

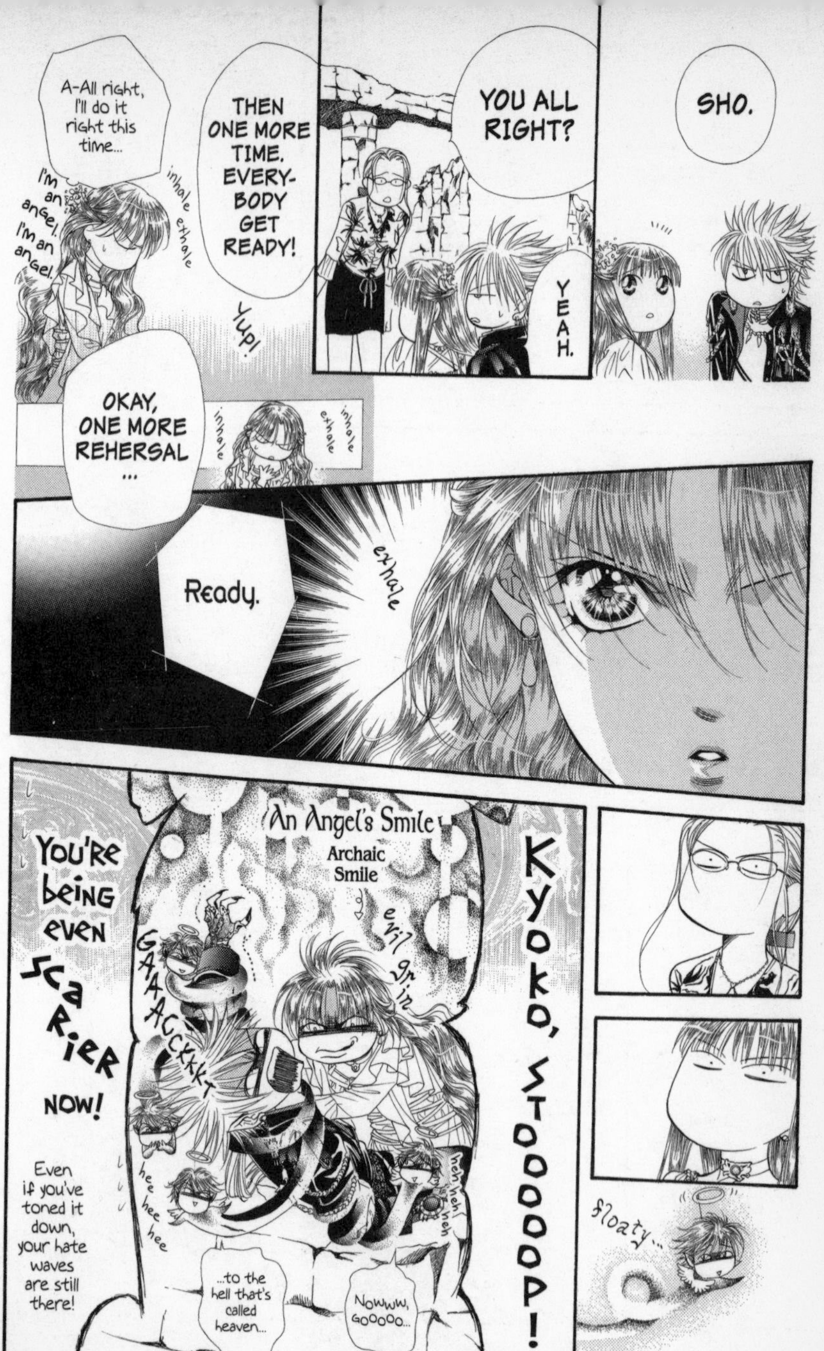
SHO.
YOU ALL RIGHT?
YEAH.
THEN ONE MORE TIME. EVERYBODY GET READY!
Yup!
A-All right, I'll do it right this time...
inhale exhale
I'm an angel. I'm an angel.
OKAY, ONE MORE REHERSAL...
inhale exhale inhale
exhale
Ready.
floaty...
Kyoko, STOOOOOOP!
An Angel's Smile
Archaic Smile
evil grin
GAAACCKKKT
heh heh heh heh
hee hee hee
Nowww, GOOOOO...
...to the hell that's called heaven...
You're being even scarier now!
Even if you've toned it down, your hate waves are still there!

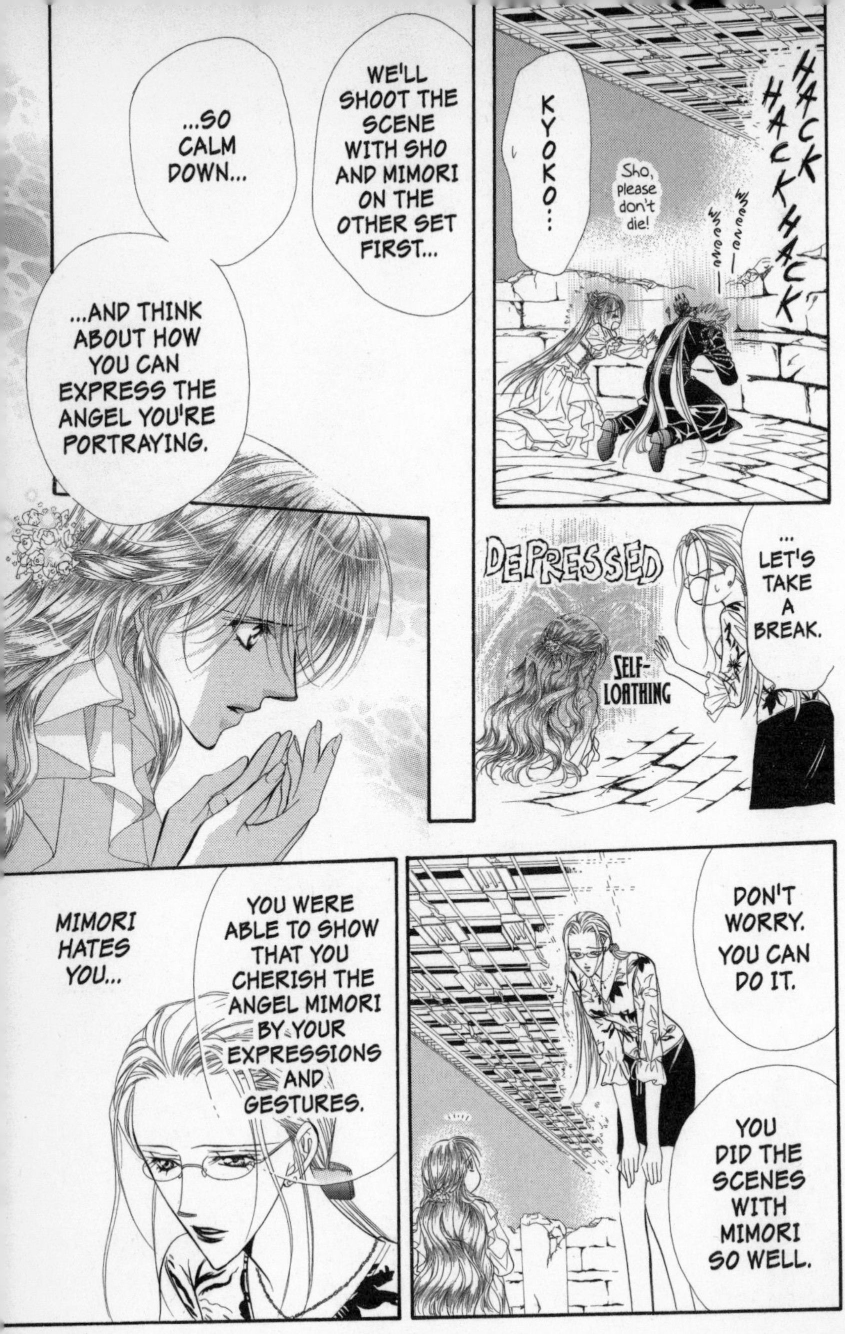
KYOKO...
Sho, please don't die!
HACK HACK HACK
wheeze— wheeze—
...LET'S TAKE A BREAK.
DEPRESSED
SELF-LOATHING
WE'LL SHOOT THE SCENE WITH SHO AND MIMORI ON THE OTHER SET FIRST...
...SO CALM DOWN...
...AND THINK ABOUT HOW YOU CAN EXPRESS THE ANGEL YOU'RE PORTRAYING.
DON'T WORRY. YOU CAN DO IT.
YOU DID THE SCENES WITH MIMORI SO WELL.
YOU WERE ABLE TO SHOW THAT YOU CHERISH THE ANGEL MIMORI BY YOUR EXPRESSIONS AND GESTURES.
MIMORI HATES YOU...

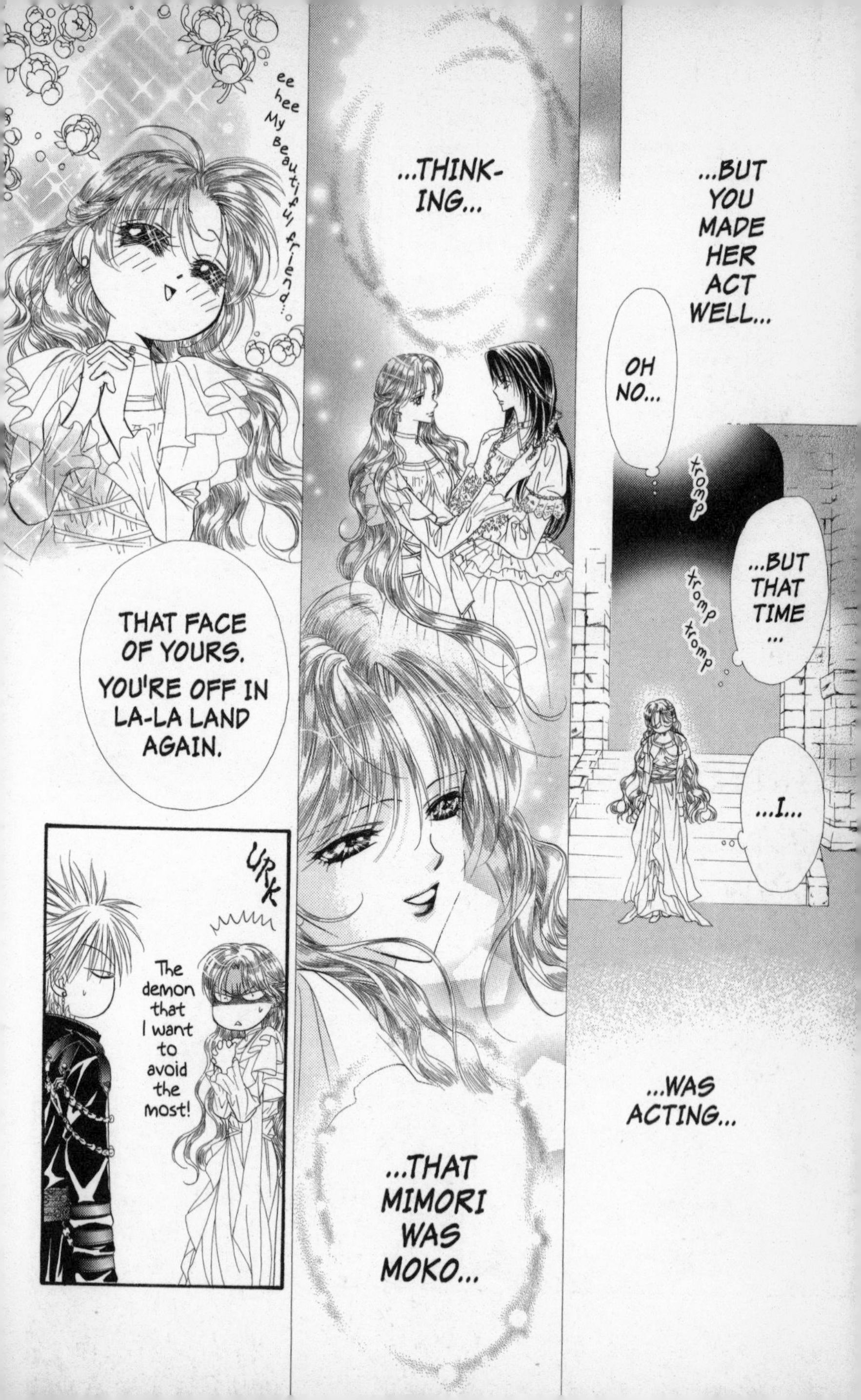
...BUT YOU MADE HER ACT WELL...
OH NO...
xromp
...BUT THAT TIME ...
xromp xromp
...I...
...WAS ACTING...
...THINK-ING...
...THAT MIMORI WAS MOKO...
ee hee My Beautiful friend...
THAT FACE OF YOURS. YOU'RE OFF IN LA-LA LAND AGAIN.
URK
The demon that I want to avoid the most!

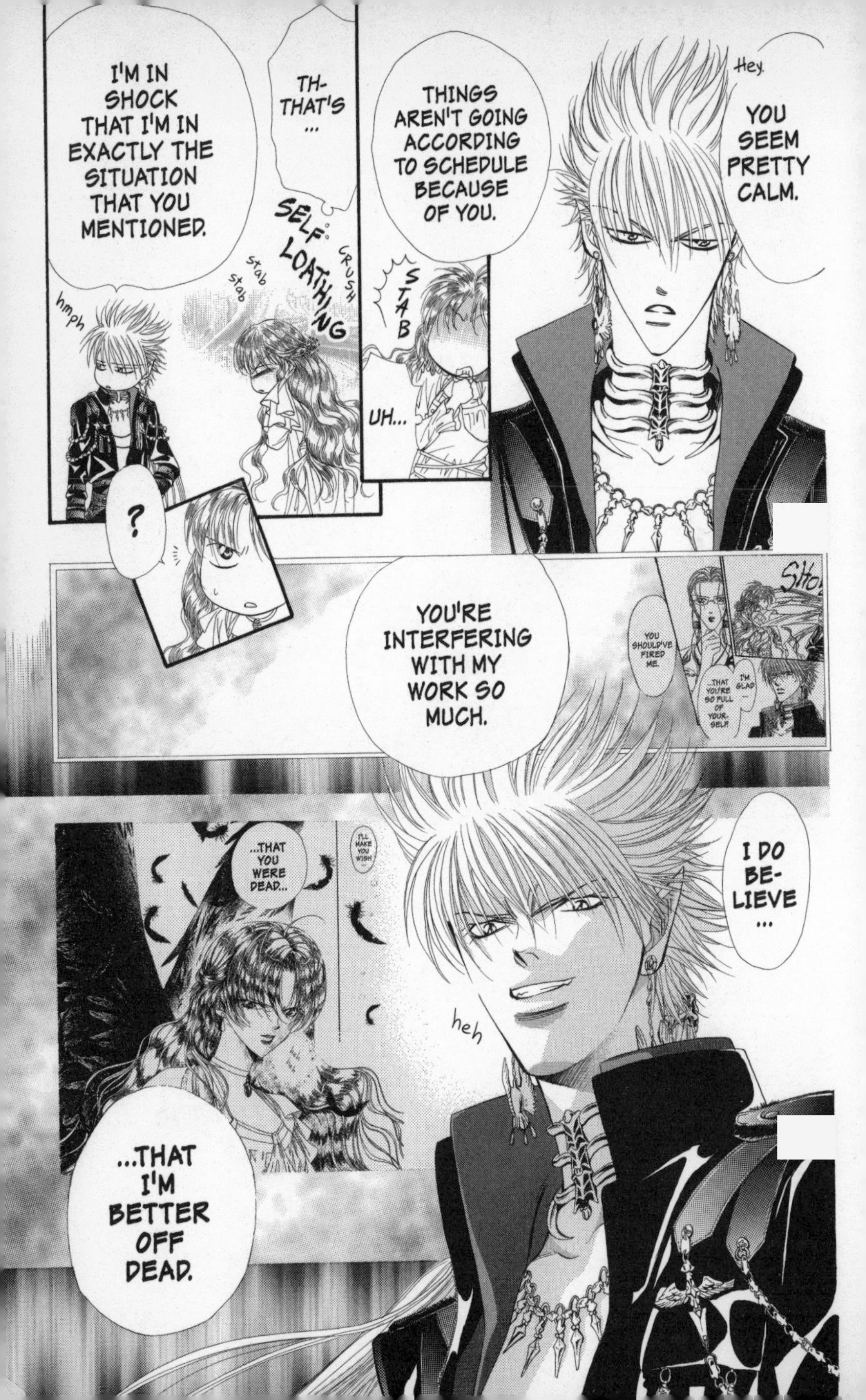
Hey.
YOU SEEM PRETTY CALM.
THINGS AREN'T GOING ACCORDING TO SCHEDULE BECAUSE OF YOU.
STAB
UH...
TH-THAT'S ...
SELF LOATHING
CRUSH
stab stab
I'M IN SHOCK THAT I'M IN EXACTLY THE SITUATION THAT YOU MENTIONED.
hmph
?
I'M GLAD ...
...THAT YOU'RE SO FULL OF YOUR-SELF
YOU SHOULD'VE FIRED ME.
YOU'RE INTERFERING WITH MY WORK SO MUCH.
I DO BE-LIEVE ...
heh
I'LL MAKE YOU WISH ...
...THAT YOU WERE DEAD...
...THAT I'M BETTER OFF DEAD.

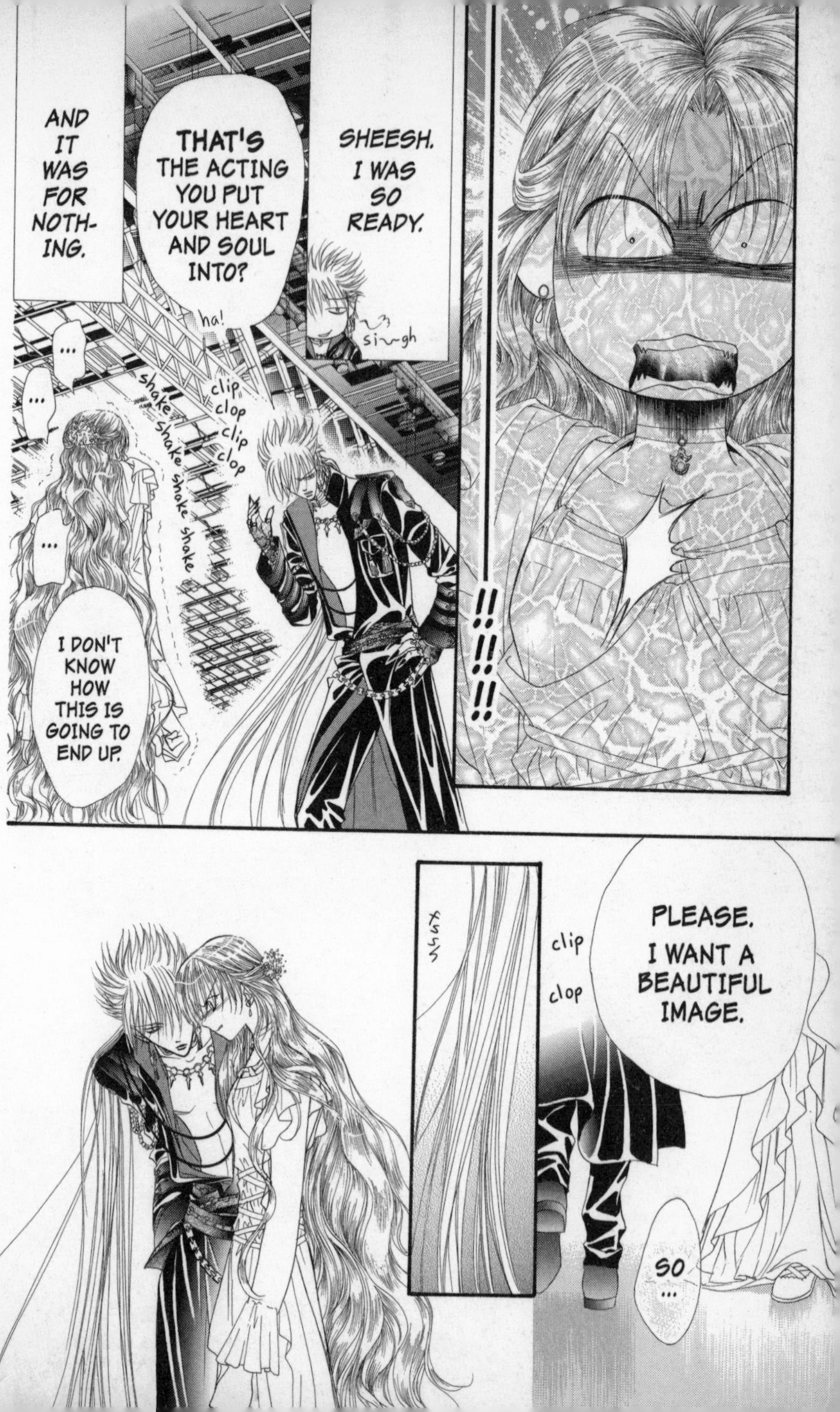
!!!!!!
SHEESH. I WAS SO READY.
si~gh
THAT'S THE ACTING YOU PUT YOUR HEART AND SOUL INTO?
ha!
AND IT WAS FOR NOTH-ING.
...
...
clip clop clip clop
shake shake shake shake
...
I DON'T KNOW HOW THIS IS GOING TO END UP.
PLEASE. I WANT A BEAUTIFUL IMAGE.
clip clop
SO...

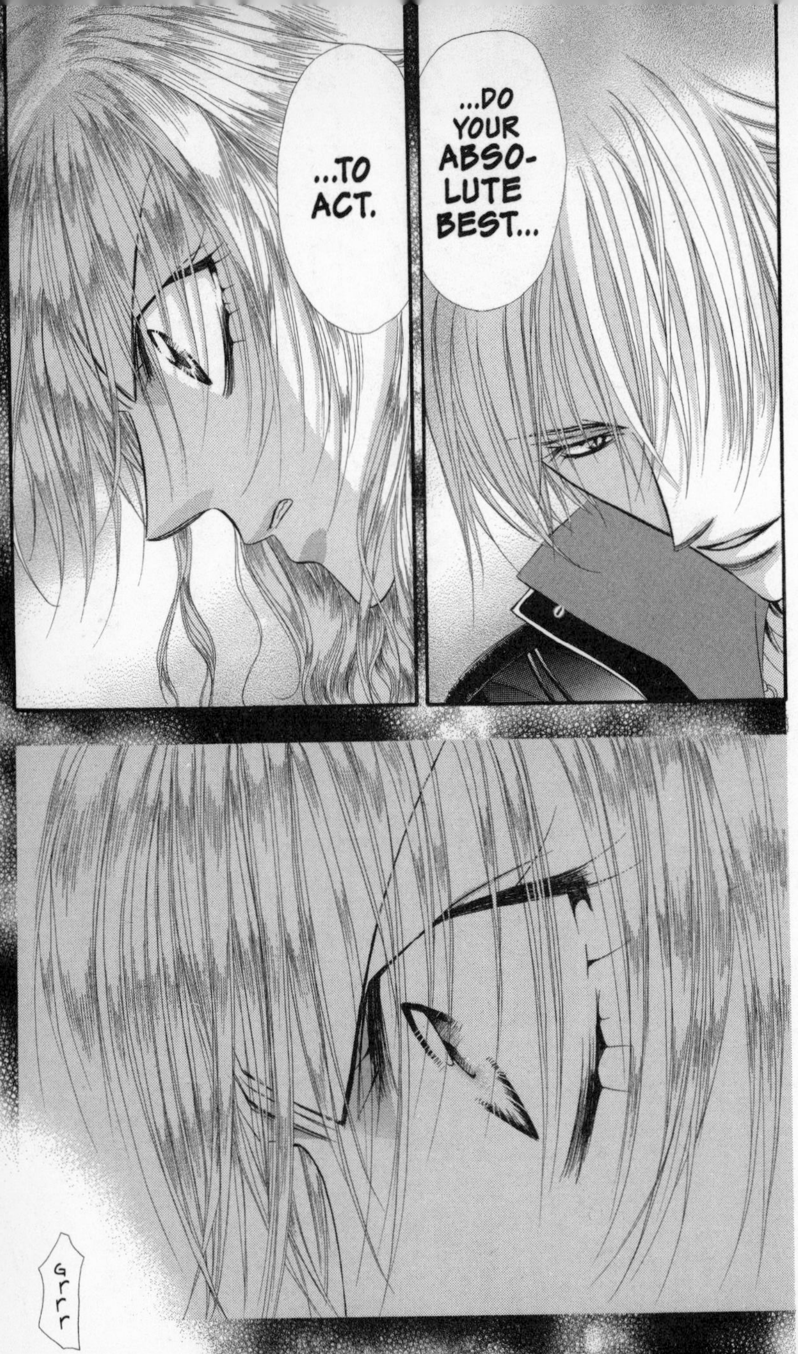
...DO YOUR ABSO-LUTE BEST...
...TO ACT.
Grrr

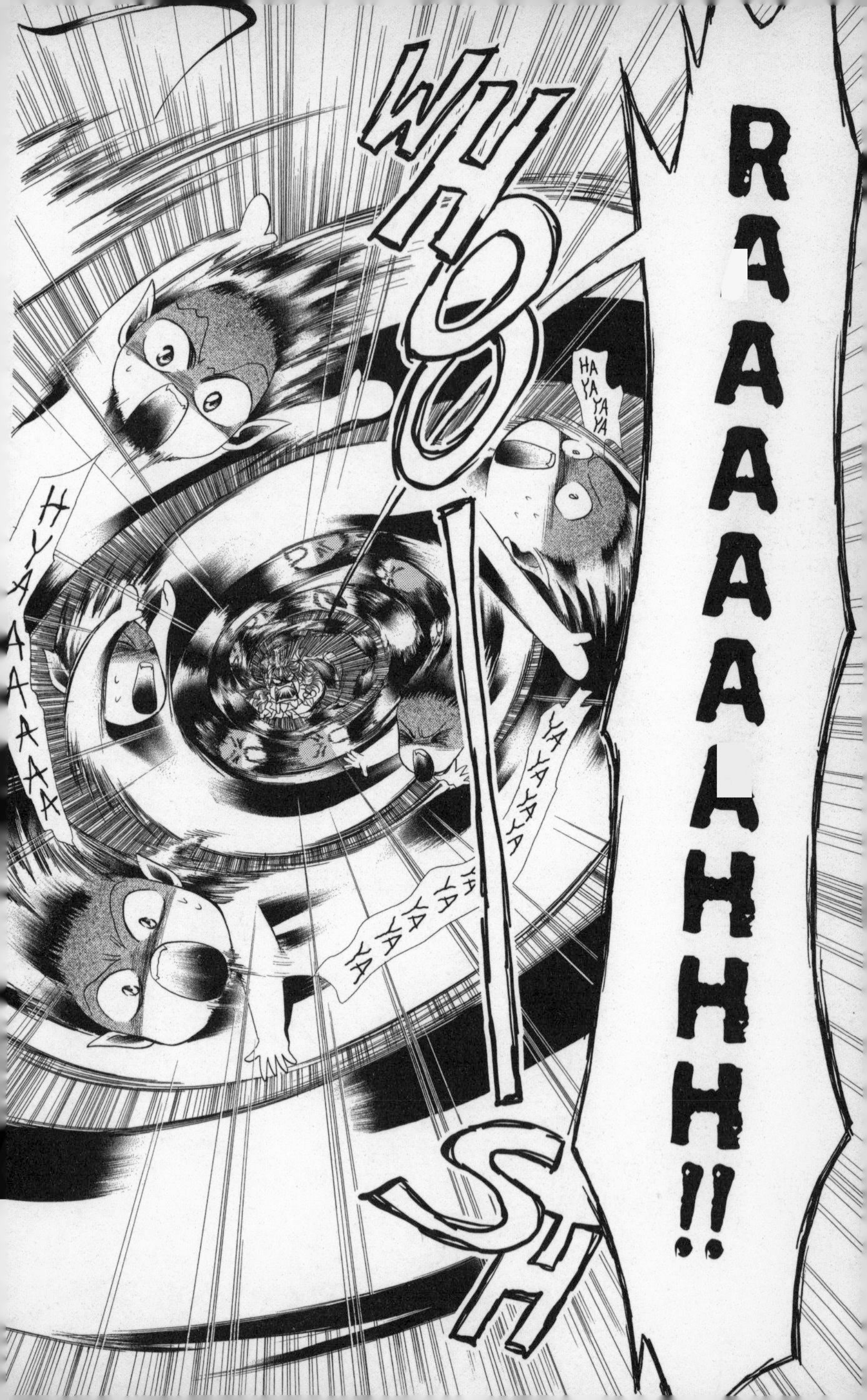
RAAAAAAHHH!!
WHOOSH
HAYAYAYAYA
YAYAYAYAYA
YAYAYAYAYA
HYAAAAAAAA

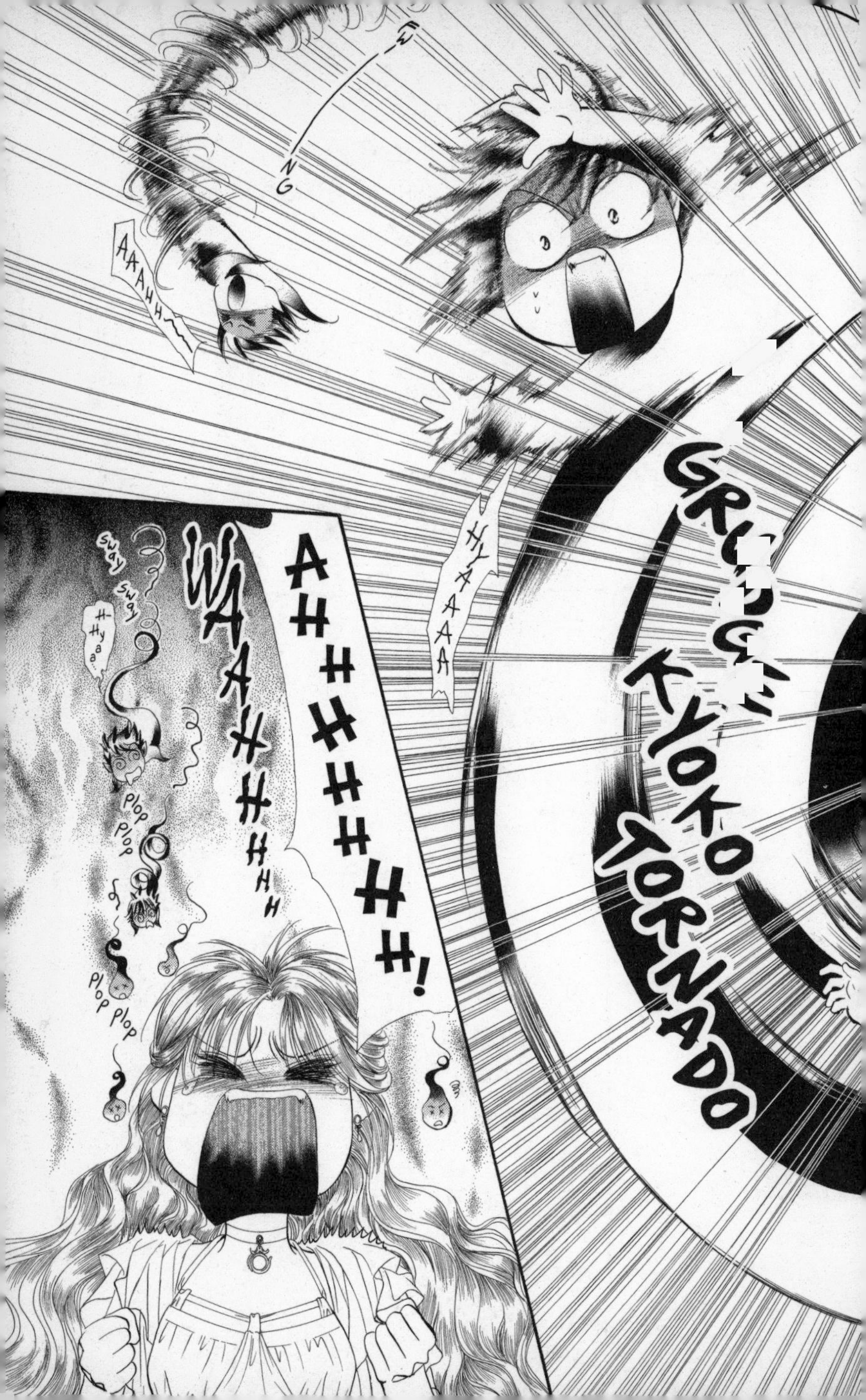
NG
AAAHH~
GRUDGE KYOKO TORNADO
HYAAAAA
AHHHHHHH!
WAAHHHHHHHH
sway
sway
H-Hyaa...
plop
plop
plop plop

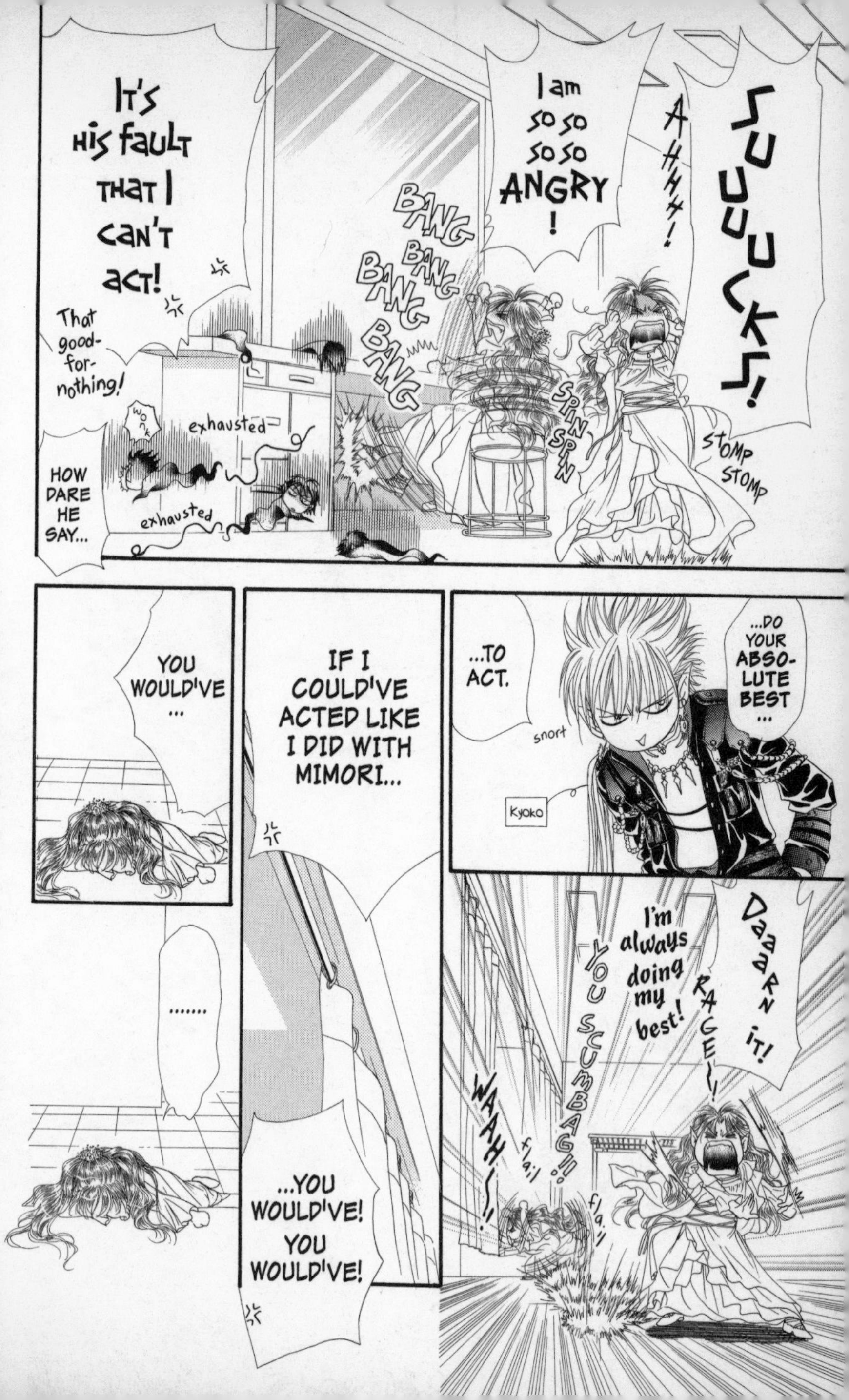
SUUUUCKS!
AHHHH!
I am so so so so ANGRY!
STOMP STOMP
SPIN SPIN
BANG BANG BANG BANG
It's his fault that I can't act!
That good-for-nothing!
wonk
exhausted
exhausted
HOW DARE HE SAY...
...DO YOUR ABSOLUTE BEST...
...TO ACT.
snort
Kyoko
Daaarn it!
RAGE~!
I'm always doing my best!
YOU SCUMBAG!!
flail
flail
WAAH~!!
IF I COULD'VE ACTED LIKE I DID WITH MIMORI...
...YOU WOULD'VE! YOU WOULD'VE!
YOU WOULD'VE...
.......

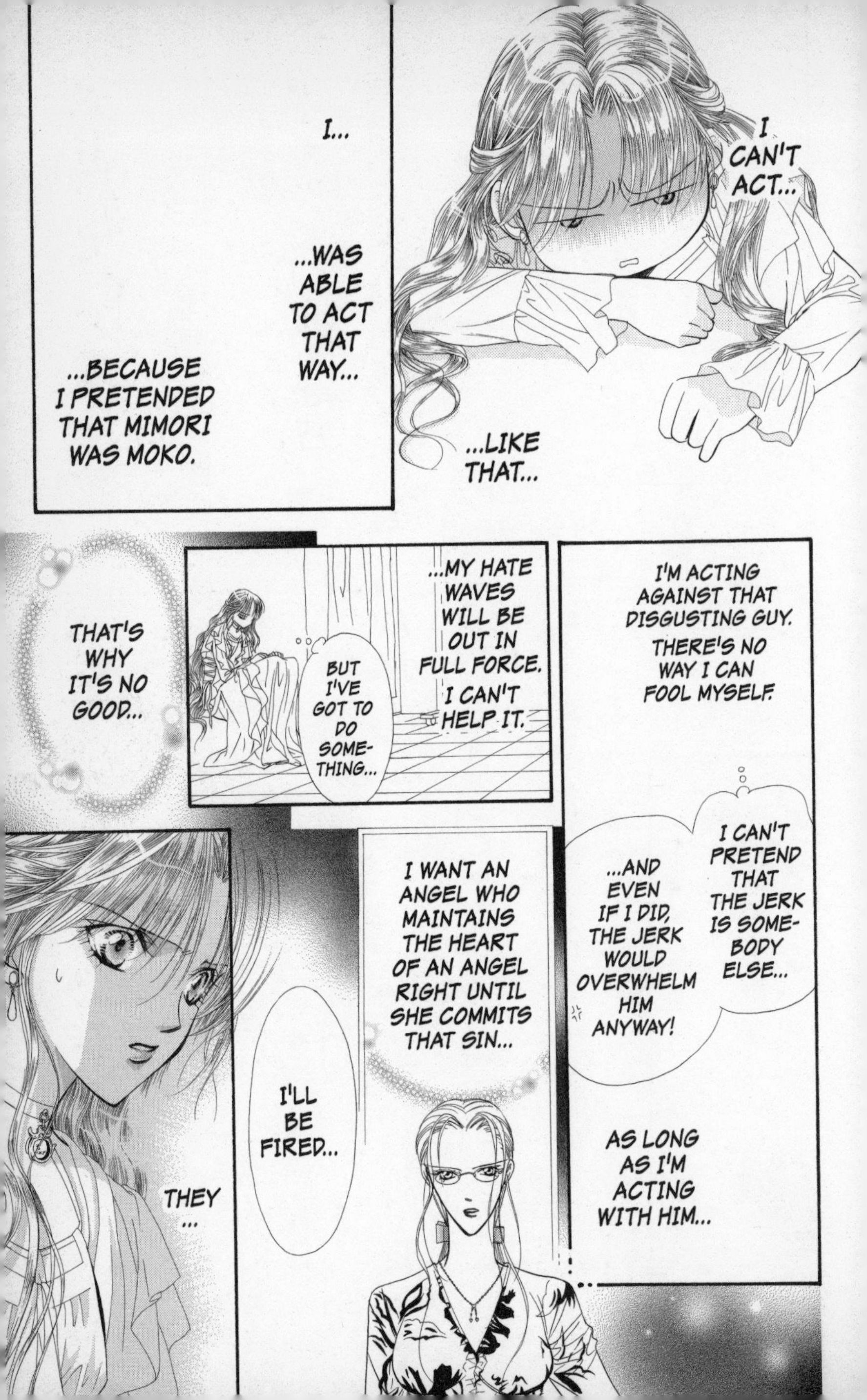
I CAN'T ACT...
...LIKE THAT...
I...
...WAS ABLE TO ACT THAT WAY...
...BECAUSE I PRETENDED THAT MIMORI WAS MOKO.
I'M ACTING AGAINST THAT DISGUSTING GUY.
THERE'S NO WAY I CAN FOOL MYSELF.
I CAN'T PRETEND THAT THE JERK IS SOMEBODY ELSE...
...AND EVEN IF I DID, THE JERK WOULD OVERWHELM HIM ANYWAY!
AS LONG AS I'M ACTING WITH HIM...
...MY HATE WAVES WILL BE OUT IN FULL FORCE.
I CAN'T HELP IT.
BUT I'VE GOT TO DO SOMETHING...
THAT'S WHY IT'S NO GOOD...
I WANT AN ANGEL WHO MAINTAINS THE HEART OF AN ANGEL RIGHT UNTIL SHE COMMITS THAT SIN...
I'LL BE FIRED...
THEY ...

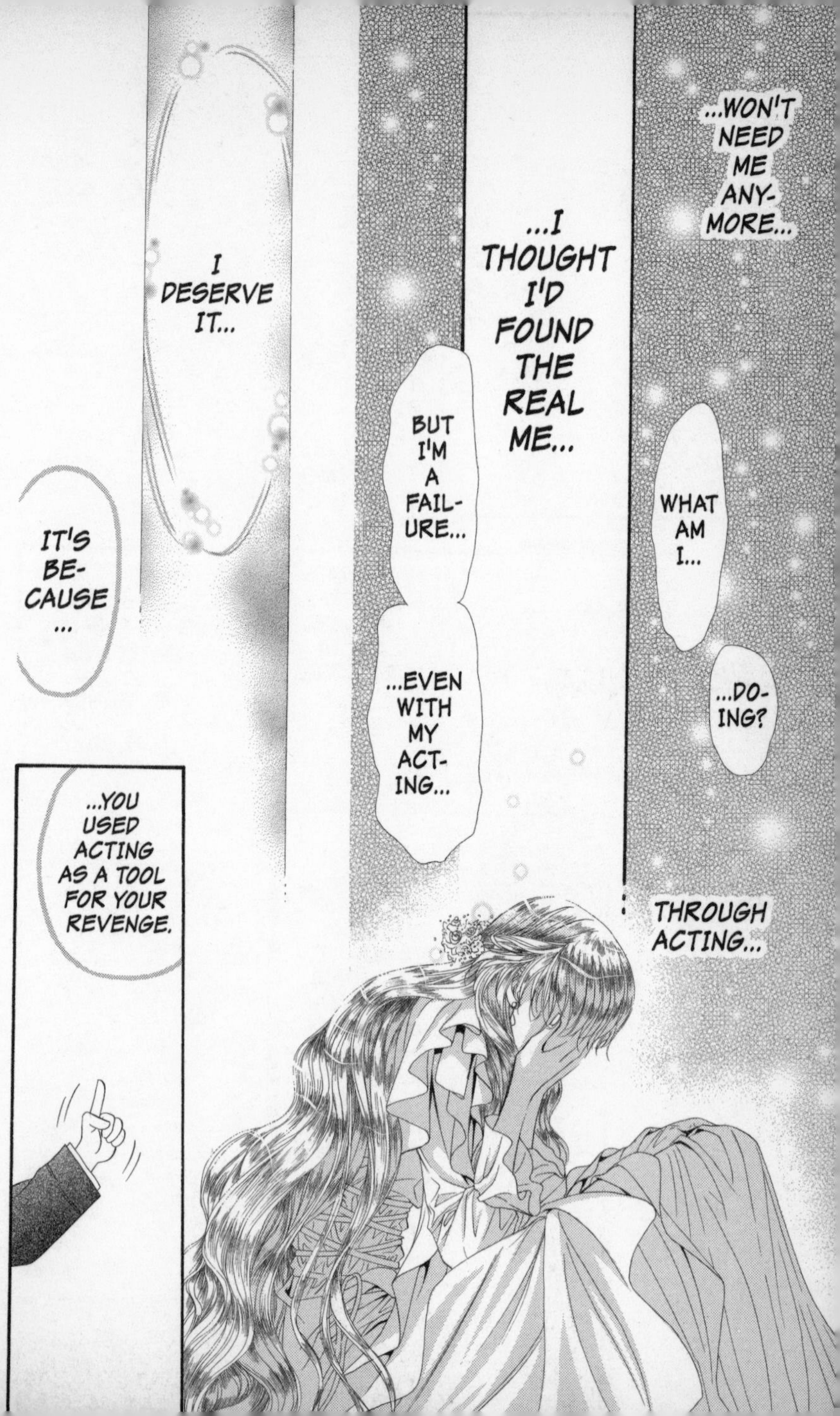

...WON'T NEED ME ANY-MORE...
WHAT AM I...
...DO-ING?
THROUGH ACTING...
...I THOUGHT I'D FOUND THE REAL ME...
BUT I'M A FAIL-URE...
...EVEN WITH MY ACT-ING...
I DESERVE IT...
IT'S BE-CAUSE...
...YOU USED ACTING AS A TOOL FOR YOUR REVENGE.

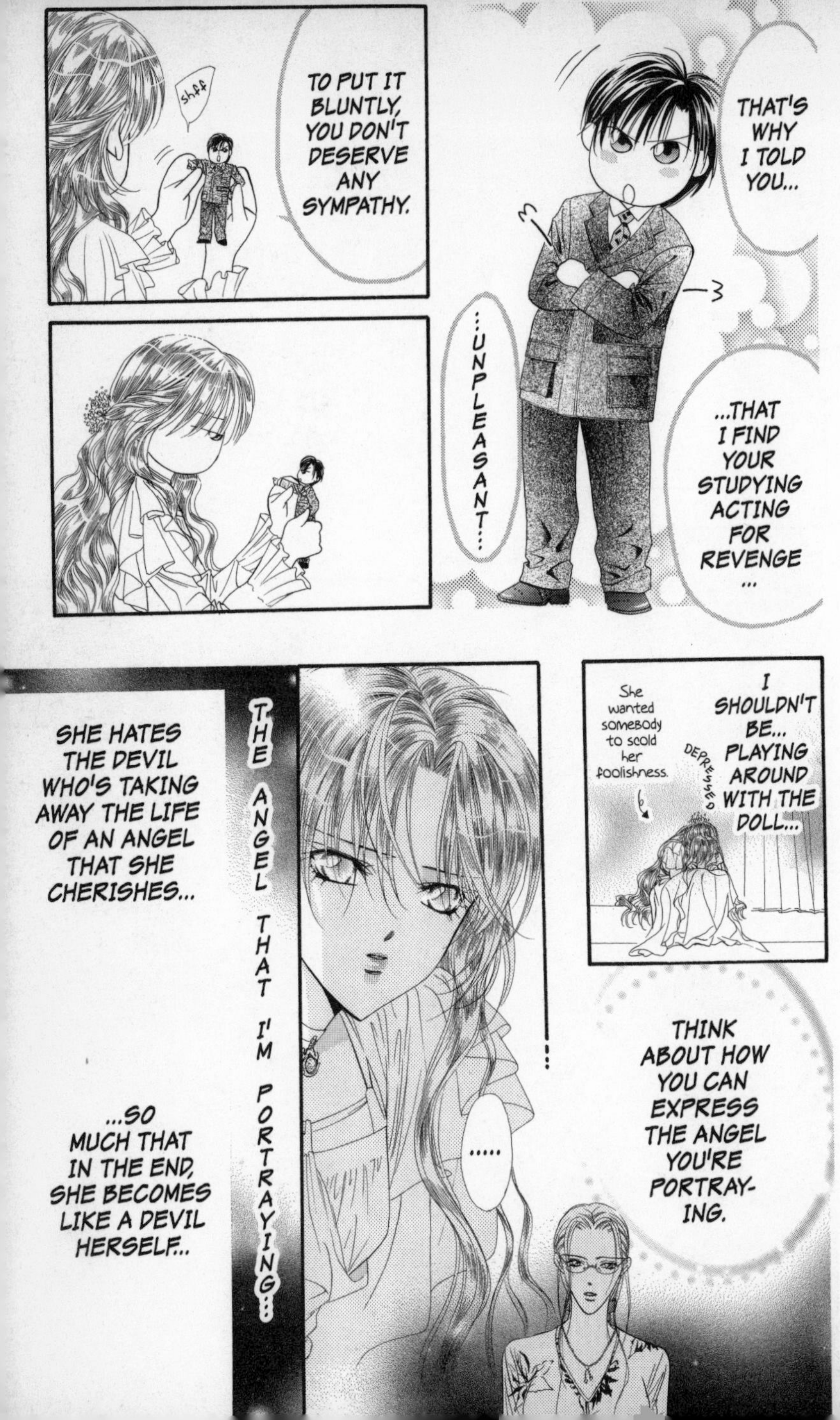
THAT'S WHY I TOLD YOU...
...THAT I FIND YOUR STUDYING ACTING FOR REVENGE ...
shff
TO PUT IT BLUNTLY, YOU DON'T DESERVE ANY SYMPATHY.
...UNPLEASANT...
I SHOULDN'T BE... PLAYING AROUND WITH THE DOLL...
She wanted somebody to scold her foolishness.
DEPRESSED
THINK ABOUT HOW YOU CAN EXPRESS THE ANGEL YOU'RE PORTRAY-ING.
.....
...
THE ANGEL THAT I'M PORTRAYING...
SHE HATES THE DEVIL WHO'S TAKING AWAY THE LIFE OF AN ANGEL THAT SHE CHERISHES...
...SO MUCH THAT IN THE END, SHE BECOMES LIKE A DEVIL HERSELF...

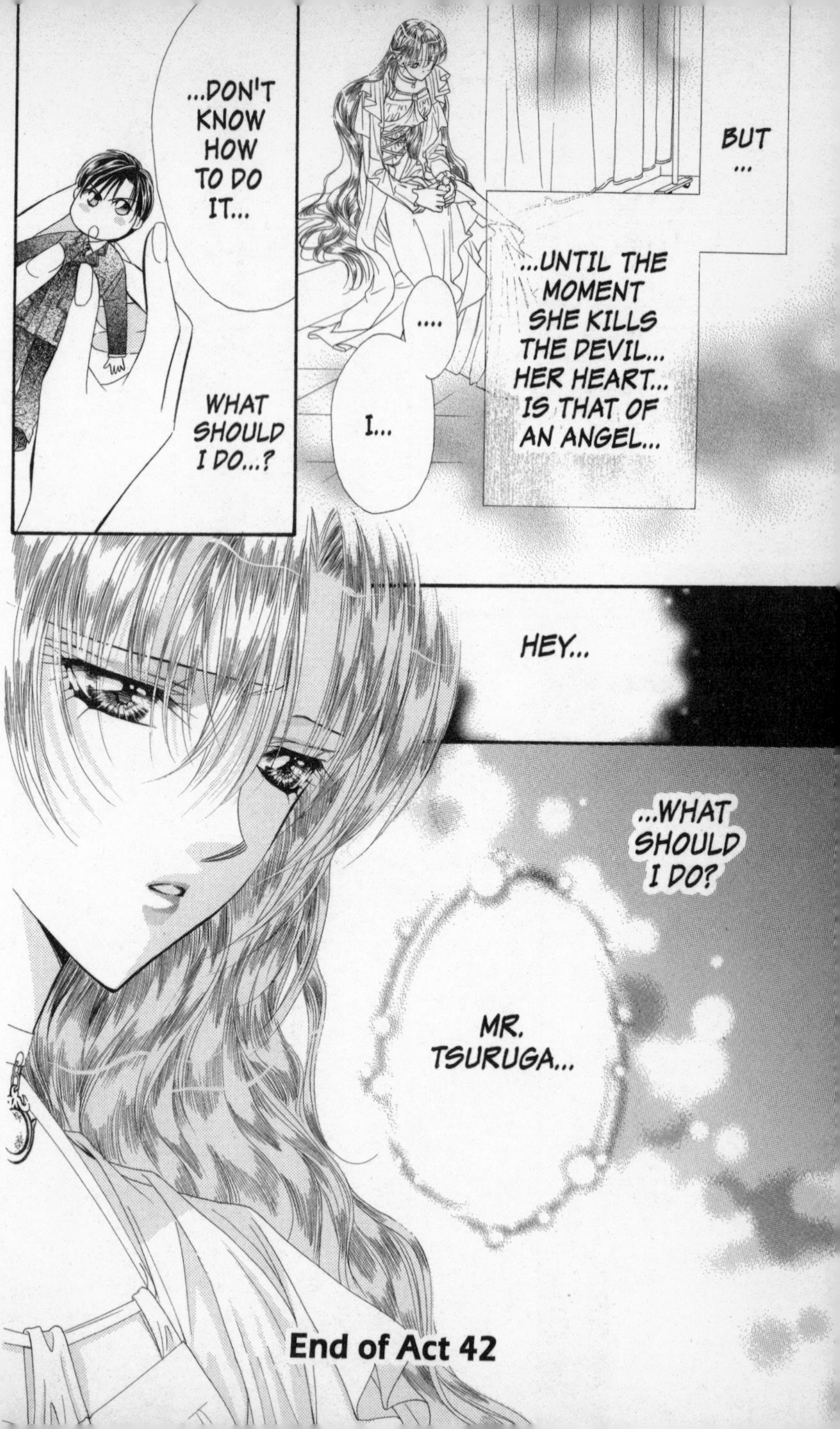
BUT ...
...UNTIL THE MOMENT SHE KILLS THE DEVIL... HER HEART... IS THAT OF AN ANGEL...
....
I...
...DON'T KNOW HOW TO DO IT...
WHAT SHOULD I DO...?
HEY...
...WHAT SHOULD I DO?
MR. TSURUGA...

End of Act 42

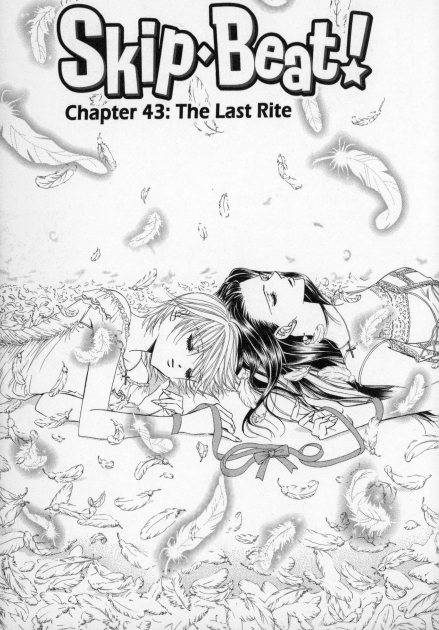

# Skip·Beat!☆

## Chapter 43: The Last Rite

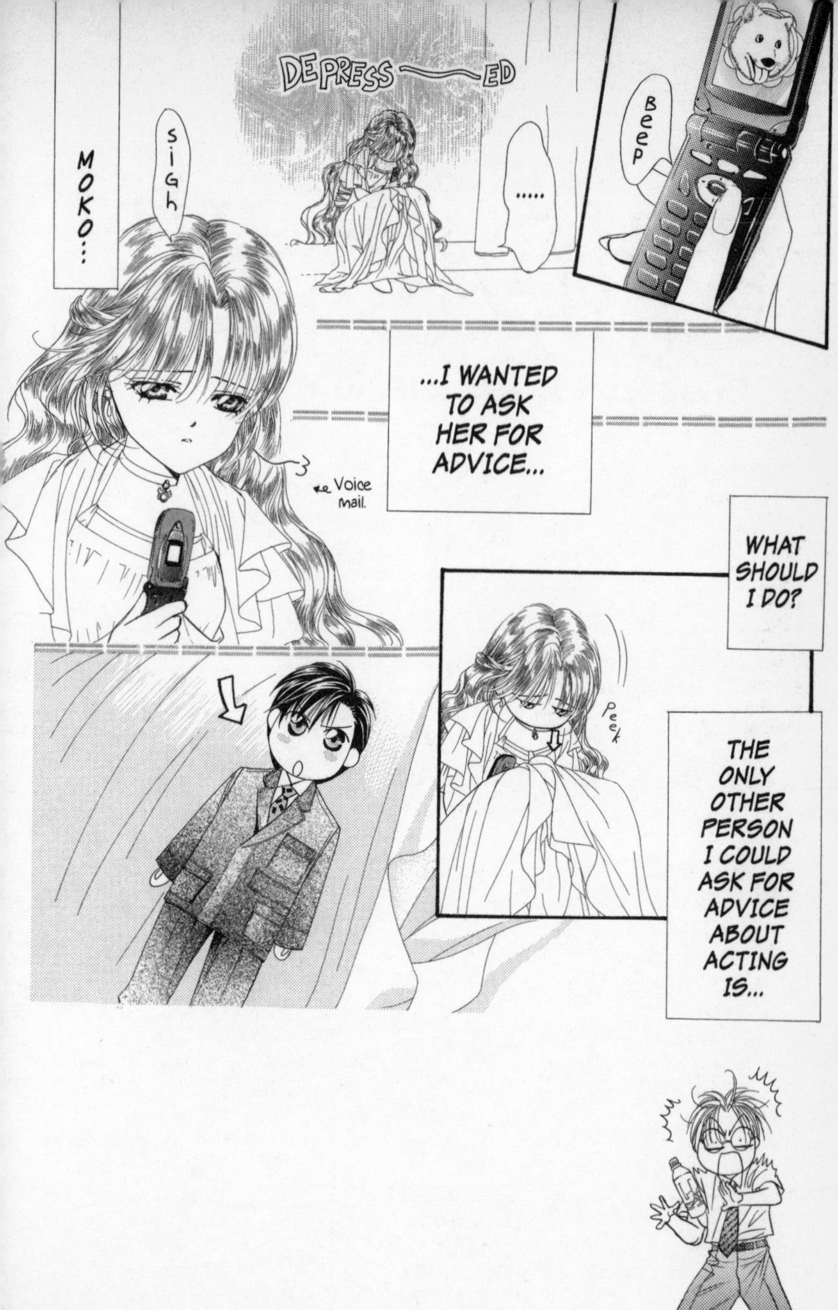
Beep
DEPRESS——ED
.....
MOKO...
sigh
...I WANTED TO ASK HER FOR ADVICE...
Voice mail.
WHAT SHOULD I DO?
Peek
THE ONLY OTHER PERSON I COULD ASK FOR ADVICE ABOUT ACTING IS...

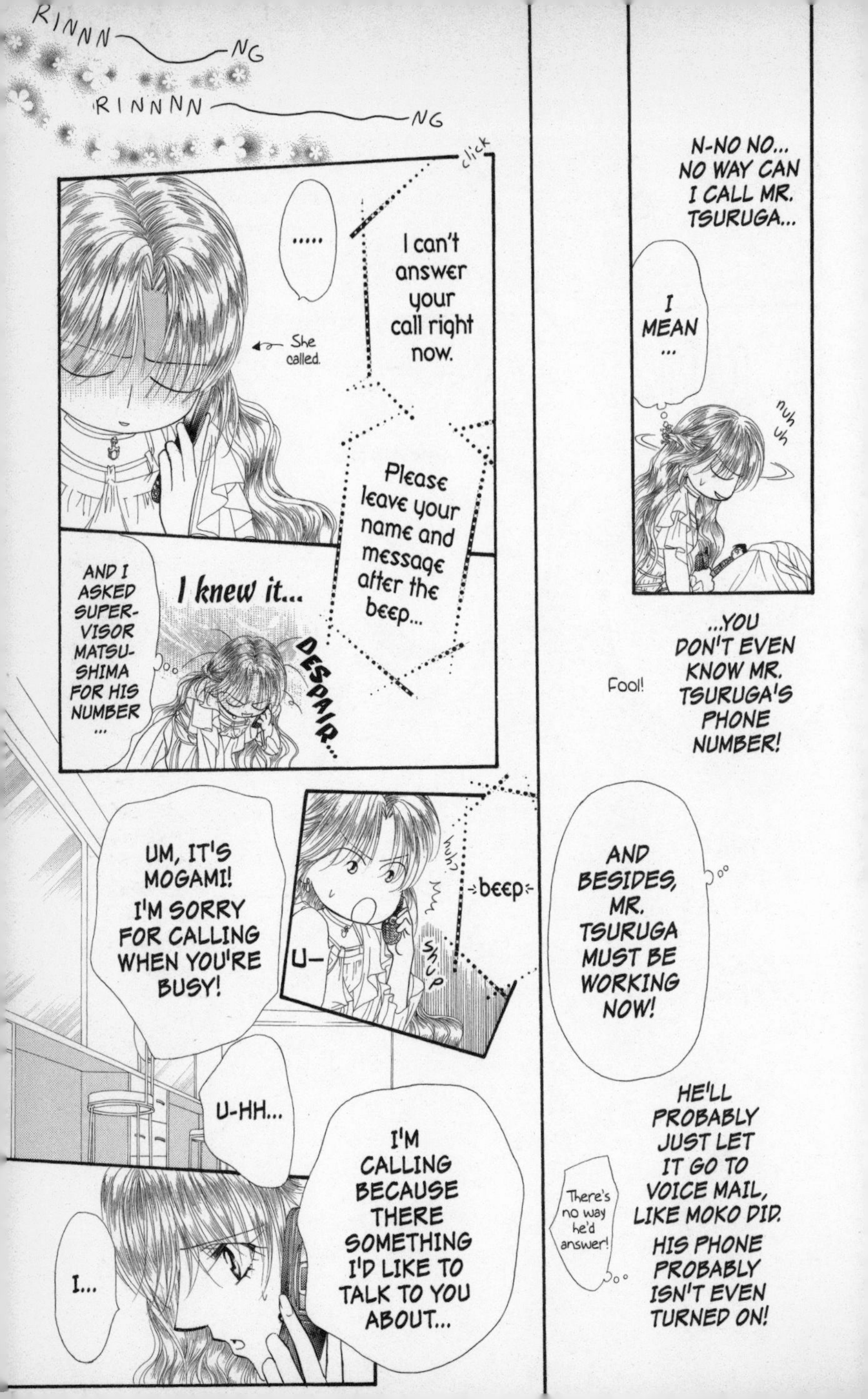
N-NO NO... NO WAY CAN I CALL MR. TSURUGA...
I MEAN...
nuh uh
...YOU DON'T EVEN KNOW MR. TSURUGA'S PHONE NUMBER!
Fool!
AND BESIDES, MR. TSURUGA MUST BE WORKING NOW!
HE'LL PROBABLY JUST LET IT GO TO VOICE MAIL, LIKE MOKO DID.
HIS PHONE PROBABLY ISN'T EVEN TURNED ON!
There's no way he'd answer!
RINNNNG
RINNNNNNG
click
I can't answer your call right now.
......
She called.
Please leave your name and message after the beep...
I knew it...
DESPAIR...
AND I ASKED SUPERVISOR MATSUSHIMA FOR HIS NUMBER...
click
beep
uh
SHUP
U—
UM, IT'S MOGAMI! I'M SORRY FOR CALLING WHEN YOU'RE BUSY!
U-HH...
I'M CALLING BECAUSE THERE SOMETHING I'D LIKE TO TALK TO YOU ABOUT...
I...

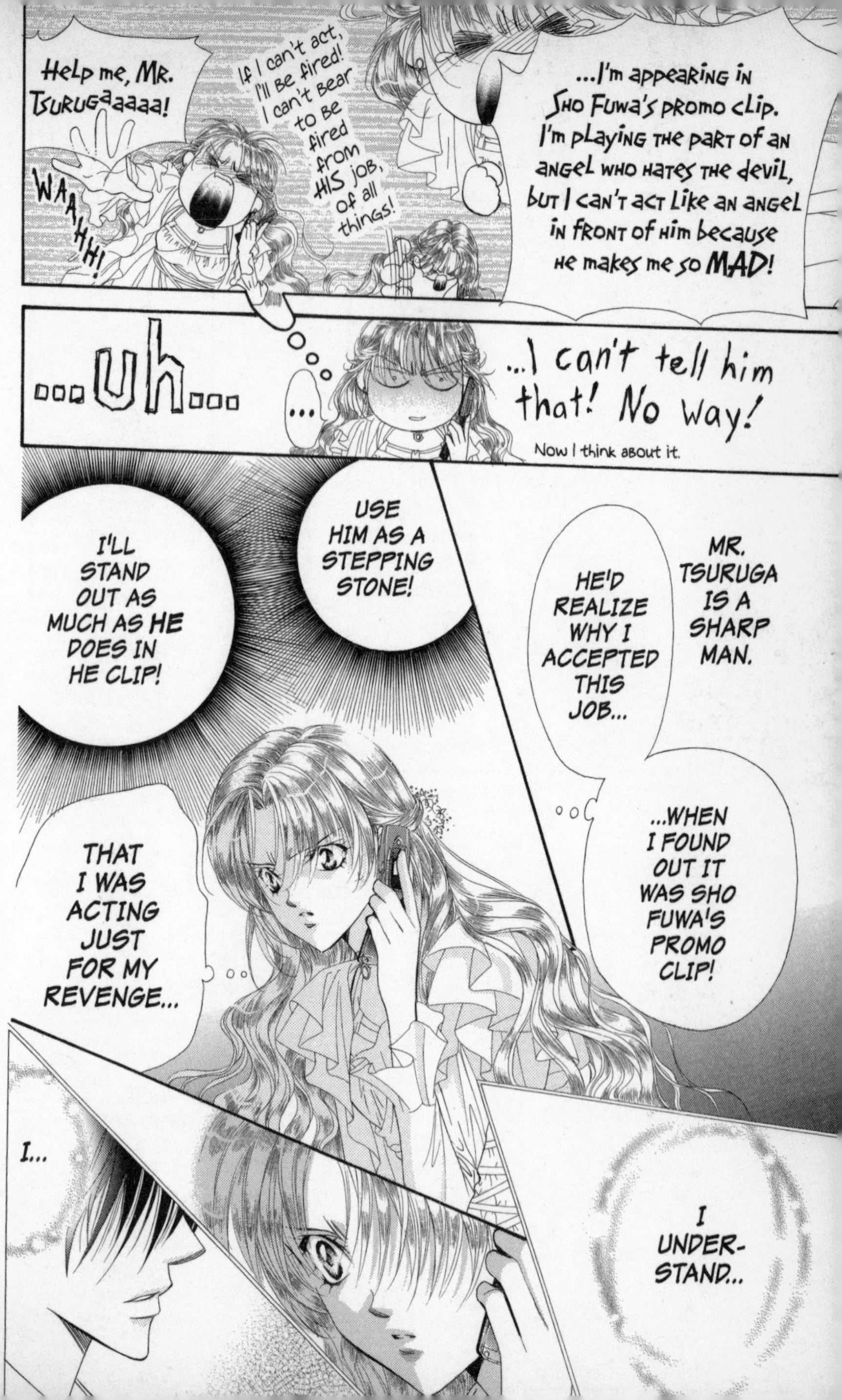
...I'm appearing in Sho Fuwa's promo clip. I'm playing the part of an angel who hates the devil, but I can't act like an angel in front of him because he makes me so MAD!
Help me, Mr. Tsurugaaaaa!
If I can't act, I'll be fired! I can't bear to be fired from HIS job, of all things!
WAAHHH!
...I can't tell him that! No way!
Now I think about it.
...
...uh...
Mr. Tsuruga is a sharp man.
He'd realize why I accepted this job...
...when I found out it was Sho Fuwa's promo clip!
That I was acting just for my revenge...
Use him as a stepping stone!
I'll stand out as much as HE does in he clip!
I understand...
I...

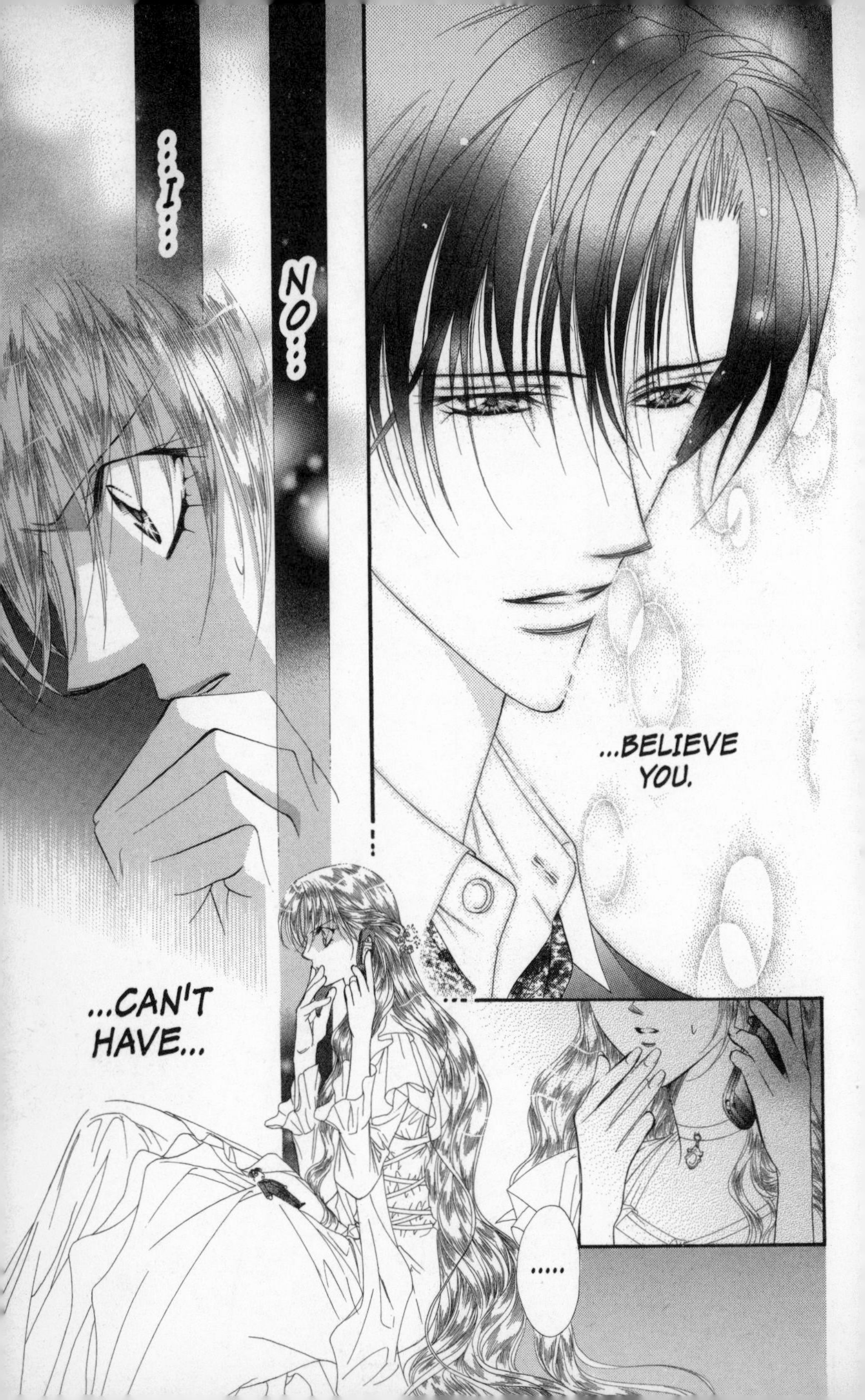
...BELIEVE YOU.
.....
...I...
NO...
...CAN'T HAVE...

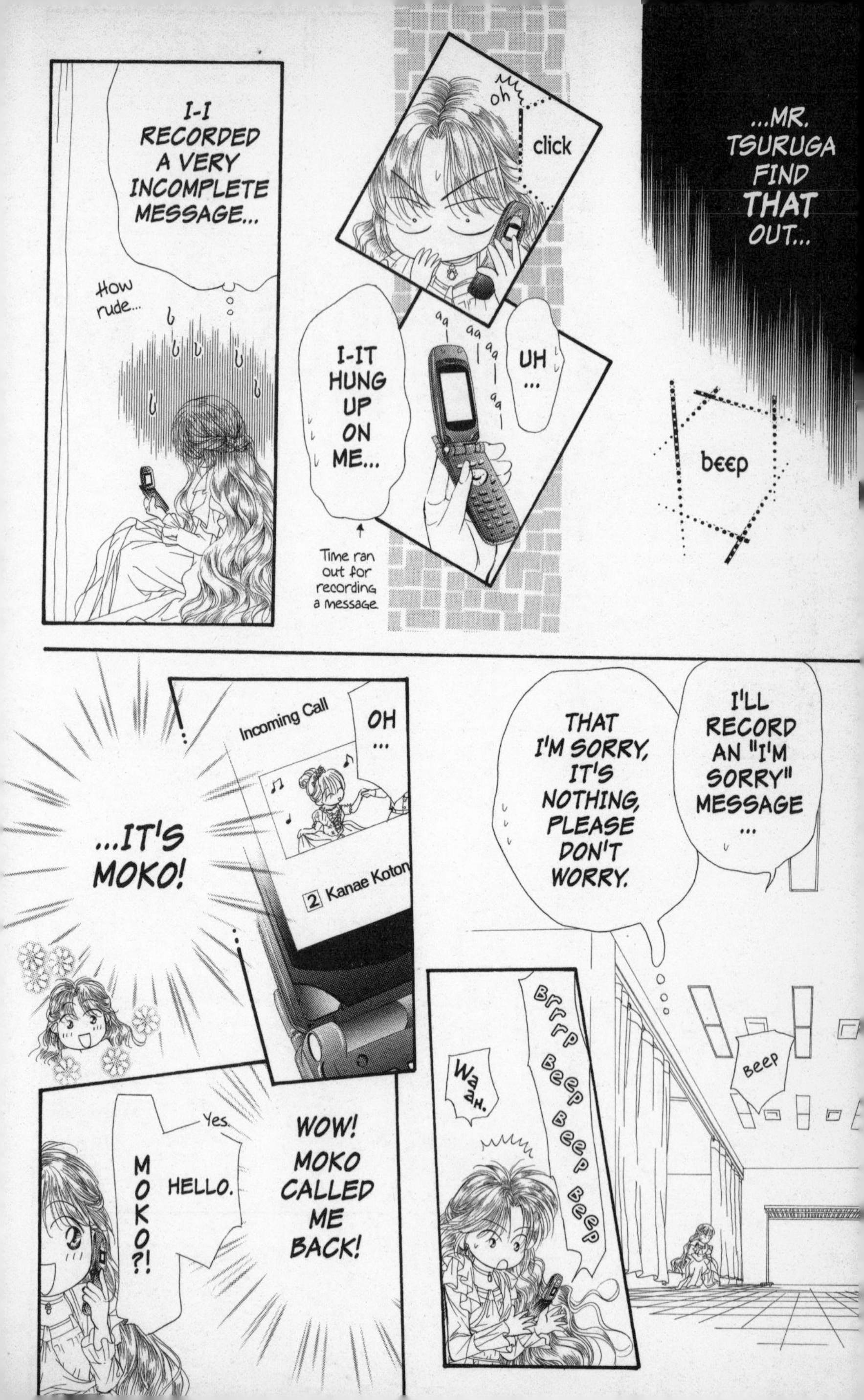
...MR. TSURUGA FIND THAT OUT...
bεεp
oh
click
UH ...
I-IT HUNG UP ON ME...
Time ran out for recording a message.
I-I RECORDED A VERY INCOMPLETE MESSAGE...
How rude...
I'LL RECORD AN "I'M SORRY" MESSAGE ...
THAT I'M SORRY, IT'S NOTHING, PLEASE DON'T WORRY.
Beep
Brrrp Beep Beep Beep Beep
Waah.
Incoming Call
OH ...
2 Kanae Koton
...IT'S MOKO!
WOW! MOKO CALLED ME BACK!
Yes.
HELLO.
MOKO?!

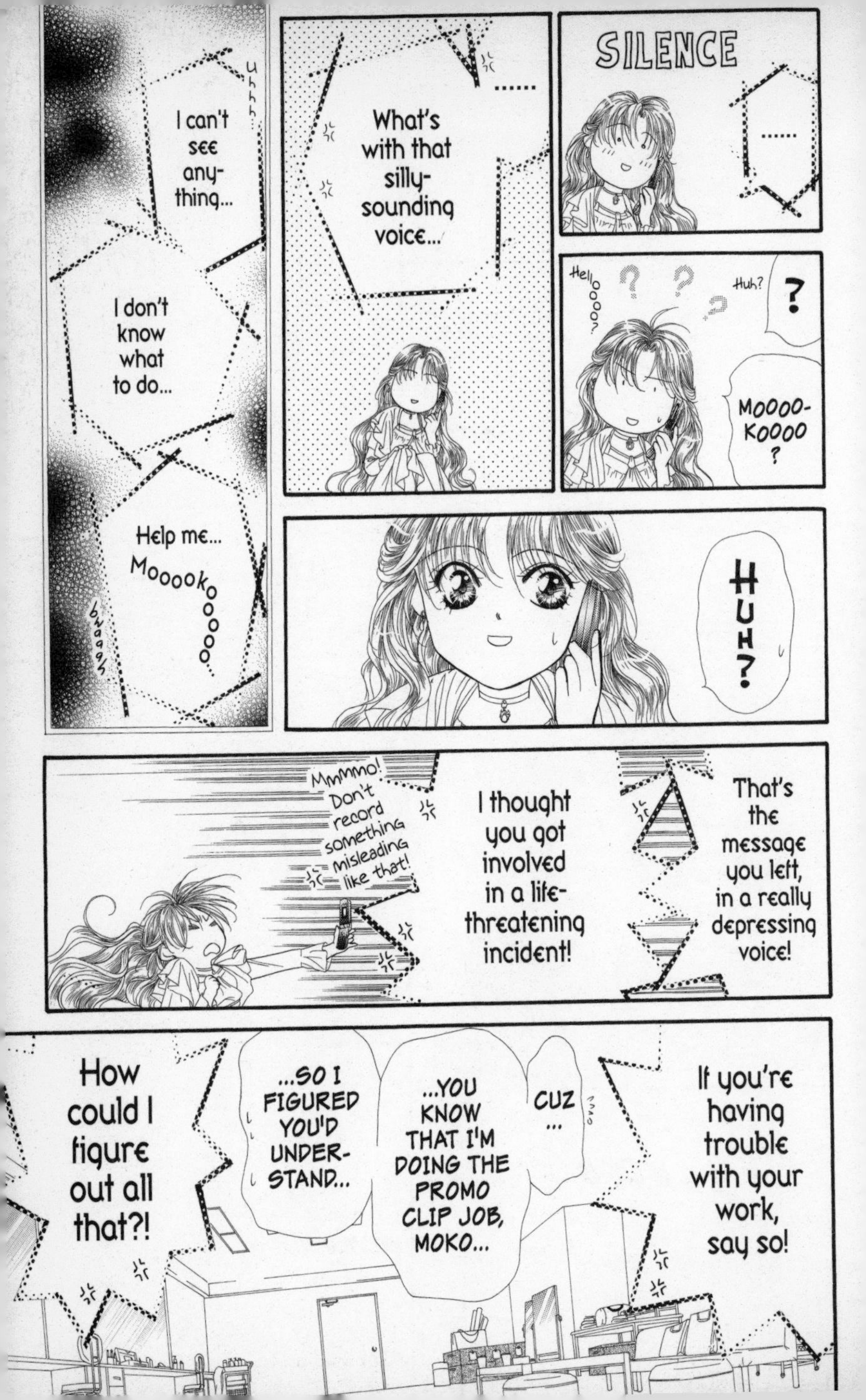
SILENCE
......
Hello o o o o ?
? ?
Huh?
?
?
MOOOO-KOOOO?
......
What's with that silly-sounding voice...!
HUH?
Uhhh
I can't see any-thing...
I don't know what to do...
Help me... Mooookooooo...
bwaaah
That's the message you left, in a really depressing voice!
I thought you got involved in a life-threatening incident!
Mmmmo! Don't record something misleading like that!
If you're having trouble with your work, say so!
CUZ...
...YOU KNOW THAT I'M DOING THE PROMO CLIP JOB, MOKO...
...SO I FIGURED YOU'D UNDER-STAND...
How could I figure out all that?!

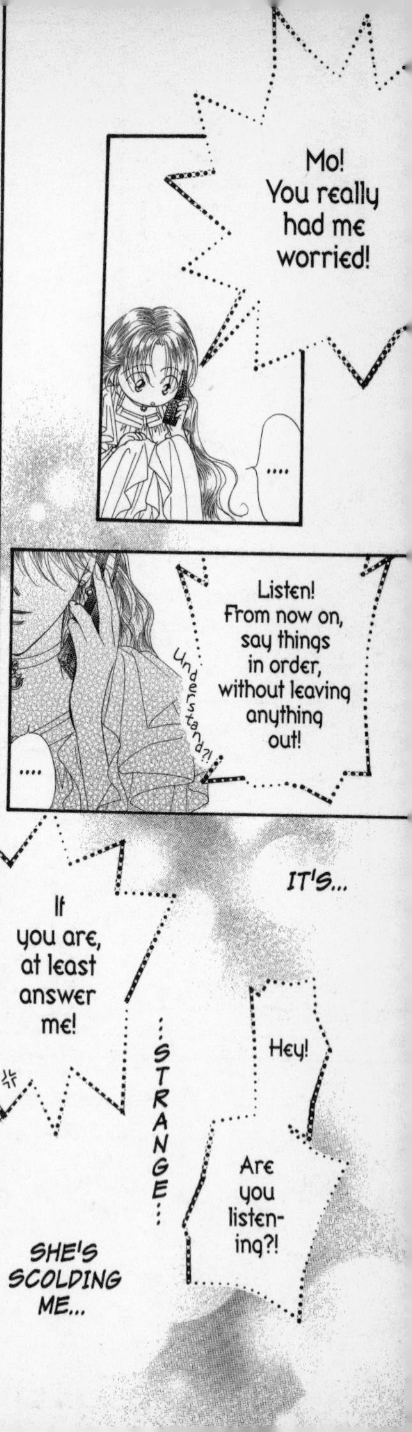
Mo! You really had me worried!
....
Listen! From now on, say things in order, without leaving anything out!
Understand?!
....
Hey!
Are you listening?!
If you are, at least answer me!
IT'S...
...STRANGE...
SHE'S SCOLDING ME...
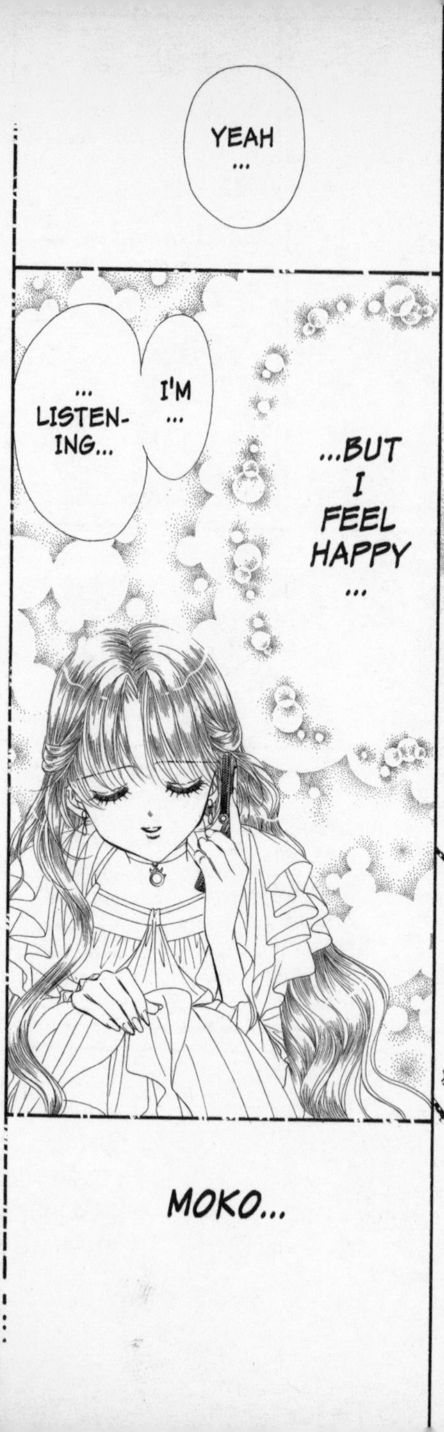
YEAH ...
I'M ...
... LISTENING...
...BUT I FEEL HAPPY ...
MOKO...

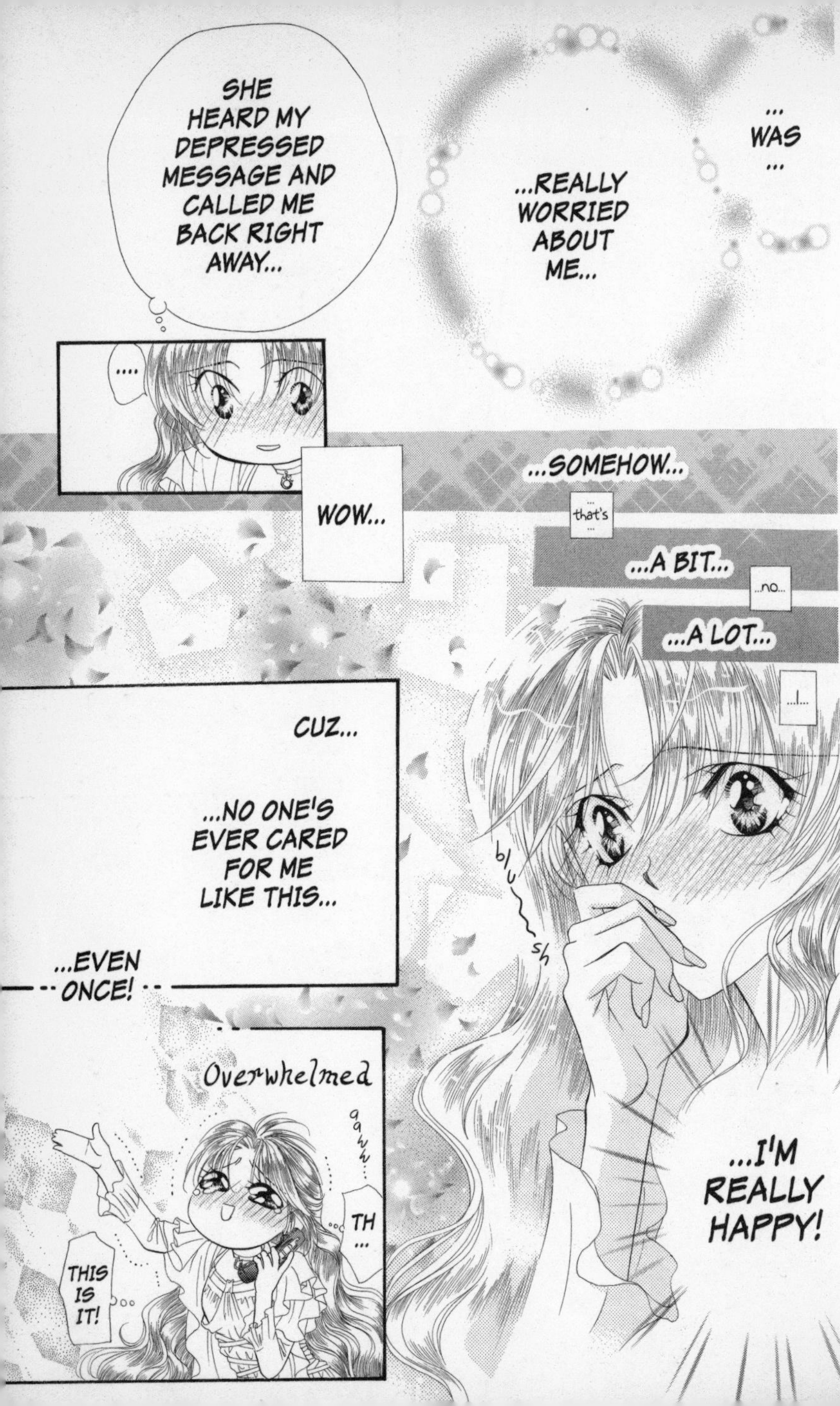

... WAS ...
...REALLY WORRIED ABOUT ME...
SHE HEARD MY DEPRESSED MESSAGE AND CALLED ME BACK RIGHT AWAY...
....
...SOMEHOW...
... that's ...
...A BIT...
...no...
...A LOT...
WOW...
...I...
blush
CUZ...
...NO ONE'S EVER CARED FOR ME LIKE THIS...
...EVEN ONCE!
...I'M REALLY HAPPY!
Overwhelmed
aaww...
TH ...
THIS IS IT!

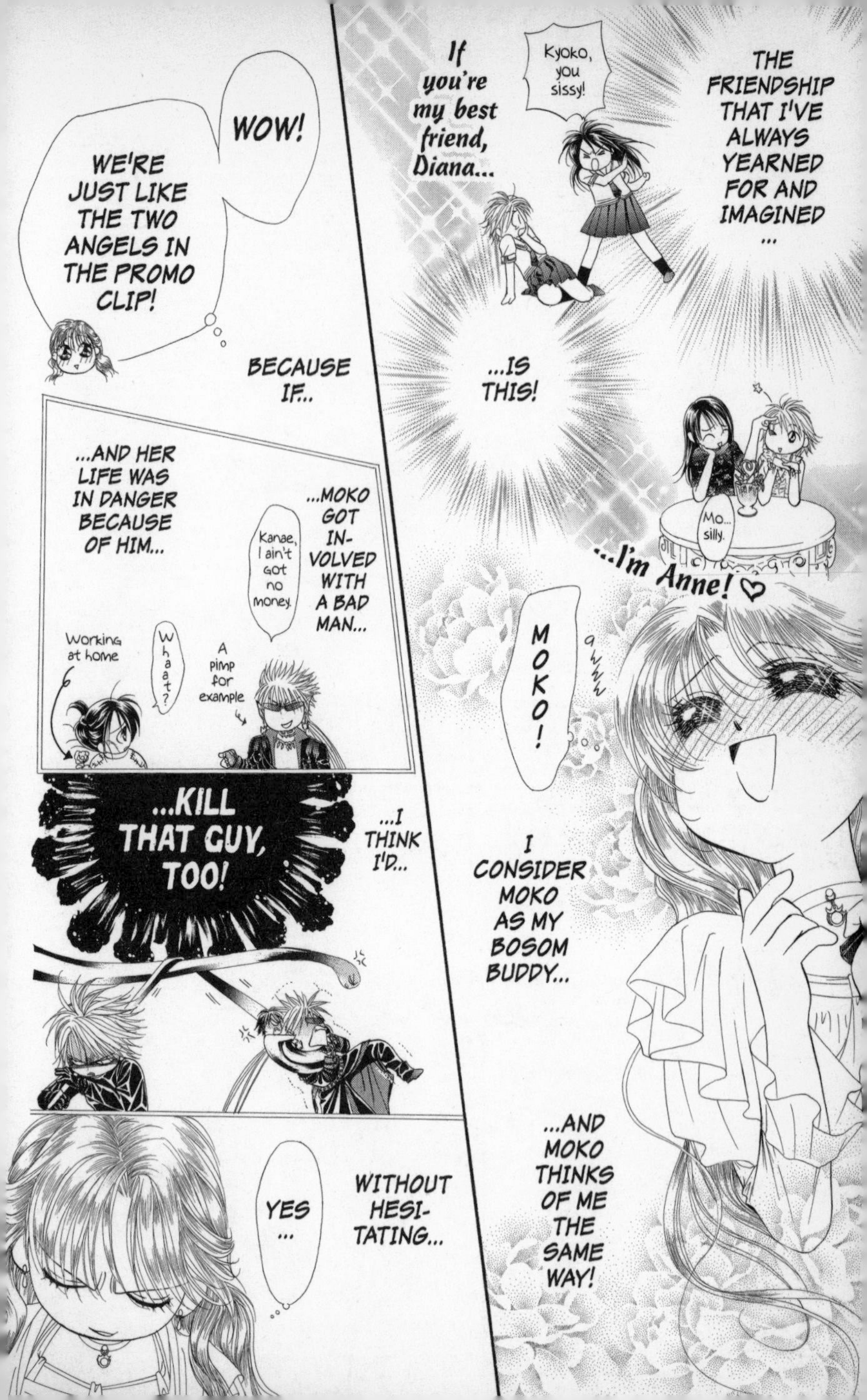
THE FRIENDSHIP THAT I'VE ALWAYS YEARNED FOR AND IMAGINED ...
Kyoko, you sissy!
If you're my best friend, Diana...
...IS THIS!
Mo... silly.
...I'm Anne! ♡
MOKO!
awww
I CONSIDER MOKO AS MY BOSOM BUDDY...
...AND MOKO THINKS OF ME THE SAME WAY!
WOW!
WE'RE JUST LIKE THE TWO ANGELS IN THE PROMO CLIP!
BECAUSE IF...
...MOKO GOT IN-VOLVED WITH A BAD MAN...
Kanae, I ain't got no money.
...AND HER LIFE WAS IN DANGER BECAUSE OF HIM...
A pimp for example
Whaat?
Working at home
...I THINK I'D...
...KILL THAT GUY, TOO!
WITHOUT HESI-TATING...
YES ...

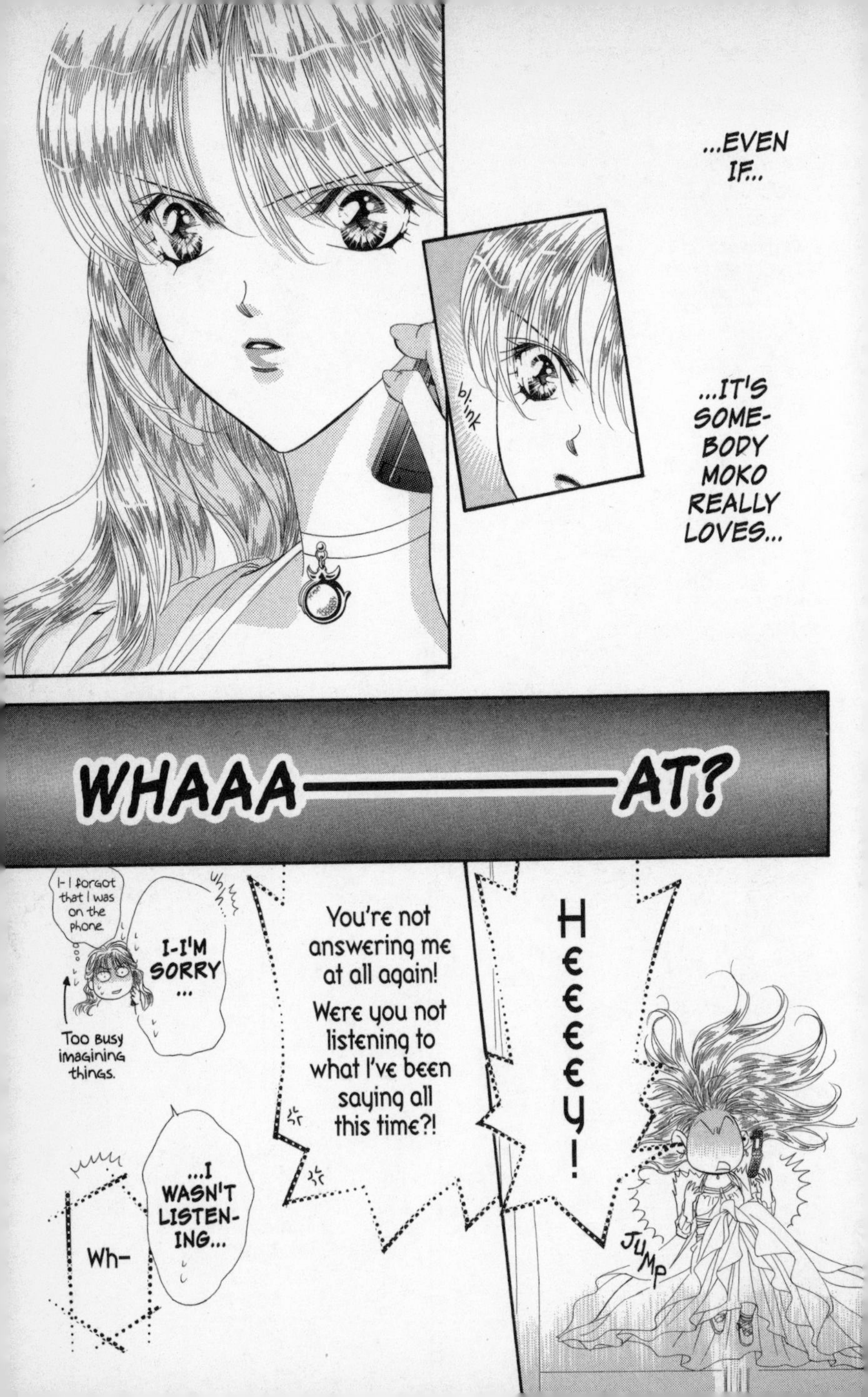
...EVEN IF...
...IT'S SOME-BODY MOKO REALLY LOVES...
blink
WHAAA——————AT?
HEEEEY!
JUMP
You're not answering me at all again! Were you not listening to what I've been saying all this time?!
I-I'M SORRY...
I-I forgot that I was on the phone
Too busy imagining things.
...I WASN'T LISTEN-ING...
Wh-

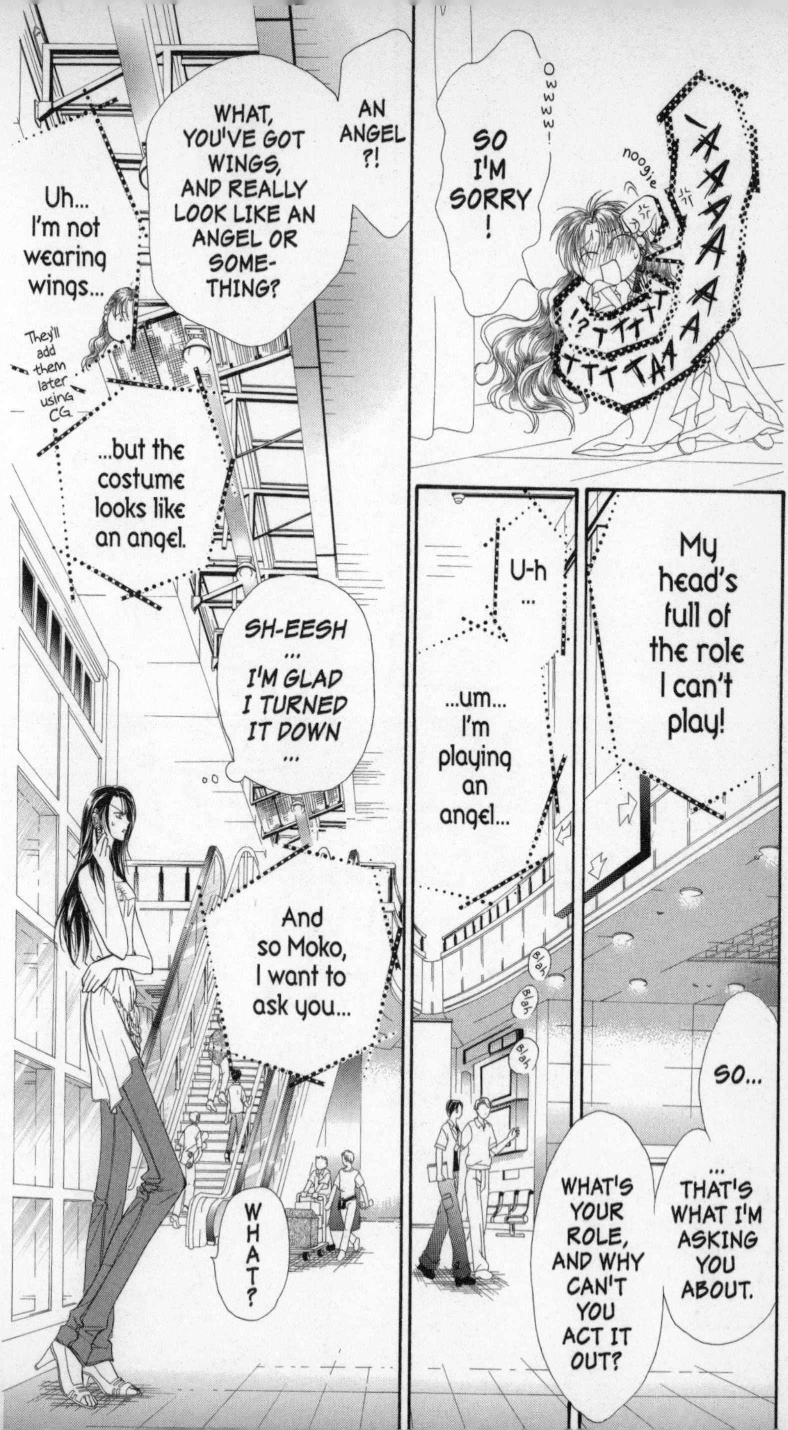
OWWWW!
SO I'M SORRY!
noogie
AAAAAAA
!? TTTTTTTTTTA
My head's full of the role I can't play!
U-h...
...um... I'm playing an angel...
SO...
...THAT'S WHAT I'M ASKING YOU ABOUT.
WHAT'S YOUR ROLE, AND WHY CAN'T YOU ACT IT OUT?
AN ANGEL?!
WHAT, YOU'VE GOT WINGS, AND REALLY LOOK LIKE AN ANGEL OR SOME-THING?
Uh... I'm not wearing wings...
They'll add them later using CG.
...but the costume looks like an angel.
SH-EESH... I'M GLAD I TURNED IT DOWN...
And so Moko, I want to ask you...
WHAT?

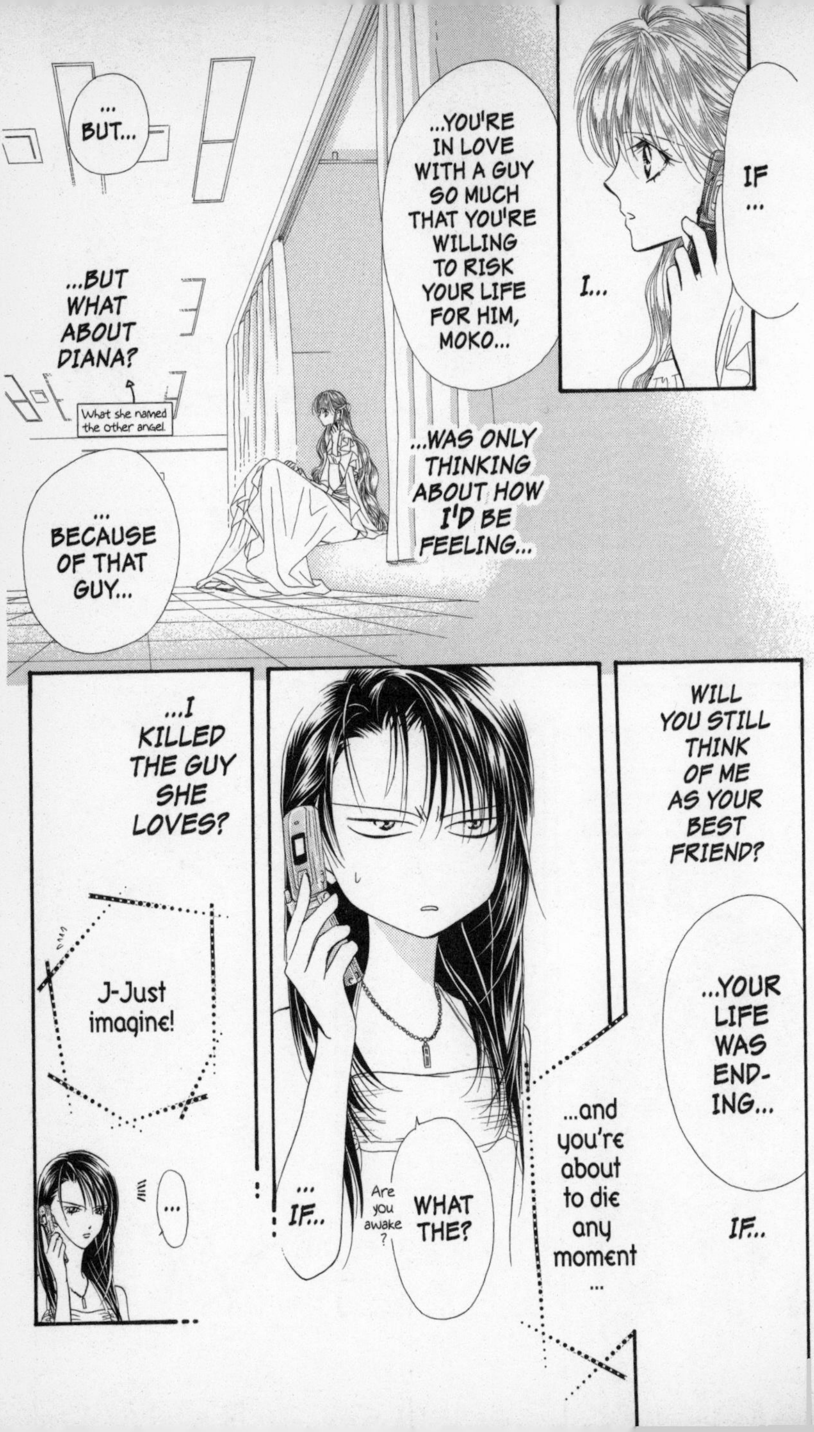
IF...
I...
...YOU'RE IN LOVE WITH A GUY SO MUCH THAT YOU'RE WILLING TO RISK YOUR LIFE FOR HIM, MOKO...
...WAS ONLY THINKING ABOUT HOW I'D BE FEELING...
... BUT...
...BUT WHAT ABOUT DIANA?
What she named the other angel.
... BECAUSE OF THAT GUY...
WILL YOU STILL THINK OF ME AS YOUR BEST FRIEND?
...YOUR LIFE WAS END-ING...
IF...
...and you're about to die any moment ...
WHAT THE?
Are you awake?
... IF...
...I KILLED THE GUY SHE LOVES?
J-Just imagine!
...

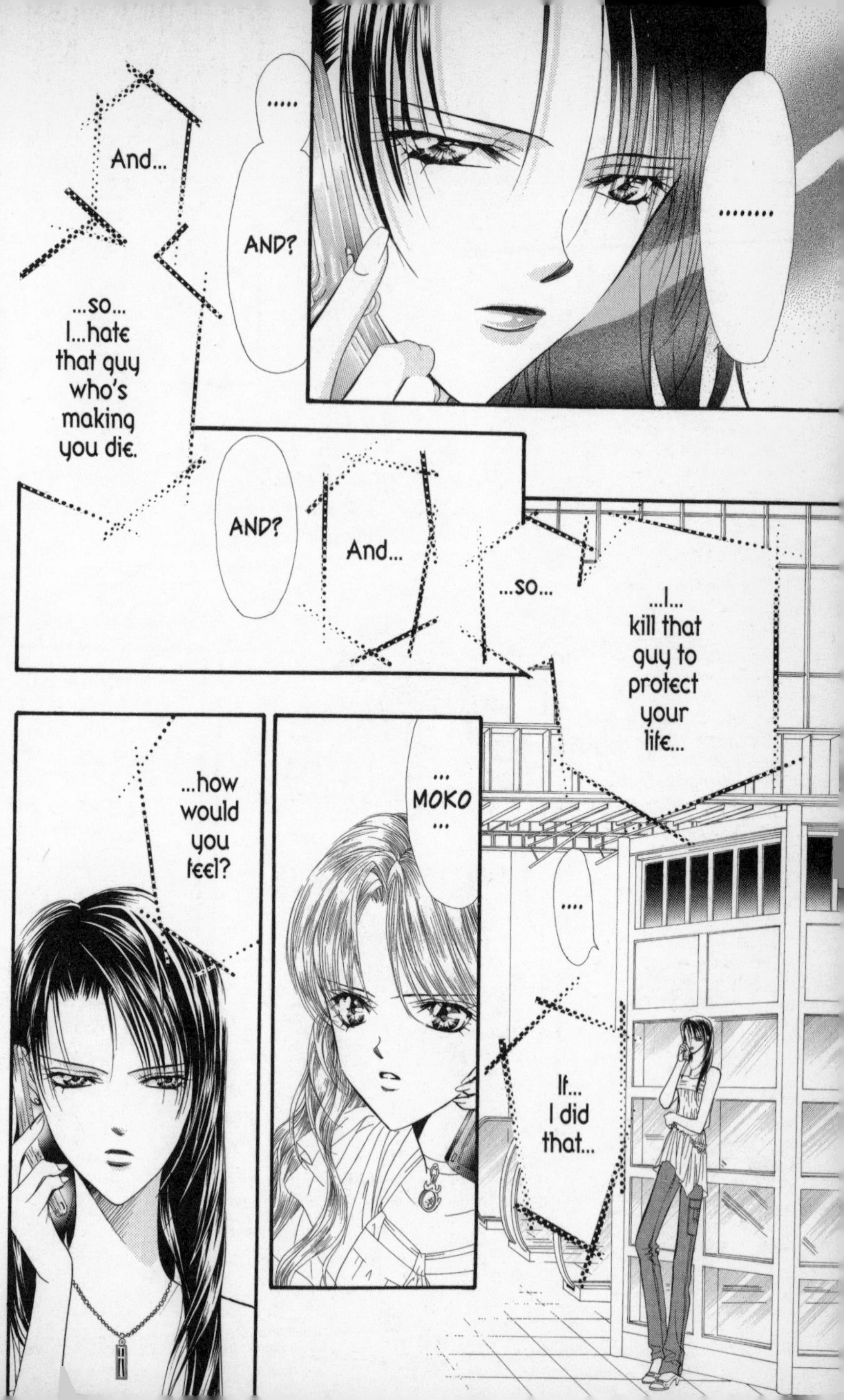
........
.....
AND?
And...
...so...
I...hate
that guy
who's
making
you die.
AND?
And...
...so...
...I...
kill that
guy to
protect
your
life...
....
If...
I did
that...
...
MOKO
...
...how
would
you
feel?

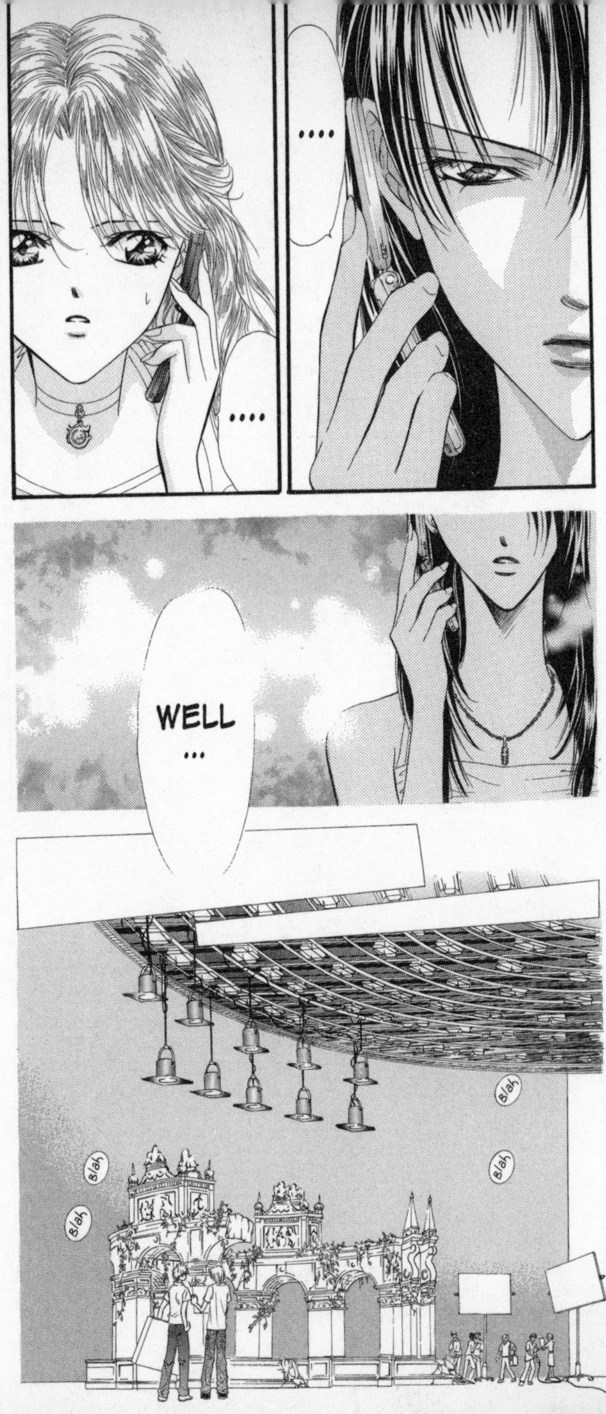
....
....
WELL ...
Blah
Blah
Blah
Blah

When I was drawing the promo clip arc, I was thinking that I wanted to do a little... of the devil version of Ren...But...I did it, But Sho looks Better in something like that..No...it's not just this time, But I always have trouble deciding what clothes Ren should wear in the story...Sho looks Good in anything, But with Ren, that doesn't work...(like Gaudy decorative stuff...) The range of clothes that he looks Good in is very narrow... especially summer clothes...I can only make him wear really simple clothes, and that's inconvenient...so with the devil Ren, the design of the clothes and accessories are very simple compared to Sho's...therefore, he doesn't look like a devil too much... oh dear... ...it's just a cosplay... ...one more thing I wanted to do was have Kanae wear the angel costume that Kyoko wore... if Kanae had accepted that job, Kanae would have worn the costume Kyoko wore...

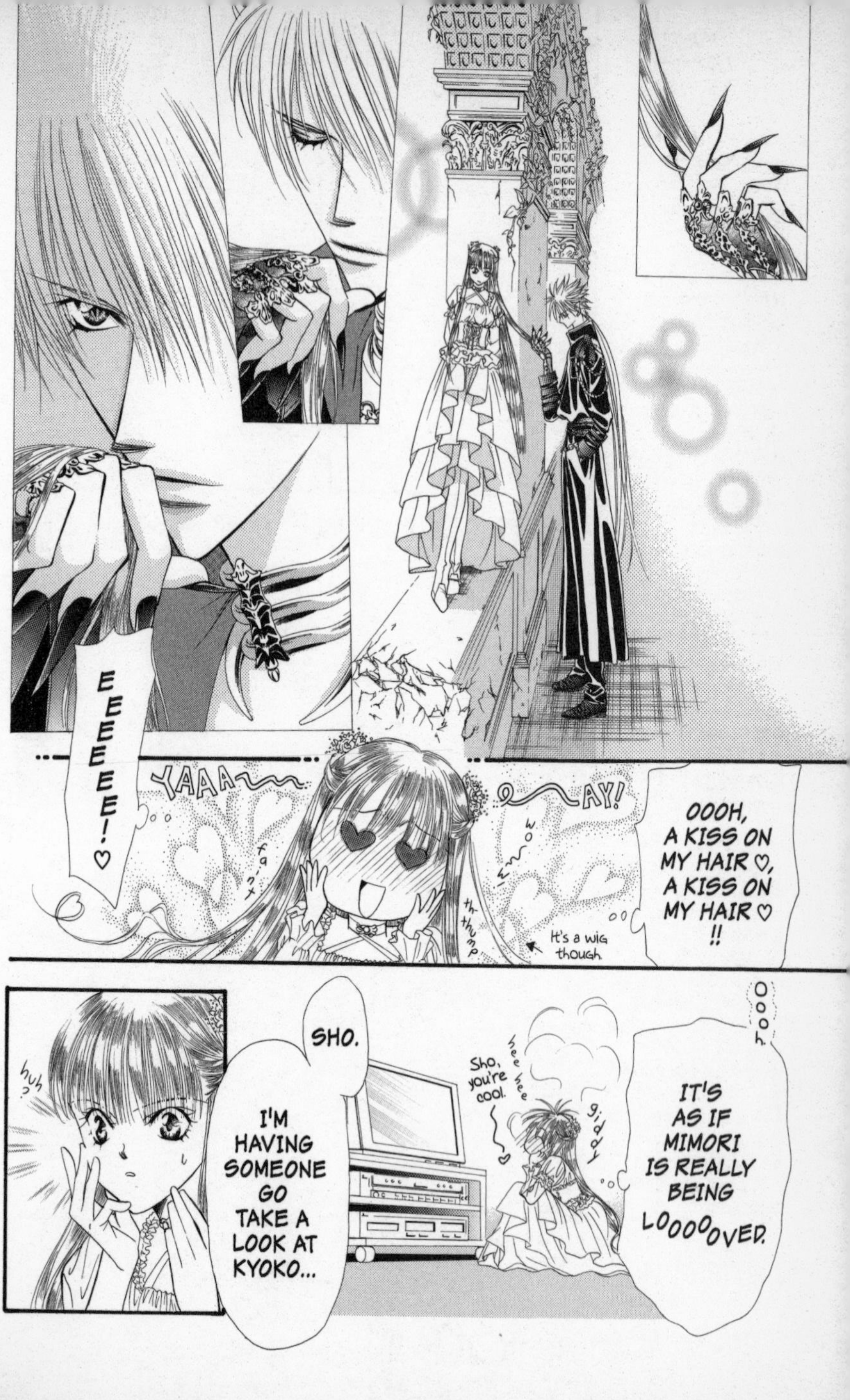
OOOH, A KISS ON MY HAIR ♡, A KISS ON MY HAIR ♡ !!
It's a wig though.
th-thump
wo-w-w!
~AY!
faint
YAAA~
EEEEEEE!♡
Oooh.
IT'S AS IF MIMORI IS REALLY BEING LOOOOOVED.
giddy
hee hee
Sho, you're cool.
SHO.
I'M HAVING SOMEONE GO TAKE A LOOK AT KYOKO...
huh?

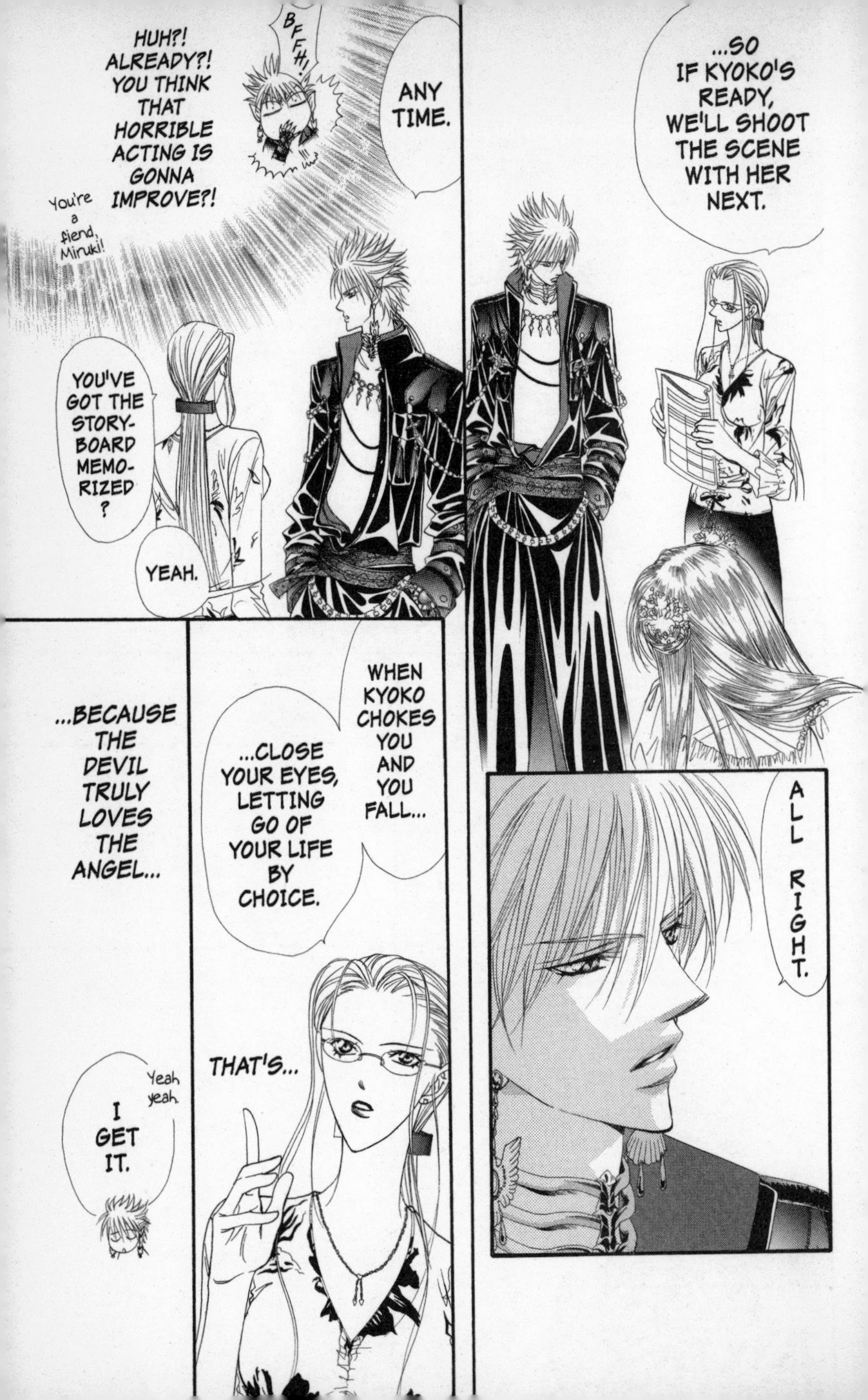
...SO IF KYOKO'S READY, WE'LL SHOOT THE SCENE WITH HER NEXT.
ANY TIME.
BFFH!
HUH?! ALREADY?! YOU THINK THAT HORRIBLE ACTING IS GONNA IMPROVE?!
You're a fiend, Miruki!
YOU'VE GOT THE STORY-BOARD MEMO-RIZED?
YEAH.
ALL RIGHT.
WHEN KYOKO CHOKES YOU AND YOU FALL...
...CLOSE YOUR EYES, LETTING GO OF YOUR LIFE BY CHOICE.
THAT'S...
...BECAUSE THE DEVIL TRULY LOVES THE ANGEL...
Yeah yeah.
I GET IT.

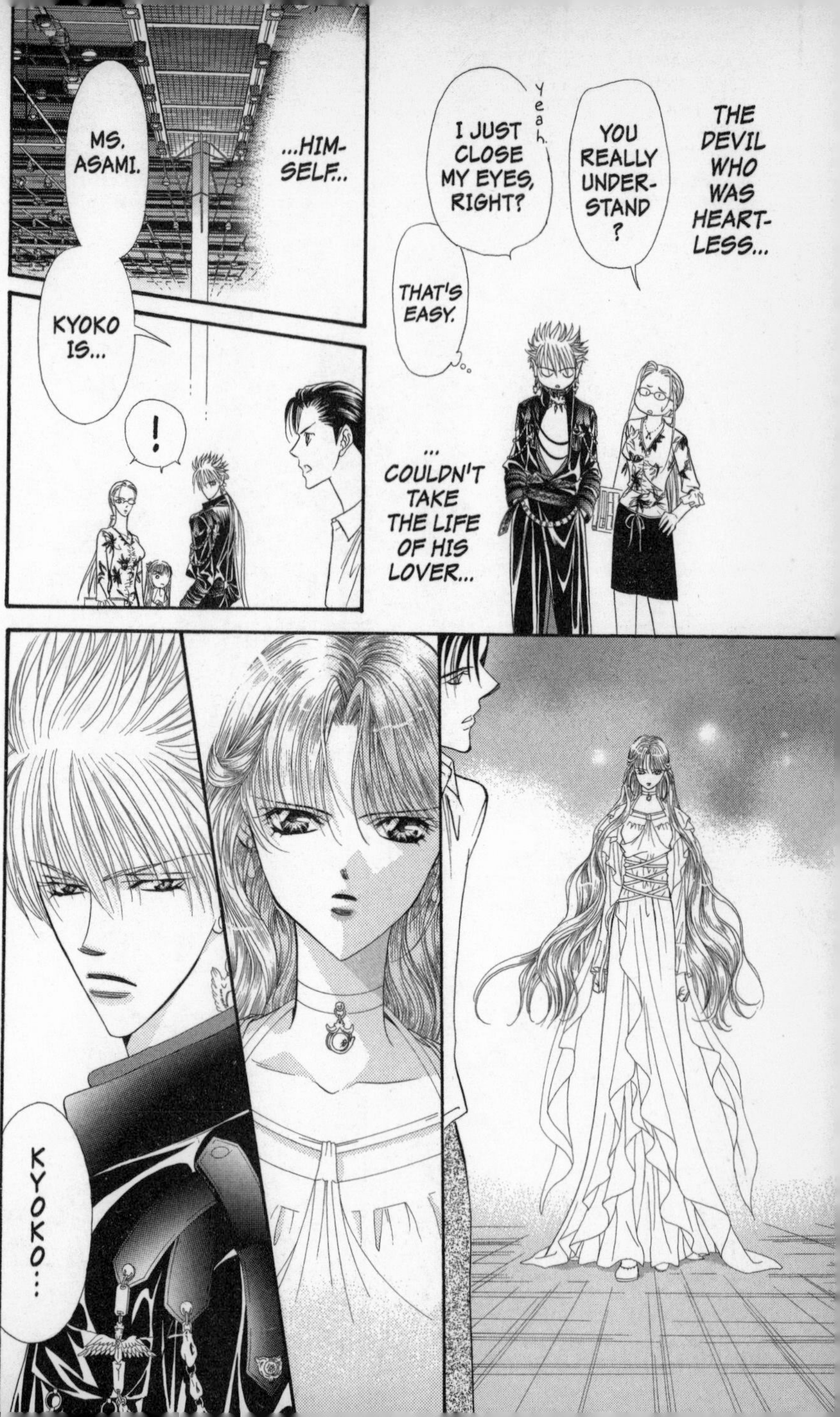
THE DEVIL WHO WAS HEART-LESS...
YOU REALLY UNDER-STAND?
Yeah.
I JUST CLOSE MY EYES, RIGHT?
THAT'S EASY.
...COULDN'T TAKE THE LIFE OF HIS LOVER...
...HIM-SELF...
MS. ASAMI.
KYOKO IS...
!
KYOKO...

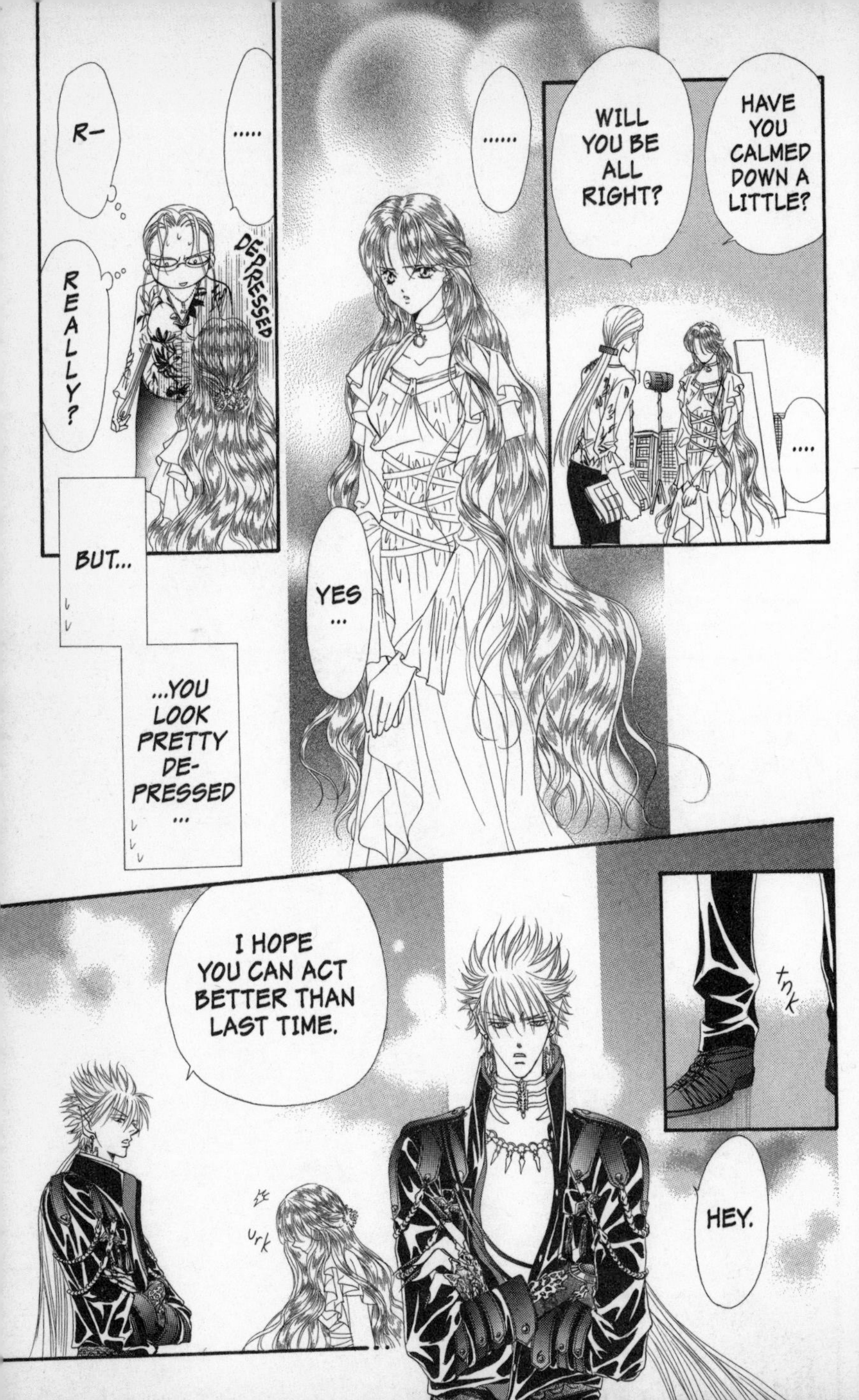
HAVE YOU CALMED DOWN A LITTLE?
WILL YOU BE ALL RIGHT?
....
......
YES ...
......
R—
DEPRESSED
REALLY?
BUT...
...YOU LOOK PRETTY DE-PRESSED ...
tnk
HEY.
I HOPE YOU CAN ACT BETTER THAN LAST TIME.
urk

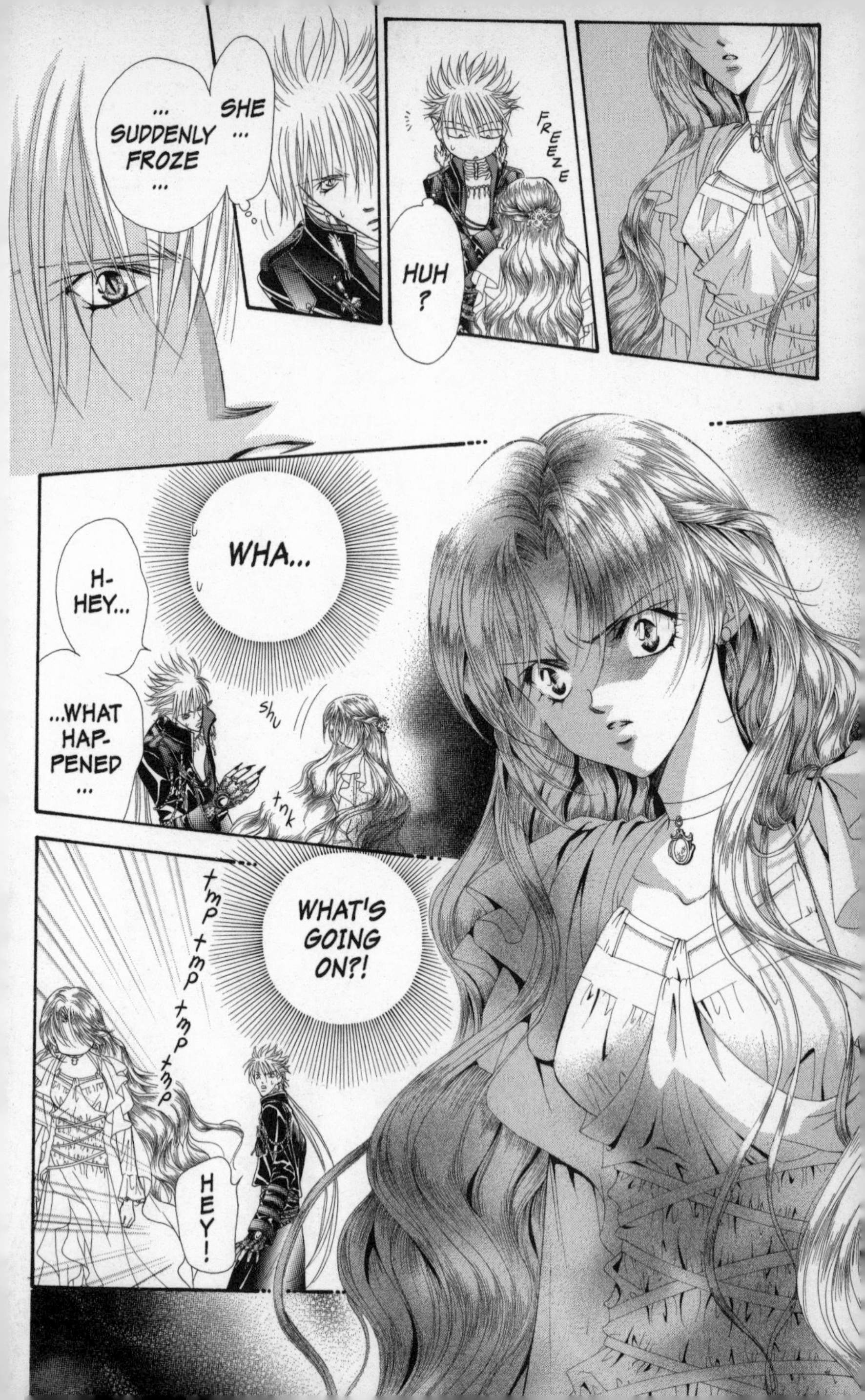
FREEZE
HUH?
SHE ...
... SUDDENLY FROZE ...
WHA...
H-HEY...
...WHAT HAPPENED ...
shu
tnk
WHAT'S GOING ON?!
tmp tmp tmp tmp
HEY!

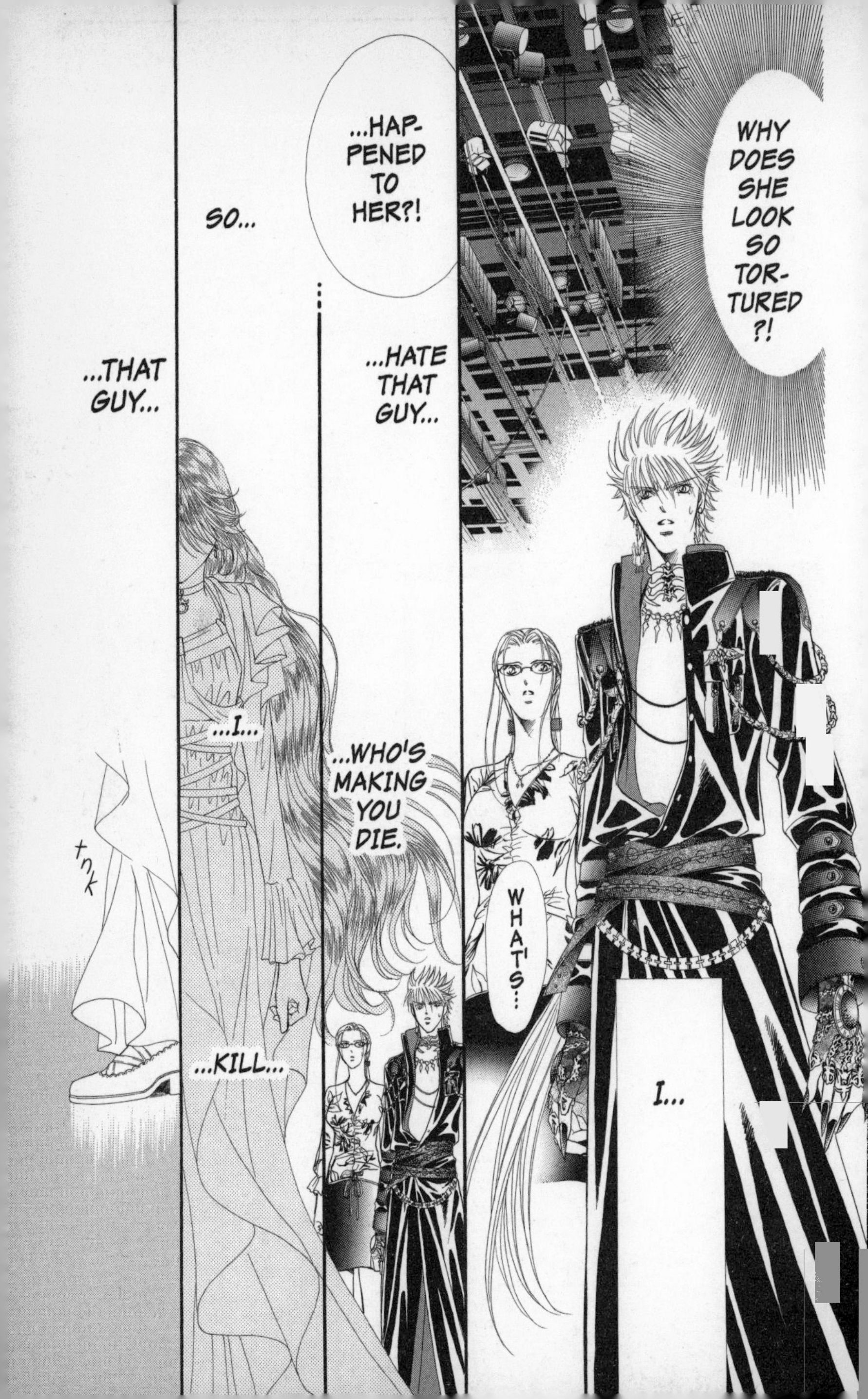
WHY DOES SHE LOOK SO TOR-TURED?!
WHAT'S...
...HAP-PENED TO HER?!
I...
...HATE THAT GUY...
...WHO'S MAKING YOU DIE.
SO...
...I...
...KILL...
...THAT GUY...
TNK

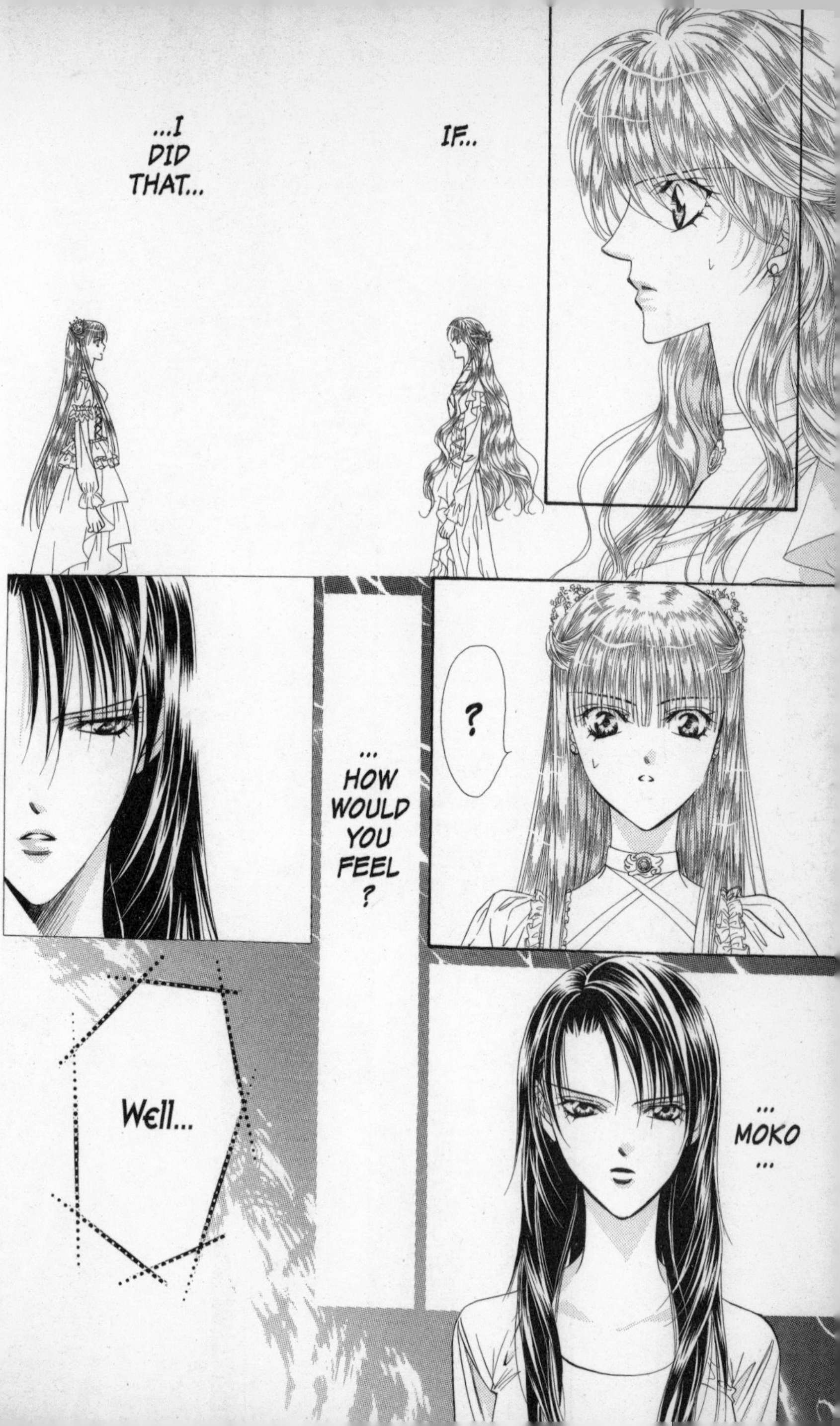
IF...
...I DID THAT...
?
...HOW WOULD YOU FEEL?
...MOKO...
Well...

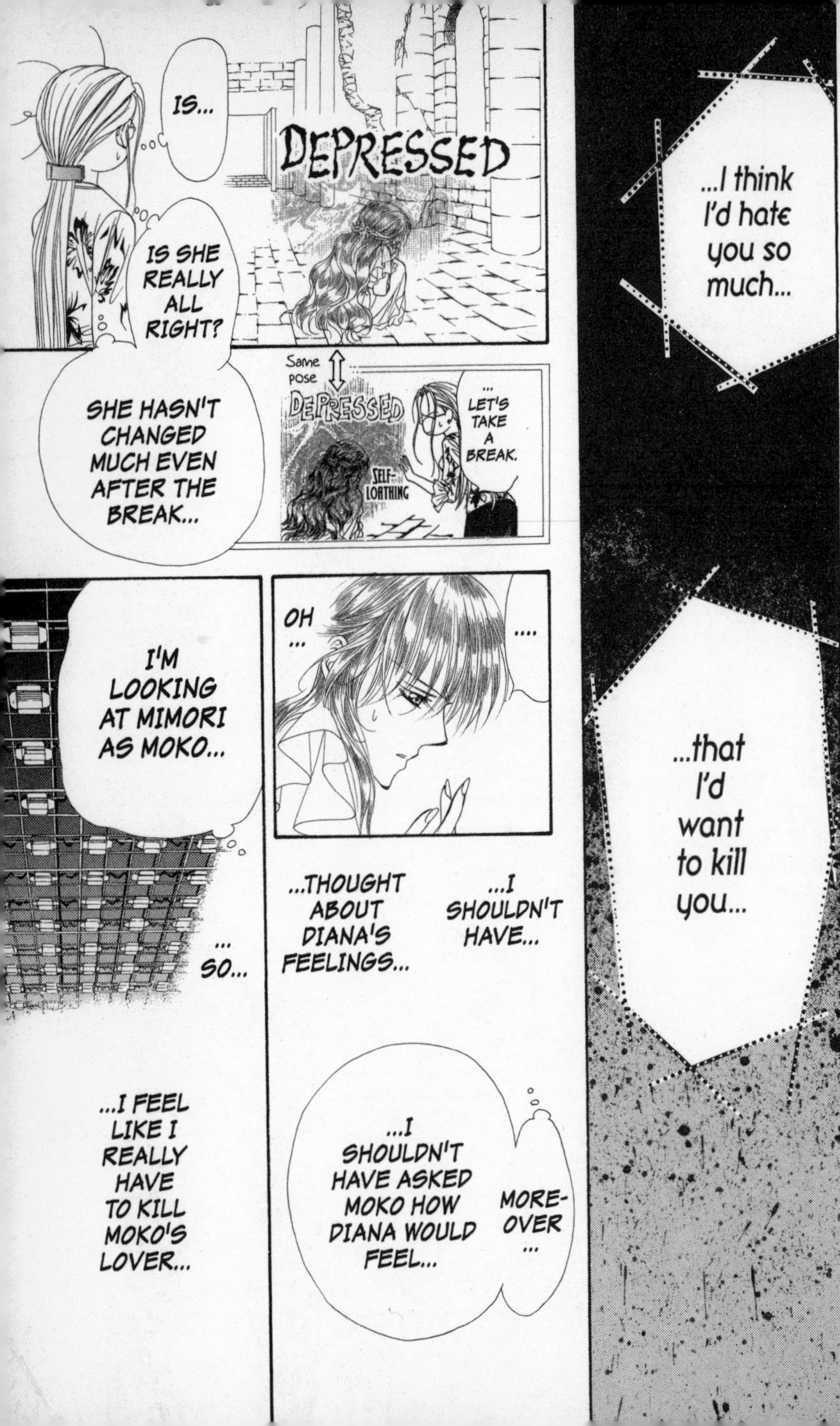
...I think I'd hate you so much...
...that I'd want to kill you...
IS...
DEPRESSED
IS SHE REALLY ALL RIGHT?
... LET'S TAKE A BREAK.
Same pose
DEPRESSED
SELF-LOATHING
SHE HASN'T CHANGED MUCH EVEN AFTER THE BREAK...
....
OH ...
I'M LOOKING AT MIMORI AS MOKO...
... SO...
...I SHOULDN'T HAVE...
...THOUGHT ABOUT DIANA'S FEELINGS...
MORE-OVER ...
...I SHOULDN'T HAVE ASKED MOKO HOW DIANA WOULD FEEL...
...I FEEL LIKE I REALLY HAVE TO KILL MOKO'S LOVER...

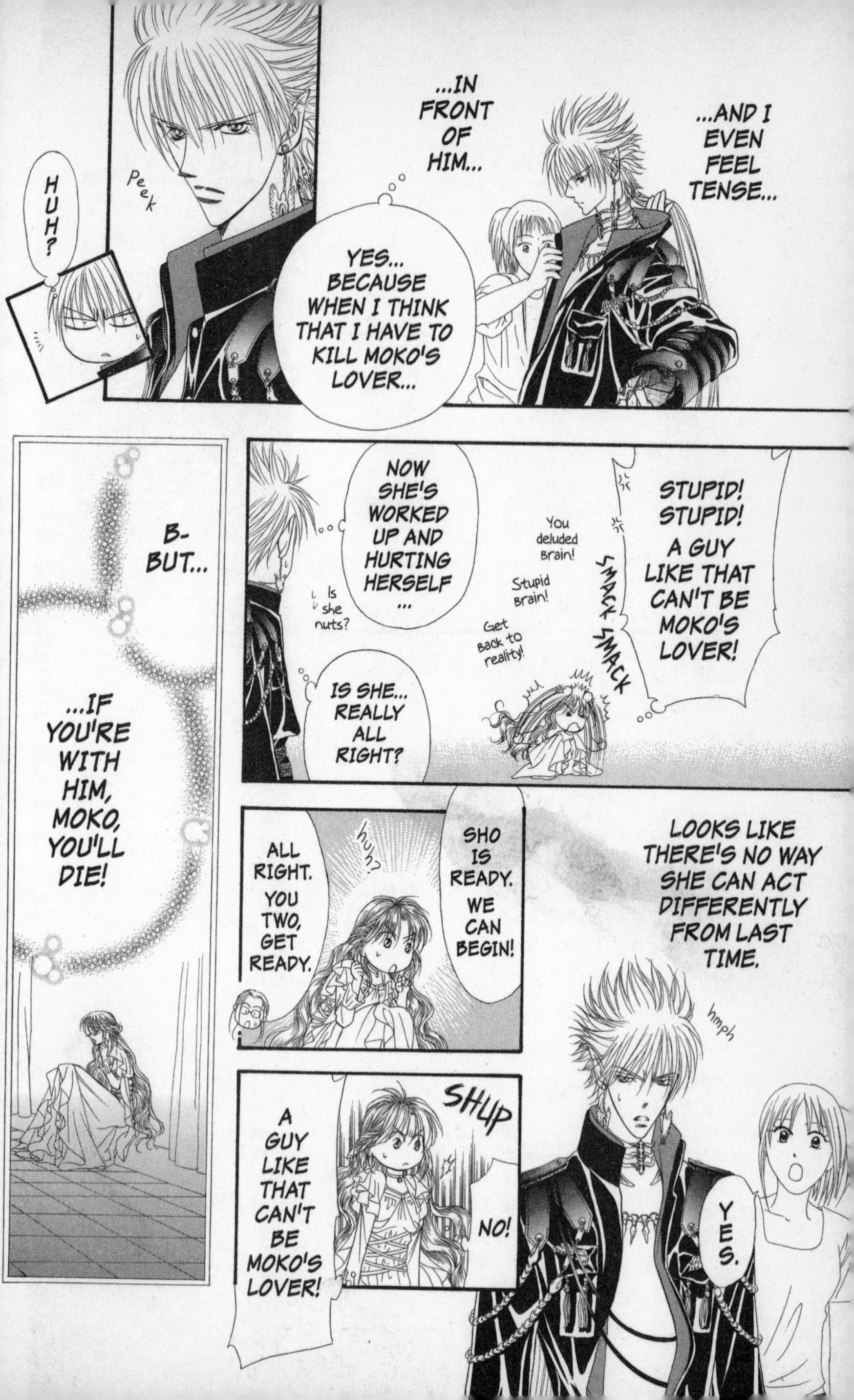
...AND I EVEN FEEL TENSE...
...IN FRONT OF HIM...
YES... BECAUSE WHEN I THINK THAT I HAVE TO KILL MOKO'S LOVER...
Peek
HUH?
STUPID! STUPID! A GUY LIKE THAT CAN'T BE MOKO'S LOVER!
SMACK SMACK
You deluded Brain!
Stupid Brain!
Get back to reality!
NOW SHE'S WORKED UP AND HURTING HERSELF...
Is she nuts?
IS SHE... REALLY ALL RIGHT?
LOOKS LIKE THERE'S NO WAY SHE CAN ACT DIFFERENTLY FROM LAST TIME.
hmph
SHO IS READY. WE CAN BEGIN!
huh?
ALL RIGHT. YOU TWO, GET READY.
YES.
NO!
SHUP
A GUY LIKE THAT CAN'T BE MOKO'S LOVER!
B-BUT...
...IF YOU'RE WITH HIM, MOKO, YOU'LL DIE!

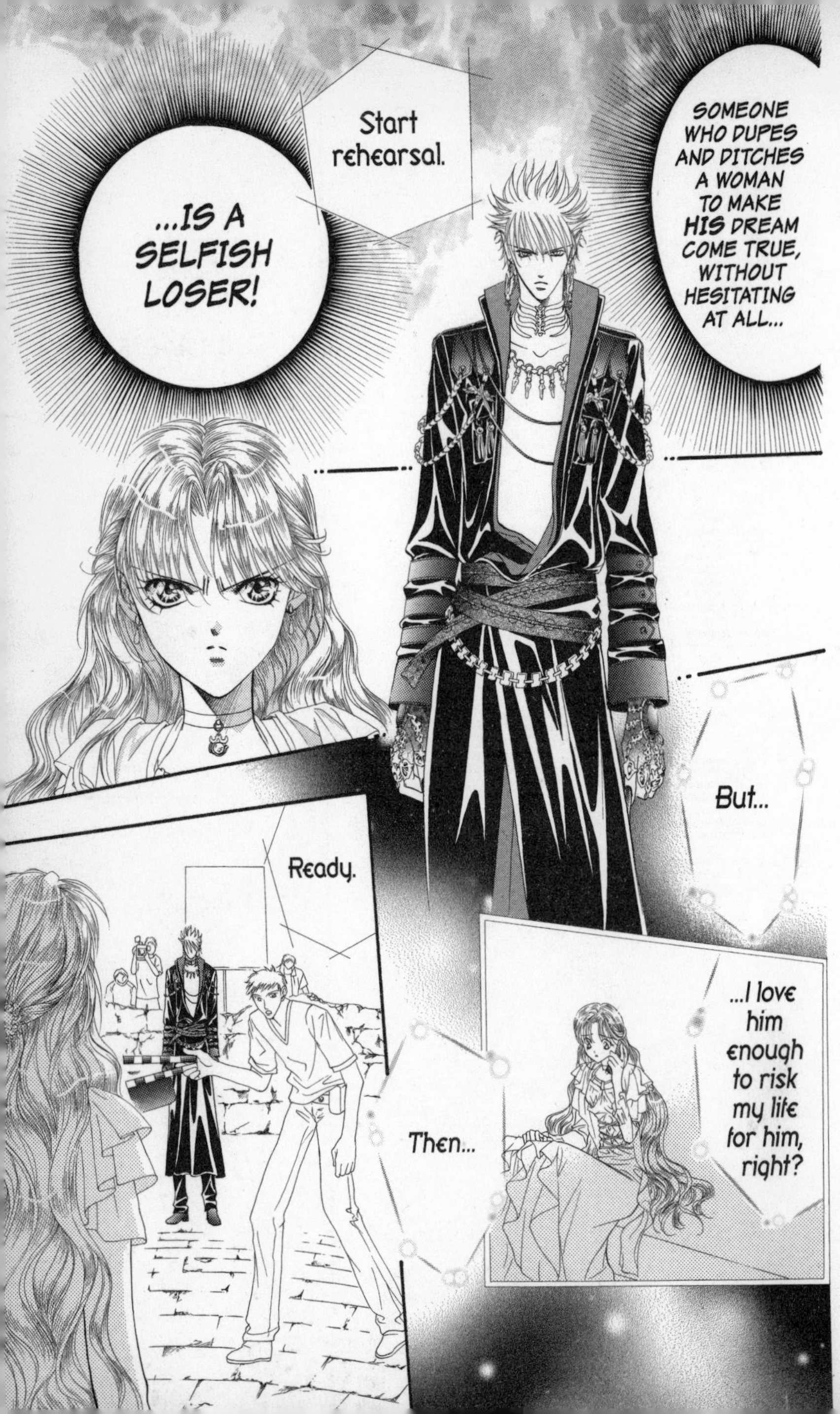
SOMEONE WHO DUPES AND DITCHES A WOMAN TO MAKE HIS DREAM COME TRUE, WITHOUT HESITATING AT ALL...
Start rehearsal.
...IS A SELFISH LOSER!
...
...
...
But...
...I love him enough to risk my life for him, right?
Then...
Ready.

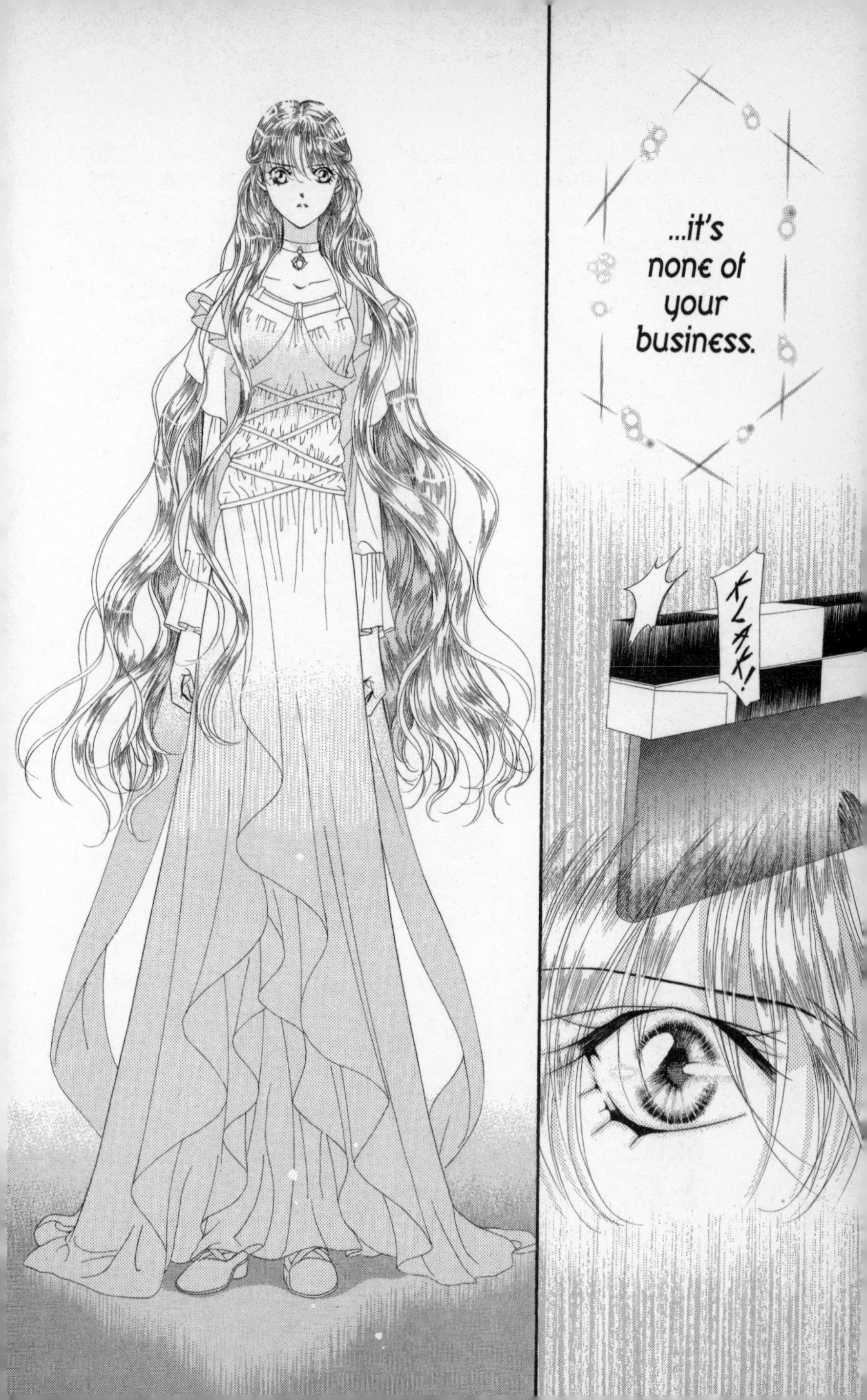
...it's none of your business.
KLAK!

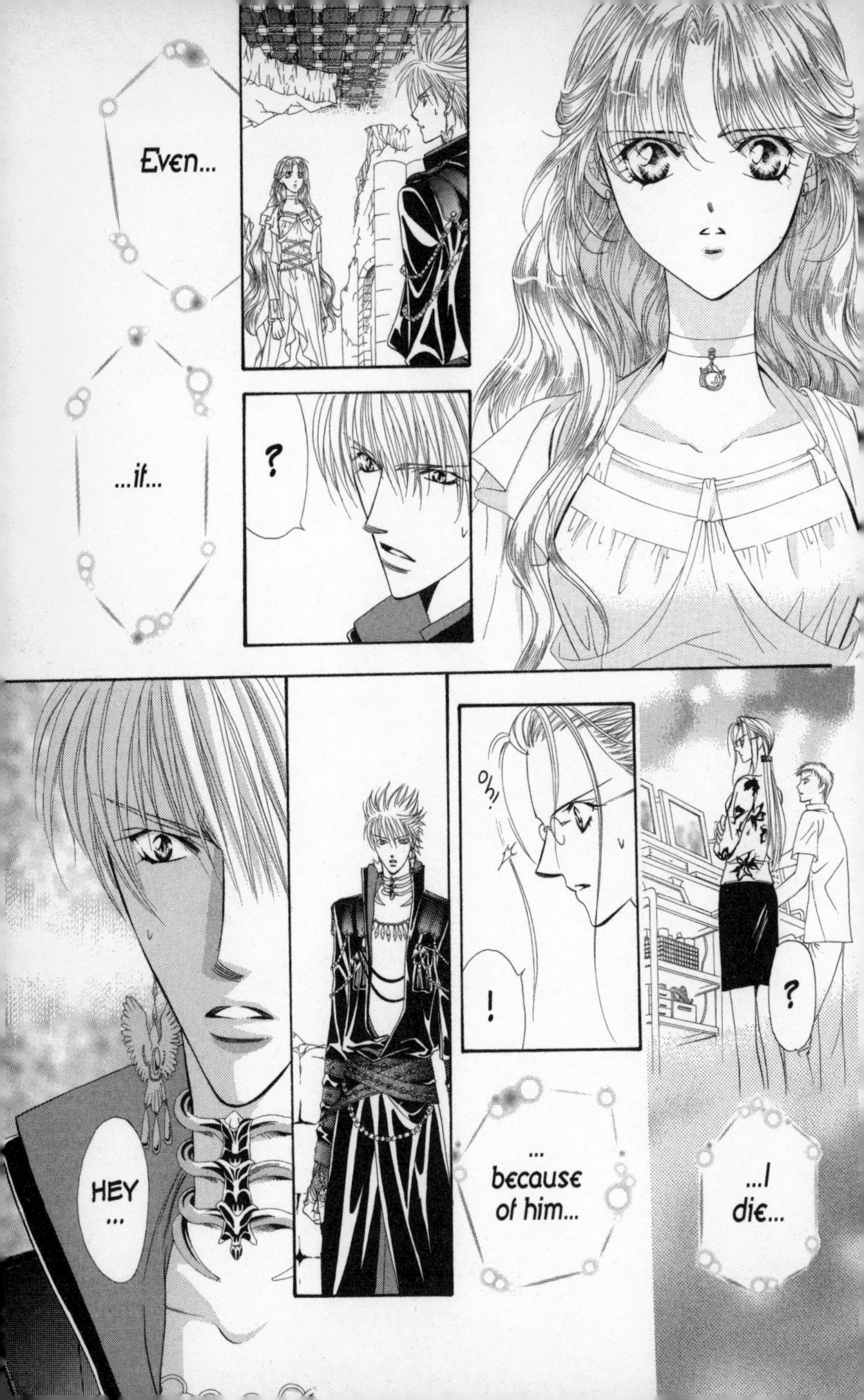
Even...
?
...if...
?
Oh!
!
...I die...
... because of him...
HEY ...

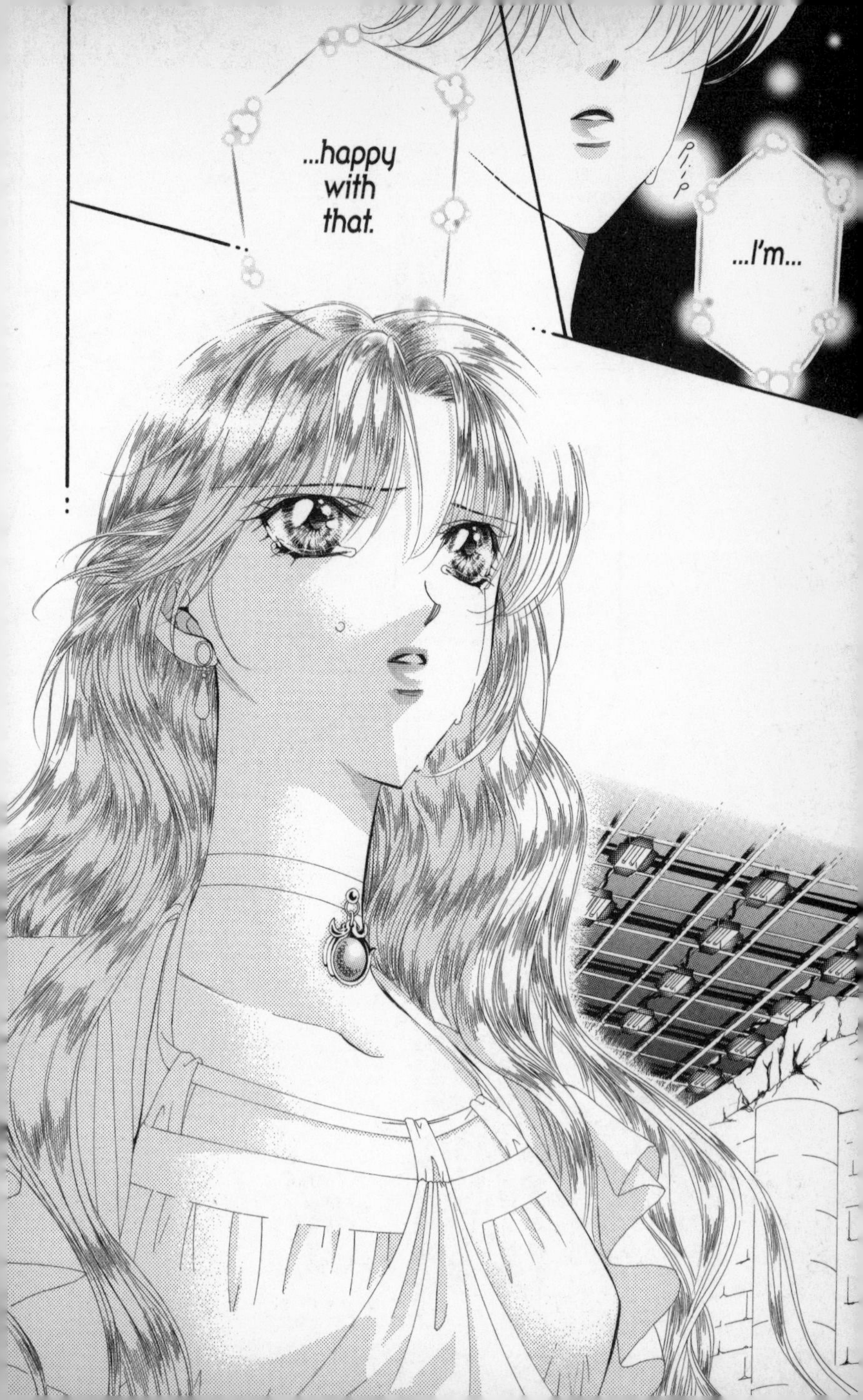
...I'm...
...happy with that.

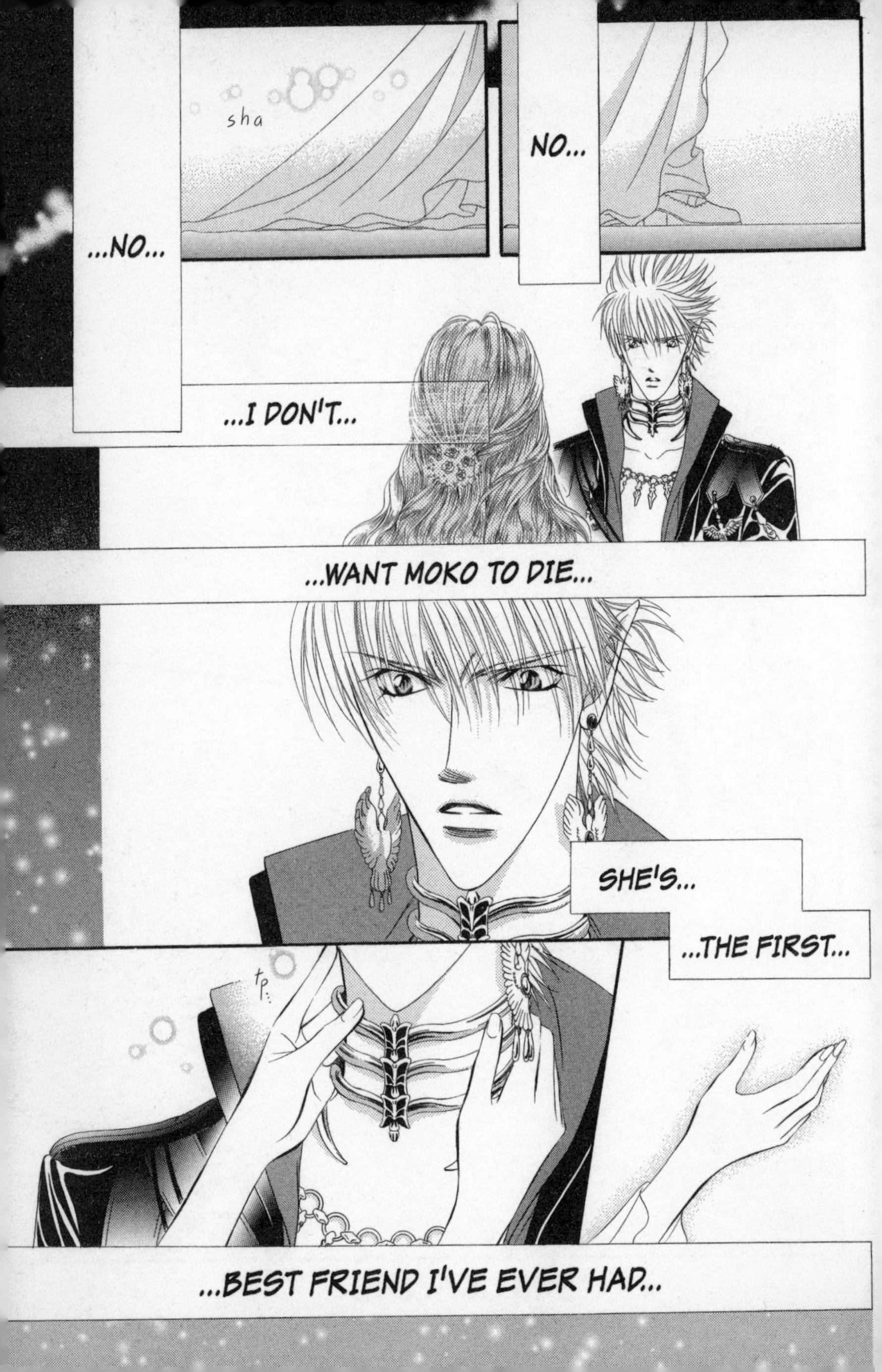
NO...
sha
...NO...
...I DON'T...
...WANT MOKO TO DIE...
SHE'S...
...THE FIRST...
tp...
...BEST FRIEND I'VE EVER HAD...

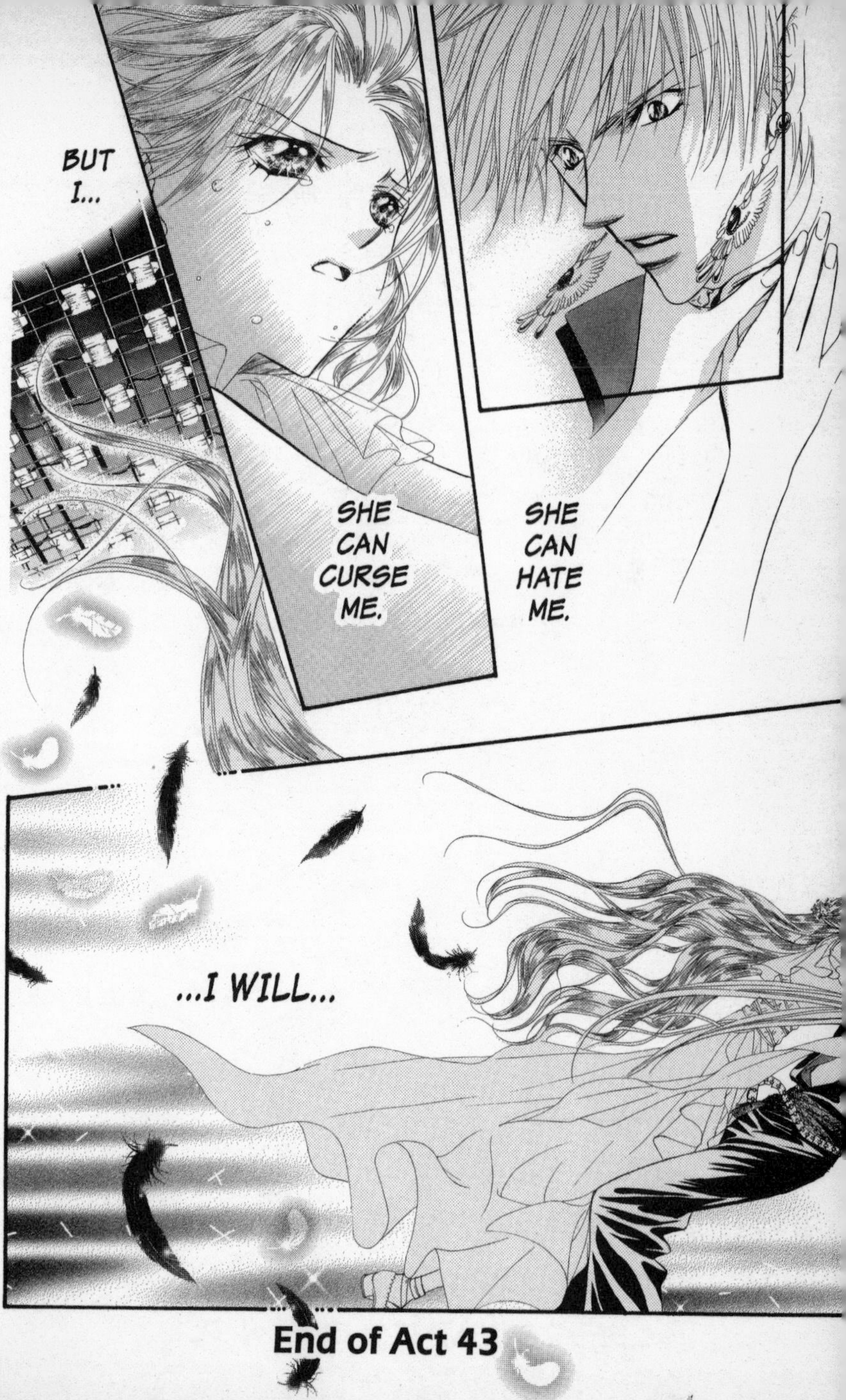
SHE CAN HATE ME.
SHE CAN CURSE ME.
BUT I...
...I WILL...

End of Act 43

# Act 44: Prisoner

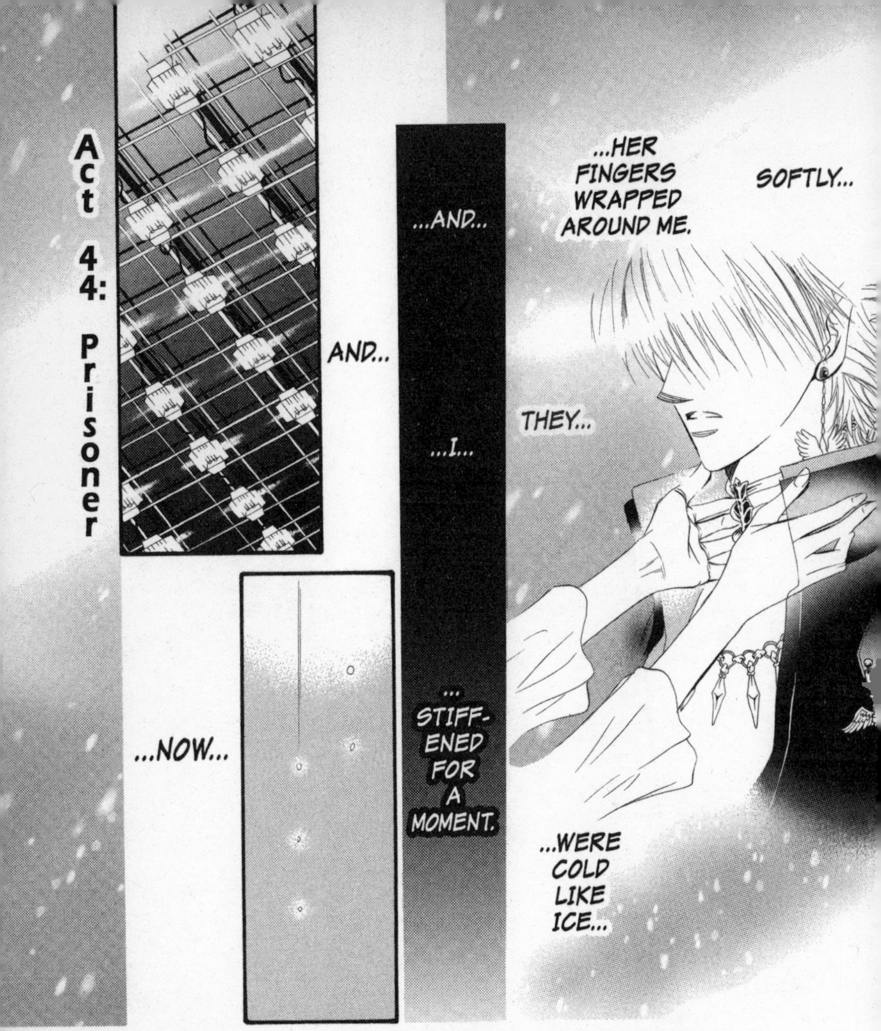
SOFTLY...
...HER FINGERS WRAPPED AROUND ME.
THEY...
...WERE COLD LIKE ICE...
...AND...
...I...
... STIFF-ENED FOR A MOMENT.
AND...
...NOW...

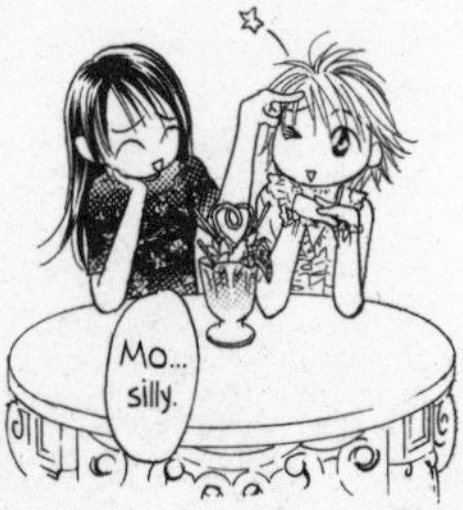
Mo... silly.

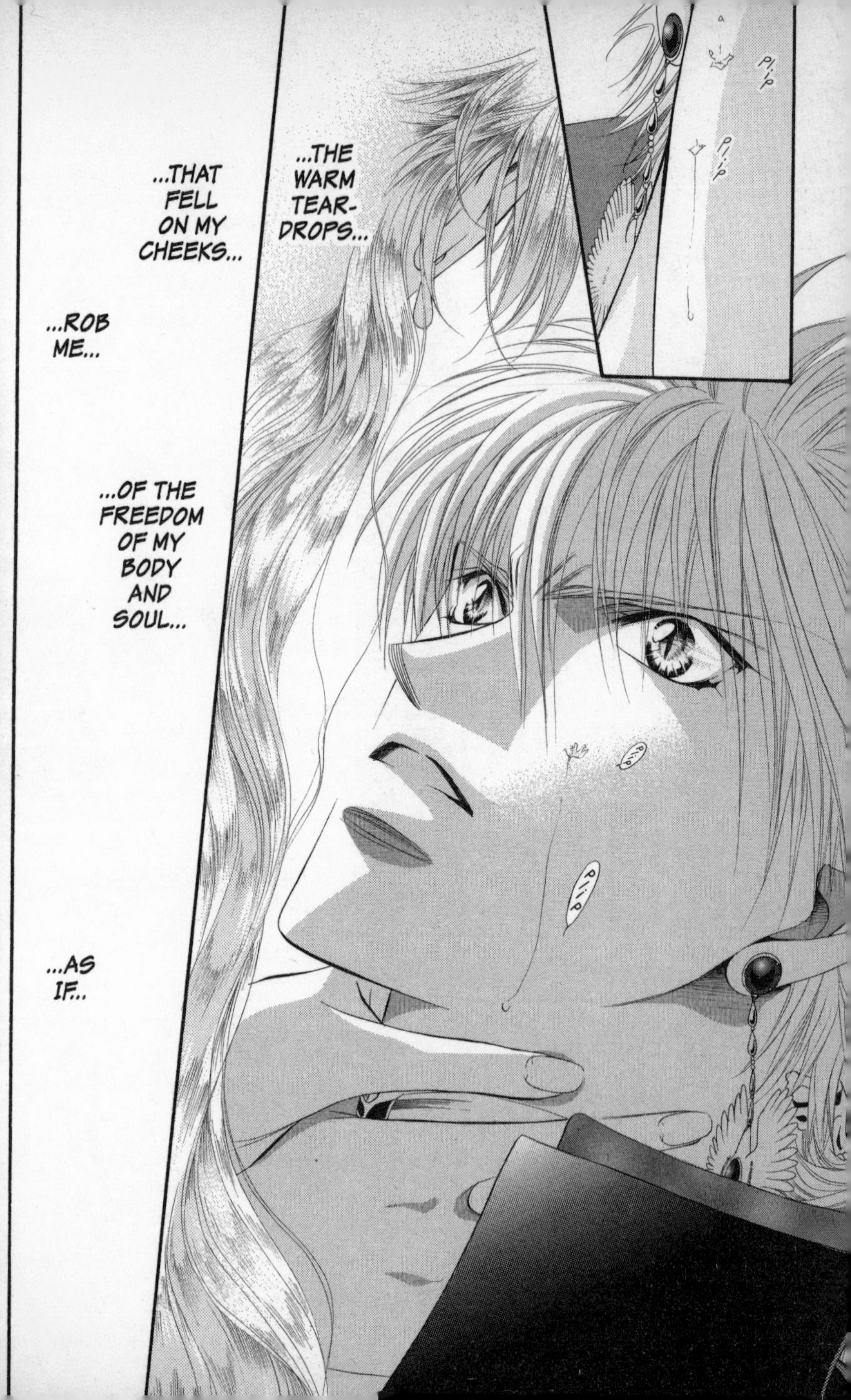

PLIP
PLIP
...THE WARM TEAR-DROPS...
...THAT FELL ON MY CHEEKS...
PLIP
PLIP
...ROB ME...
...OF THE FREEDOM OF MY BODY AND SOUL...
...AS IF...

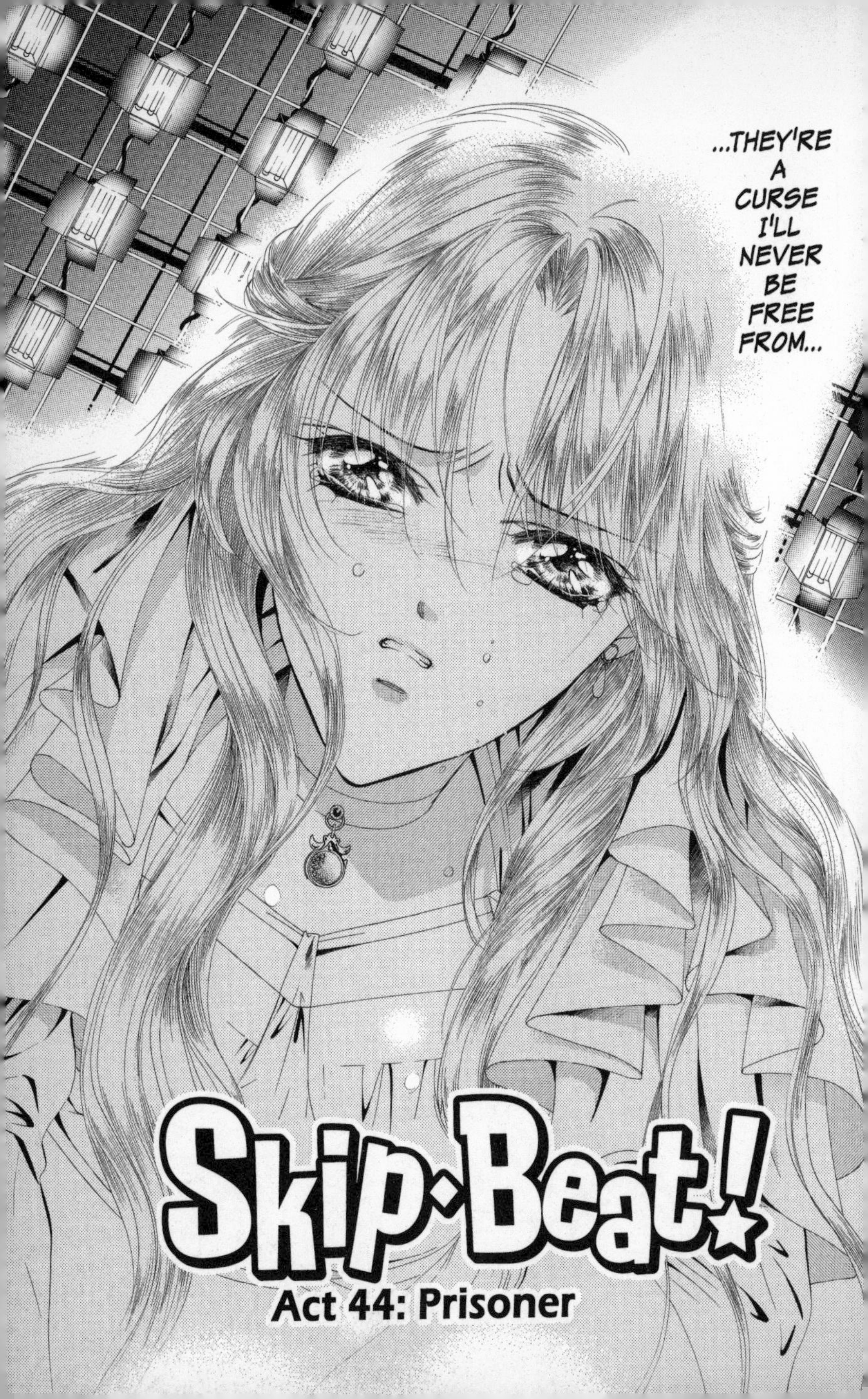
...THEY'RE A CURSE I'LL NEVER BE FREE FROM...
Skip·Beat!
Act 44: Prisoner

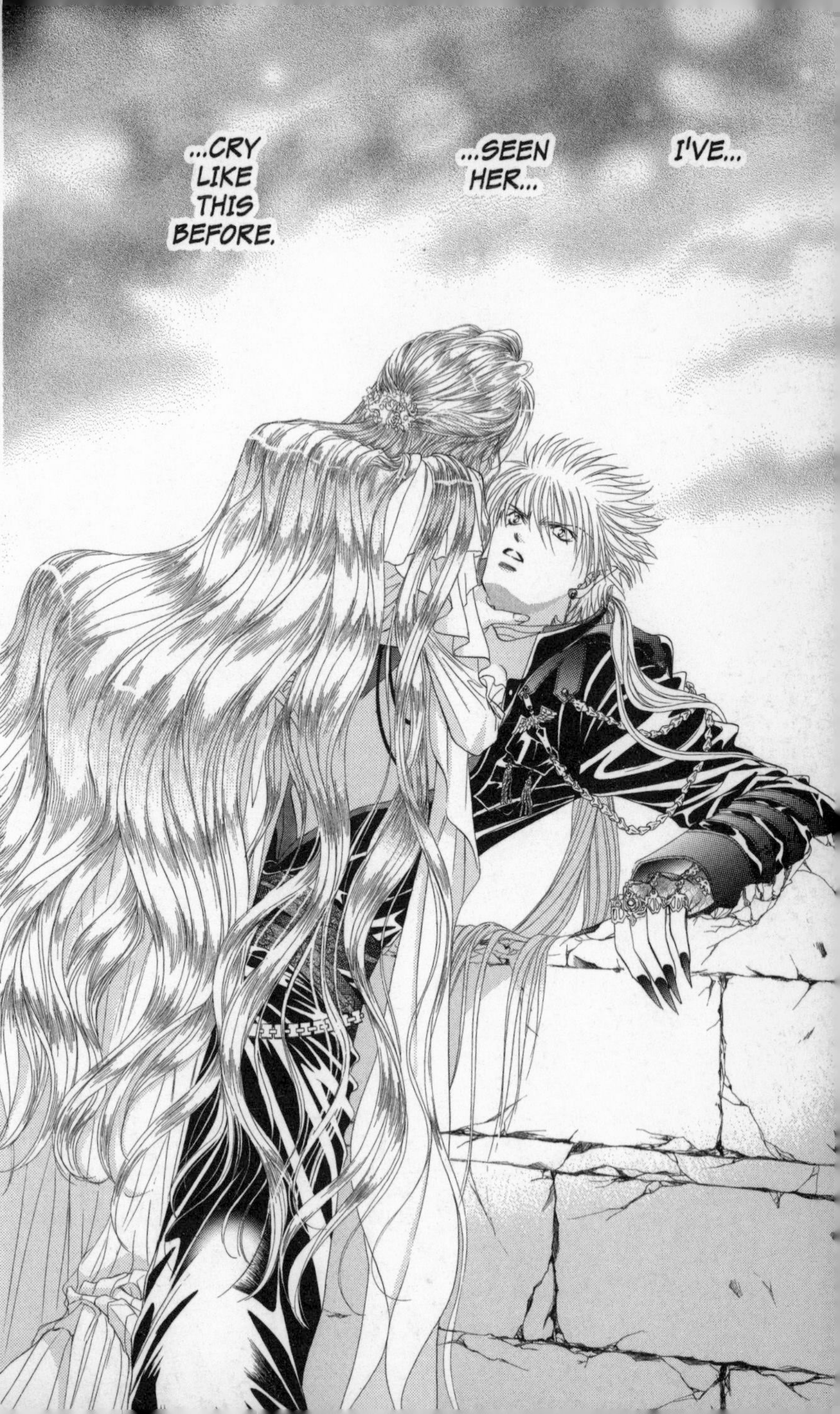
I'VE...
...SEEN HER...
...CRY LIKE THIS BEFORE.

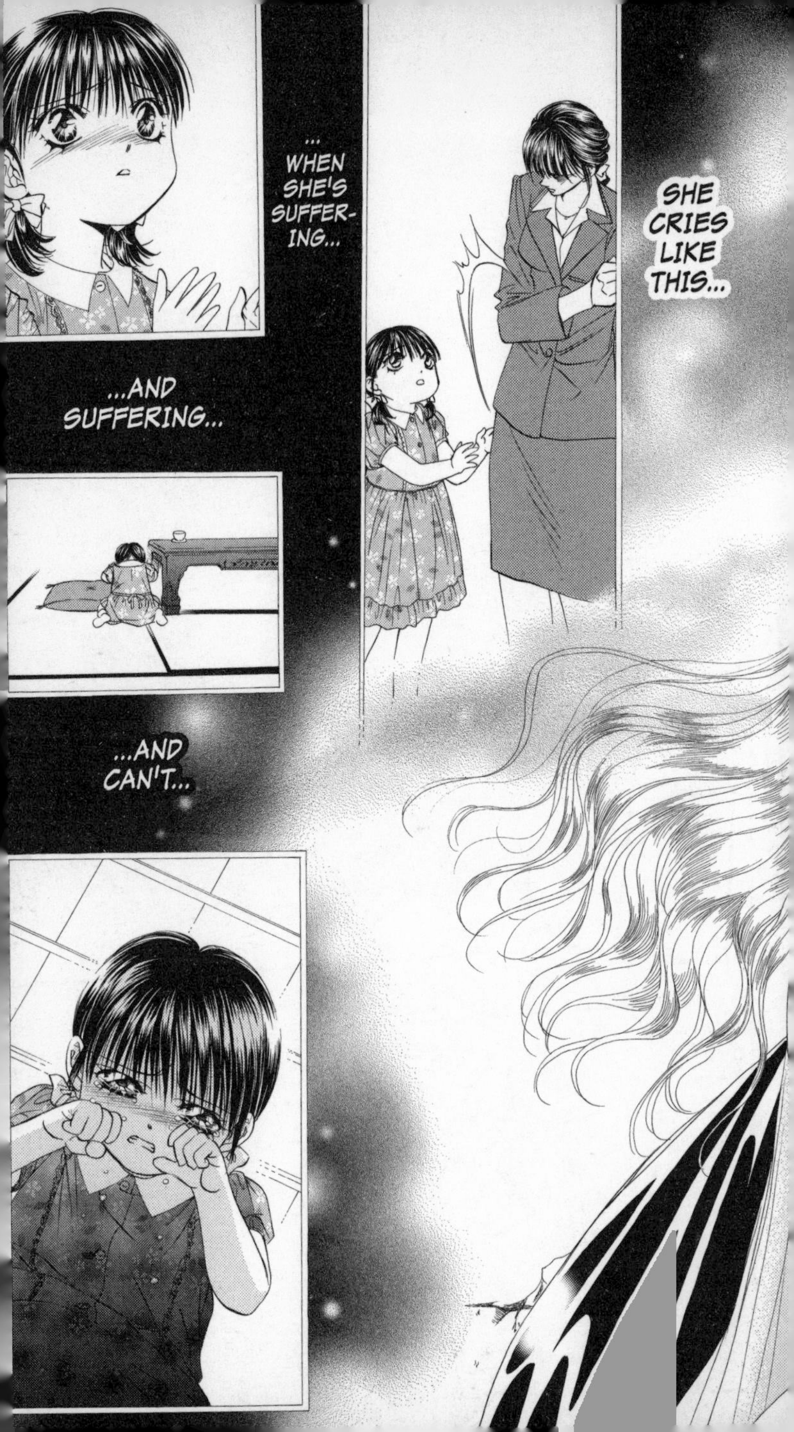
SHE CRIES LIKE THIS...
... WHEN SHE'S SUFFER-ING...
...AND SUFFERING...
...AND CAN'T...

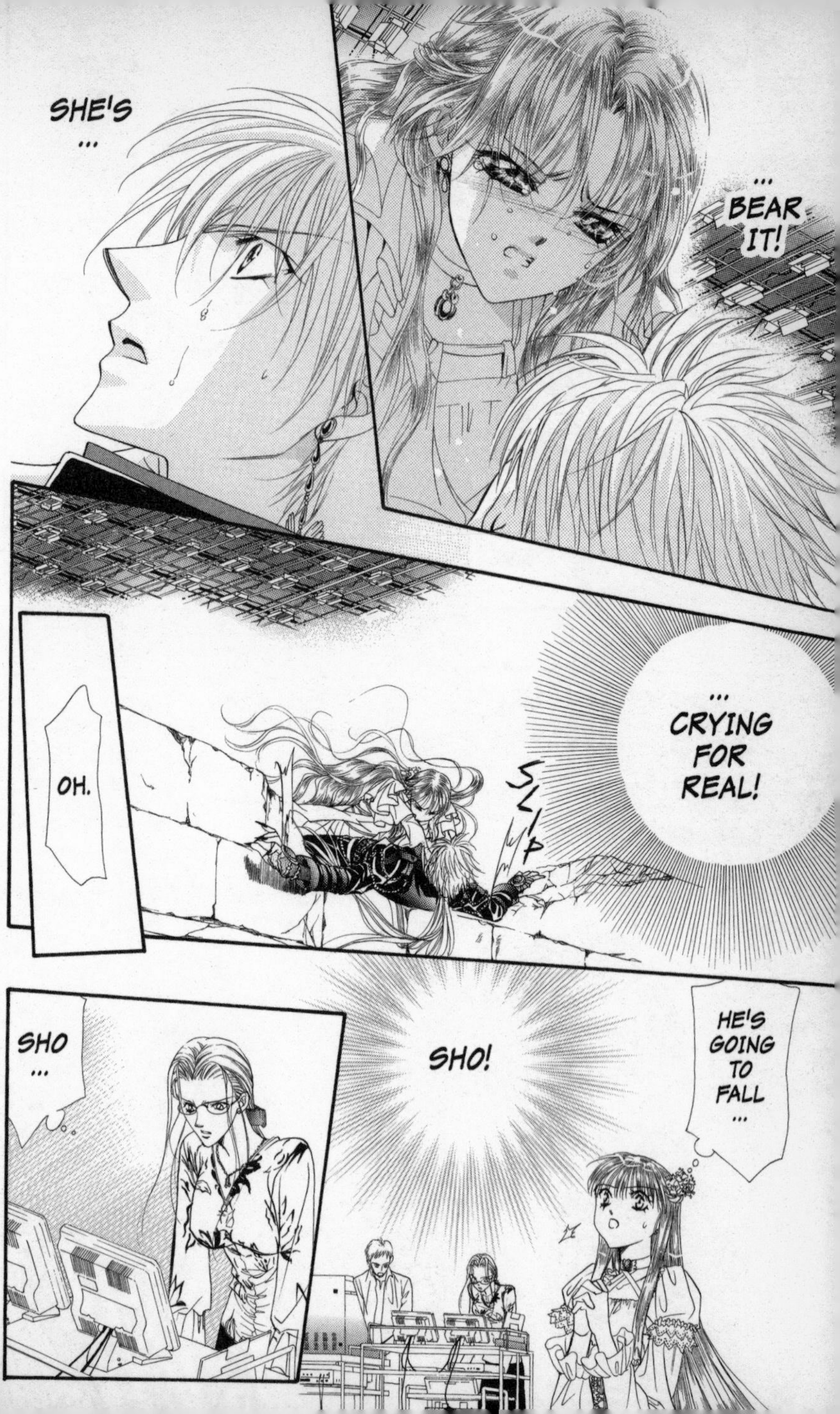
... BEAR IT!
SHE'S ...
... CRYING FOR REAL!
SLIP
OH.
HE'S GOING TO FALL ...
SHO!
SHO ...

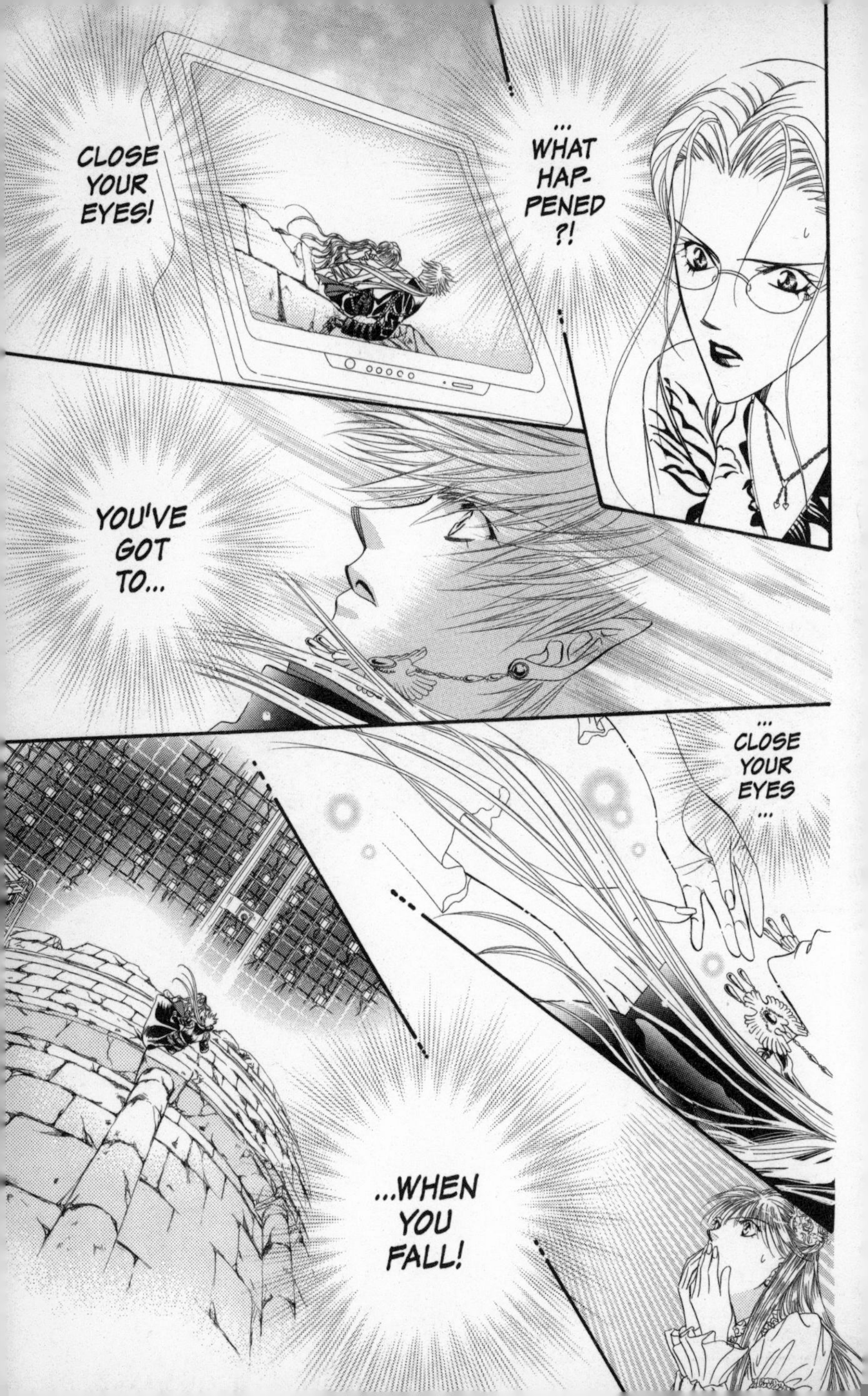
...WHAT HAP-PENED?!
CLOSE YOUR EYES!
YOU'VE GOT TO...
...CLOSE YOUR EYES...
...WHEN YOU FALL!

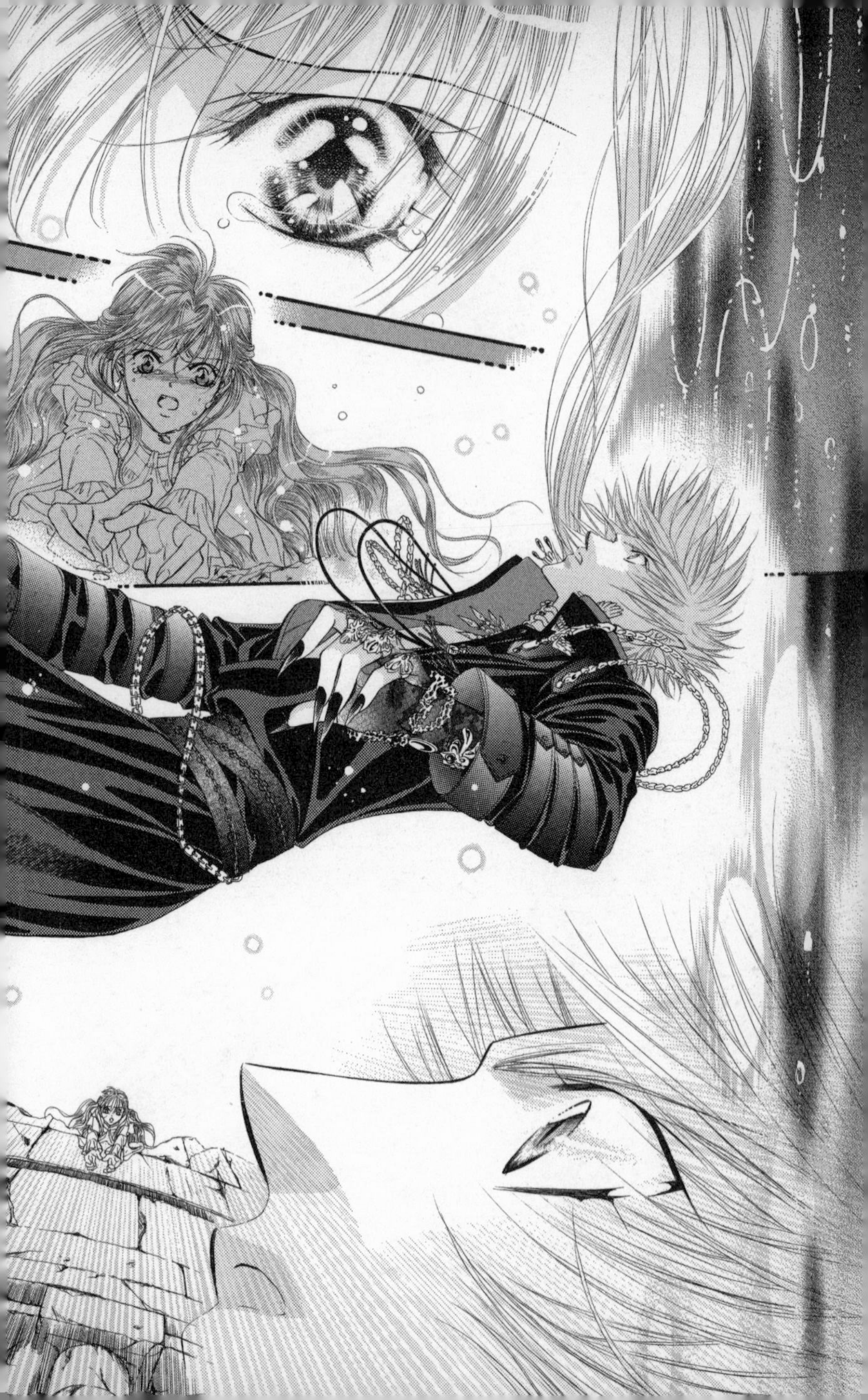

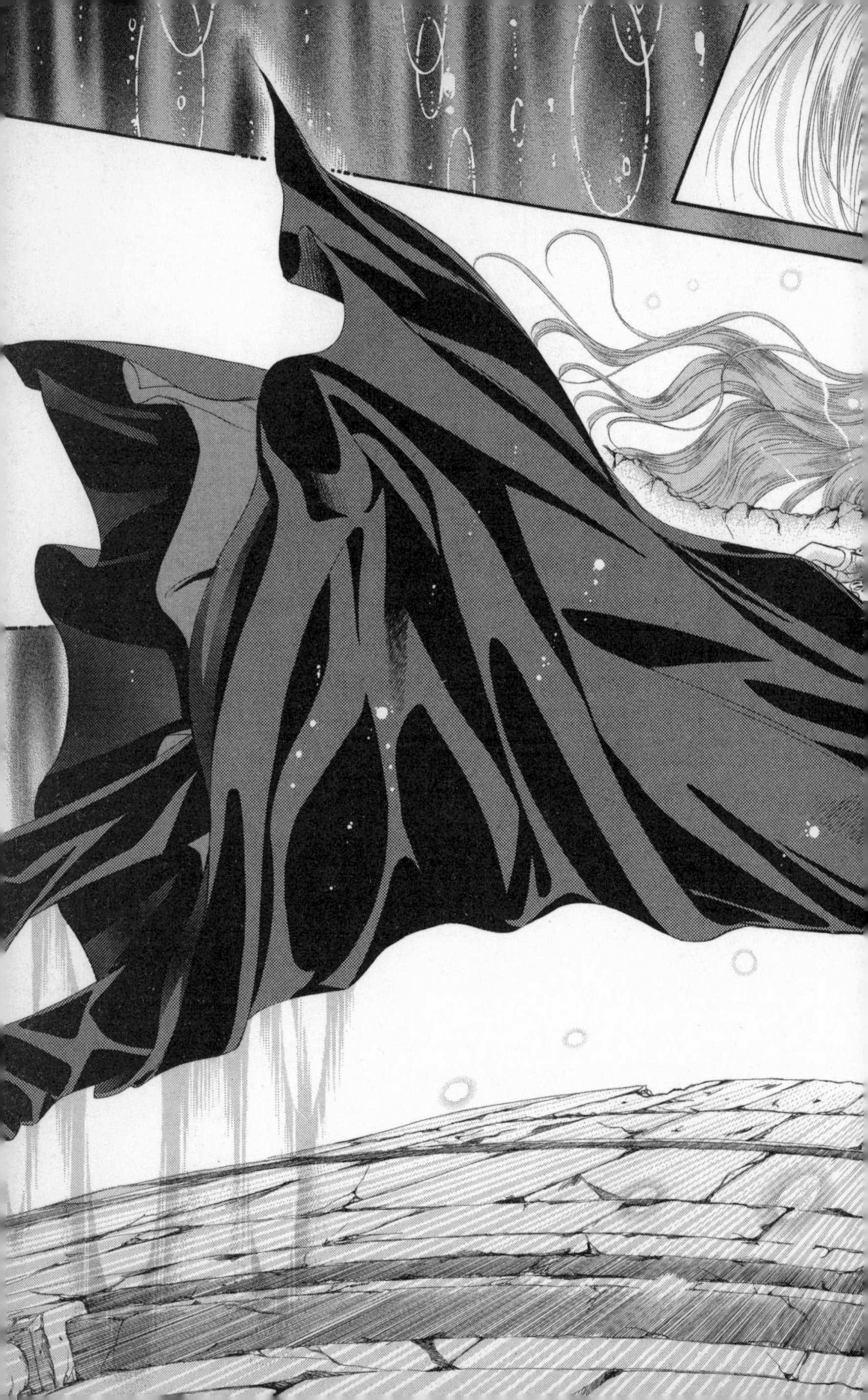

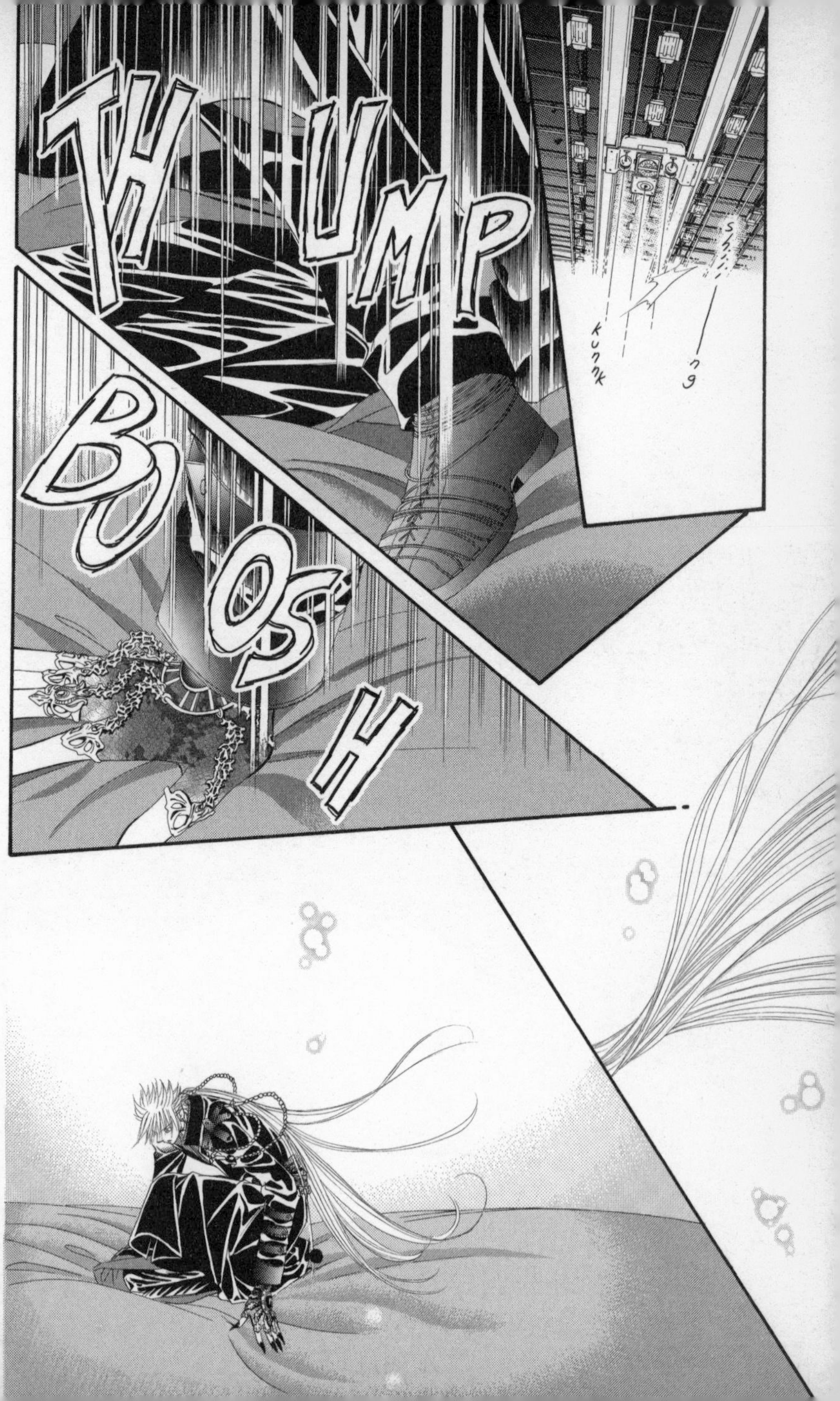
shiiing
kunnk
THUMP
BOOSH

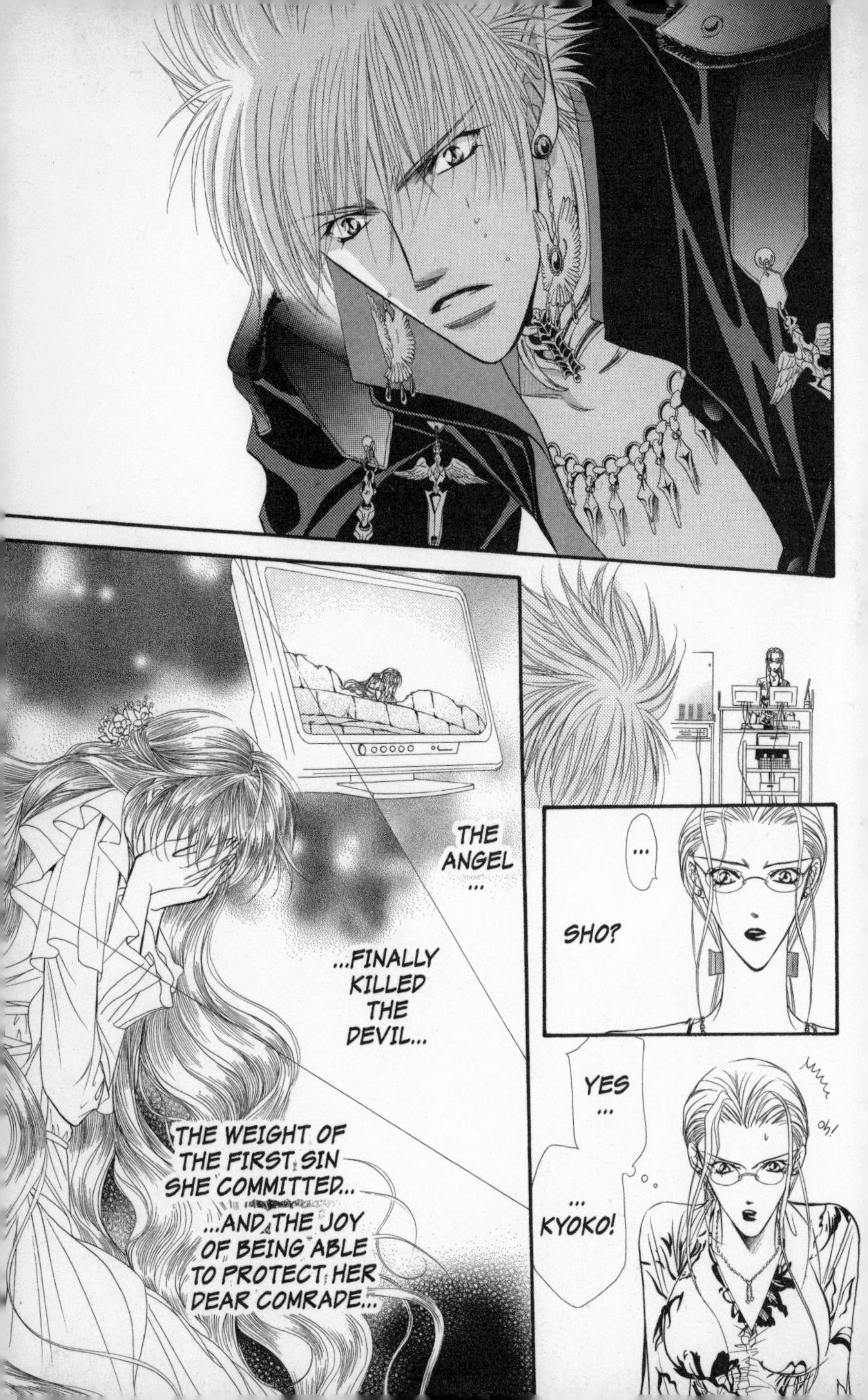
...
SHO?
YES ...
... KYOKO!
oh!
THE ANGEL ...
...FINALLY KILLED THE DEVIL...
THE WEIGHT OF THE FIRST SIN SHE COMMITTED...
...AND THE JOY OF BEING ABLE TO PROTECT HER DEAR COMRADE...

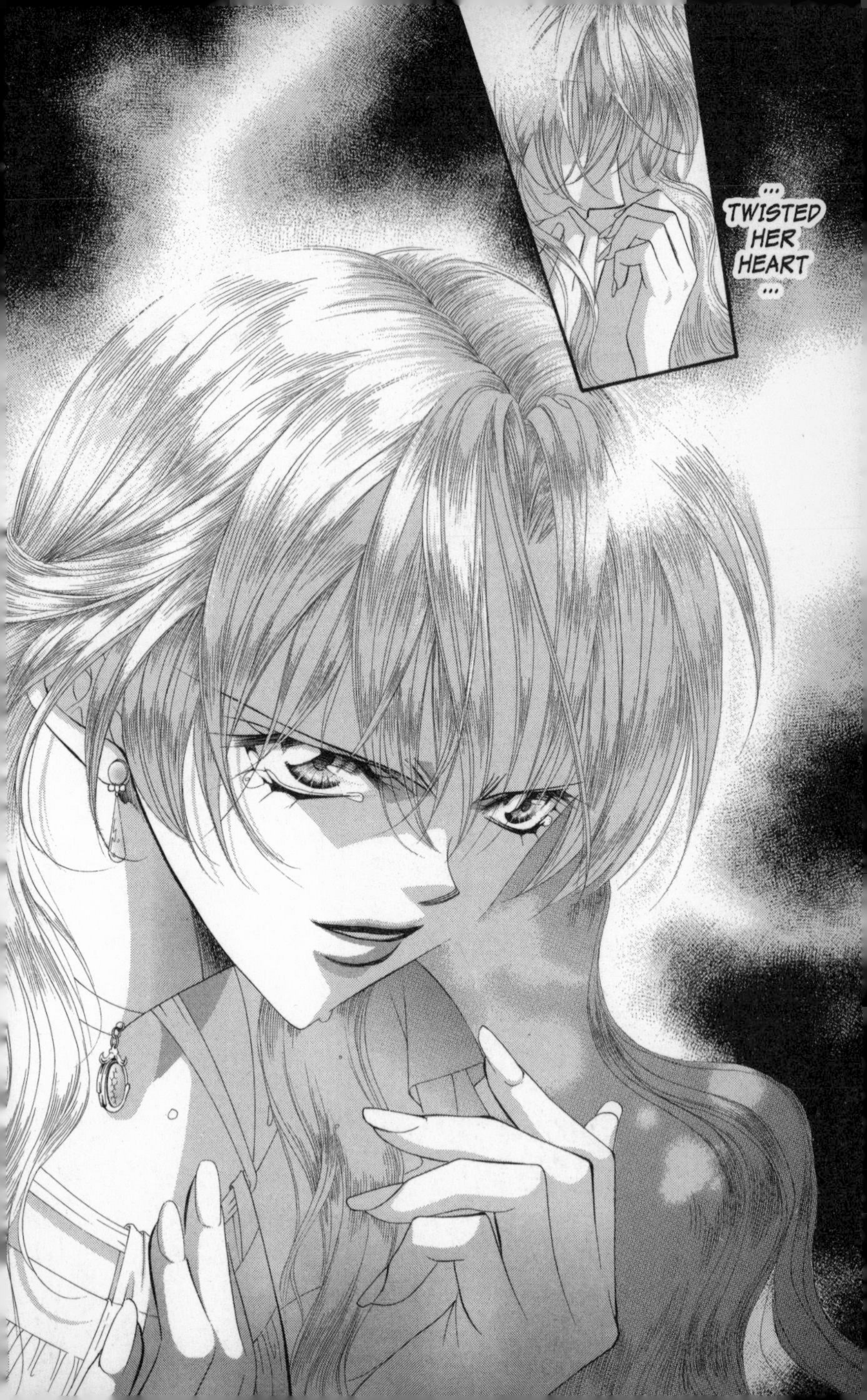
...TWISTED HER HEART...

...and Kyoko would have worn the costume Pochi wore...and when I thought about that, I wanted to draw it... But...a blonde Kanae... that's scary too, since she might not look good...

...therefore...

I tried drawing... Kyoko wearing Pochi's costume...

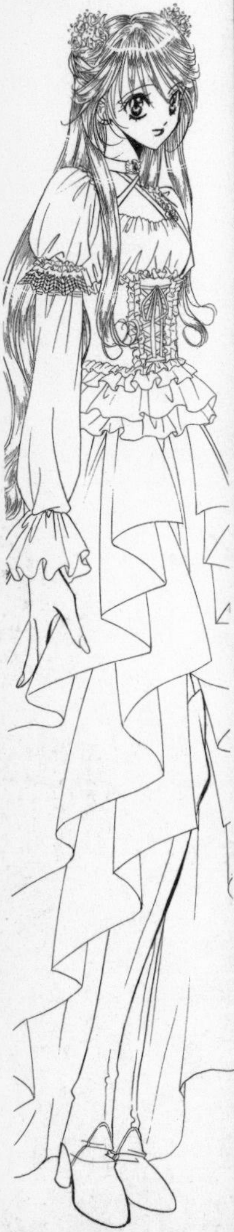

...AND MADE HER GO MAD...

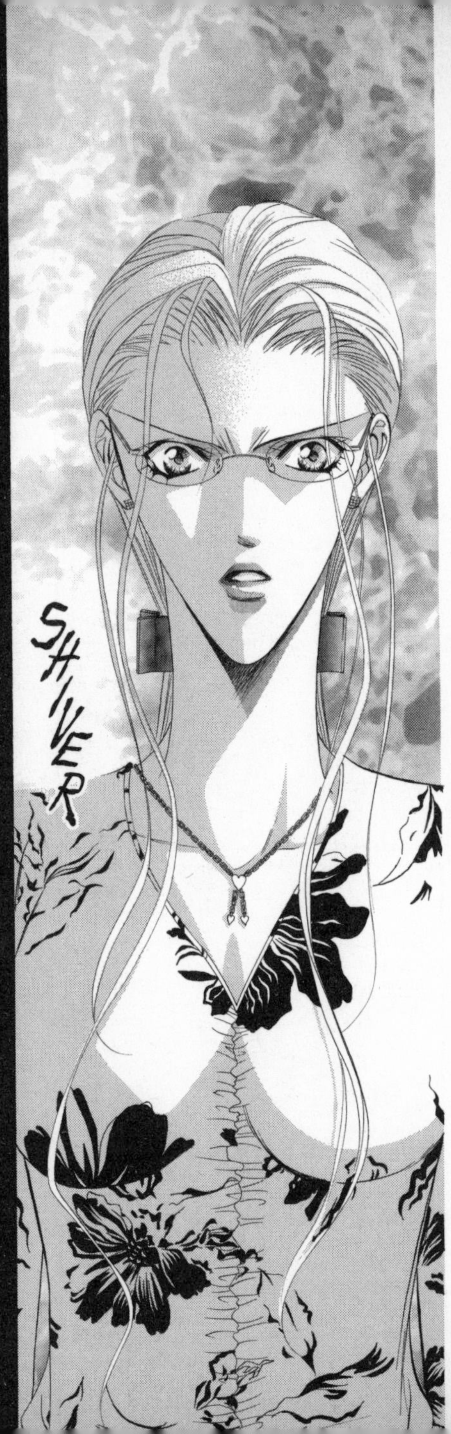
SHIVER

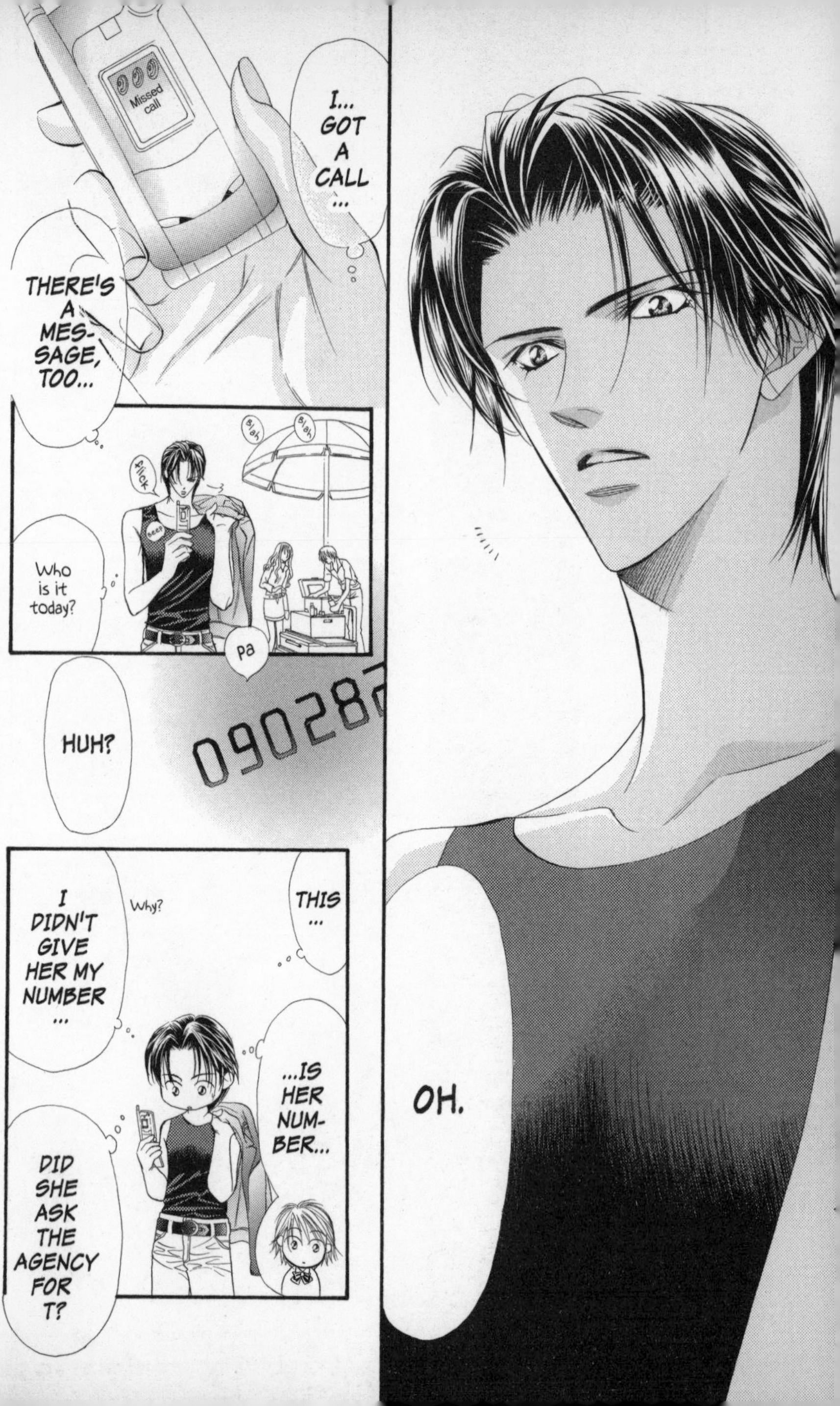
OH.
Missed call
I... GOT A CALL...
THERE'S A MES-SAGE, TOO...
Blah
Blah
Flick
Beep
Who is it today?
Pa
HUH?
090282
THIS...
...IS HER NUM-BER...
Why?
I DIDN'T GIVE HER MY NUMBER...
DID SHE ASK THE AGENCY FOR T?

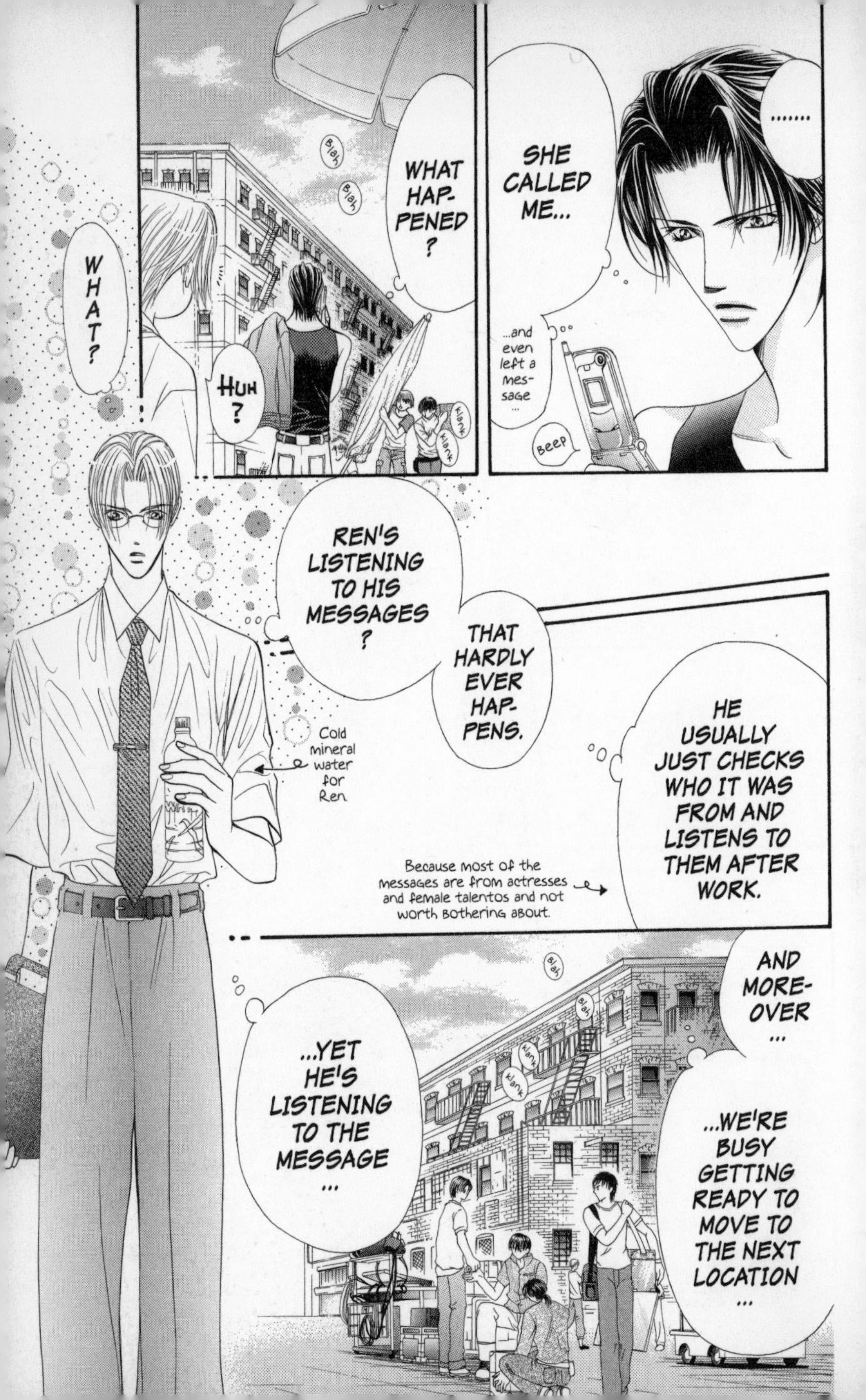
.......
SHE CALLED ME...
...and even left a message...
Beep
WHAT HAPPENED?
Blah
Blah
Klank
Klank
HUH?
WHAT?
REN'S LISTENING TO HIS MESSAGES?
THAT HARDLY EVER HAPPENS.
HE USUALLY JUST CHECKS WHO IT WAS FROM AND LISTENS TO THEM AFTER WORK.
Because most of the messages are from actresses and female talentos and not worth bothering about.
Cold mineral water for Ren.
Blah
Blah
Klank
Klank
AND MOREOVER...
...WE'RE BUSY GETTING READY TO MOVE TO THE NEXT LOCATION...
...YET HE'S LISTENING TO THE MESSAGE...

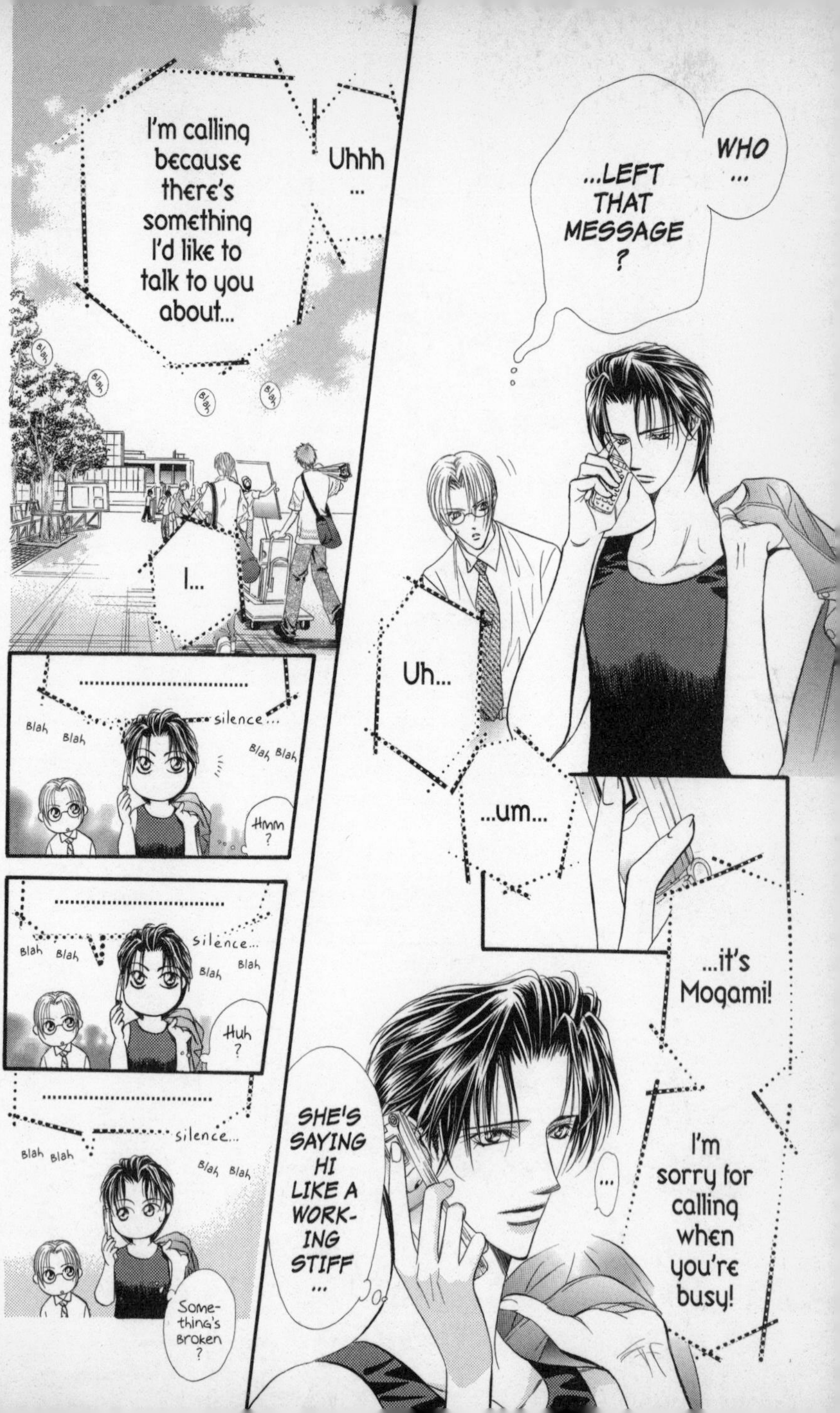
WHO ...
...LEFT THAT MESSAGE ?
Uh...
...um...
...it's Mogami!
I'm sorry for calling when you're busy!
...
SHE'S SAYING HI LIKE A WORK-ING STIFF ...
Uhhh ...
I'm calling because there's something I'd like to talk to you about...
Blah
Blah
Blah
Blah
I...
..........................
silence...
Blah Blah
Blah Blah
Hmm ?
..........................
silence...
Blah Blah
Blah Blah
Huh ?
..........................
silence...
Blah Blah
Blah Blah
Some-thing's broken ?

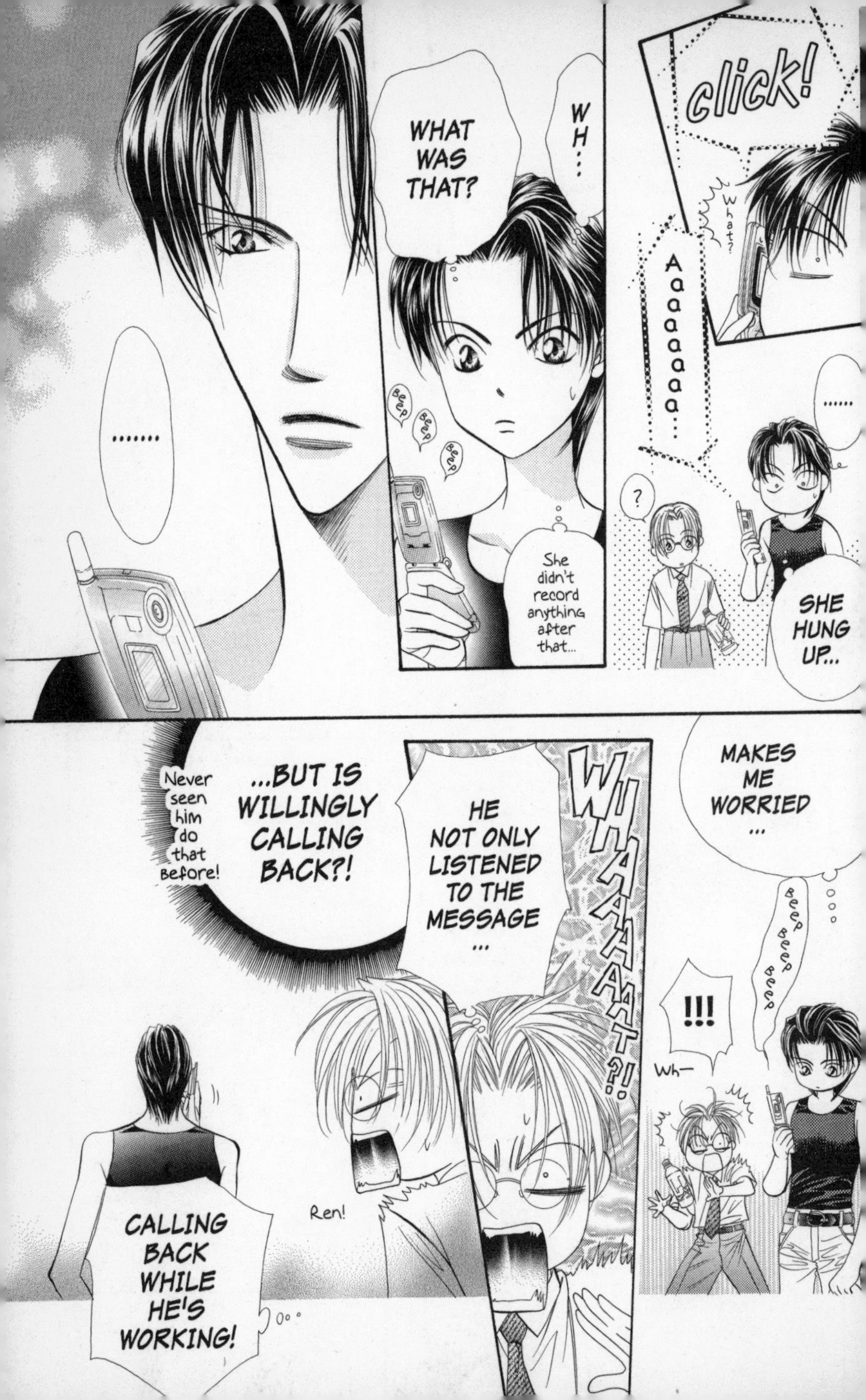
click!
What?
Aaaaaaaa...
......
?
SHE HUNG UP...
WH...
WHAT WAS THAT?
Beep
Beep
Beep
She didn't record anything after that...
.......
MAKES ME WORRIED...
Beep beep beep
!!!
Wh—
WHAAAAAAT?!
HE NOT ONLY LISTENED TO THE MESSAGE...
...BUT IS WILLINGLY CALLING BACK?!
Never seen him do that before!
Ren!
CALLING BACK WHILE HE'S WORKING!

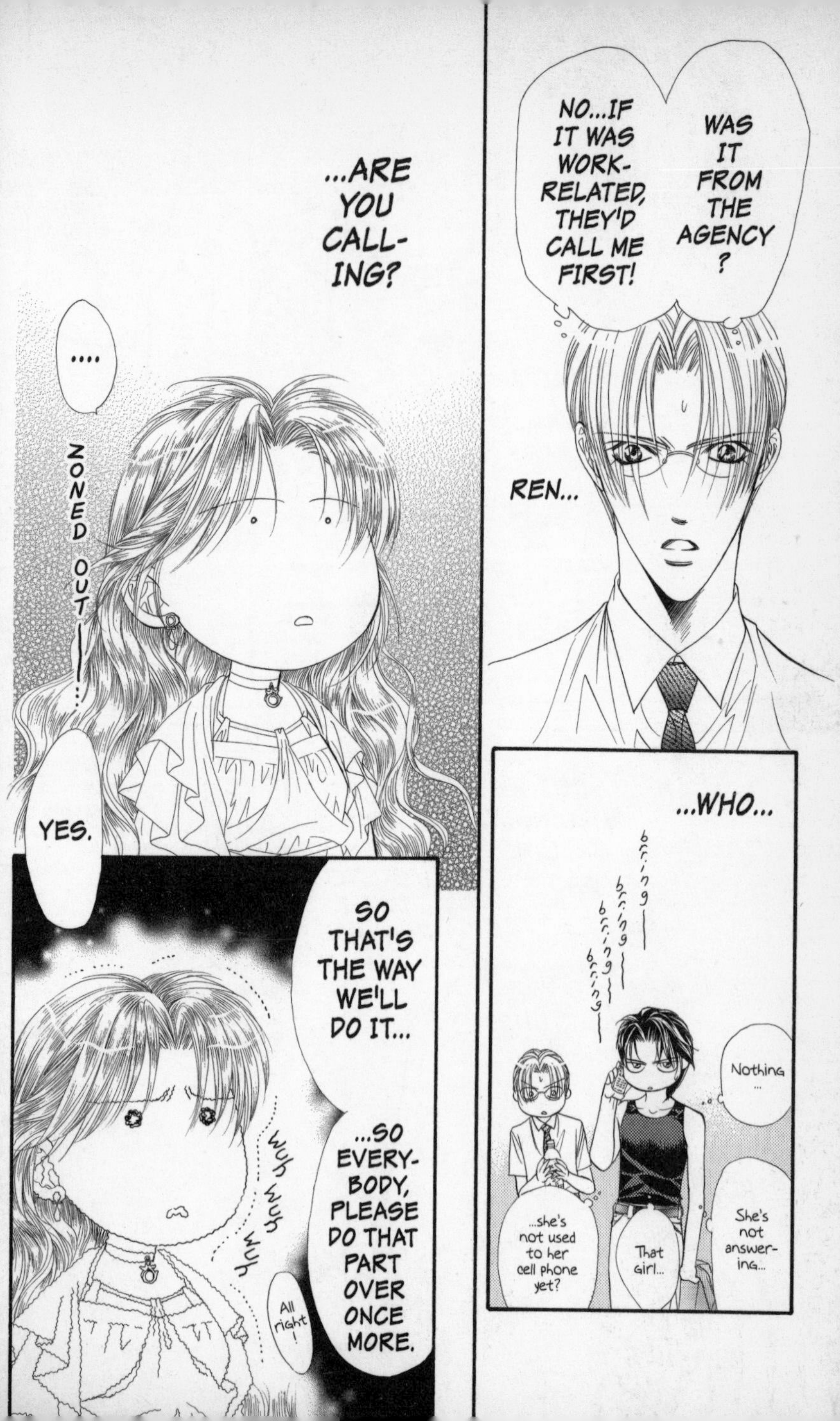
WAS IT FROM THE AGENCY?
NO...IF IT WAS WORK-RELATED, THEY'D CALL ME FIRST!
REN...
...WHO...
brring— brring— brring— brring—
Nothing...
She's not answering...
That Girl...
...she's not used to her cell phone yet?
...ARE YOU CALLING?
....
ZONED OUT—
YES.
SO THAT'S THE WAY WE'LL DO IT...
...SO EVERYBODY, PLEASE DO THAT PART OVER ONCE MORE.
wuh wuh wuh
All right!

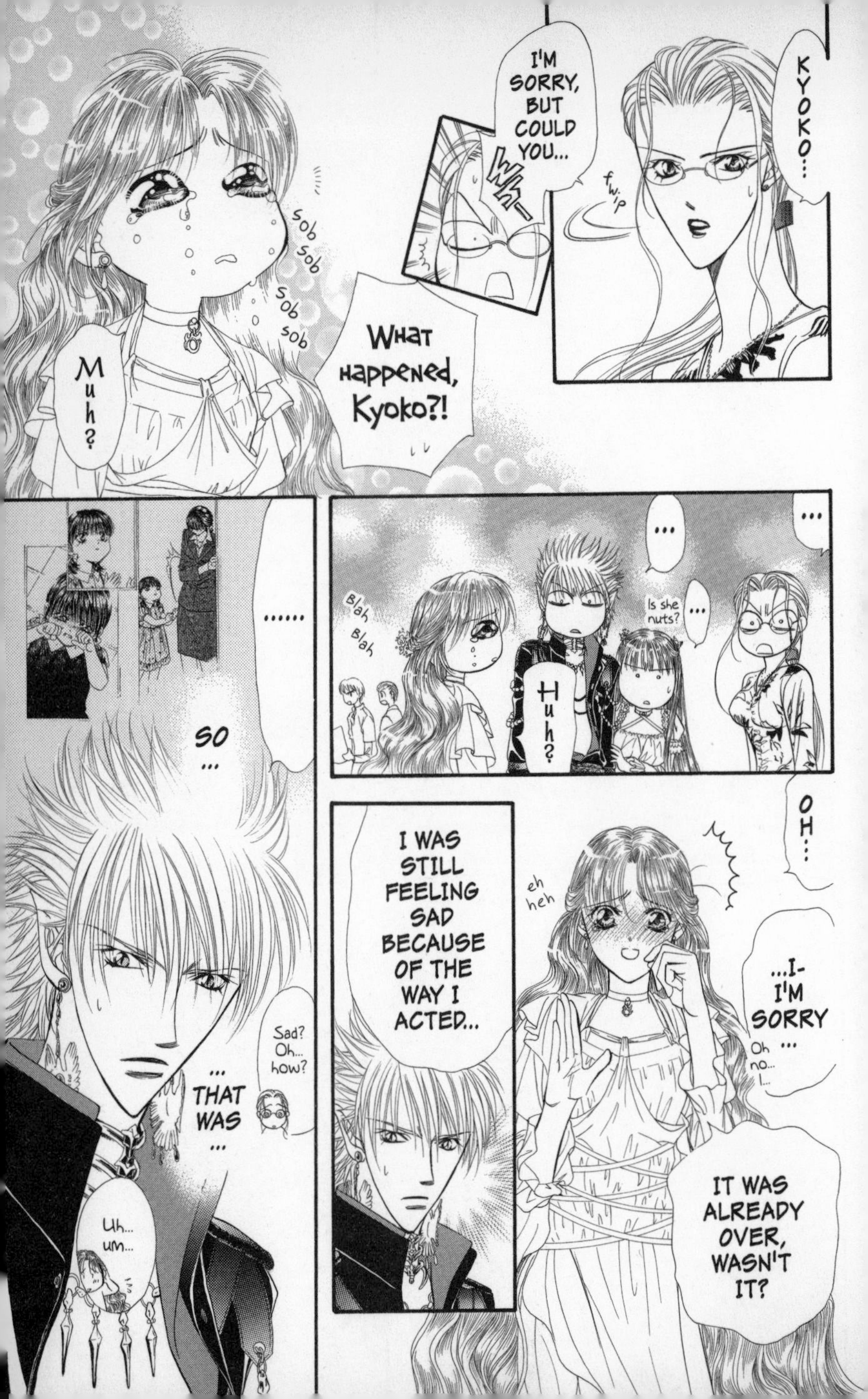
KYOKO...
fwip
I'M SORRY, BUT COULD YOU...
WH—
What happened, Kyoko?!
sob sob
sob sob
Muh?
...
...
Is she nuts?
...
Huh?
Blah Blah
OH...
...I- I'M SORRY ...
Oh no... I...
eh heh
I WAS STILL FEELING SAD BECAUSE OF THE WAY I ACTED...
IT WAS ALREADY OVER, WASN'T IT?
......
SO ...
... THAT WAS ...
Sad? Oh... how?
Uh... um...

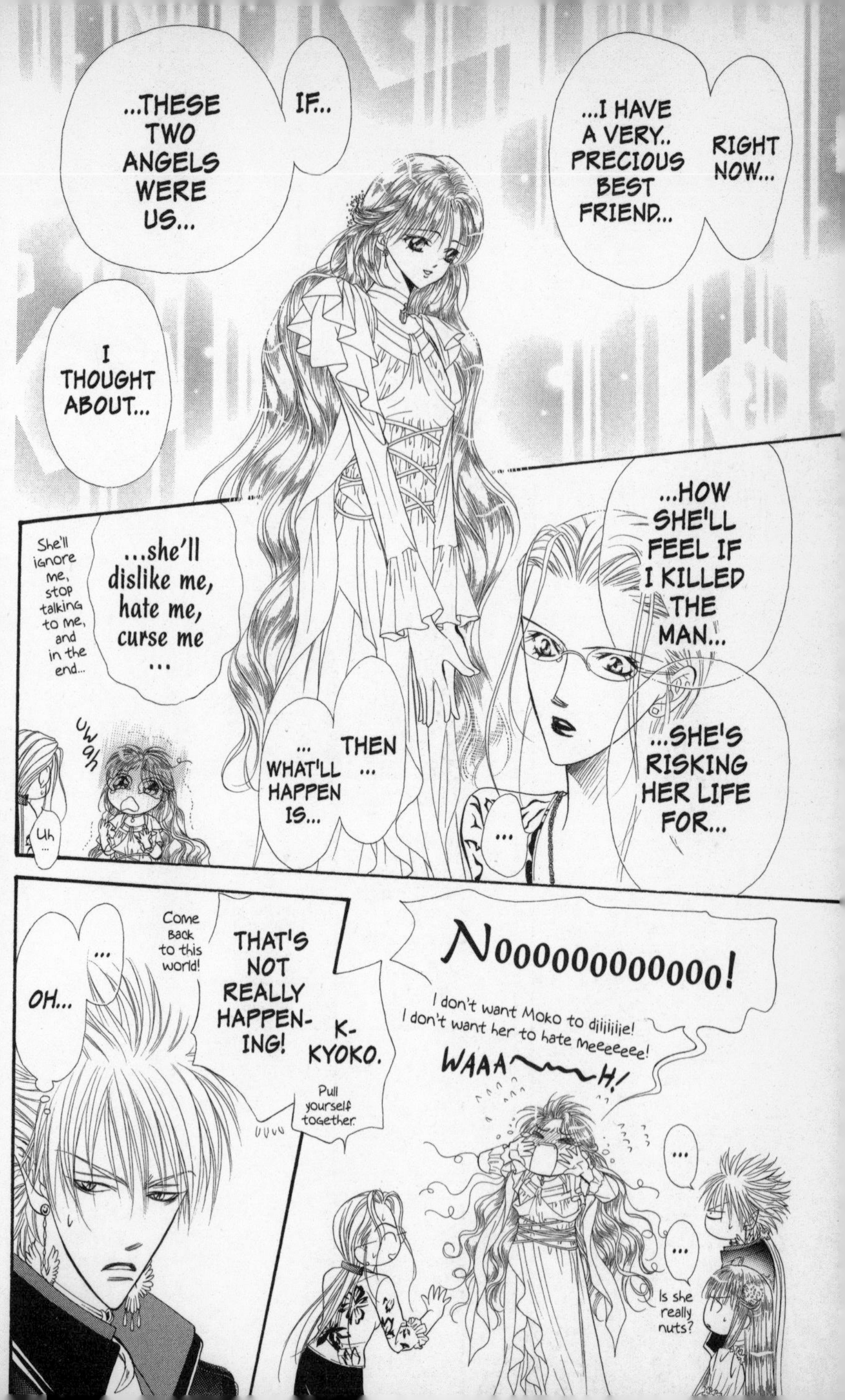
RIGHT NOW...
...I HAVE A VERY.. PRECIOUS BEST FRIEND...
IF..
...THESE TWO ANGELS WERE US...
I THOUGHT ABOUT...
...HOW SHE'LL FEEL IF I KILLED THE MAN...
...SHE'S RISKING HER LIFE FOR...
...
THEN ... WHAT'LL HAPPEN IS...
...she'll dislike me, hate me, curse me ...
She'll ignore me, stop talking to me, and in the end...
Uwah
Uh ...
Noooooooooooo!
I don't want Moko to diiiiiiie! I don't want her to hate meeeeeee!
WAAA~H!
...
...
Is she really nuts?
K-KYOKO.
Pull yourself together.
THAT'S NOT REALLY HAPPENING!
Come back to this world!
...
OH...

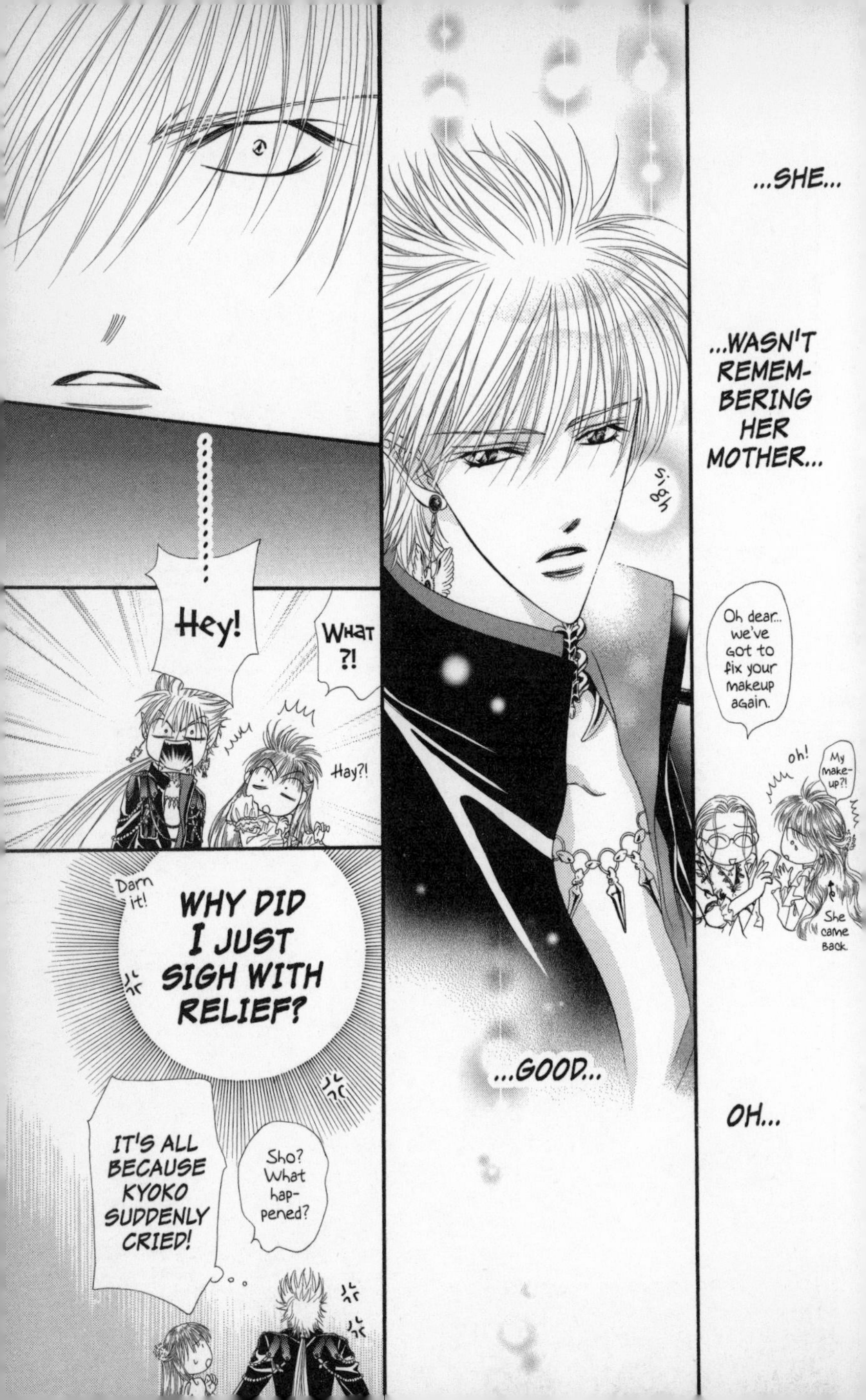

...SHE...
...WASN'T REMEM-BERING HER MOTHER...
Oh dear... we've got to fix your makeup again.
Oh!
My make-up?!
She came back.
OH...
sigh
...GOOD...
......
Hey!
WHAT?!
Hay?!
Darn it!
WHY DID I JUST SIGH WITH RELIEF?
IT'S ALL BECAUSE KYOKO SUDDENLY CRIED!
Sho? What hap-pened?

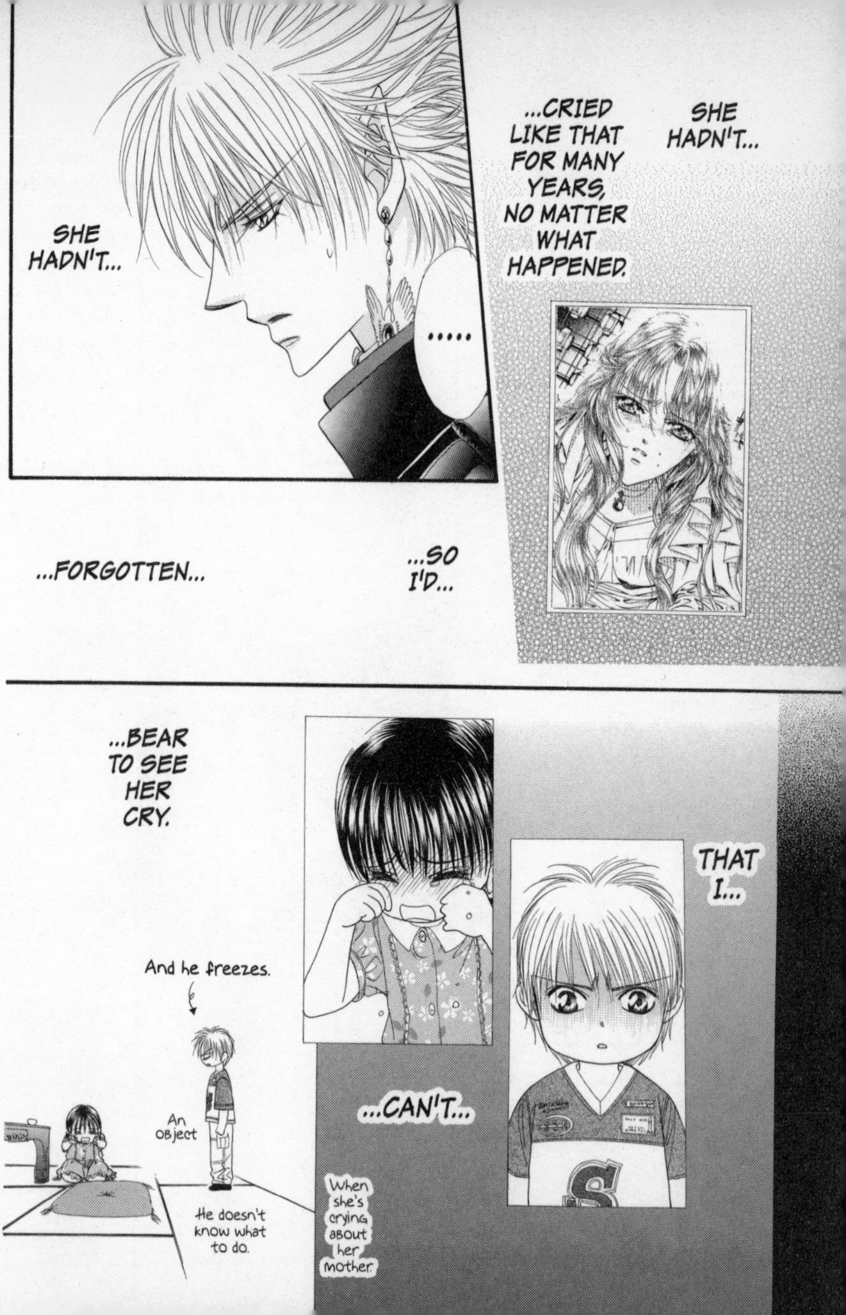
SHE HADN'T...
...CRIED LIKE THAT FOR MANY YEARS, NO MATTER WHAT HAPPENED.
SHE HADN'T...
.....
...SO I'D...
...FORGOTTEN...
THAT I...
...CAN'T...
...BEAR TO SEE HER CRY.
When she's crying about her mother.
And he freezes.
An object
He doesn't know what to do.

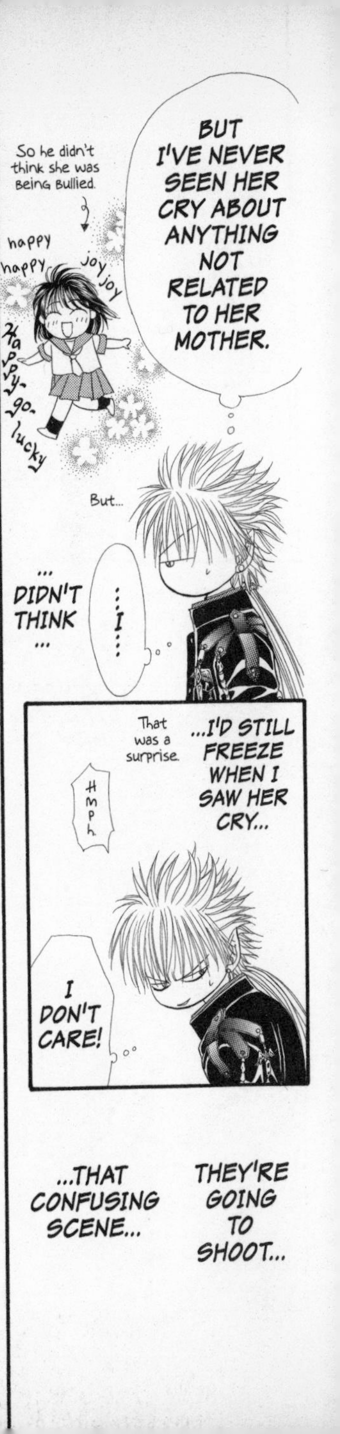
BUT I'VE NEVER SEEN HER CRY ABOUT ANYTHING NOT RELATED TO HER MOTHER.
So he didn't think she was being bullied.
happy happy
joy joy
Happy-go-lucky
But...
...I...
...DIDN'T THINK...
...I'D STILL FREEZE WHEN I SAW HER CRY...
That was a surprise.
Hmph.
I DON'T CARE!
THEY'RE GOING TO SHOOT...
...THAT CONFUSING SCENE...
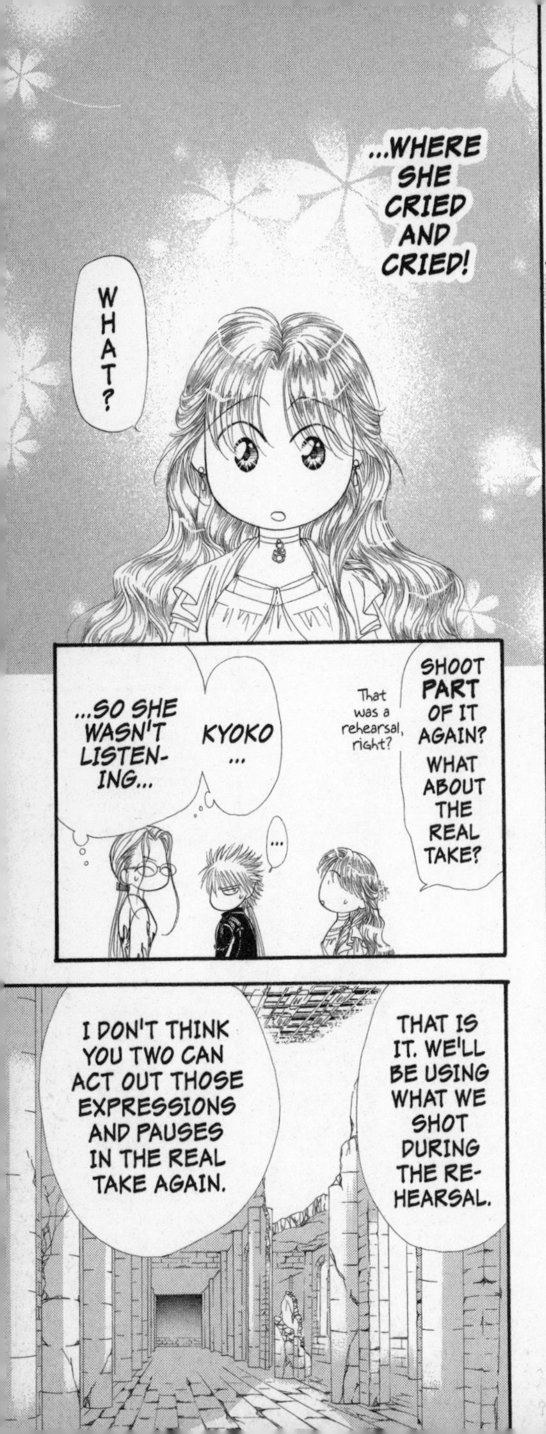
...WHERE SHE CRIED AND CRIED!
WHAT?
SHOOT PART OF IT AGAIN? WHAT ABOUT THE REAL TAKE?
That was a rehearsal, right?
KYOKO...
...
...SO SHE WASN'T LISTENING...
THAT IS IT. WE'LL BE USING WHAT WE SHOT DURING THE REHEARSAL.
I DON'T THINK YOU TWO CAN ACT OUT THOSE EXPRESSIONS AND PAUSES IN THE REAL TAKE AGAIN.

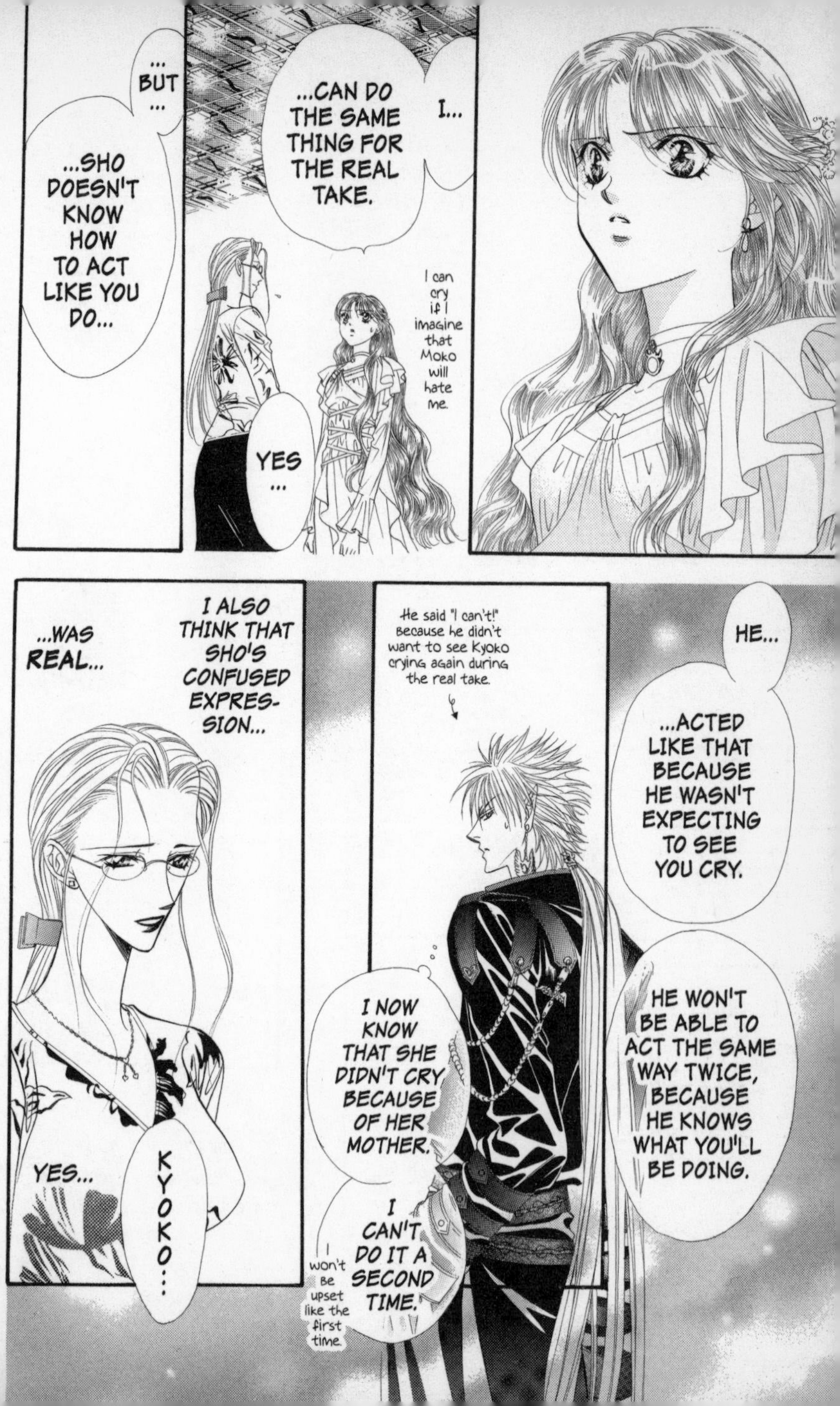

I...
...CAN DO THE SAME THING FOR THE REAL TAKE.
I can cry if I imagine that Moko will hate me.
YES...
...BUT...
...SHO DOESN'T KNOW HOW TO ACT LIKE YOU DO...
HE...
...ACTED LIKE THAT BECAUSE HE WASN'T EXPECTING TO SEE YOU CRY.
He said "I can't!" because he didn't want to see Kyoko crying again during the real take.
HE WON'T BE ABLE TO ACT THE SAME WAY TWICE, BECAUSE HE KNOWS WHAT YOU'LL BE DOING.
I NOW KNOW THAT SHE DIDN'T CRY BECAUSE OF HER MOTHER.
I CAN'T DO IT A SECOND TIME.
I won't be upset like the first time.
I ALSO THINK THAT SHO'S CONFUSED EXPRESSION...
...WAS REAL...
KYOKO...
YES...

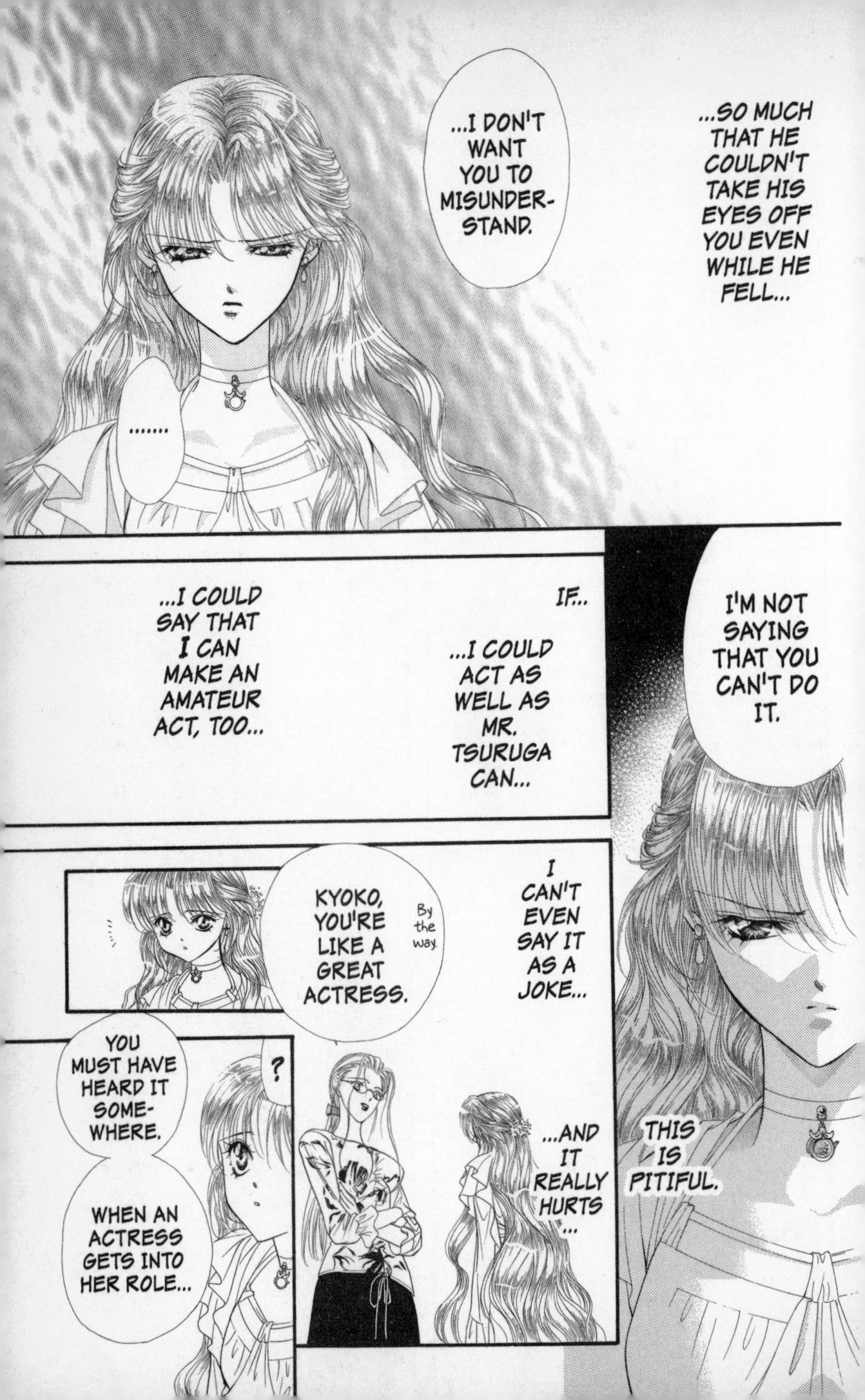
...SO MUCH THAT HE COULDN'T TAKE HIS EYES OFF YOU EVEN WHILE HE FELL...
...I DON'T WANT YOU TO MISUNDERSTAND.
.......
I'M NOT SAYING THAT YOU CAN'T DO IT.
THIS IS PITIFUL.
IF...
...I COULD ACT AS WELL AS MR. TSURUGA CAN...
...I COULD SAY THAT I CAN MAKE AN AMATEUR ACT, TOO...
I CAN'T EVEN SAY IT AS A JOKE...
...AND IT REALLY HURTS...
By the way.
KYOKO, YOU'RE LIKE A GREAT ACTRESS.
?
YOU MUST HAVE HEARD IT SOMEWHERE.
WHEN AN ACTRESS GETS INTO HER ROLE...

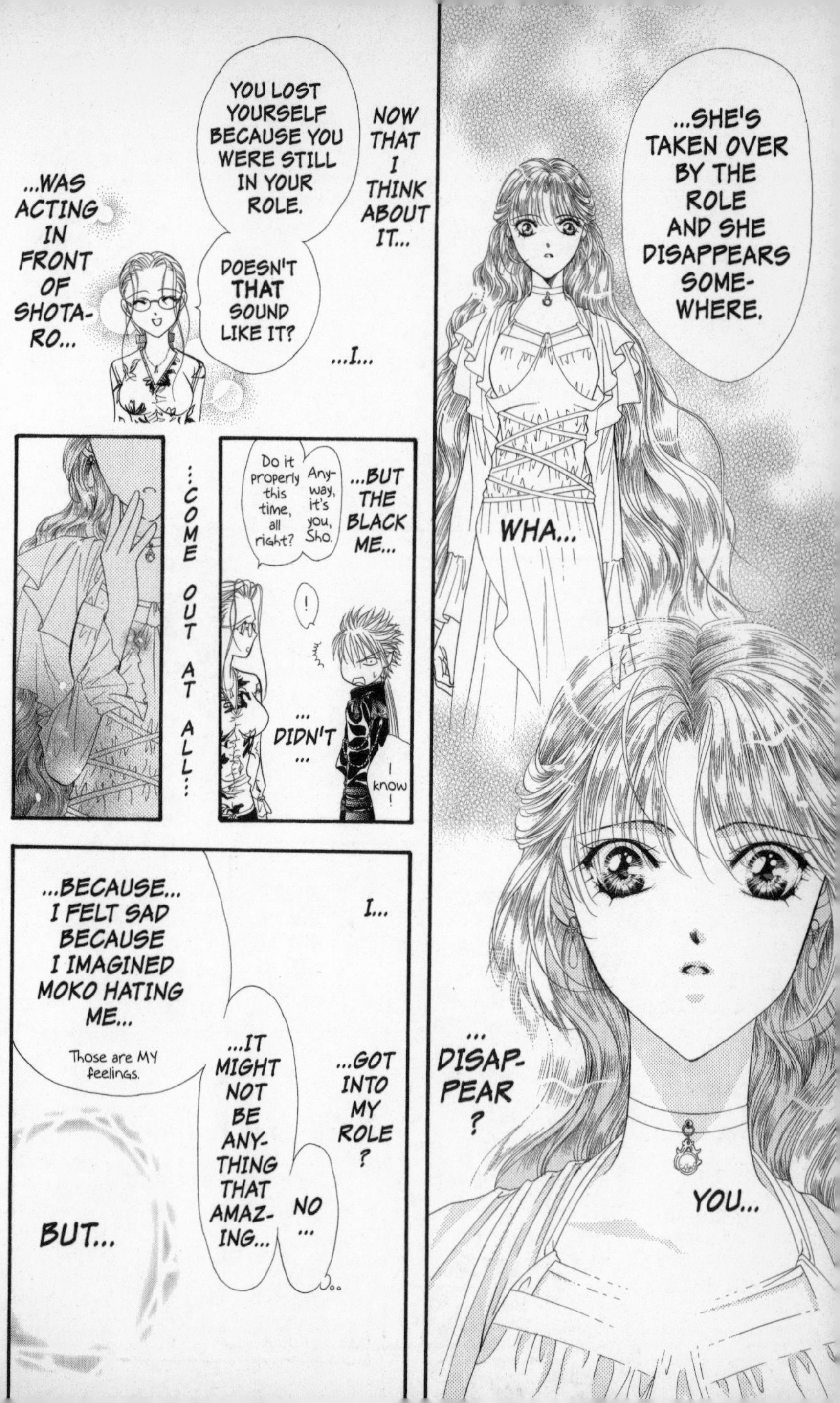
NOW THAT I THINK ABOUT IT...
YOU LOST YOURSELF BECAUSE YOU WERE STILL IN YOUR ROLE.
DOESN'T THAT SOUND LIKE IT?
...I...
...WAS ACTING IN FRONT OF SHOTARO...
...BUT THE BLACK ME...
Any-way, it's you, Sho.
Do it properly this time, all right?
!
...DIDN'T...
I know!
...COME OUT AT ALL...
I...
...GOT INTO MY ROLE?
...IT MIGHT NOT BE ANYTHING THAT AMAZING...
NO...
...BECAUSE... I FELT SAD BECAUSE I IMAGINED MOKO HATING ME...
Those are MY feelings.
BUT...
...SHE'S TAKEN OVER BY THE ROLE AND SHE DISAPPEARS SOME-WHERE.
WHA...
...DISAP-PEAR?
YOU...

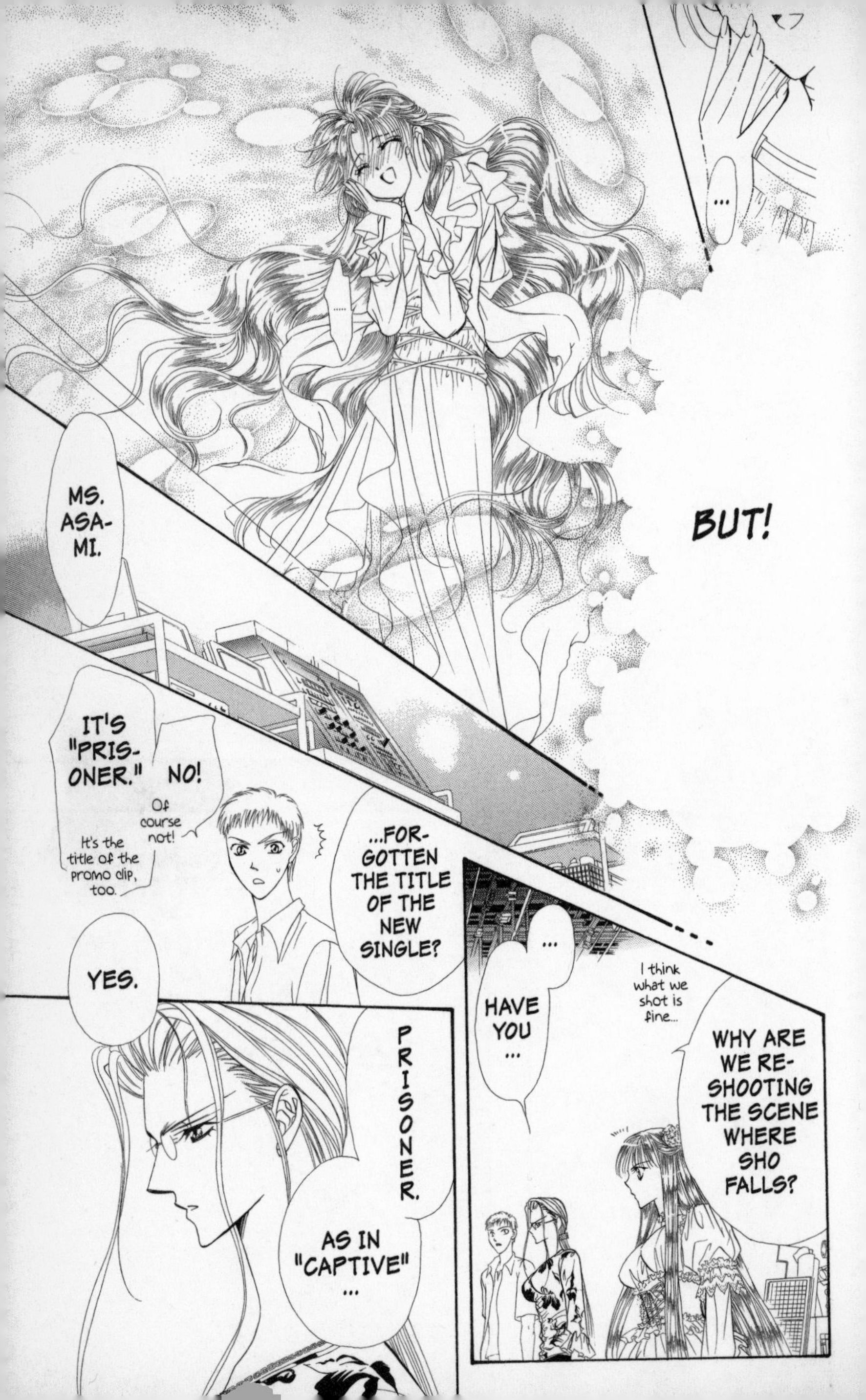
...
BUT!
......
MS. ASAMI.
I think what we shot is fine...
WHY ARE WE RE-SHOOTING THE SCENE WHERE SHO FALLS?
...
HAVE YOU ...
...FORGOTTEN THE TITLE OF THE NEW SINGLE?
YES.
IT'S "PRISONER."
NO!
Of course not!
It's the title of the promo clip, too.
PRISONER.
AS IN "CAPTIVE" ...

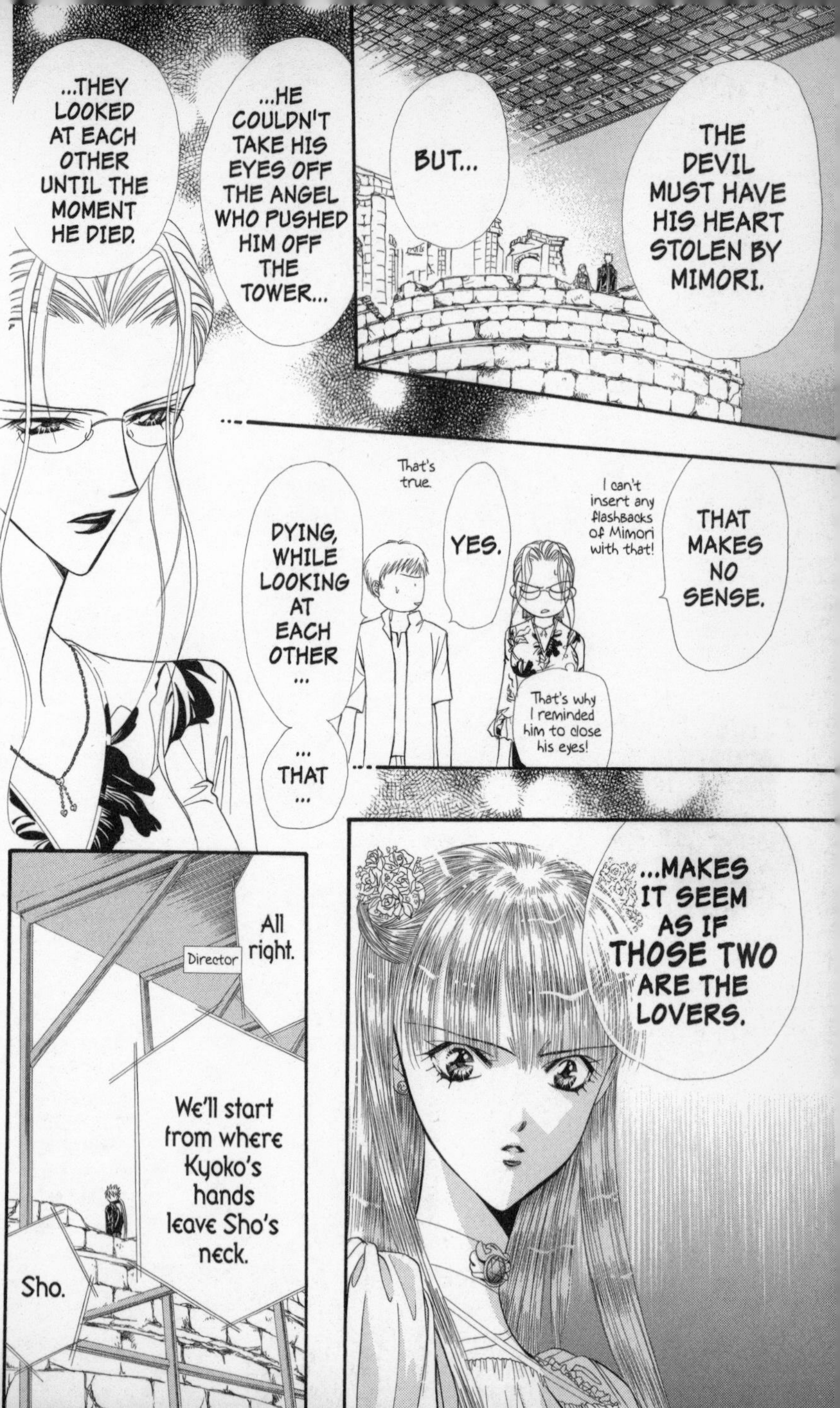
THE DEVIL MUST HAVE HIS HEART STOLEN BY MIMORI.
BUT...
...HE COULDN'T TAKE HIS EYES OFF THE ANGEL WHO PUSHED HIM OFF THE TOWER...
...THEY LOOKED AT EACH OTHER UNTIL THE MOMENT HE DIED.
...
THAT MAKES NO SENSE.
I can't insert any flashbacks of Mimori with that!
That's why I reminded him to close his eyes!
YES.
That's true.
DYING, WHILE LOOKING AT EACH OTHER ...
... THAT ...
...MAKES IT SEEM AS IF THOSE TWO ARE THE LOVERS.
Director
All right.
We'll start from where Kyoko's hands leave Sho's neck.
Sho.

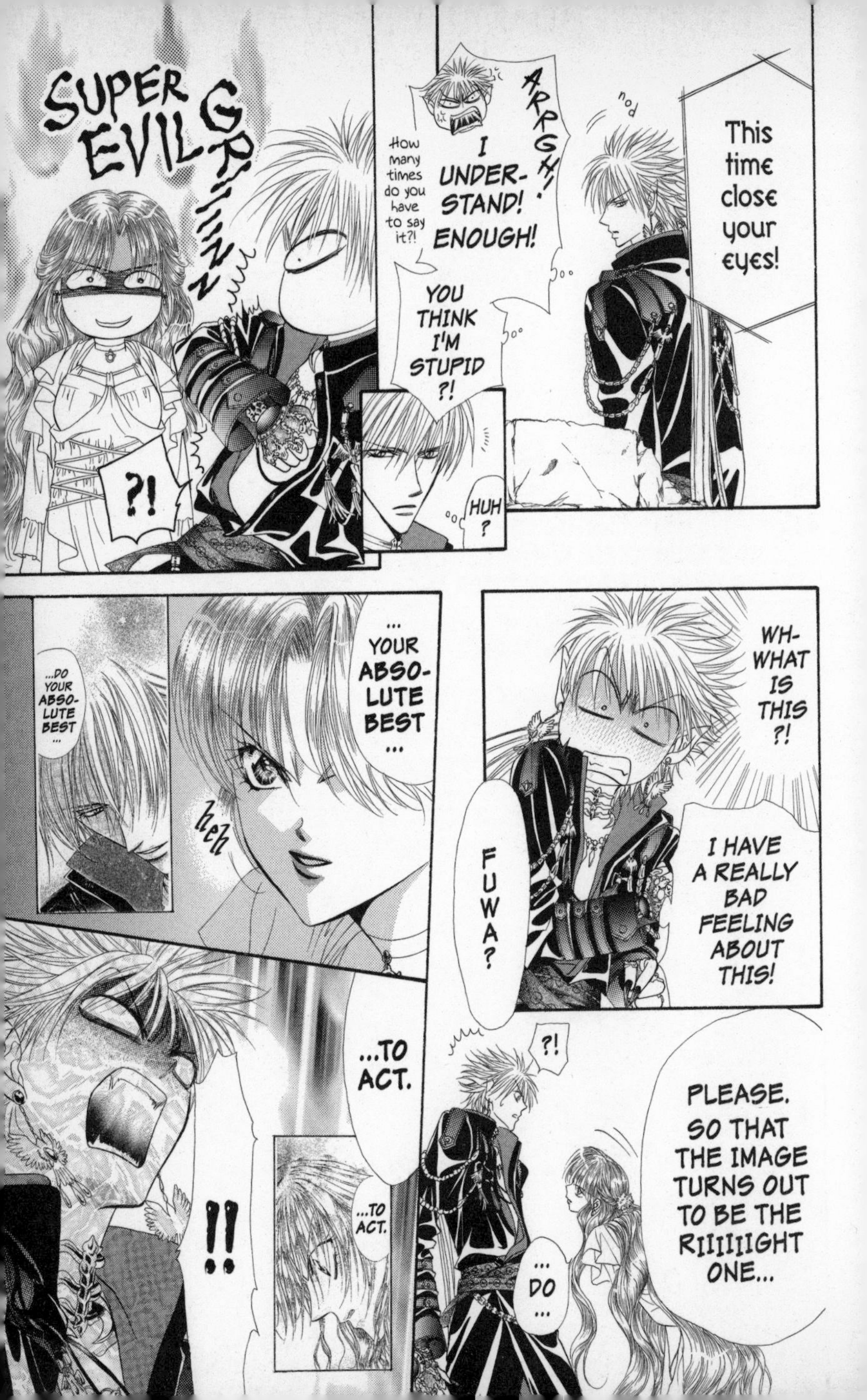

nod
This time close your eyes!
ARRGH!
I UNDERSTAND! ENOUGH!
How many times do you have to say it?!
YOU THINK I'M STUPID?!
HUH?
SUPER EVIL GRIIIINN
?!
WH-WHAT IS THIS?!
I HAVE A REALLY BAD FEELING ABOUT THIS!
FUWA?
...YOUR ABSOLUTE BEST...
heh
...DO YOUR ABSOLUTE BEST...
?!
PLEASE. SO THAT THE IMAGE TURNS OUT TO BE THE RIIIIIIGHT ONE...
...DO...
...TO ACT.
...TO ACT.
!!

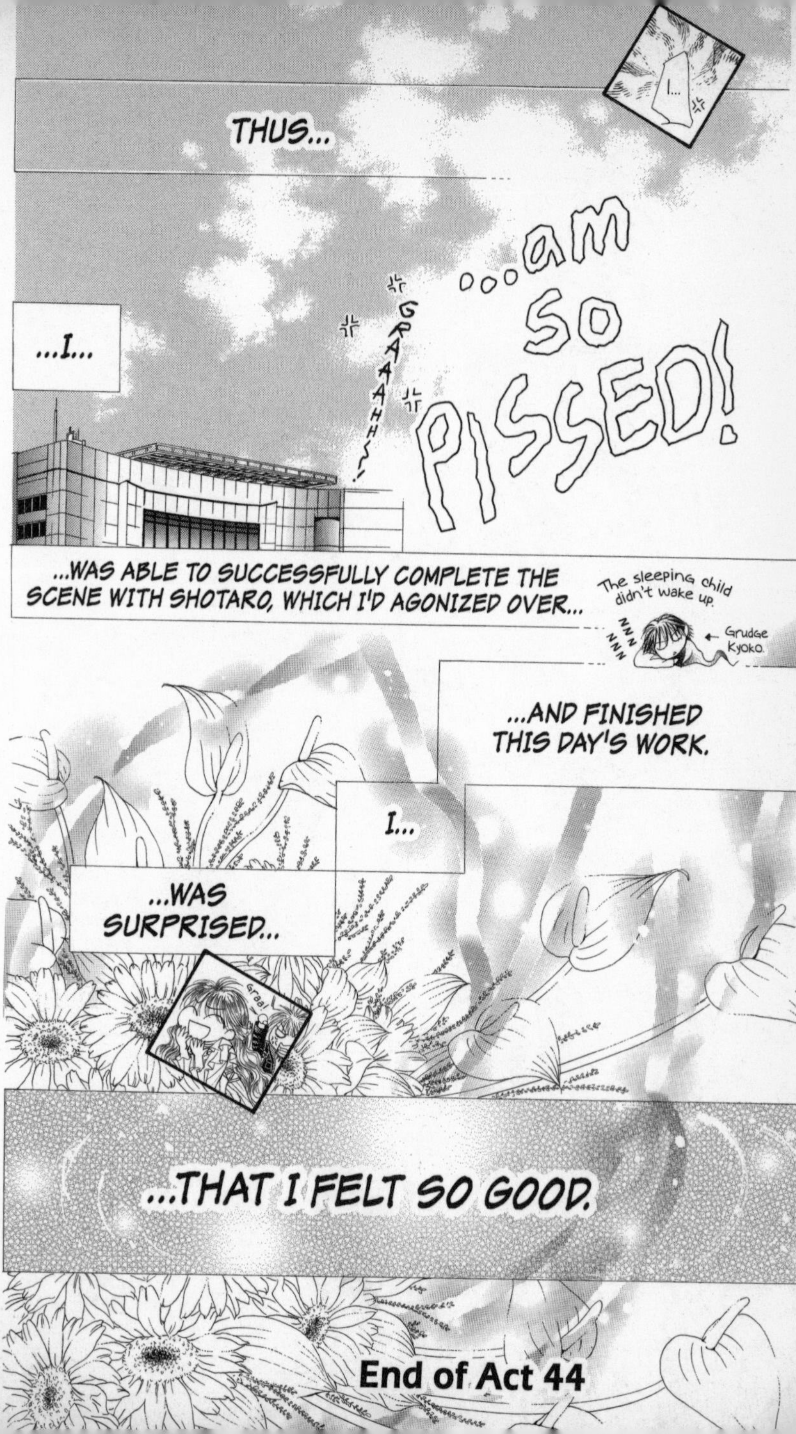
I...
THUS...
...I...
GRAAAAHH~!
...am so PISSED!
...WAS ABLE TO SUCCESSFULLY COMPLETE THE SCENE WITH SHOTARO, WHICH I'D AGONIZED OVER...
The sleeping child didn't wake up.
NNN NNN
Grudge Kyoko.
...AND FINISHED THIS DAY'S WORK.
I...
...WAS SURPRISED...
Graa!
...THAT I FELT SO GOOD.
End of Act 44

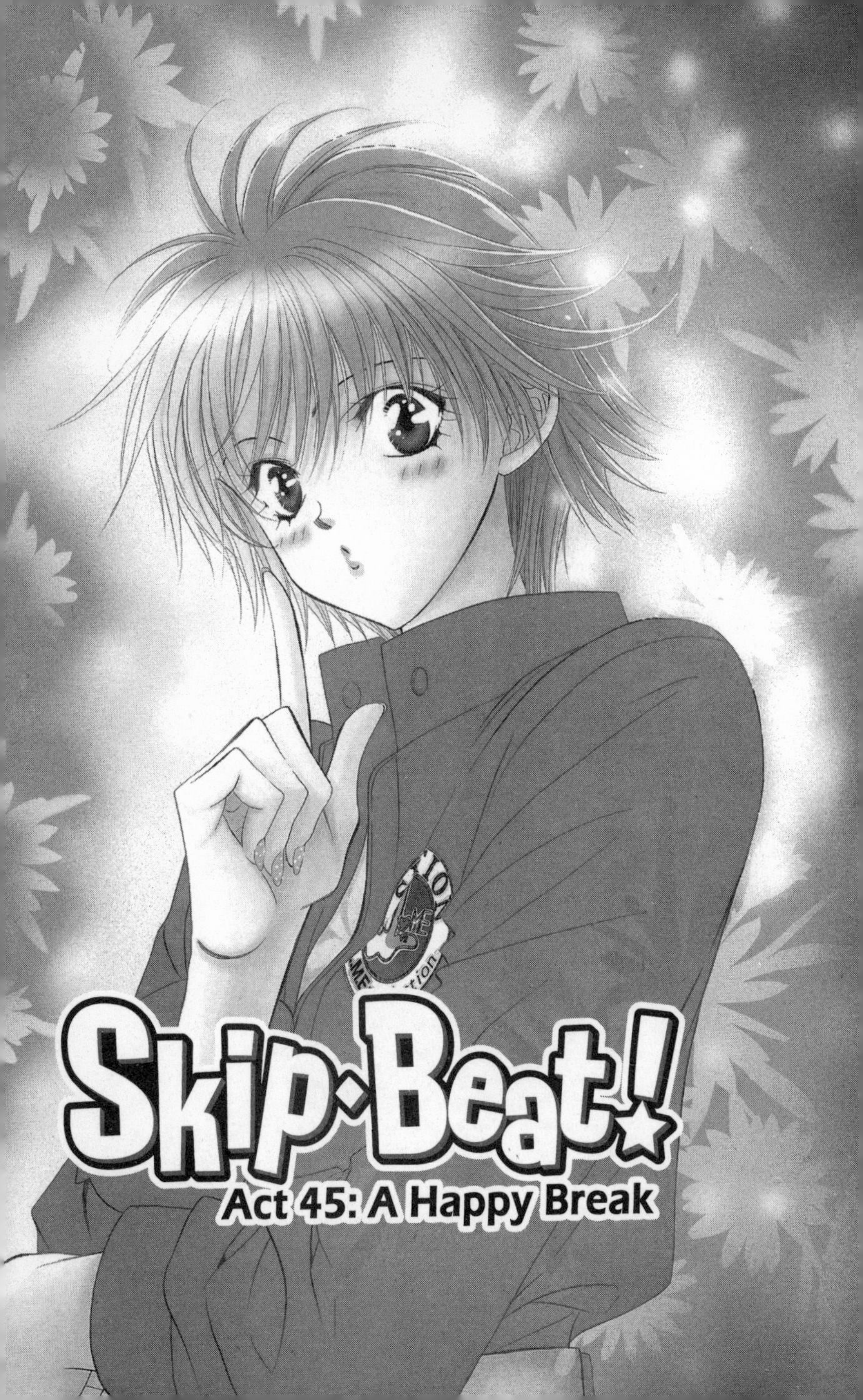
Skip·Beat!
Act 45: A Happy Break

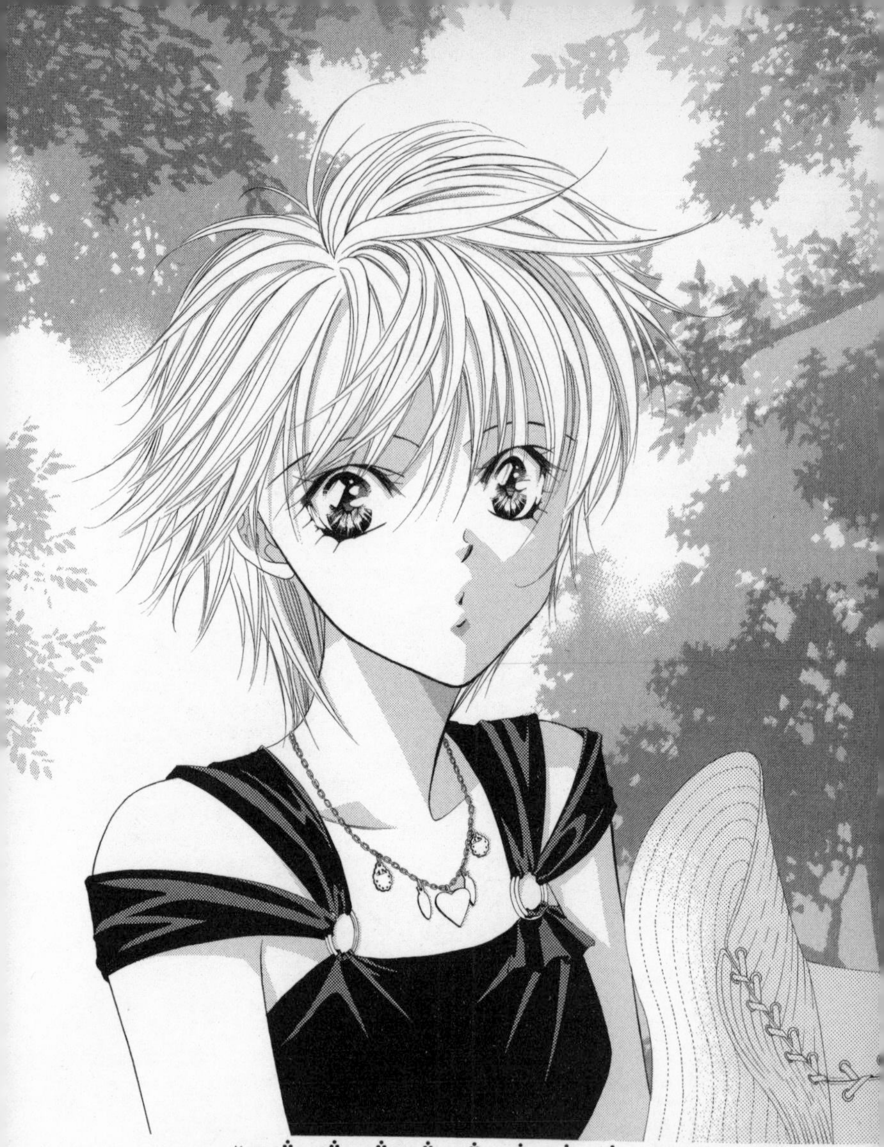

# Skip•Beat!

Volume 8

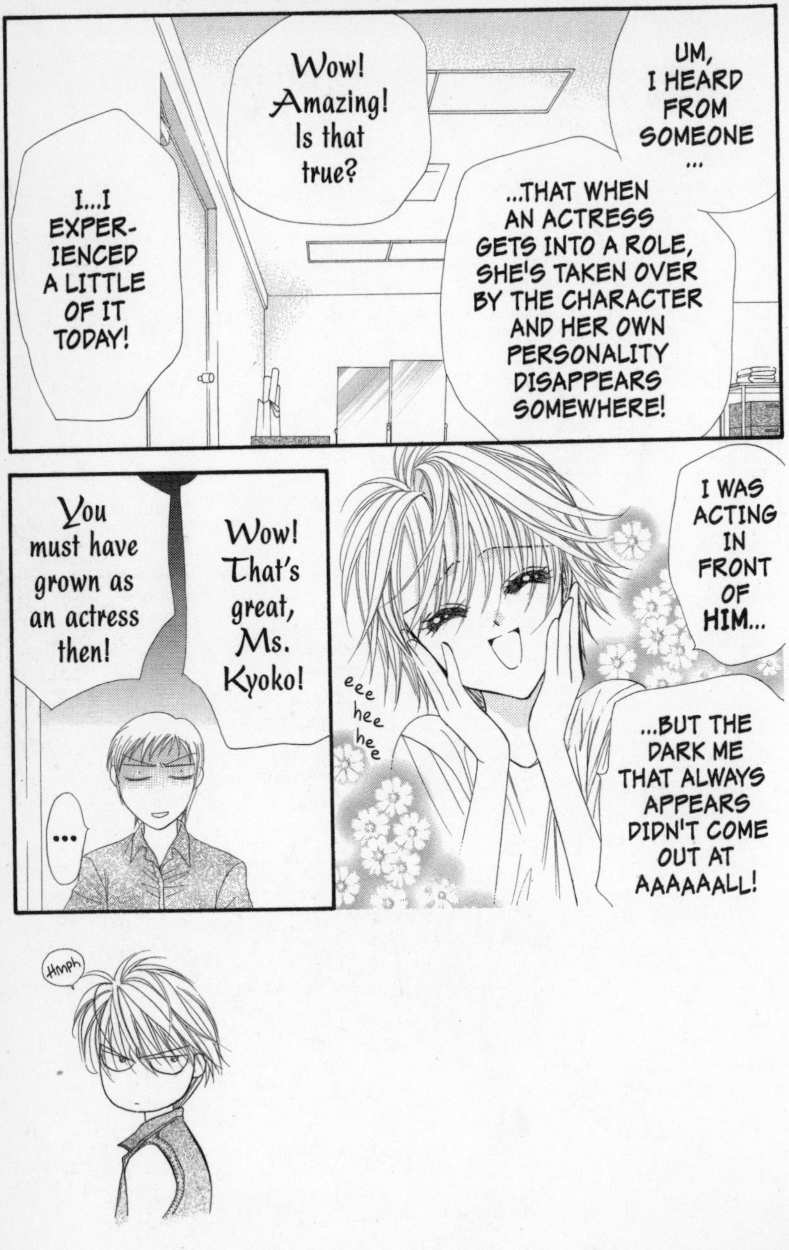
UM, I HEARD FROM SOMEONE ...
...THAT WHEN AN ACTRESS GETS INTO A ROLE, SHE'S TAKEN OVER BY THE CHARACTER AND HER OWN PERSONALITY DISAPPEARS SOMEWHERE!
Wow! Amazing! Is that true?
I...I EXPERIENCED A LITTLE OF IT TODAY!
I WAS ACTING IN FRONT OF HIM...
...BUT THE DARK ME THAT ALWAYS APPEARS DIDN'T COME OUT AT AAAAAALL!
eee hee hee
Wow! That's great, Ms. Kyoko!
You must have grown as an actress then!
...
Hmph

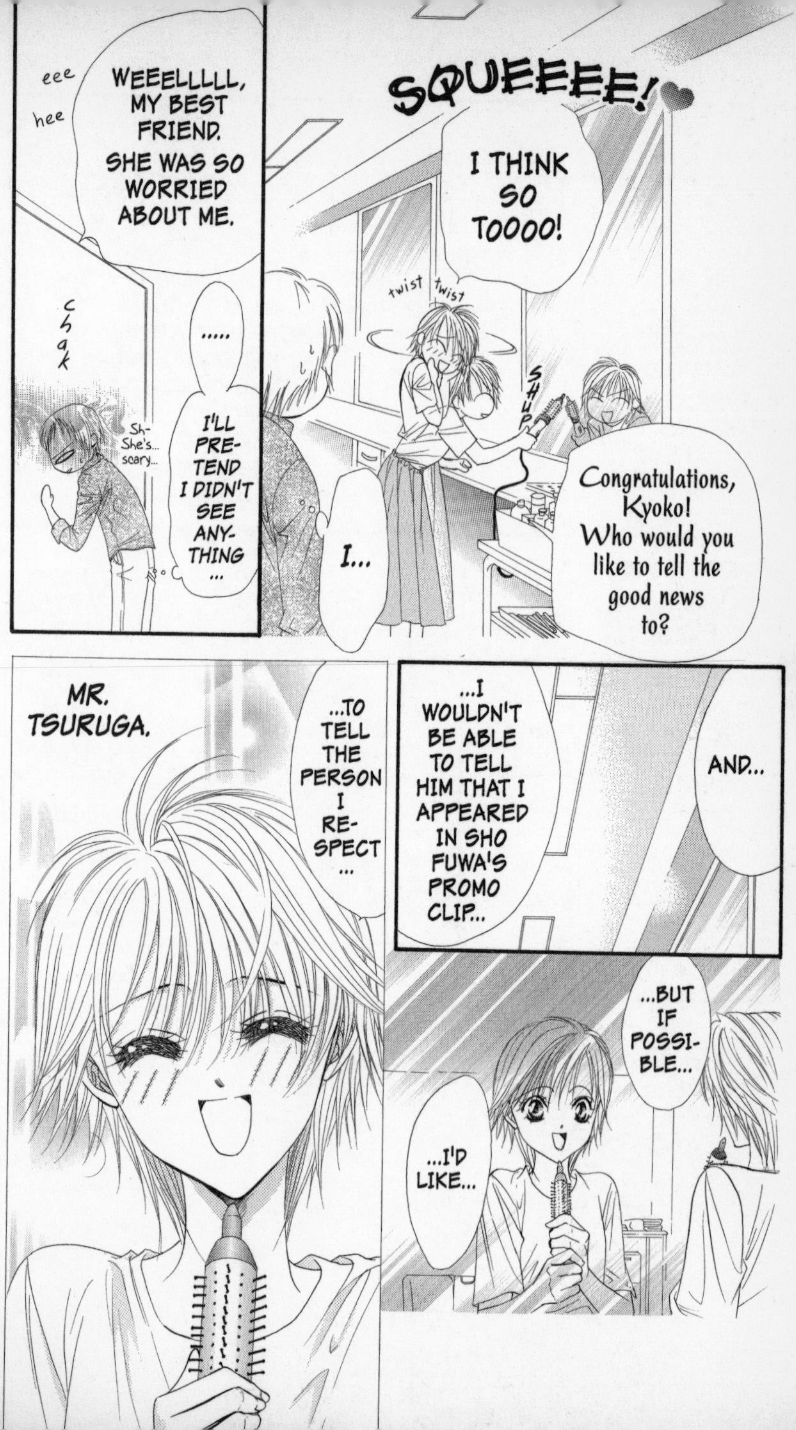
SQUEEEE!
I THINK SO TOOOO!
twist twist
SHUP
Congratulations, Kyoko! Who would you like to tell the good news to?
I...
eee hee
WEEELLLLL, MY BEST FRIEND. SHE WAS SO WORRIED ABOUT ME.
.....
chak
I'LL PRETEND I DIDN'T SEE ANYTHING...
Sh- She's... scary...
AND...
...I WOULDN'T BE ABLE TO TELL HIM THAT I APPEARED IN SHO FUWA'S PROMO CLIP...
...BUT IF POSSIBLE...
...I'D LIKE...
...TO TELL THE PERSON I RESPECT...
MR. TSURUGA.

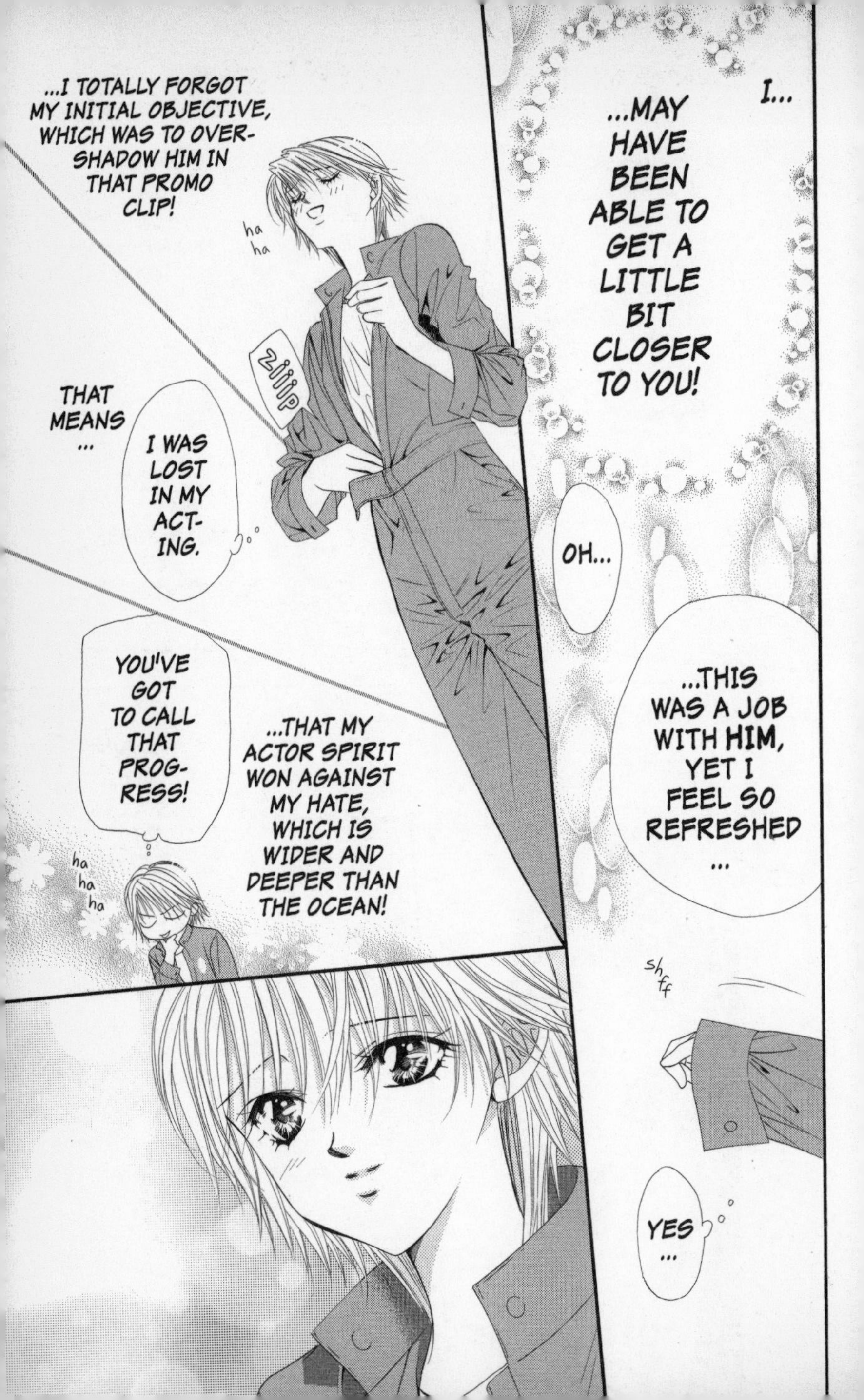
I...
...MAY HAVE BEEN ABLE TO GET A LITTLE BIT CLOSER TO YOU!
OH...
...THIS WAS A JOB WITH HIM, YET I FEEL SO REFRESHED ...
...I TOTALLY FORGOT MY INITIAL OBJECTIVE, WHICH WAS TO OVER-SHADOW HIM IN THAT PROMO CLIP!
ha ha
ziiip
I WAS LOST IN MY ACT-ING.
THAT MEANS ...
...THAT MY ACTOR SPIRIT WON AGAINST MY HATE, WHICH IS WIDER AND DEEPER THAN THE OCEAN!
YOU'VE GOT TO CALL THAT PROG-RESS!
ha ha ha
shff
YES ...

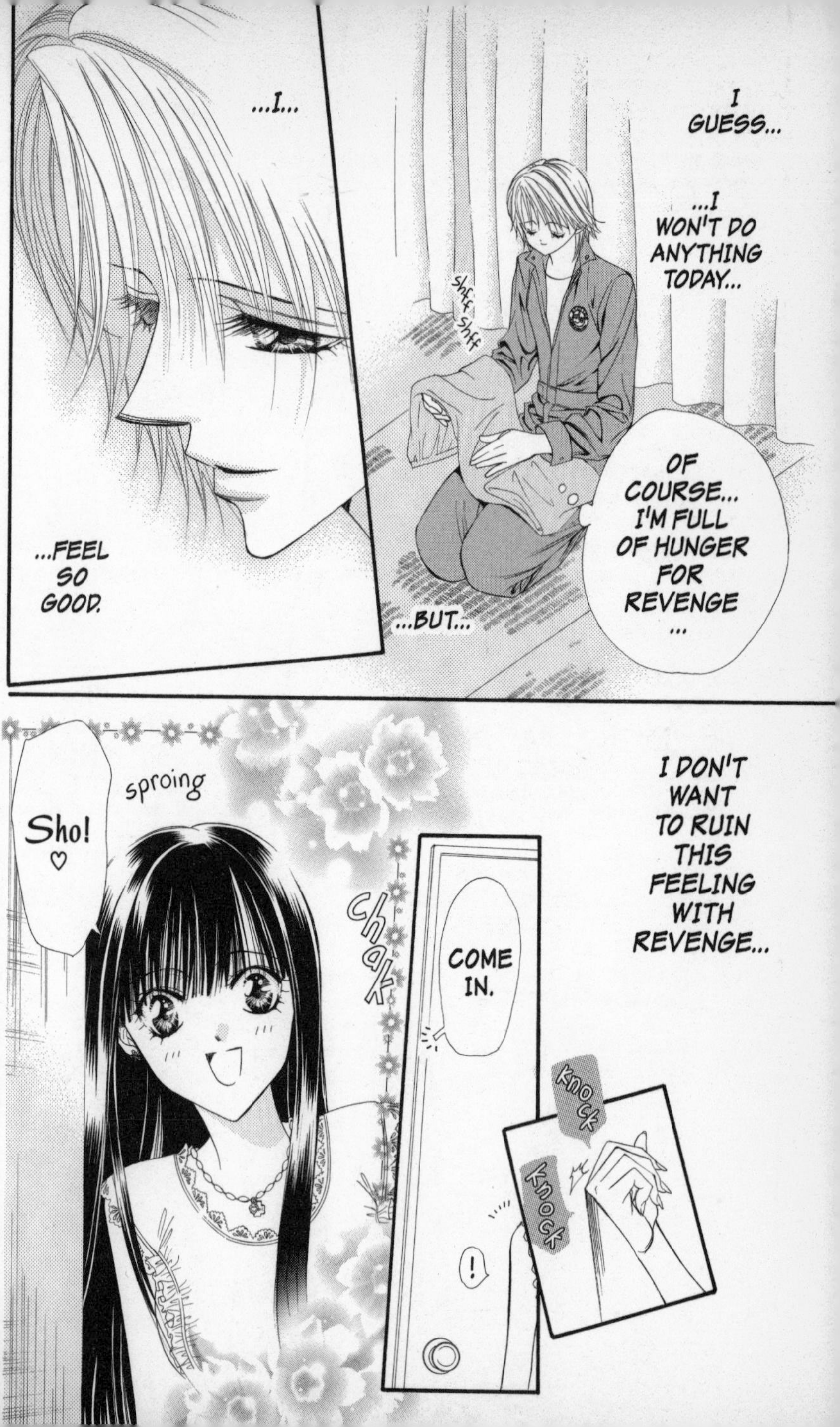
I GUESS...
...I WON'T DO ANYTHING TODAY...
shff shff
OF COURSE... I'M FULL OF HUNGER FOR REVENGE ...
...BUT...
...I...
...FEEL SO GOOD.
I DON'T WANT TO RUIN THIS FEELING WITH REVENGE...
knock knock
!
COME IN.
chak
sproing
Sho! ♡

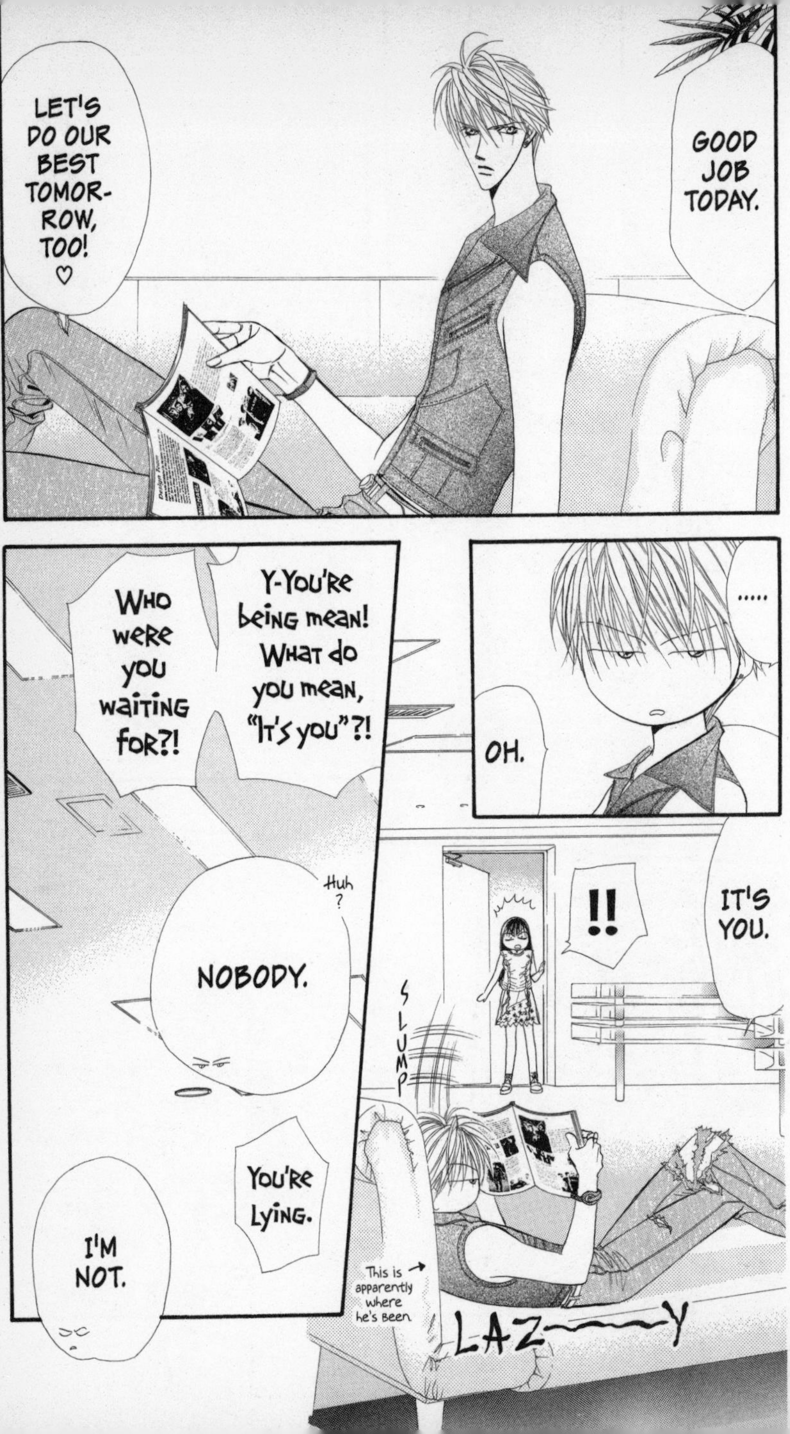
GOOD JOB TODAY.
LET'S DO OUR BEST TOMORROW, TOO! ♡
.....
OH.
IT'S YOU.
!!
SLUMP
This is apparently where he's been →
LAZ————Y
Y-You're being mean! What do you mean, "It's you"?!
Who were you waiting for?!
Huh?
NOBODY.
You're lying.
I'M NOT.

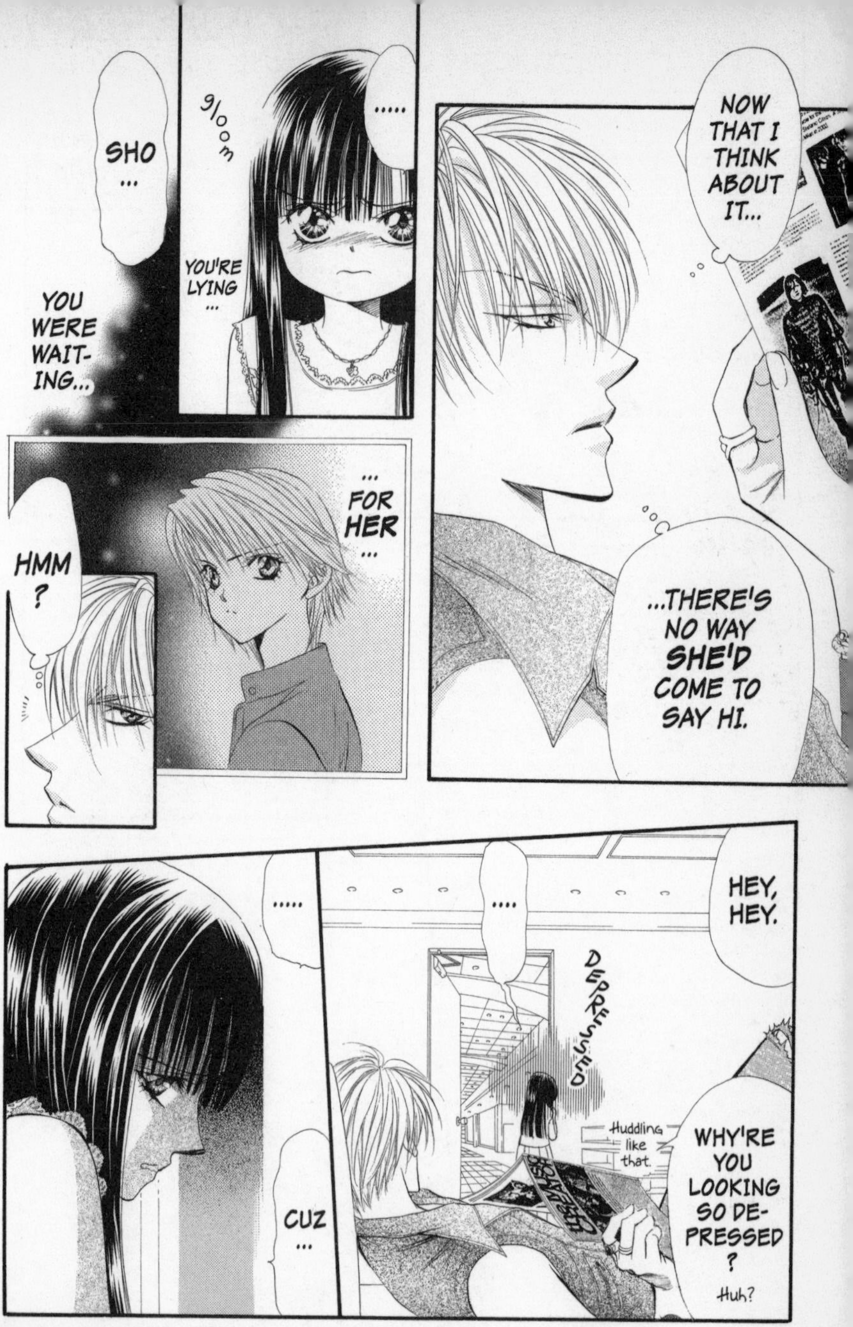
NOW THAT I THINK ABOUT IT...
...THERE'S NO WAY SHE'D COME TO SAY HI.
.....
gloom
YOU'RE LYING ...
SHO ...
YOU WERE WAIT- ING...
... FOR HER ...
HMM ?
HEY, HEY.
WHY'RE YOU LOOKING SO DE- PRESSED ?
Huh?
Huddling like that.
....
DEPRESSED
.....
CUZ ...

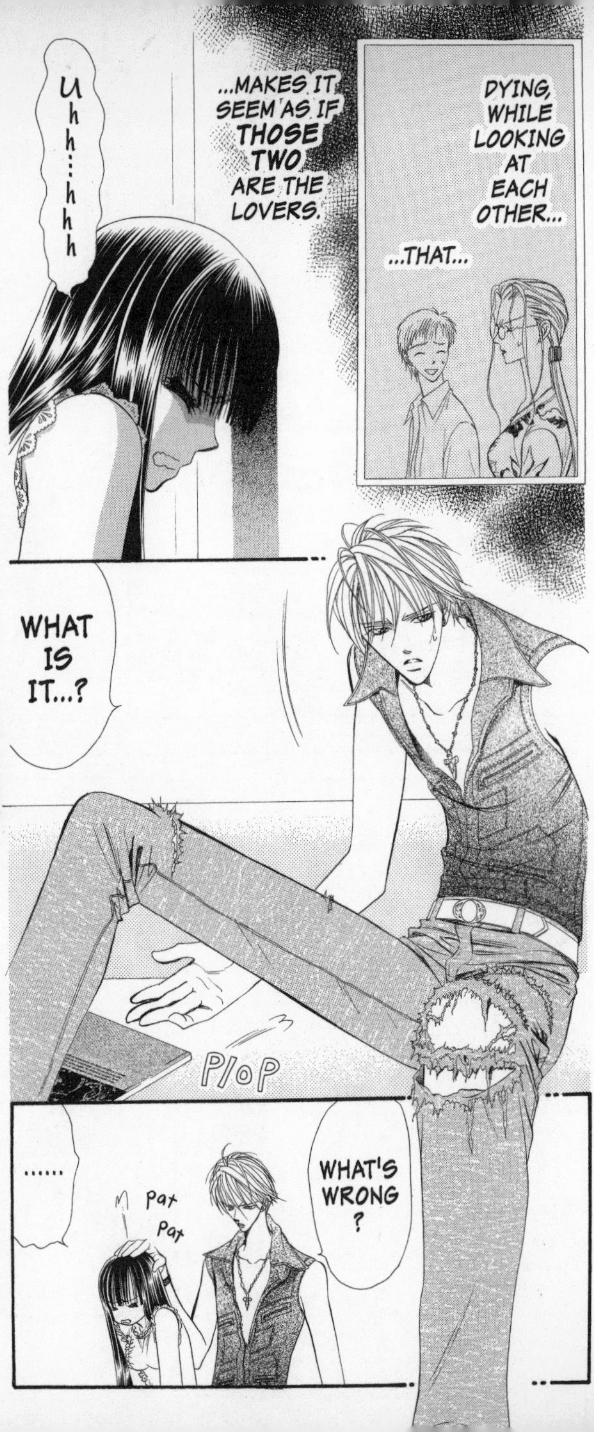
DYING, WHILE LOOKING AT EACH OTHER...
...THAT...
...MAKES IT SEEM AS IF THOSE TWO ARE THE LOVERS.
Uhh...hhh
WHAT IS IT...?
PLOP
WHAT'S WRONG?
Pat Pat
......

## Mimori Nanokura

For some reason, my assistants liked her...I myself don't hate her either, so I'm thinking about having her appear in Kyoko's school scenes again...

POCHIRI

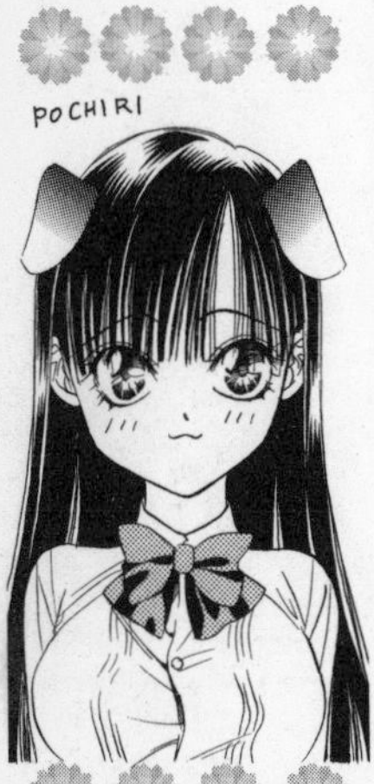

If I have the time to have Pochi, who has nothing to do with the main story, interact and play around with Kyoko... That is...in my case, I'm so obsessed with the "ending" of each chapter, I run out of pages, so I cut things here and there...and episodes disappear often...

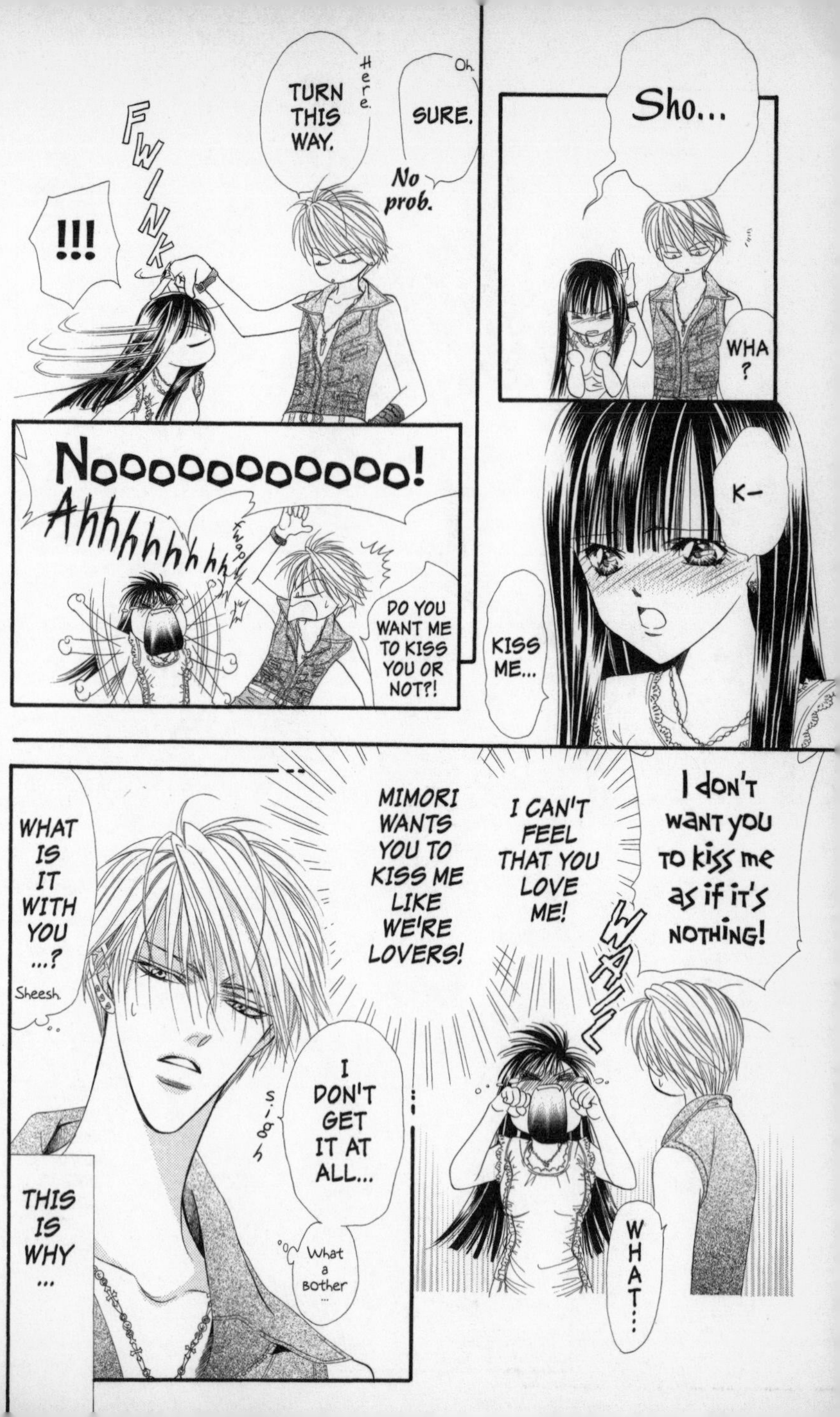
Sho...
WHA?
K-
KISS ME...
Oh.
SURE.
No prob.
Here.
TURN THIS WAY.
FWINK
!!!
Nooooooooooo!
Ahhhhhhhh
DO YOU WANT ME TO KISS YOU OR NOT?!
I don't want you to kiss me as if it's nothing!
WAIL
I CAN'T FEEL THAT YOU LOVE ME!
MIMORI WANTS YOU TO KISS ME LIKE WE'RE LOVERS!
WHAT...
I DON'T GET IT AT ALL...
sigh
What a bother...
WHAT IS IT WITH YOU...?
Sheesh.
THIS IS WHY...

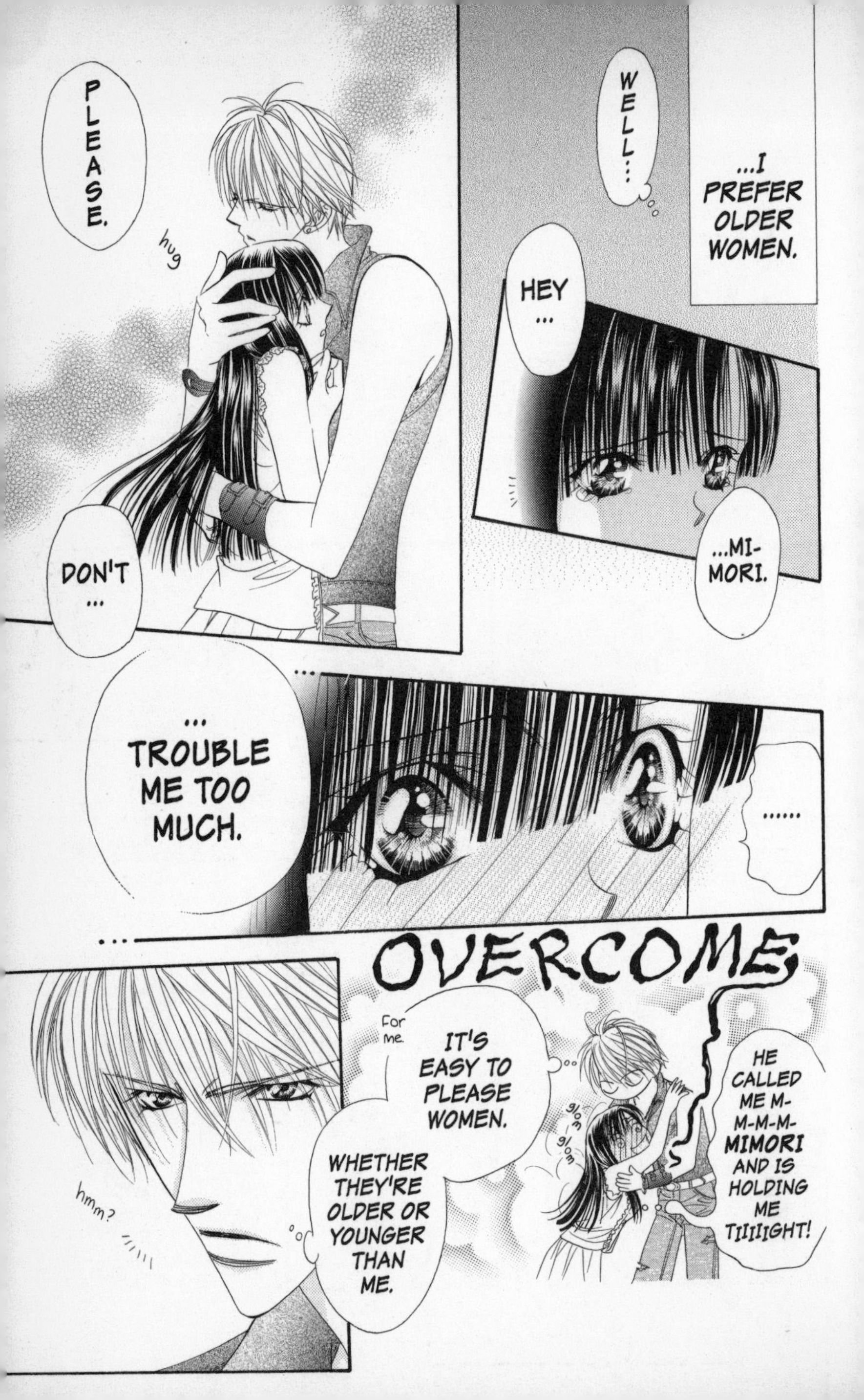
...I PREFER OLDER WOMEN.
WELL...
HEY ...
...MI-MORI.
PLEASE.
hug
DON'T ...
......
...
... TROUBLE ME TOO MUCH.
...
OVERCOME
HE CALLED ME M-M-M-M-MIMORI AND IS HOLDING ME TIIIIIGHT!
glom glom
For me.
IT'S EASY TO PLEASE WOMEN.
WHETHER THEY'RE OLDER OR YOUNGER THAN ME.
hmm?

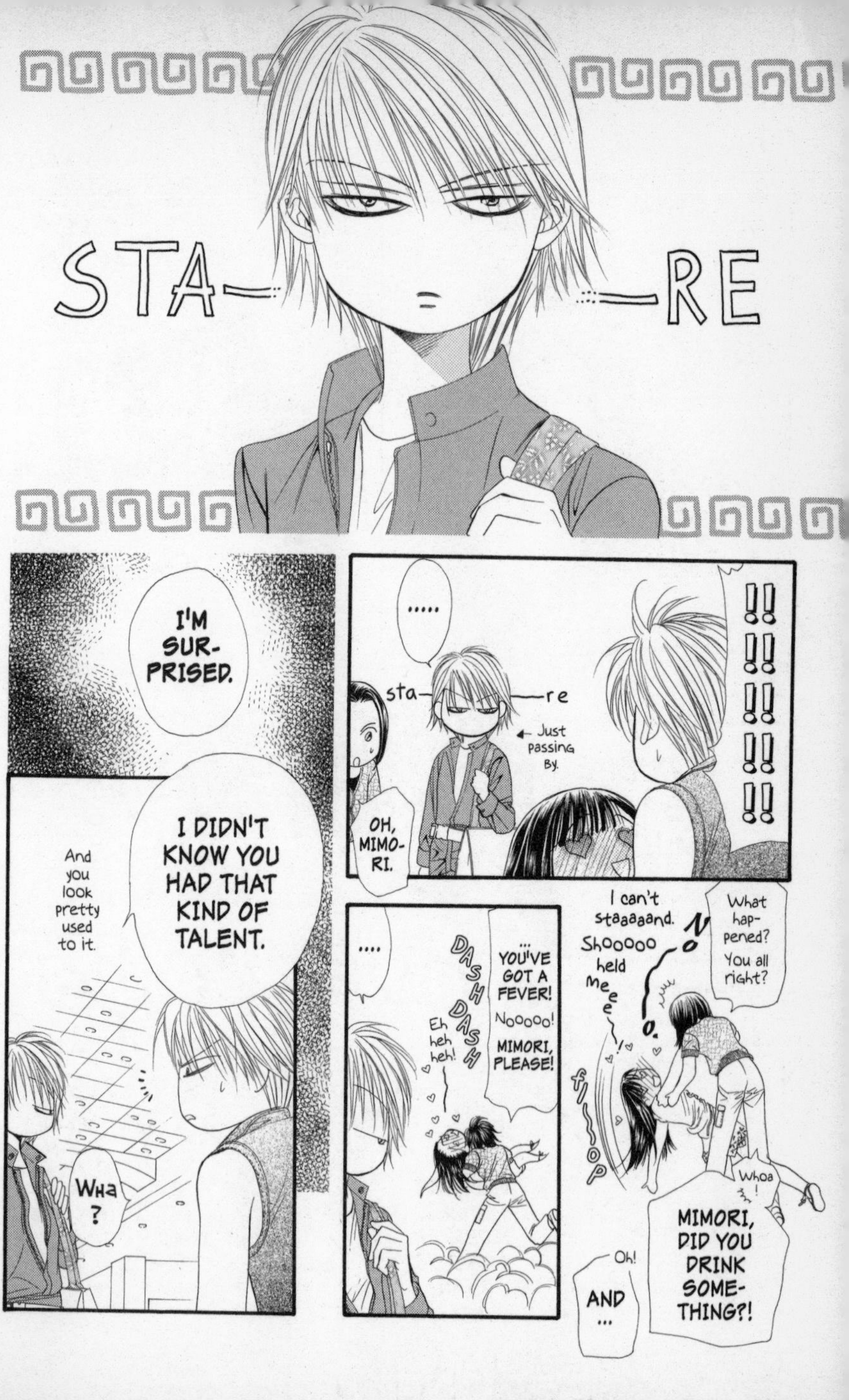
STA— —RE
!! !! !! !! !!
.....
sta— —re
Just passing by.
OH, MIMORI.
What happened? You all right?
I can't staaaaand.
Shoooooo held meeee~!
NO
fl~op
Whoa!
MIMORI, DID YOU DRINK SOMETHING?!
Oh!
AND ...
... YOU'VE GOT A FEVER!
Noooooo!
MIMORI, PLEASE!
DASH DASH
Eh heh heh!
....
I'M SURPRISED.
I DIDN'T KNOW YOU HAD THAT KIND OF TALENT.
And you look pretty used to it.
Wha?

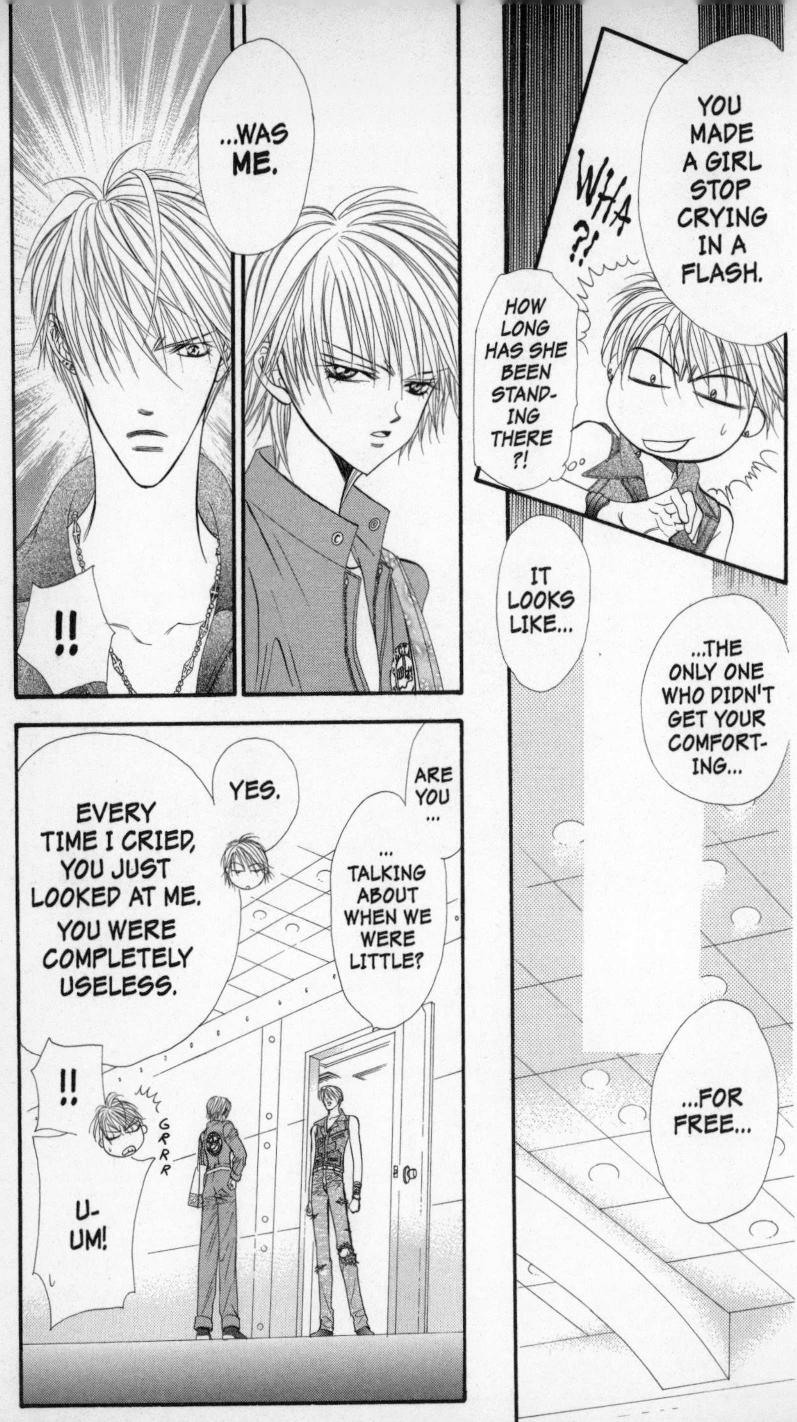
YOU MADE A GIRL STOP CRYING IN A FLASH.
WHA ?!
HOW LONG HAS SHE BEEN STAND-ING THERE ?!
IT LOOKS LIKE...
...THE ONLY ONE WHO DIDN'T GET YOUR COMFORT-ING...
...FOR FREE...
...WAS ME.
!!
ARE YOU ...
... TALKING ABOUT WHEN WE WERE LITTLE?
YES.
EVERY TIME I CRIED, YOU JUST LOOKED AT ME.
YOU WERE COMPLETELY USELESS.
!!
GRRR
U-UM!

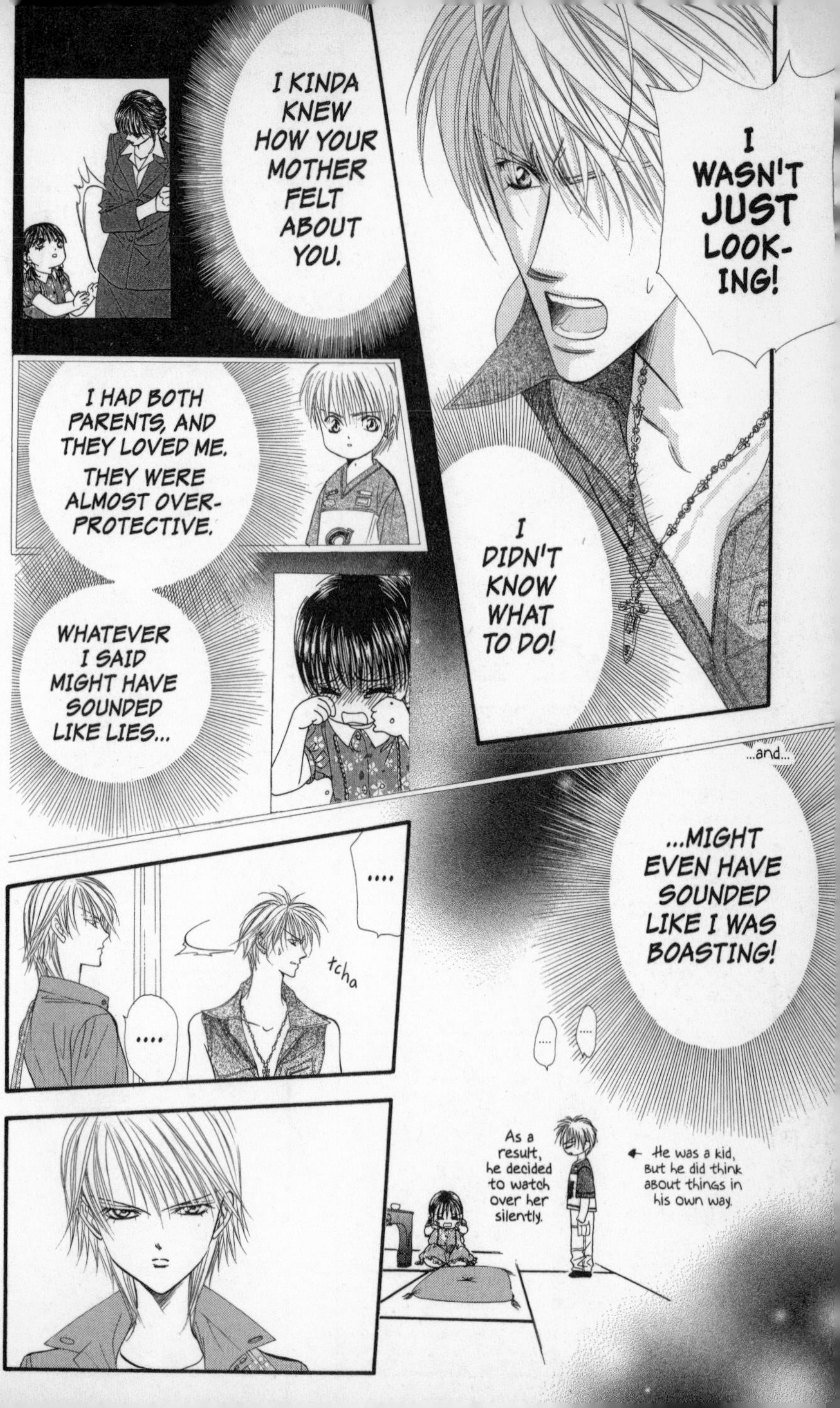
I WASN'T JUST LOOKING!
I DIDN'T KNOW WHAT TO DO!
I KINDA KNEW HOW YOUR MOTHER FELT ABOUT YOU.
I HAD BOTH PARENTS, AND THEY LOVED ME.
THEY WERE ALMOST OVER-PROTECTIVE.
WHATEVER I SAID MIGHT HAVE SOUNDED LIKE LIES...
...and...
...MIGHT EVEN HAVE SOUNDED LIKE I WAS BOASTING!
....
....
....
tcha
....
He was a kid, but he did think about things in his own way.
As a result, he decided to watch over her silently.

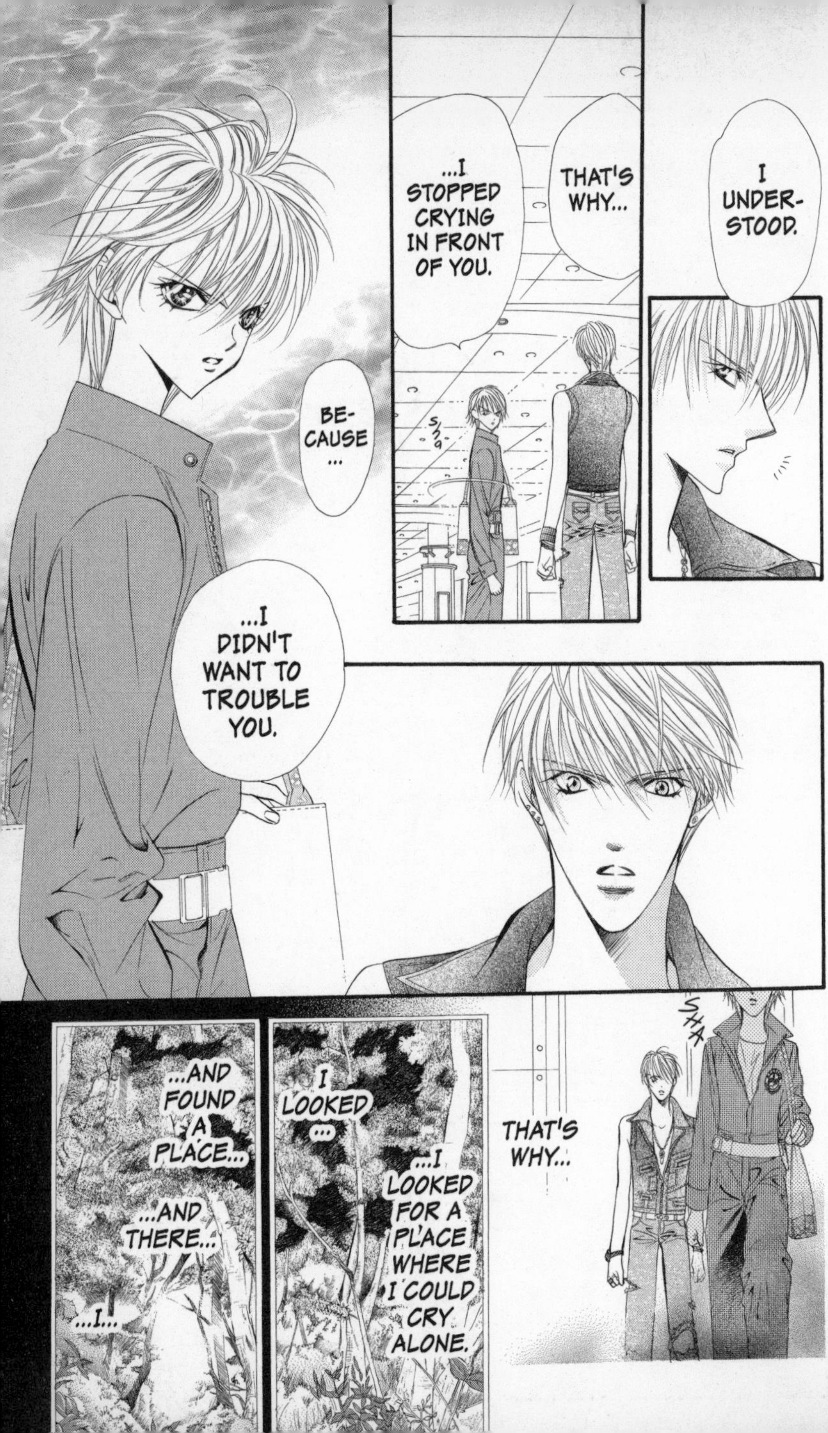
I UNDERSTOOD.
THAT'S WHY...
...I STOPPED CRYING IN FRONT OF YOU.
BECAUSE...
...I DIDN'T WANT TO TROUBLE YOU.
SHA
THAT'S WHY...
I LOOKED...
...I LOOKED FOR A PLACE WHERE I COULD CRY ALONE.
...AND FOUND A PLACE...
...AND THERE...
...I...

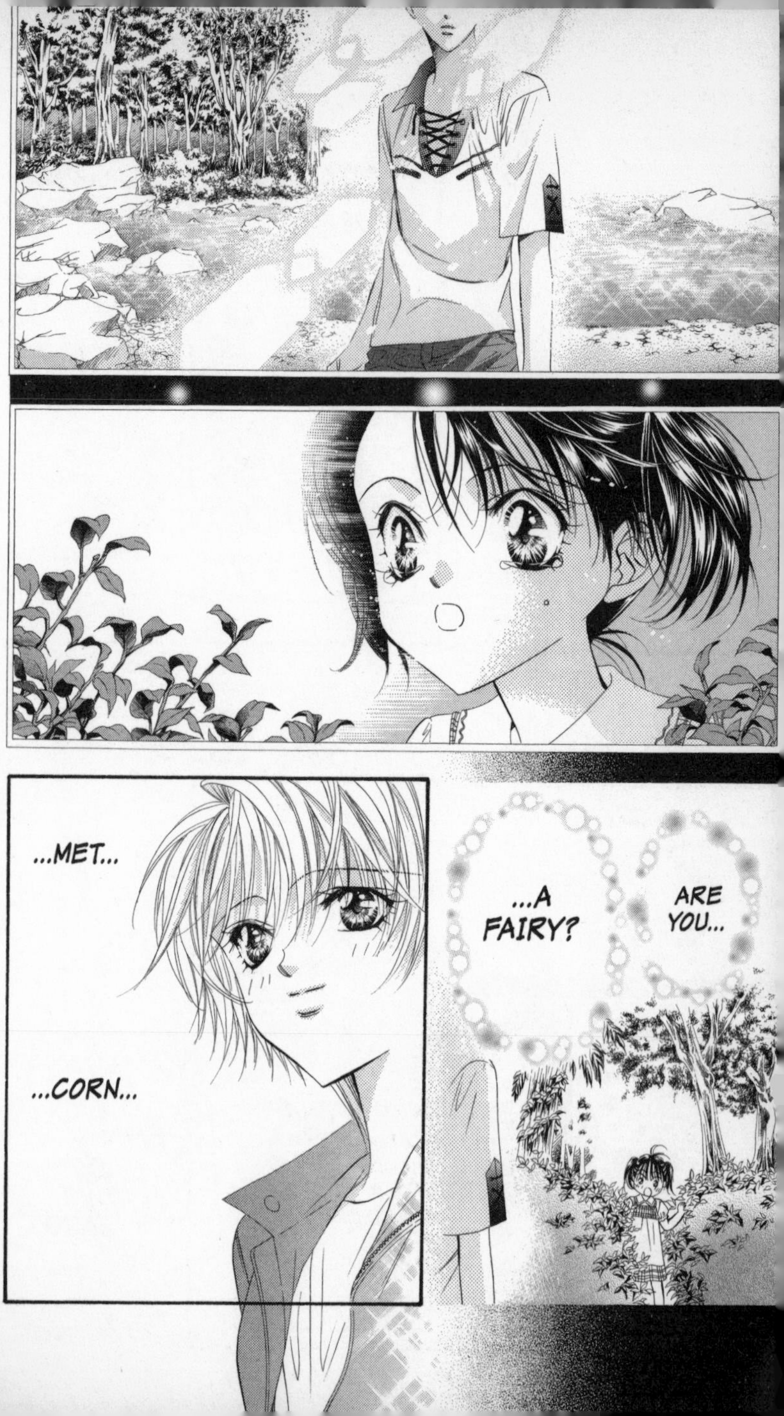
ARE YOU...
...A FAIRY?
...MET...
...CORN...

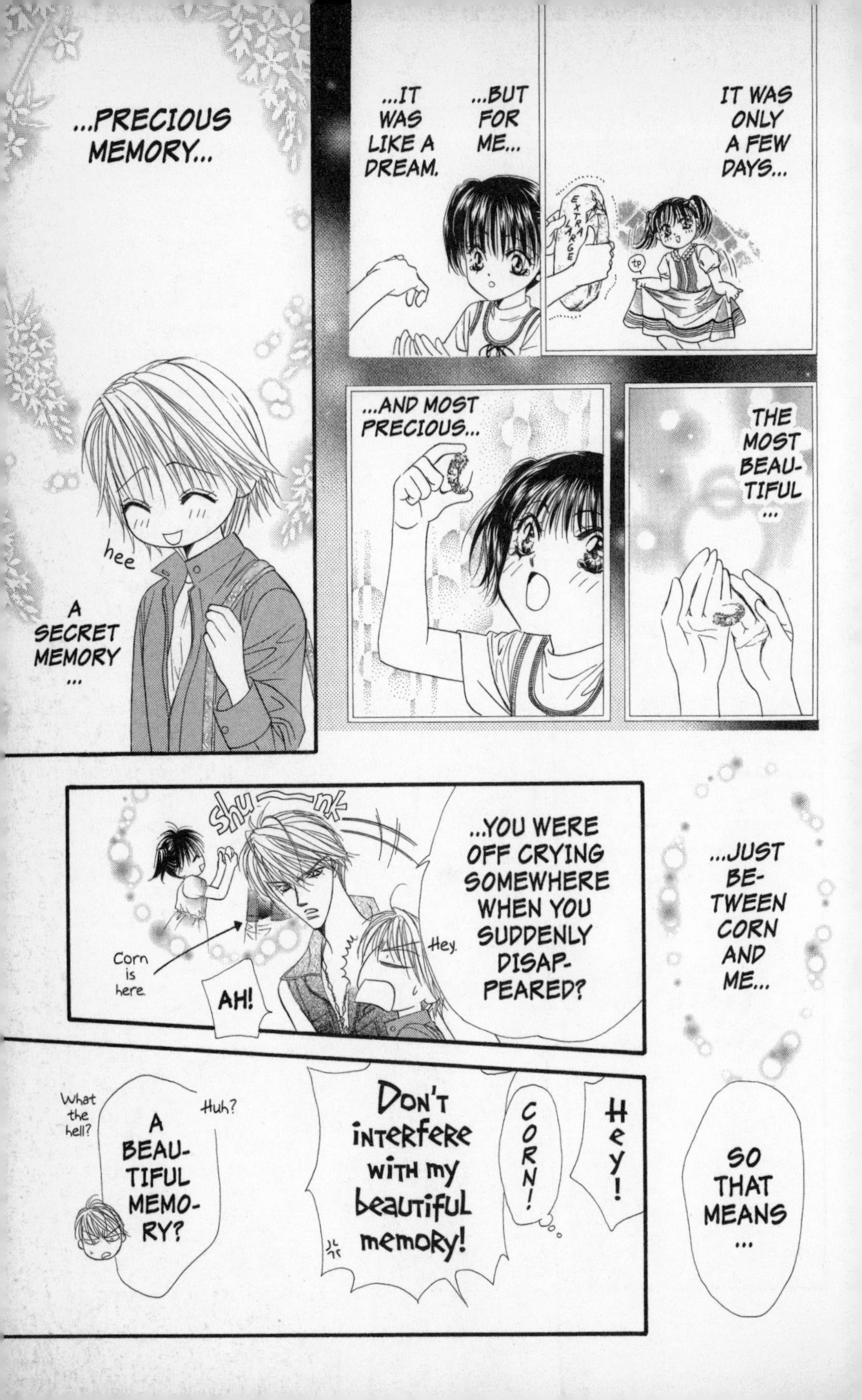
IT WAS ONLY A FEW DAYS...
tp
EXTRA LARGE
...BUT FOR ME...
...IT WAS LIKE A DREAM.
THE MOST BEAUTIFUL...
...AND MOST PRECIOUS...
...PRECIOUS MEMORY...
hee
A SECRET MEMORY...
...JUST BETWEEN CORN AND ME...
SHU—NK
...YOU WERE OFF CRYING SOMEWHERE WHEN YOU SUDDENLY DISAPPEARED?
Hey.
Corn is here.
AH!
SO THAT MEANS...
Hey!
CORN!
Don't interfere with my beautiful memory!
Huh?
A BEAUTIFUL MEMORY?
What the hell?

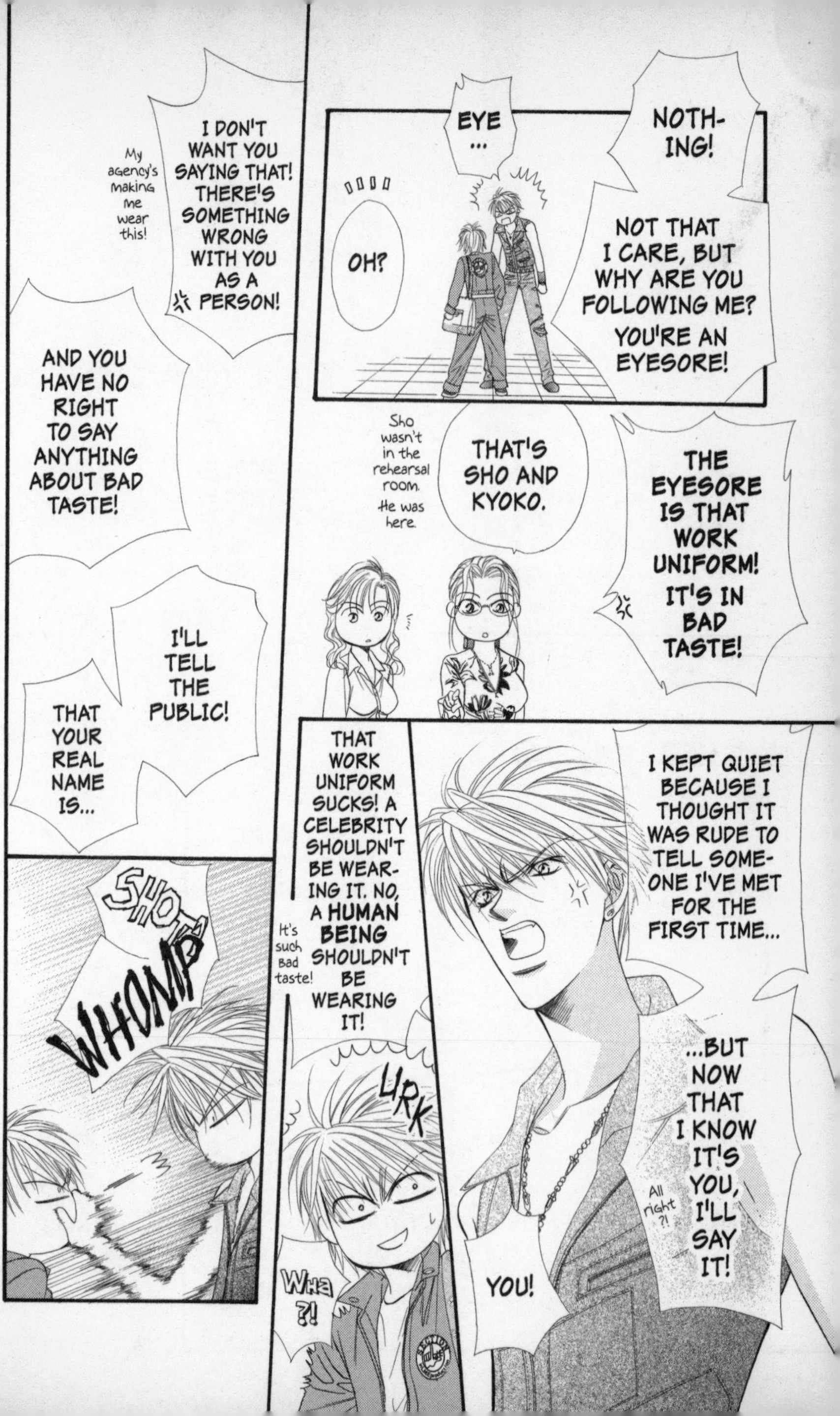
NOTH-ING!
EYE...
NOT THAT I CARE, BUT WHY ARE YOU FOLLOWING ME?
YOU'RE AN EYESORE!
OH?
THE EYESORE IS THAT WORK UNIFORM!
IT'S IN BAD TASTE!
THAT'S SHO AND KYOKO.
Sho wasn't in the rehearsal room.
He was here.
I KEPT QUIET BECAUSE I THOUGHT IT WAS RUDE TO TELL SOME-ONE I'VE MET FOR THE FIRST TIME...
...BUT NOW THAT I KNOW IT'S YOU, I'LL SAY IT!
All right?!
YOU!
THAT WORK UNIFORM SUCKS! A CELEBRITY SHOULDN'T BE WEAR-ING IT. NO, A HUMAN BEING SHOULDN'T BE WEARING IT!
It's such Bad taste!
URK
Wha ?!
I DON'T WANT YOU SAYING THAT! THERE'S SOMETHING WRONG WITH YOU AS A PERSON!
My agency's making me wear this!
AND YOU HAVE NO RIGHT TO SAY ANYTHING ABOUT BAD TASTE!
I'LL TELL THE PUBLIC!
THAT YOUR REAL NAME IS...
SHOTA
WHOMP

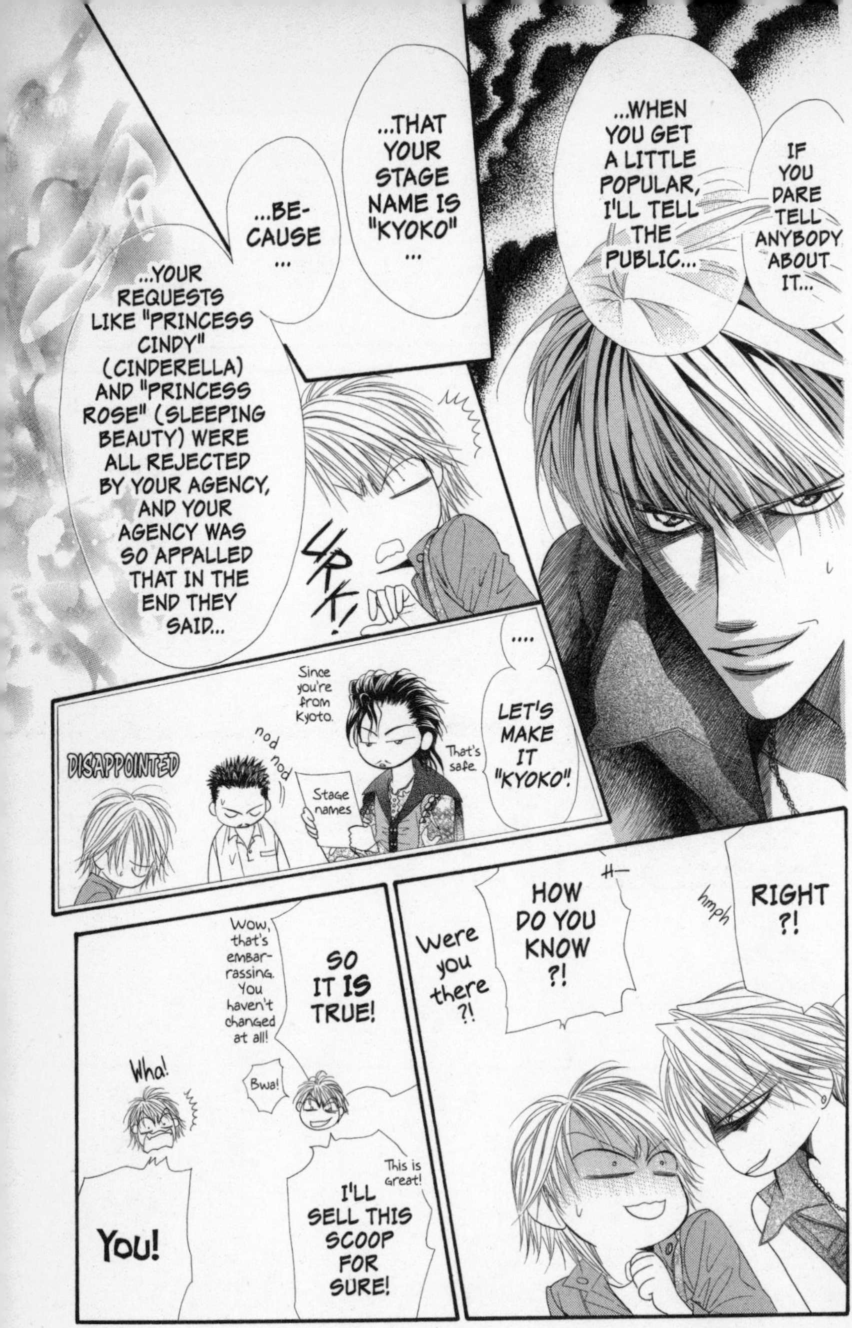
IF YOU DARE TELL ANYBODY ABOUT IT...
...WHEN YOU GET A LITTLE POPULAR, I'LL TELL THE PUBLIC...
...THAT YOUR STAGE NAME IS "KYOKO"...
...BE-CAUSE...
...YOUR REQUESTS LIKE "PRINCESS CINDY" (CINDERELLA) AND "PRINCESS ROSE" (SLEEPING BEAUTY) WERE ALL REJECTED BY YOUR AGENCY, AND YOUR AGENCY WAS SO APPALLED THAT IN THE END THEY SAID...
URK!
....
LET'S MAKE IT "KYOKO".
That's safe.
Since you're from Kyoto.
Stage names
nod nod
DISAPPOINTED
RIGHT?!
hmph
HOW DO YOU KNOW?!
Were you there?!
H—
SO IT IS TRUE!
Wow, that's embarrassing. You haven't changed at all!
Bwa!
Wha!
This is Great!
I'LL SELL THIS SCOOP FOR SURE!
YOU!

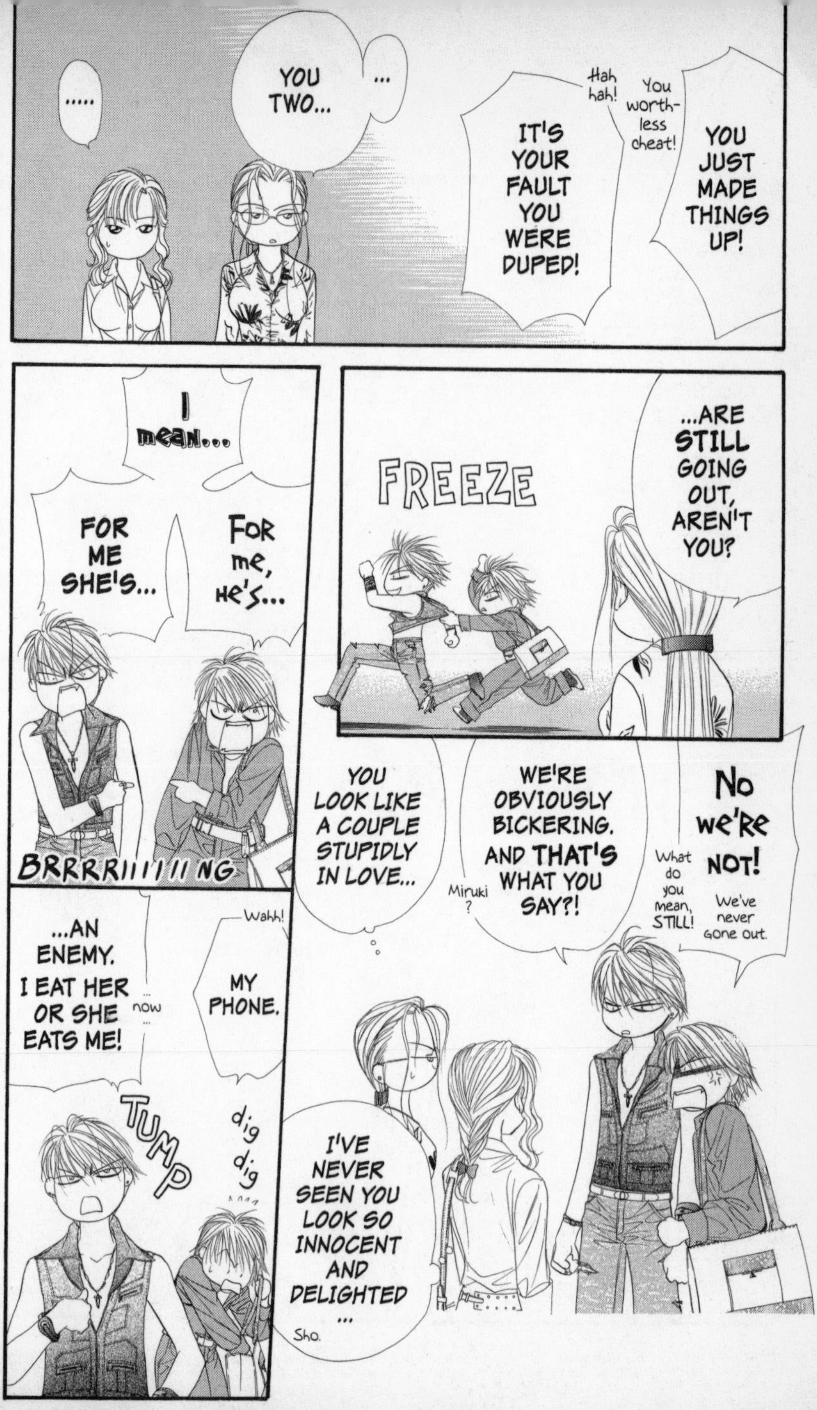
YOU JUST MADE THINGS UP!
You worthless cheat!
Hah hah!
IT'S YOUR FAULT YOU WERE DUPED!
...
YOU TWO...
......
...ARE STILL GOING OUT, AREN'T YOU?
FREEZE
No we're NOT!
We've never gone out.
What do you mean, STILL!
WE'RE OBVIOUSLY BICKERING. AND THAT'S WHAT YOU SAY?!
Miruki?
YOU LOOK LIKE A COUPLE STUPIDLY IN LOVE...
I'VE NEVER SEEN YOU LOOK SO INNOCENT AND DELIGHTED...
Sho.
I mean...
For me, he's...
FOR ME SHE'S...
BRRRRIIIIIIING
Wahh!
MY PHONE.
...now...
...AN ENEMY. I EAT HER OR SHE EATS ME!
dig dig
TUMP

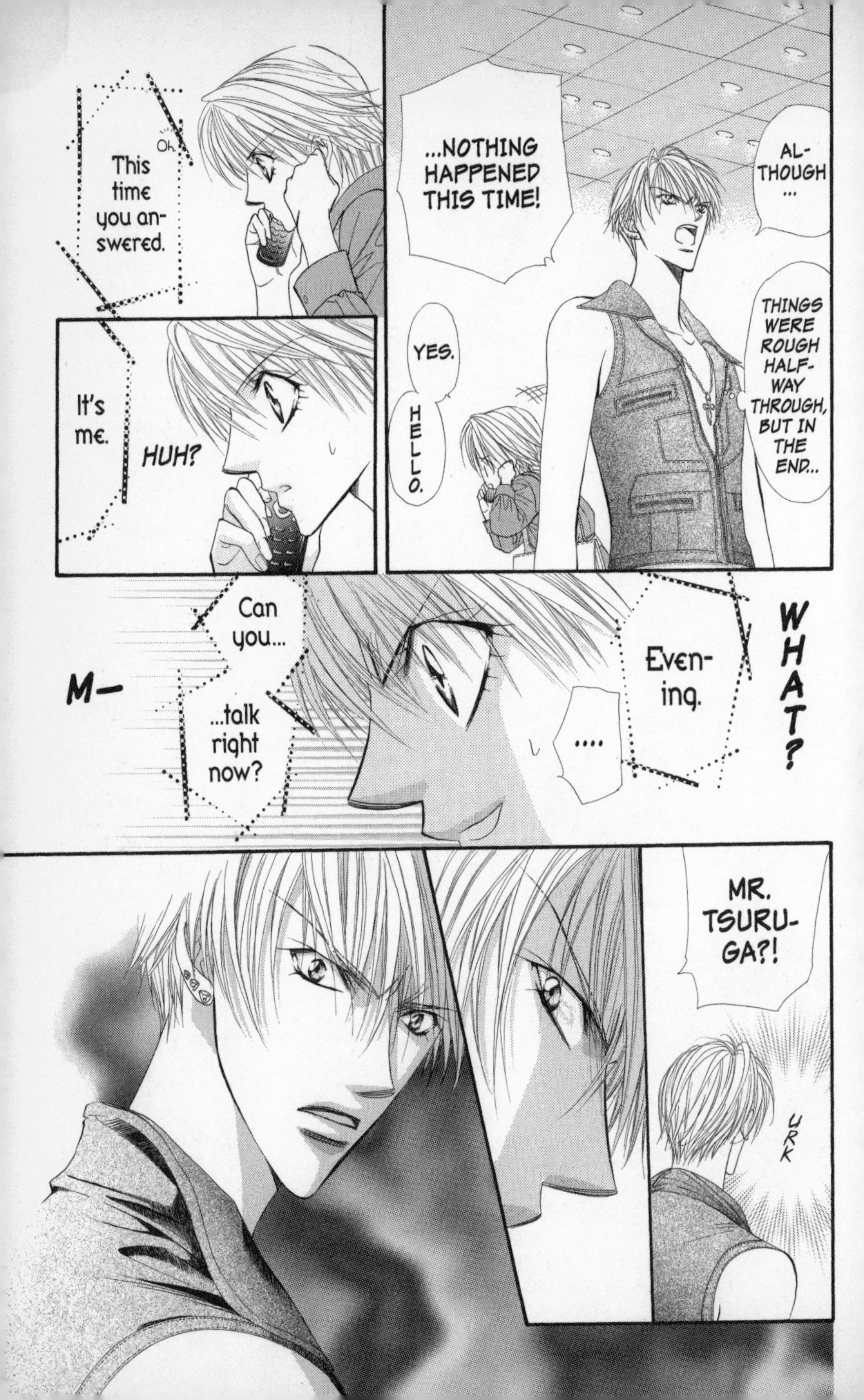
AL-THOUGH...
THINGS WERE ROUGH HALF-WAY THROUGH, BUT IN THE END...
...NOTHING HAPPENED THIS TIME!
YES.
HELLO.
Oh.
This time you an-swered.
It's me.
HUH?
WHAT?
Even-ing.
....
Can you...
...talk right now?
M—
MR. TSURU-GA?!
URK

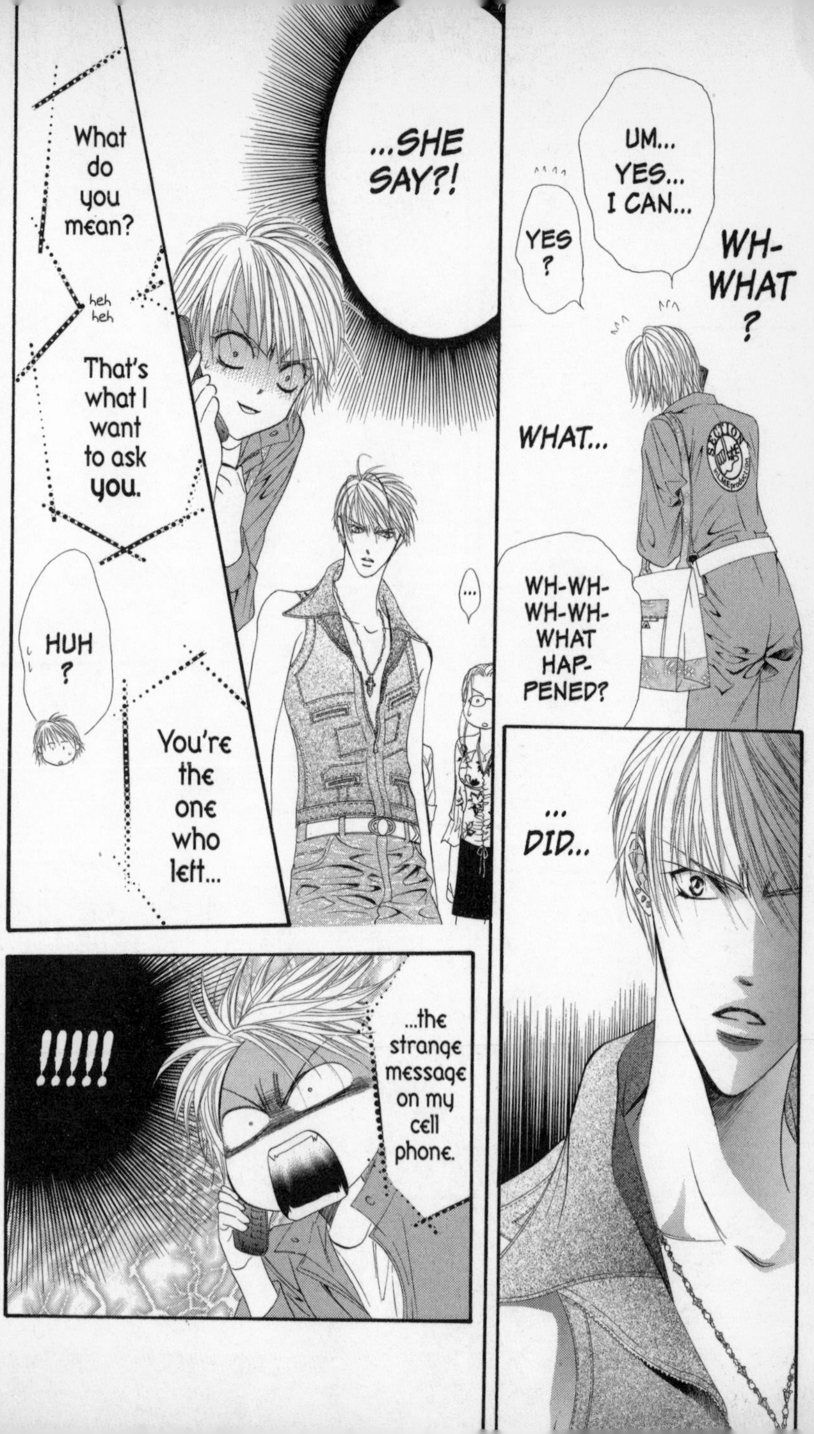
UM... YES... I CAN...
YES?
WH-WHAT?
WHAT...
WH-WH-WH-WH-WHAT HAP-PENED?
...DID...
...SHE SAY?!
What do you mean?
heh heh
That's what I want to ask you.
HUH?
...
You're the one who left...
...the strange message on my cell phone.
!!!!!

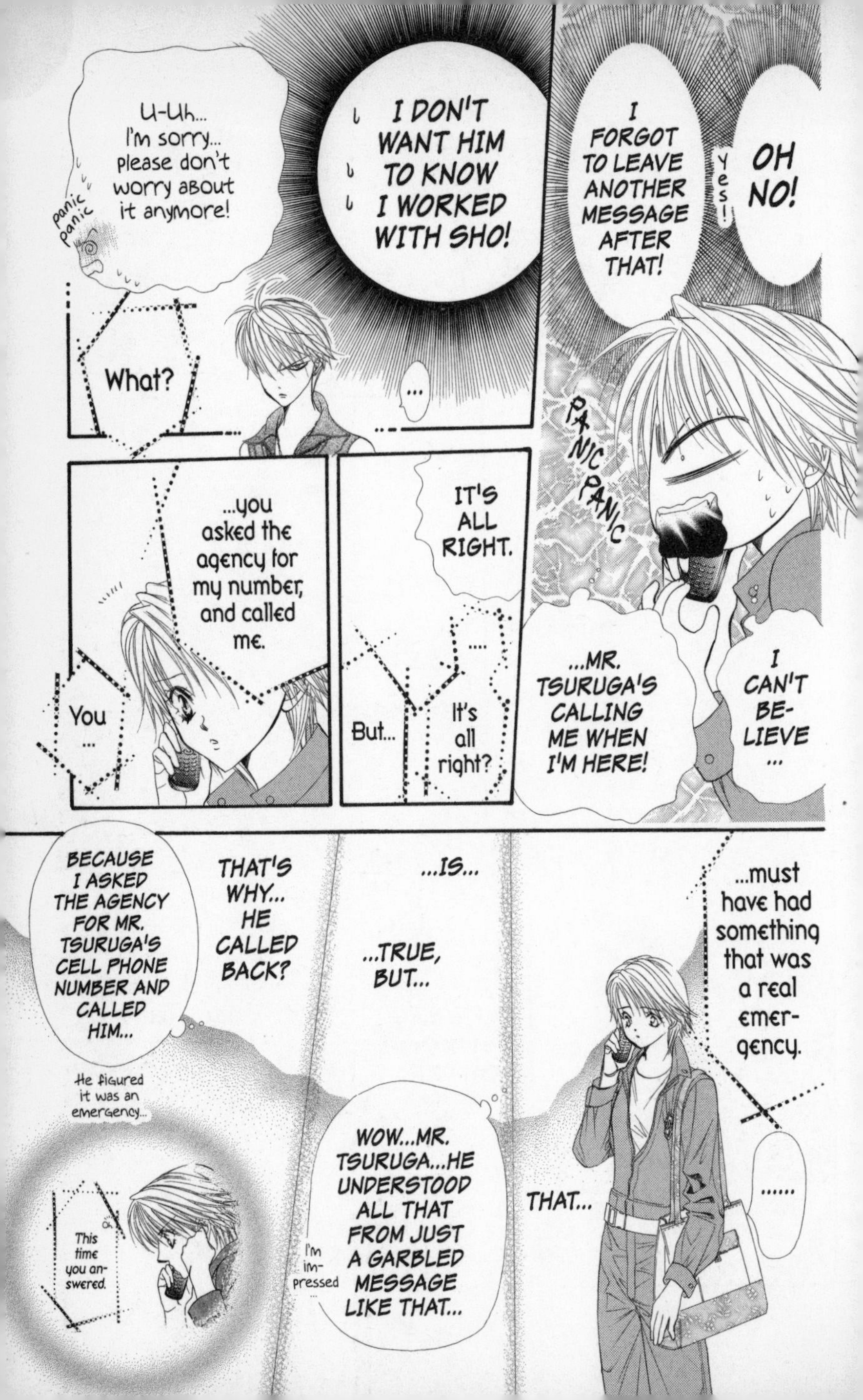
OH NO!
Yes!
I FORGOT TO LEAVE ANOTHER MESSAGE AFTER THAT!
PANIC PANIC
I CAN'T BE-LIEVE...
...MR. TSURUGA'S CALLING ME WHEN I'M HERE!
I DON'T WANT HIM TO KNOW I WORKED WITH SHO!
U-Uh... I'm sorry... please don't worry about it anymore!
panic panic
...
What?
IT'S ALL RIGHT.
...
It's all right?
But...
...you asked the agency for my number, and called me.
You...
...must have had something that was a real emer-gency.
......
THAT...
...IS...
...TRUE, BUT...
WOW...MR. TSURUGA...HE UNDERSTOOD ALL THAT FROM JUST A GARBLED MESSAGE LIKE THAT...
I'm im-pressed...
THAT'S WHY... HE CALLED BACK?
BECAUSE I ASKED THE AGENCY FOR MR. TSURUGA'S CELL PHONE NUMBER AND CALLED HIM...
He figured it was an emergency...
OK
This time you an-swered.

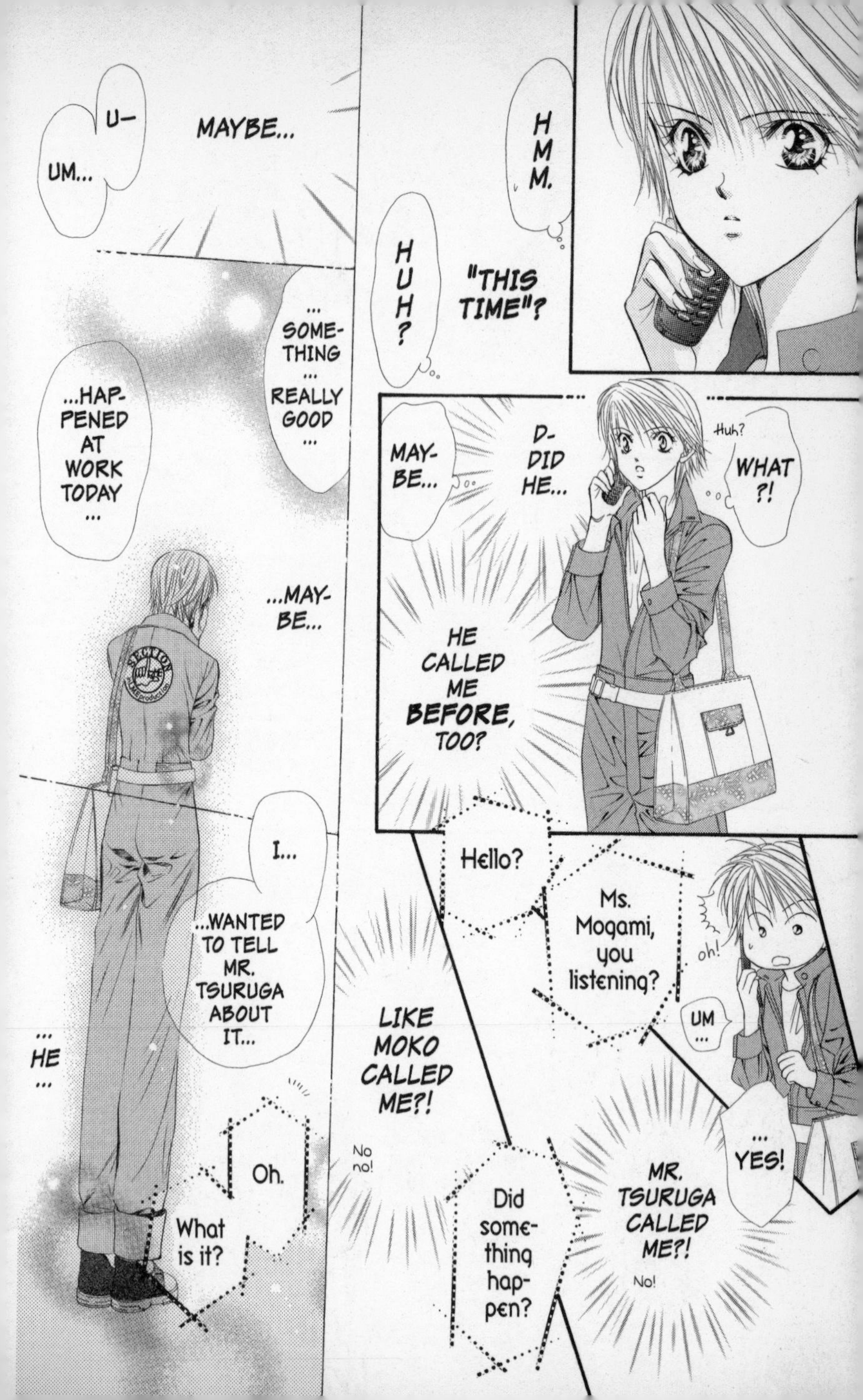
HMM.
"THIS TIME"?
HUH?
Huh?
WHAT?!
D-DID HE...
MAYBE...
HE CALLED ME BEFORE, TOO?
Hello?
Ms. Mogami, you listening?
oh!
UM...
...YES!
MR. TSURUGA CALLED ME?!
No!
Did something happen?
LIKE MOKO CALLED ME?!
No no!
U-
UM...
MAYBE...
...SOMETHING...REALLY GOOD...
...HAPPENED AT WORK TODAY...
...MAYBE...
I...
...WANTED TO TELL MR. TSURUGA ABOUT IT...
Oh.
What is it?
...HE...

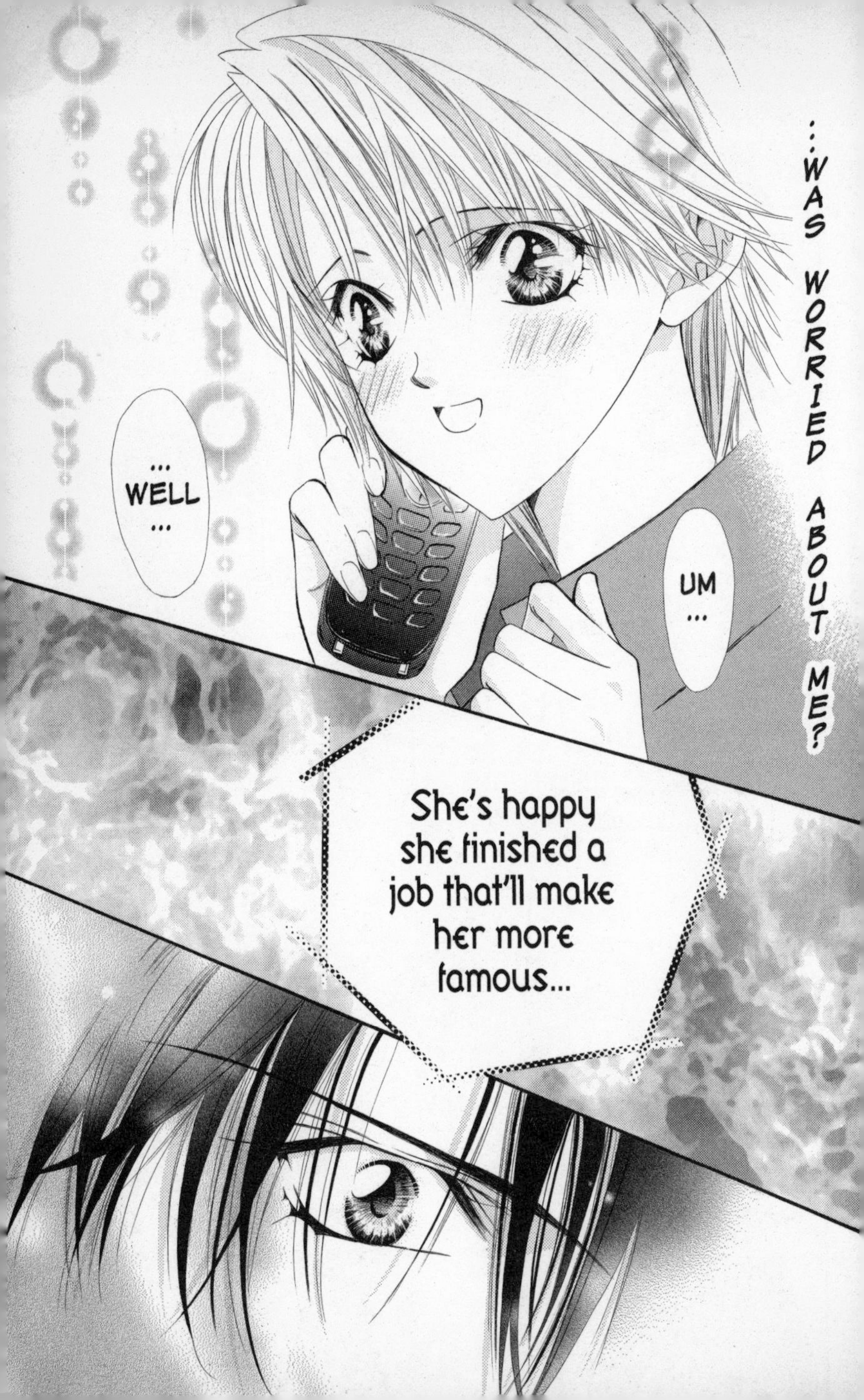
...WAS WORRIED ABOUT ME?
UM ...
... WELL ...
She's happy she finished a job that'll make her more famous...

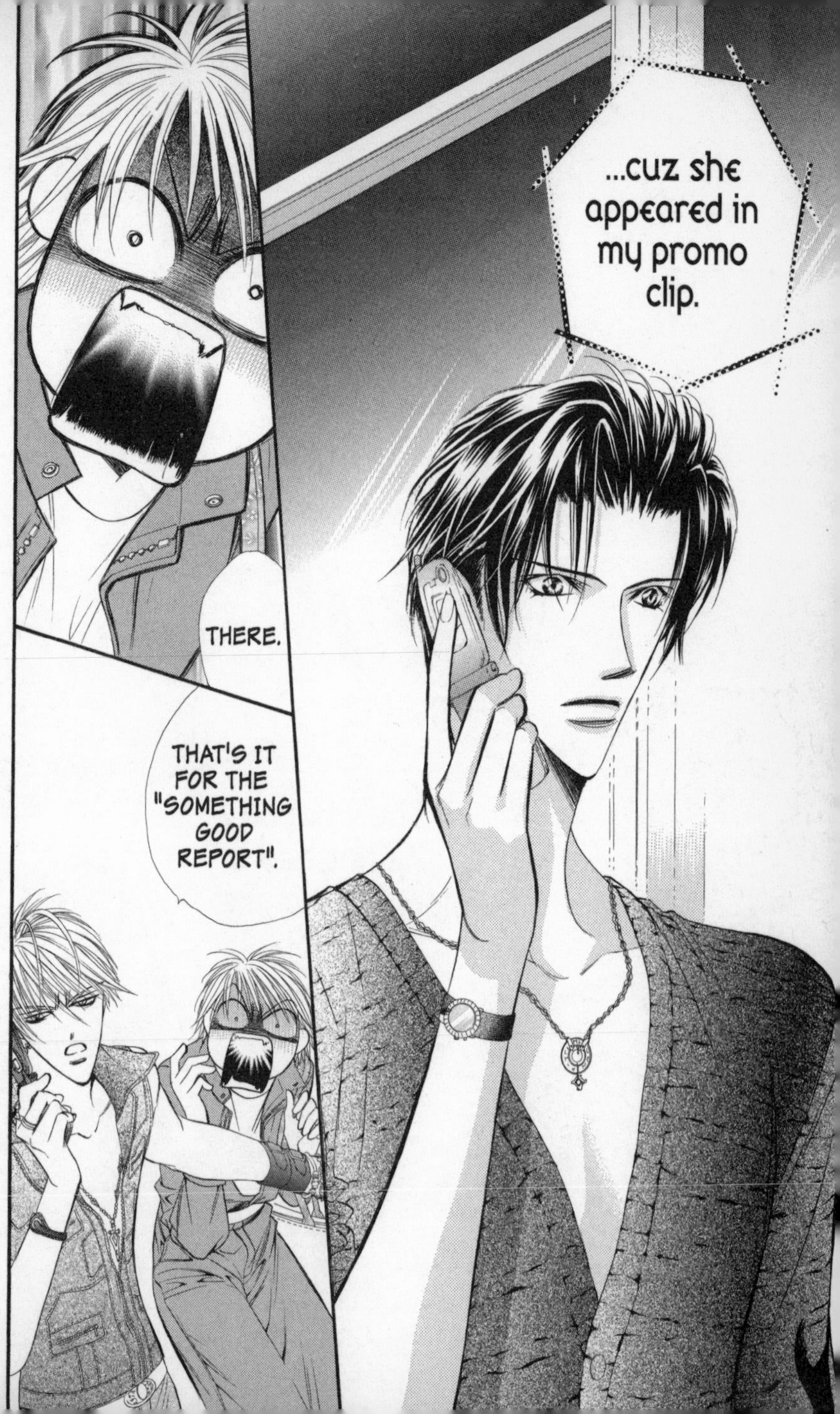
...cuz she appeared in my promo clip.
THERE.
THAT'S IT FOR THE "SOMETHING GOOD REPORT".

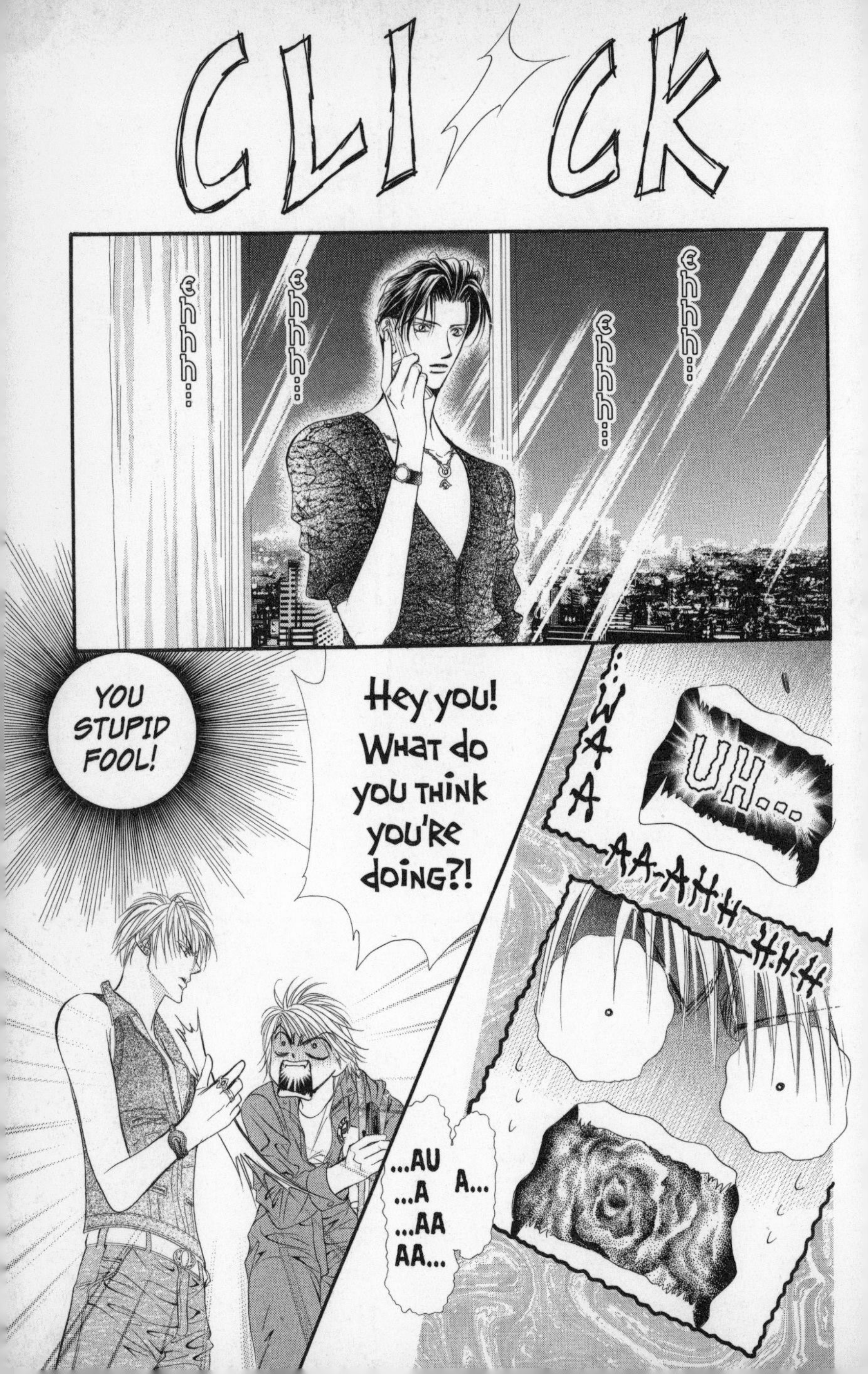
CLICK
Mhhhh...
Mhhhh...
Mhhhh...
Mhhhh...
...WAAA
AA-AHHHHHH
UH...
...AU A...
...A
...AA
AA...
Hey you! What do you think you're doing?!
YOU STUPID FOOL!

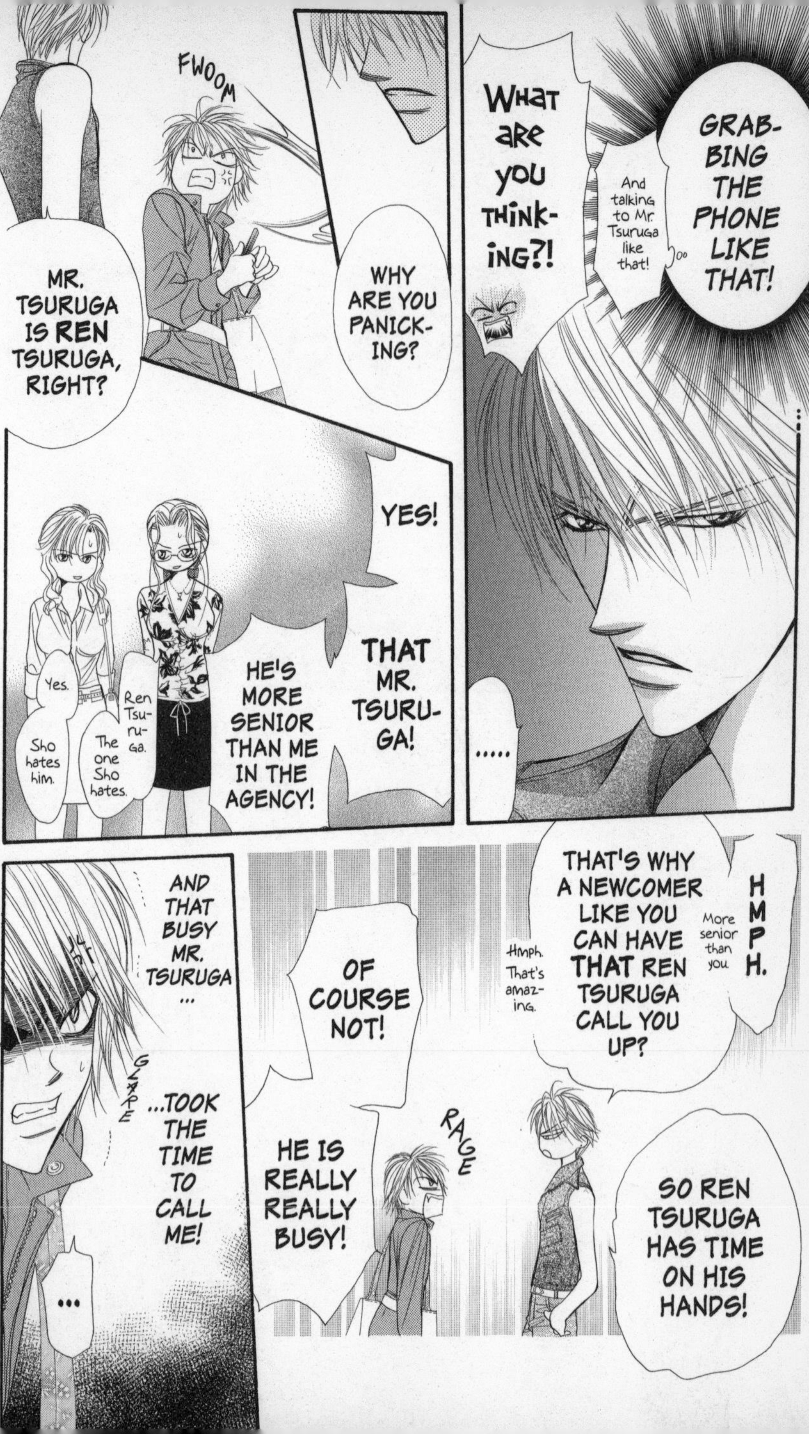
GRAB-BING THE PHONE LIKE THAT!
And talking to Mr. Tsuruga like that!
What are you think-ing?!
.....
FWOOM
WHY ARE YOU PANICK-ING?
MR. TSURUGA IS REN TSURUGA, RIGHT?
YES!
THAT MR. TSURU-GA!
HE'S MORE SENIOR THAN ME IN THE AGENCY!
Ren Tsu-ru-ga.
Yes.
The one Sho hates.
Sho hates him.
HMPH.
More senior than you
THAT'S WHY A NEWCOMER LIKE YOU CAN HAVE THAT REN TSURUGA CALL YOU UP?
Hmph. That's amaz-ing.
SO REN TSURUGA HAS TIME ON HIS HANDS!
RAGE
OF COURSE NOT!
HE IS REALLY REALLY BUSY!
AND THAT BUSY MR. TSURUGA ...
GLARE
...TOOK THE TIME TO CALL ME!
...

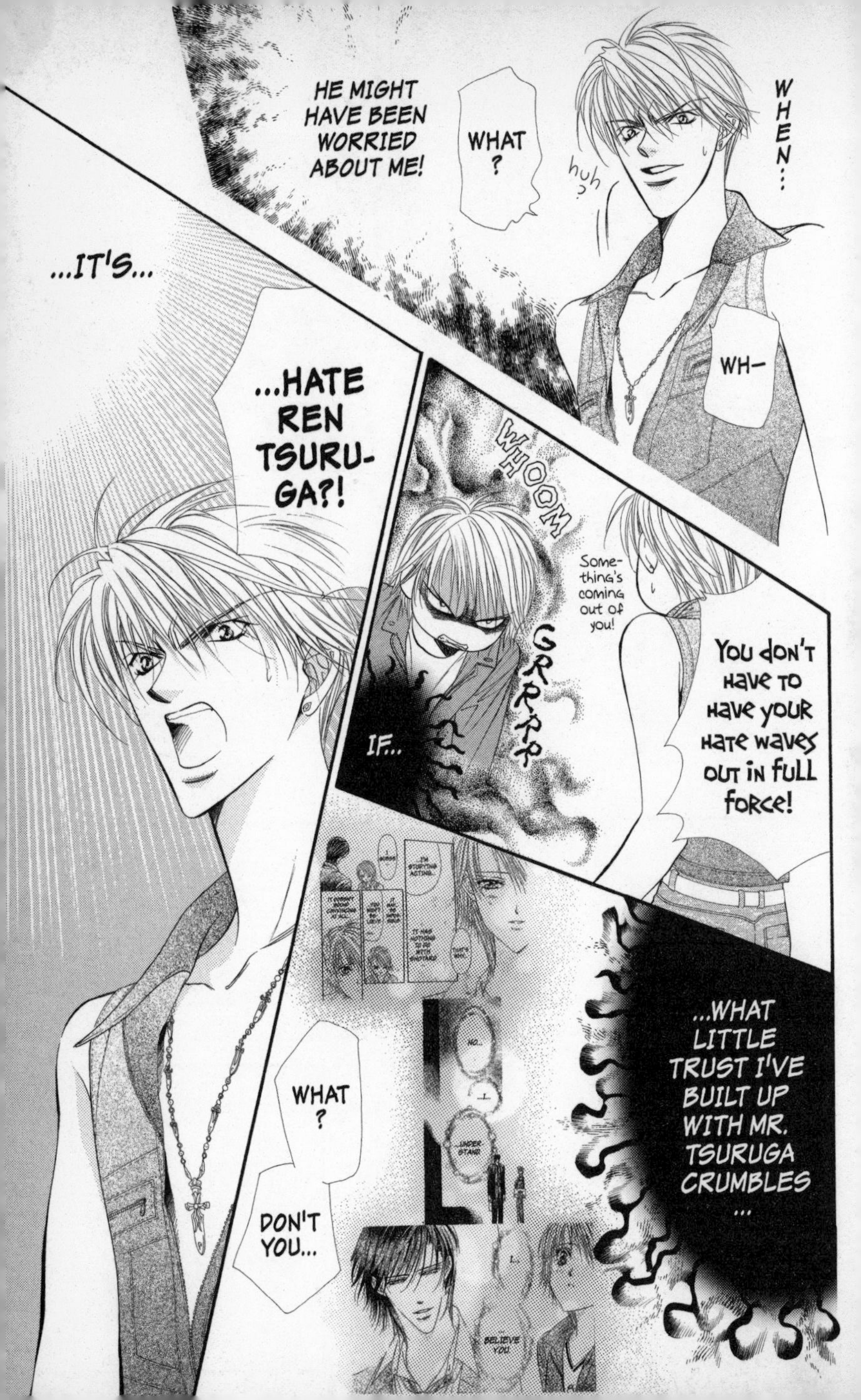
WHEN...
huh?
WHAT?
HE MIGHT HAVE BEEN WORRIED ABOUT ME!
...IT'S...
WH–
You don't have to have your hate waves out in full force!
Something's coming out of you!
WHOOM
GRRRR
IF...
...HATE REN TSURUGA?!
...WHAT LITTLE TRUST I'VE BUILT UP WITH MR. TSURUGA CRUMBLES ...
WHAT?
DON'T YOU...

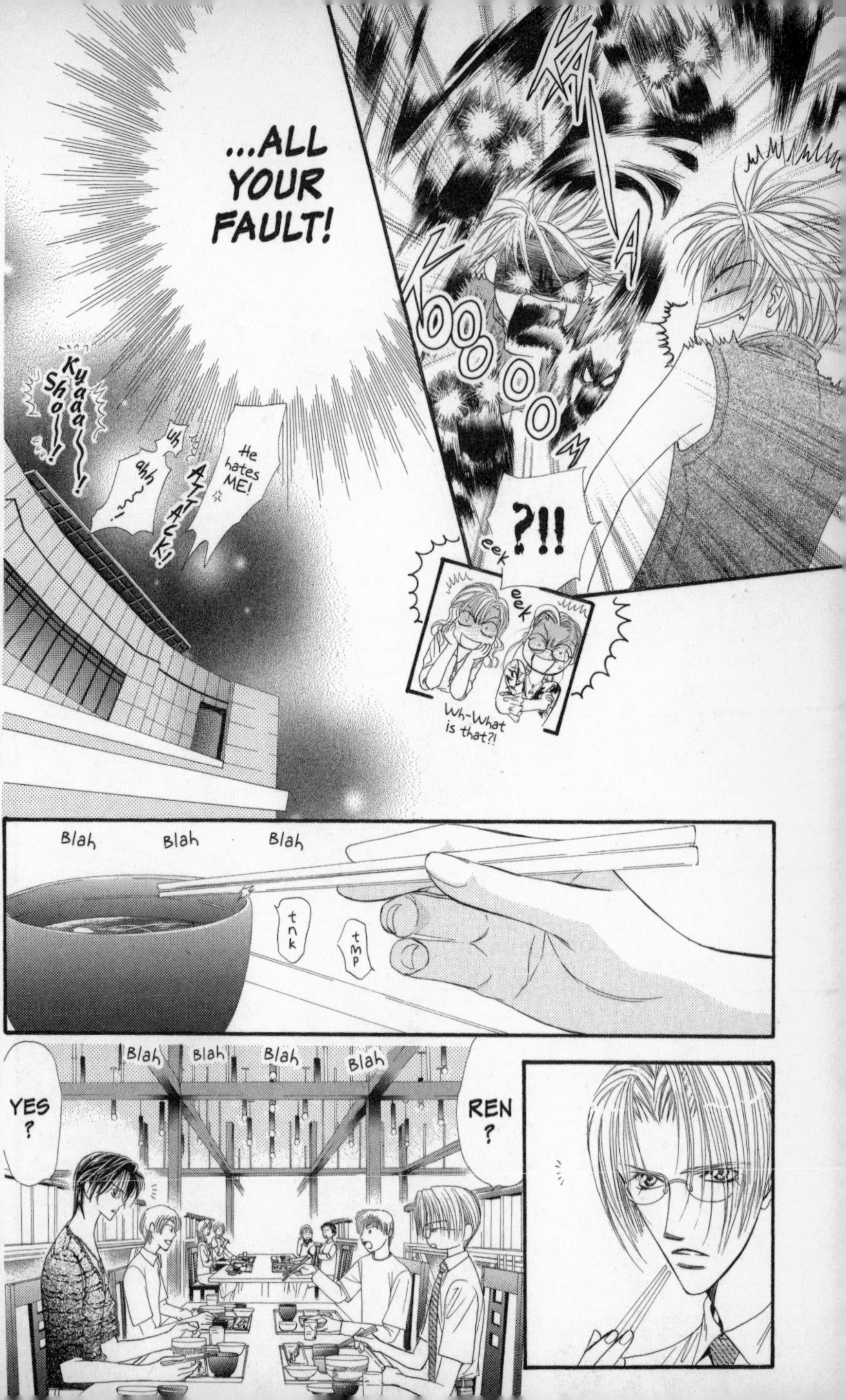
KAAA
KOOOOOOM
?!!
eek
eek
Wh-What is that?!
...ALL YOUR FAULT!
He hates ME!
ATTACK!
uh ahh~!
Kyaaa~! Sho~!
Blah
Blah
Blah
tnk
tmp
Blah
Blah
Blah
Blah
REN?
YES?

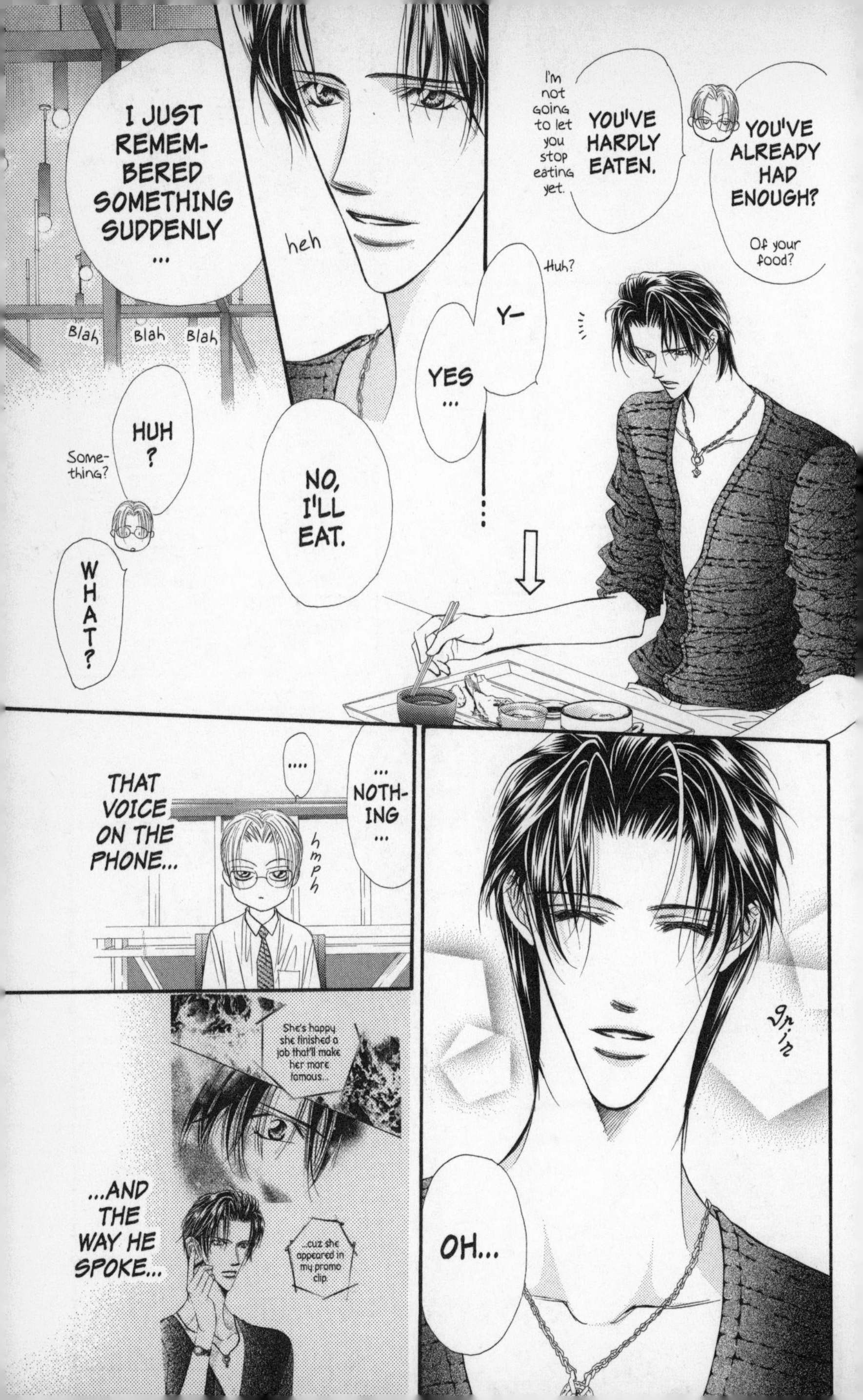
YOU'VE ALREADY HAD ENOUGH?
Of your food?
YOU'VE HARDLY EATEN.
I'm not going to let you stop eating yet.
Huh?
Y-
YES...
...
heh
I JUST REMEMBERED SOMETHING SUDDENLY...
Blah Blah Blah
WHAT?
HUH?
Something?
NO, I'LL EAT.
OH...
grin
....
...NOTHING...
hmph
THAT VOICE ON THE PHONE...
She's happy she finished a job that'll make her more famous...
...cuz she appeared in my promo clip.
...AND THE WAY HE SPOKE...

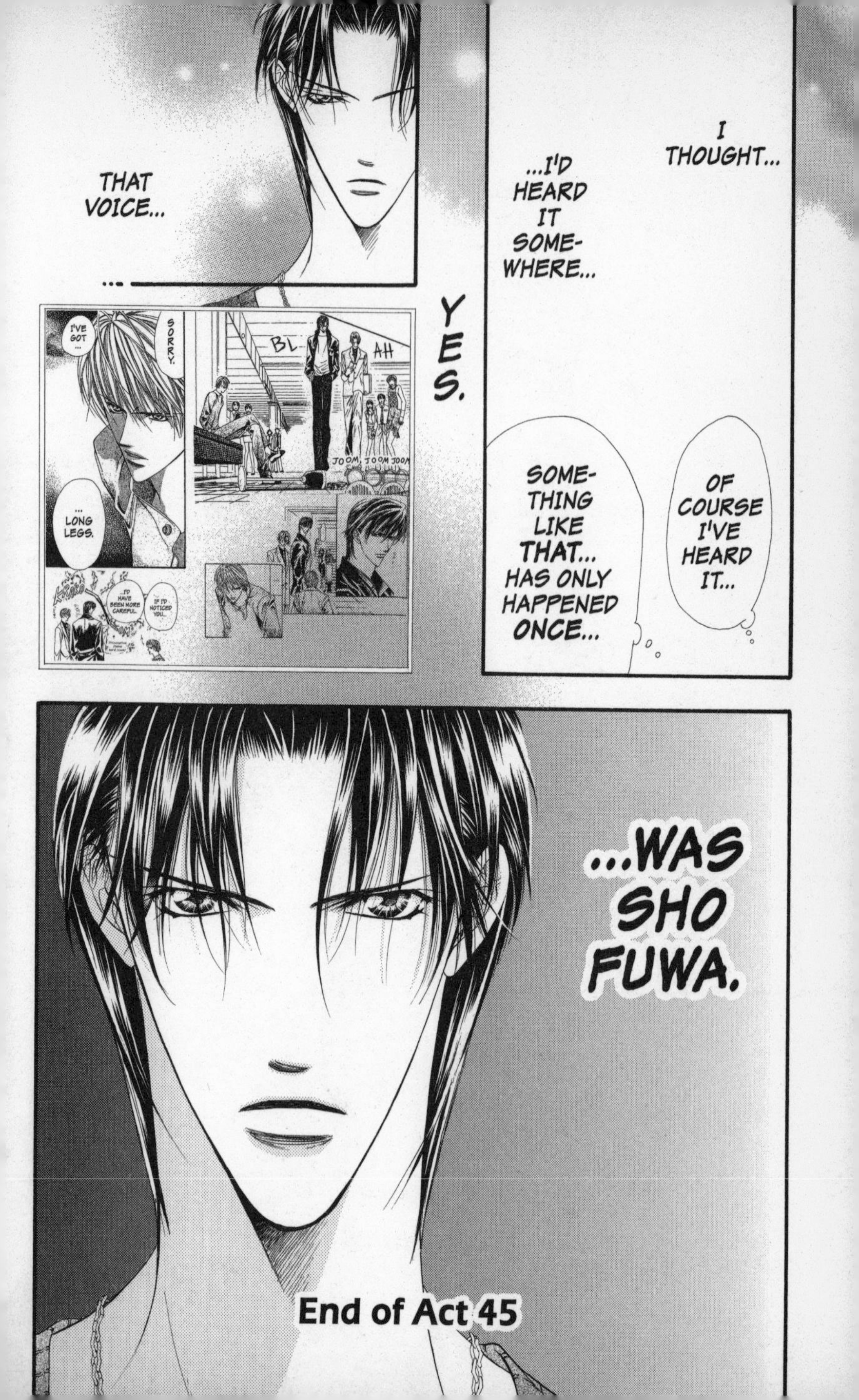
I THOUGHT...
...I'D HEARD IT SOME-WHERE...
THAT VOICE...
...
OF COURSE I'VE HEARD IT...
SOMETHING LIKE THAT... HAS ONLY HAPPENED ONCE...
YES.
AH
BL
JOOM JOOM JOOM
SORRY.
I'VE GOT ...
... LONG LEGS.
IF I'D NOTICED YOU...
...I'D HAVE BEEN MORE CAREFUL.
...WAS SHO FUWA.
End of Act 45

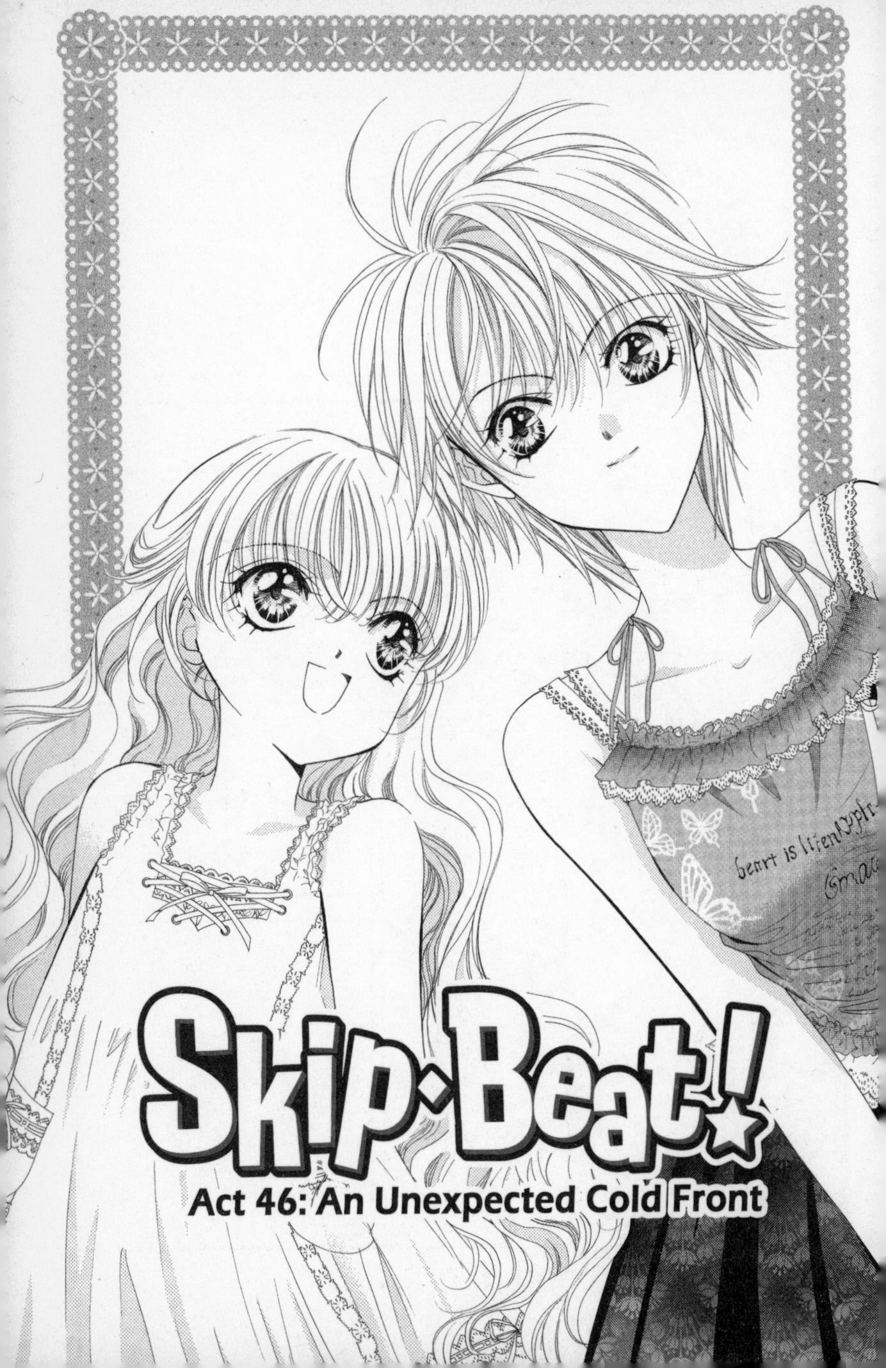
Skip·Beat!
Act 46: An Unexpected Cold Front

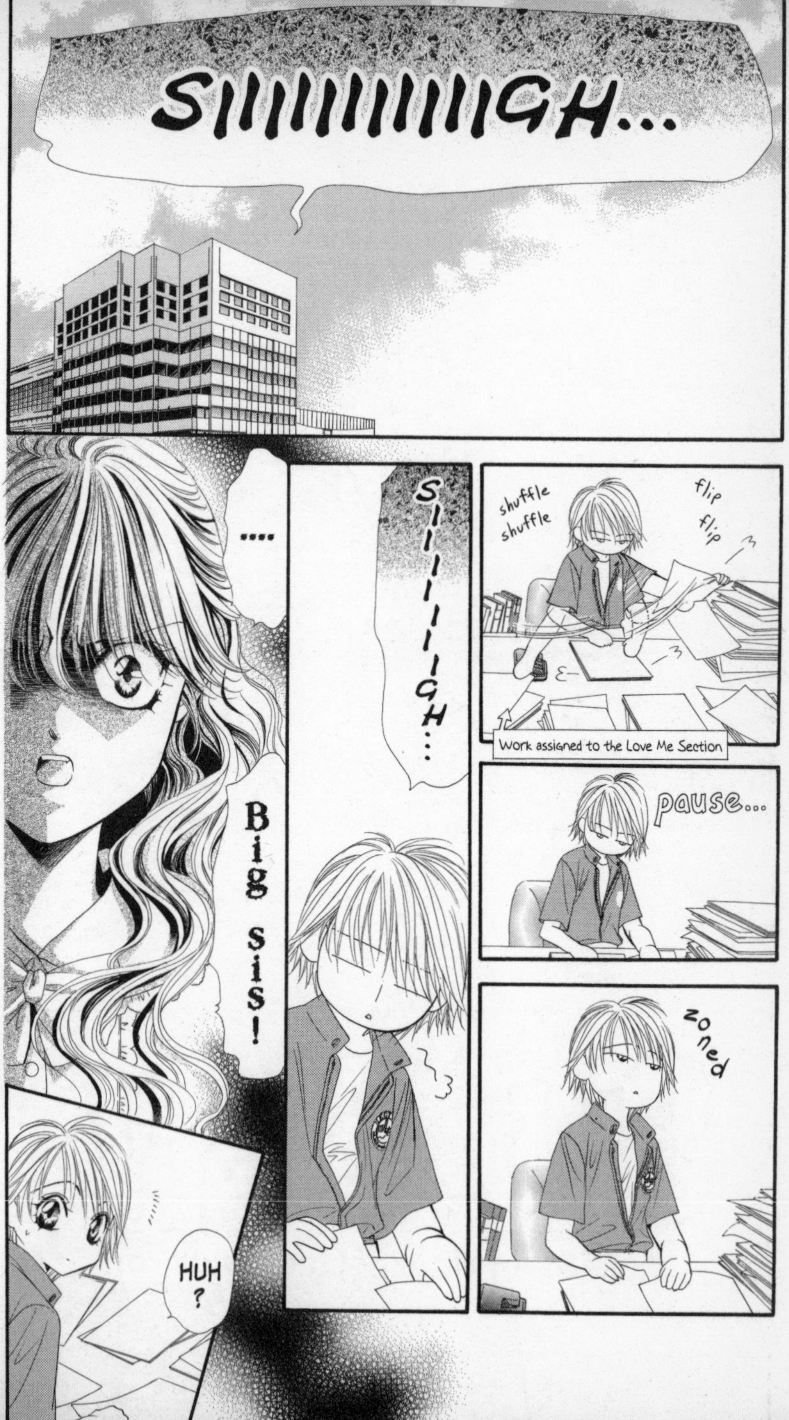
SIIIIIIIIIGH...
flip flip
shuffle shuffle
Work assigned to the Love Me Section
pause...
zoned
SIIIIIIIGH...
....
Big sis!
HUH?

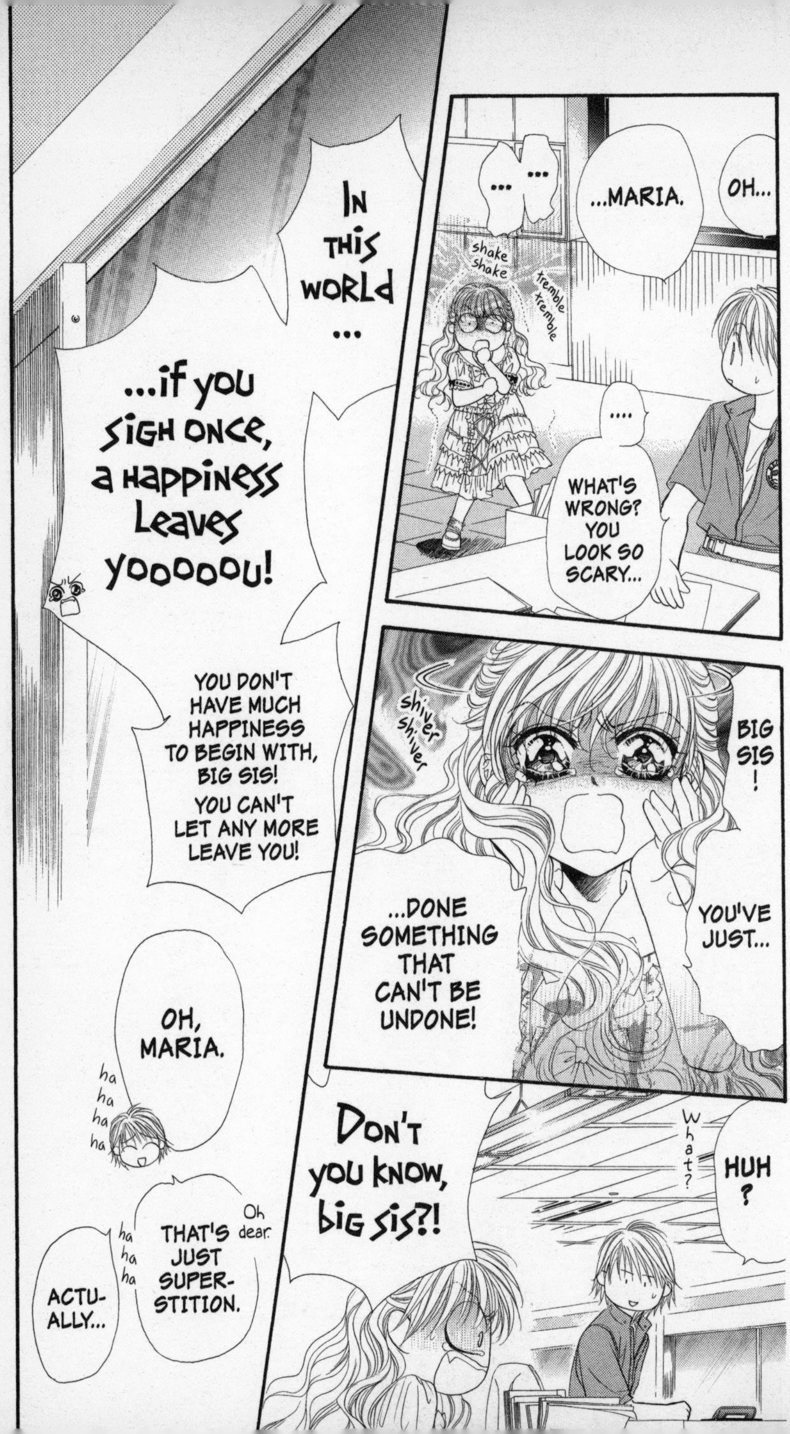

OH...
...MARIA.
... ...
shake shake
tremble tremble
....
WHAT'S WRONG? YOU LOOK SO SCARY...
BIG SIS!
shiver shiver
YOU'VE JUST...
...DONE SOMETHING THAT CAN'T BE UNDONE!
HUH?
What?
Don't you know, big sis?!
In this world...
...if you sigh once, a happiness leaves yoooooou!
YOU DON'T HAVE MUCH HAPPINESS TO BEGIN WITH, BIG SIS! YOU CAN'T LET ANY MORE LEAVE YOU!
OH, MARIA.
ha ha ha ha
Oh dear.
THAT'S JUST SUPER-STITION.
ha ha ha
ACTU-ALLY...

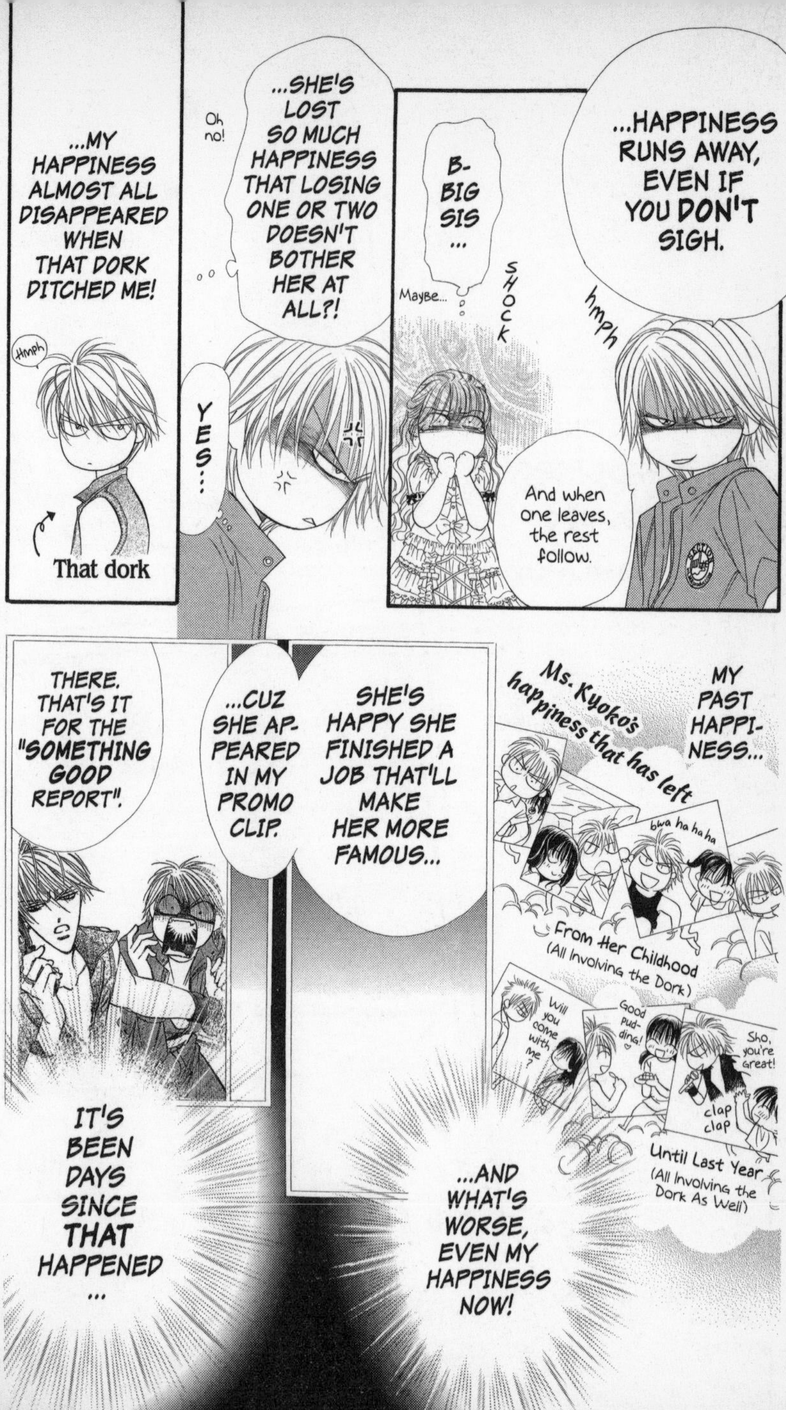
...HAPPINESS RUNS AWAY, EVEN IF YOU DON'T SIGH.
hmph
And when one leaves, the rest follow.
B-BIG SIS...
SHOCK
Maybe...
...SHE'S LOST SO MUCH HAPPINESS THAT LOSING ONE OR TWO DOESN'T BOTHER HER AT ALL?!
Oh no!
YES...
...MY HAPPINESS ALMOST ALL DISAPPEARED WHEN THAT DORK DITCHED ME!
Hmph
That dork
MY PAST HAPPINESS...
Ms. Kyoko's happiness that has left
bwa ha ha ha
From Her Childhood (All Involving the Dork)
Sho, you're great!
clap clap
Good pudding!
Will you come with me?
Until Last Year (All Involving the Dork As Well)
SHE'S HAPPY SHE FINISHED A JOB THAT'LL MAKE HER MORE FAMOUS...
...CUZ SHE APPEARED IN MY PROMO CLIP.
THERE. THAT'S IT FOR THE "SOMETHING GOOD REPORT".
...AND WHAT'S WORSE, EVEN MY HAPPINESS NOW!
IT'S BEEN DAYS SINCE THAT HAPPENED...

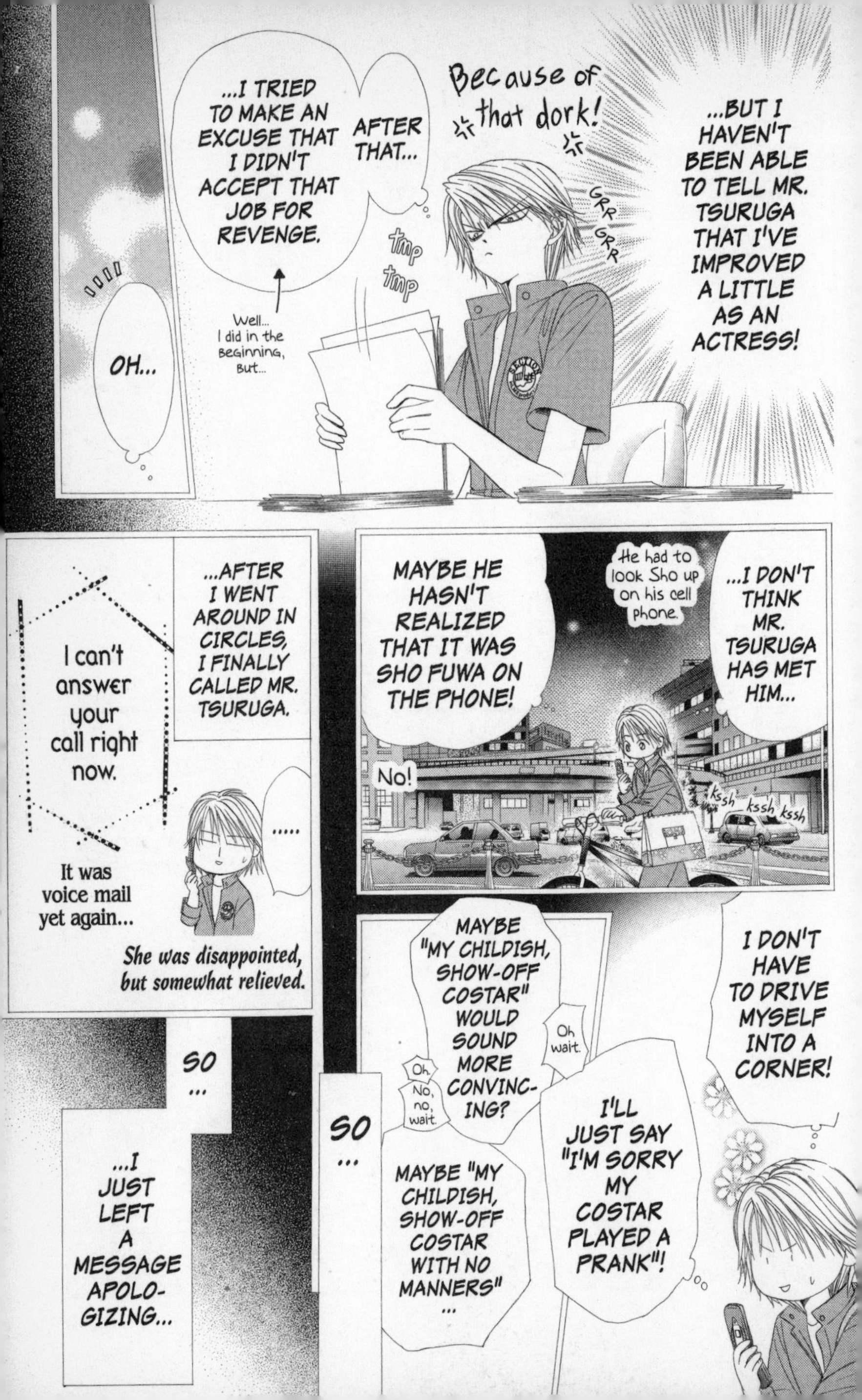

...BUT I HAVEN'T BEEN ABLE TO TELL MR. TSURUGA THAT I'VE IMPROVED A LITTLE AS AN ACTRESS!
Because of that dork!
GRR GRR
AFTER THAT...
...I TRIED TO MAKE AN EXCUSE THAT I DIDN'T ACCEPT THAT JOB FOR REVENGE.
tmp tmp
Well... I did in the beginning, but...
OH...
...I DON'T THINK MR. TSURUGA HAS MET HIM...
He had to look Sho up on his cell phone.
MAYBE HE HASN'T REALIZED THAT IT WAS SHO FUWA ON THE PHONE!
No!
kssh kssh kssh
...AFTER I WENT AROUND IN CIRCLES, I FINALLY CALLED MR. TSURUGA.
I can't answer your call right now.
.....
It was voice mail yet again...
She was disappointed, but somewhat relieved.
I DON'T HAVE TO DRIVE MYSELF INTO A CORNER!
MAYBE "MY CHILDISH, SHOW-OFF COSTAR" WOULD SOUND MORE CONVINCING?
Oh wait.
I'LL JUST SAY "I'M SORRY MY COSTAR PLAYED A PRANK"!
Oh. No, no, wait.
SO...
MAYBE "MY CHILDISH, SHOW-OFF COSTAR WITH NO MANNERS"...
SO...
...I JUST LEFT A MESSAGE APOLOGIZING...

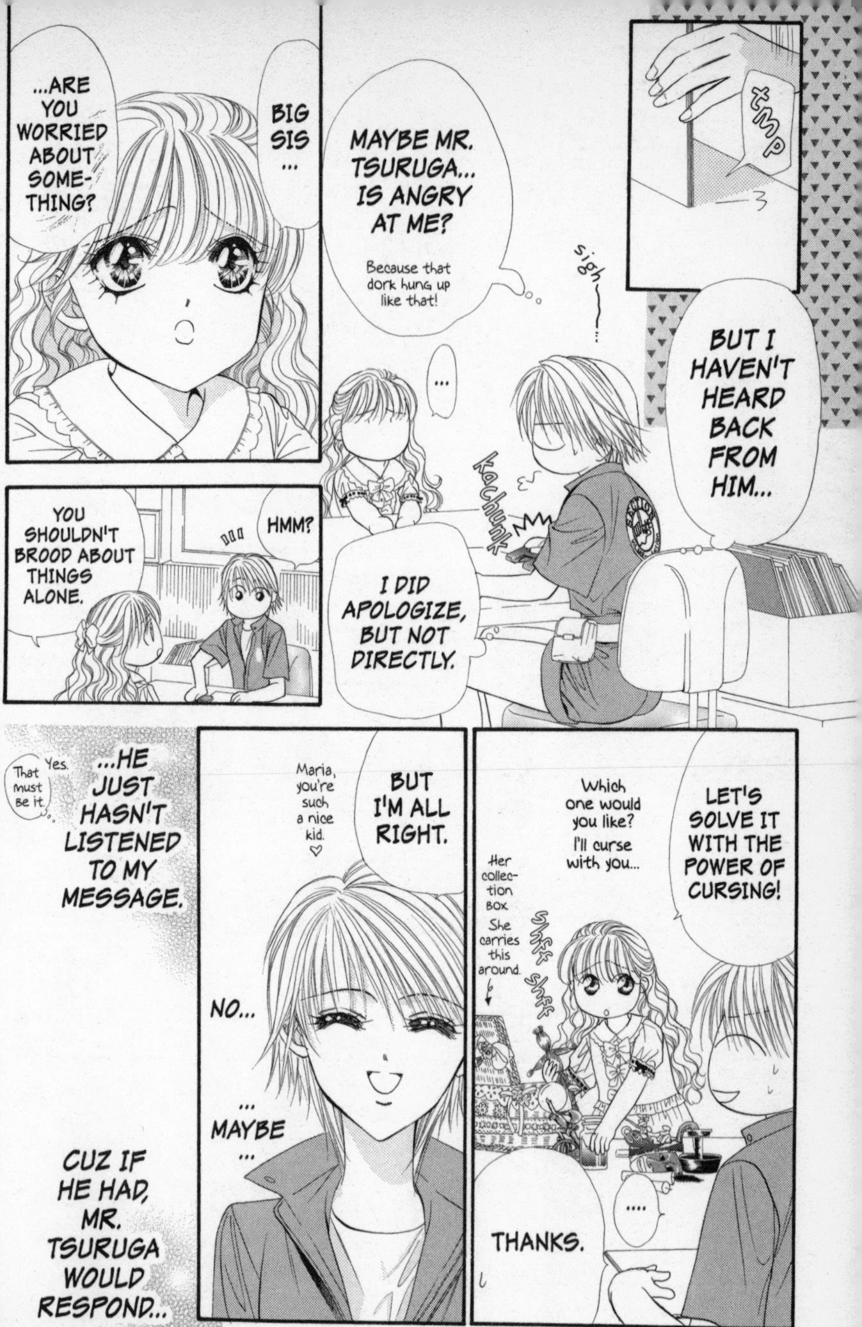
tmp
BUT I HAVEN'T HEARD BACK FROM HIM...
sigh—...
MAYBE MR. TSURUGA... IS ANGRY AT ME?
Because that dork hung up like that!
...
kachunk
I DID APOLOGIZE, BUT NOT DIRECTLY.
BIG SIS...
...ARE YOU WORRIED ABOUT SOMETHING?
HMM?
YOU SHOULDN'T BROOD ABOUT THINGS ALONE.
LET'S SOLVE IT WITH THE POWER OF CURSING!
Which one would you like? I'll curse with you...
Her collection box
She carries this around.
shff shff
....
THANKS.
BUT I'M ALL RIGHT.
Maria, you're such a nice kid ♡
NO...
...MAYBE...
...HE JUST HASN'T LISTENED TO MY MESSAGE.
Yes.
That must be it.
CUZ IF HE HAD, MR. TSURUGA WOULD RESPOND...

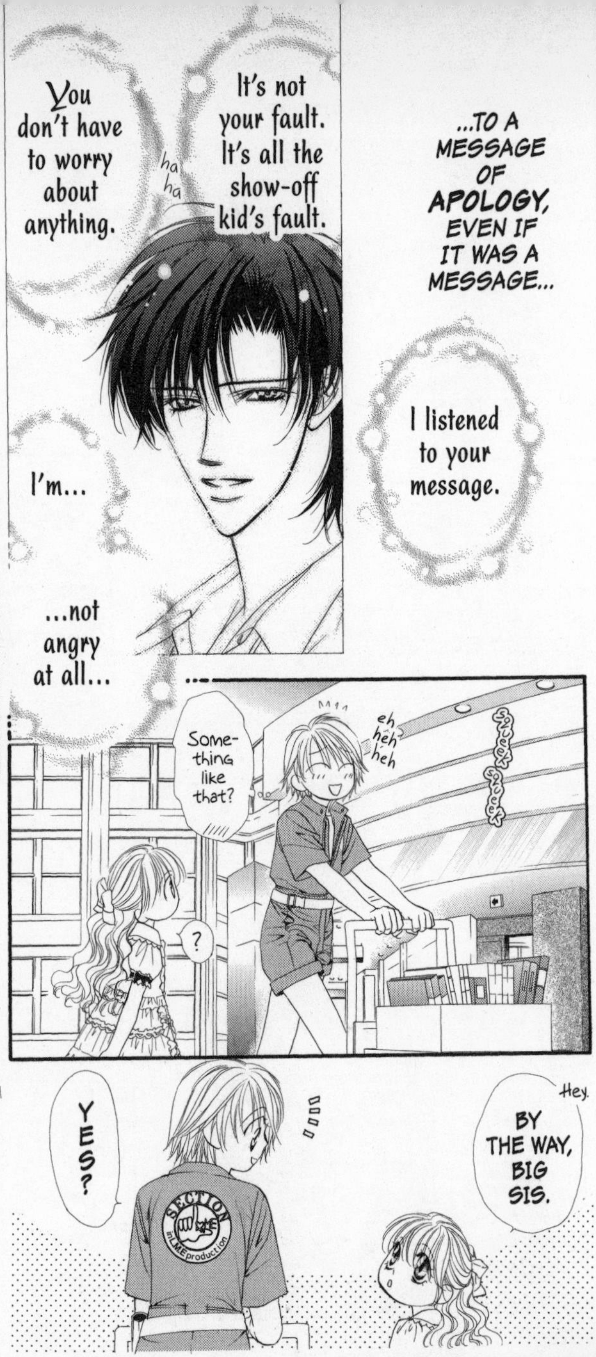
...TO A MESSAGE OF APOLOGY, EVEN IF IT WAS A MESSAGE...
I listened to your message.
It's not your fault. It's all the show-off kid's fault.
ha ha
You don't have to worry about anything.
I'm...
...not angry at all...
eh heh heh
squeek squeek
Something like that?
?
Hey.
BY THE WAY, BIG SIS.
YES?

Haruki Asami

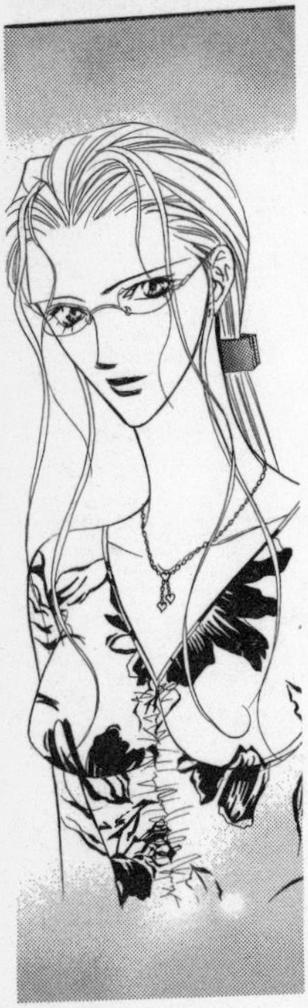

This woman... ♪ I basically prefer women to have breasts than have none at all...but if they're this big... her shoulders become wide, and I'm scared she looks like a sumo wrestler...and...as I continue drawing her, I feel that her breasts are getting even bigger, so I'm even more scared... anyway, like Ren, this woman is a bother, because I have to pay attention to her... ♪

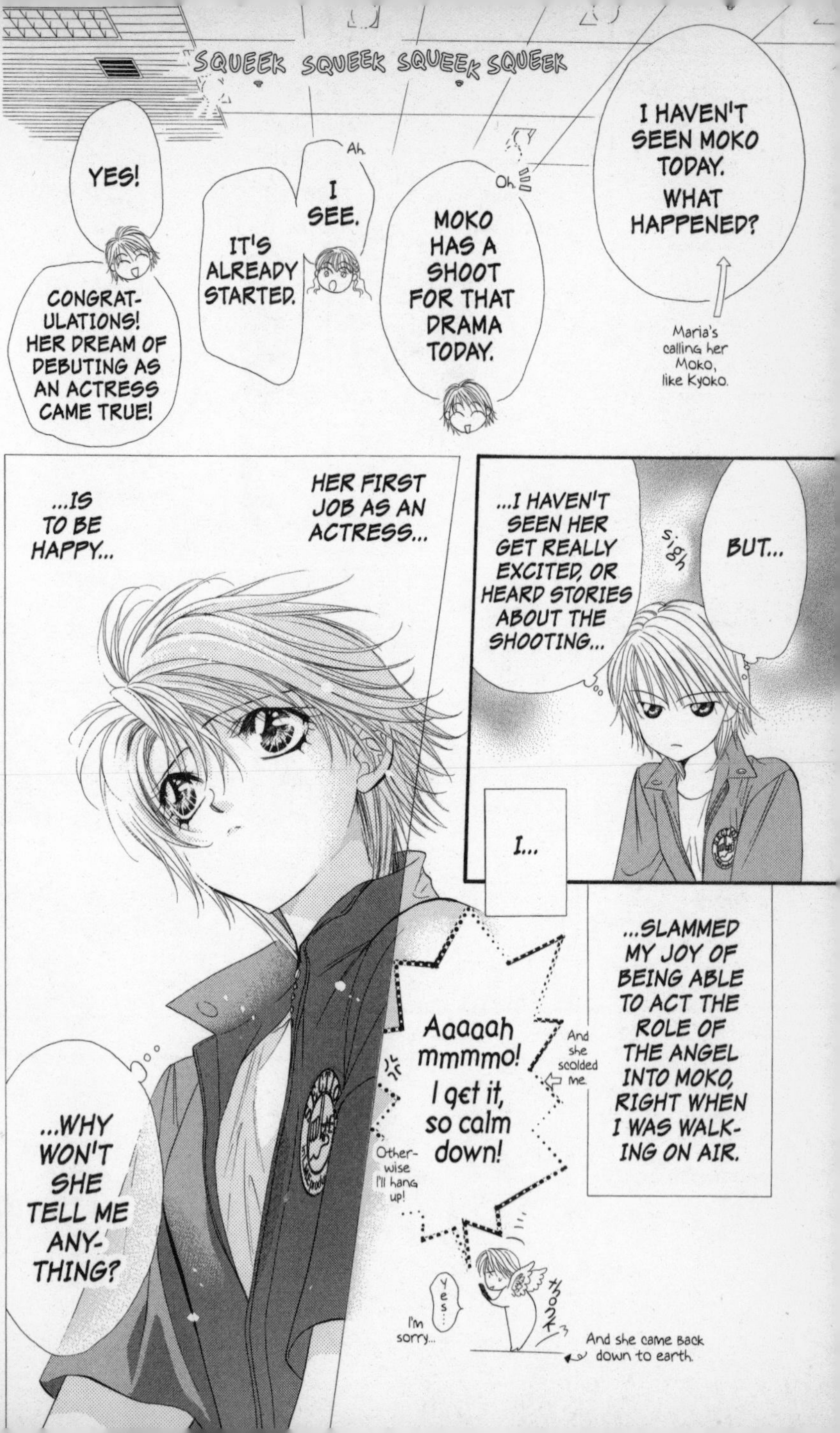
SQUEEK SQUEEK SQUEEK SQUEEK
I HAVEN'T SEEN MOKO TODAY. WHAT HAPPENED?
Maria's calling her Moko, like Kyoko.
Oh.
MOKO HAS A SHOOT FOR THAT DRAMA TODAY.
Ah.
I SEE.
IT'S ALREADY STARTED.
YES!
CONGRATULATIONS! HER DREAM OF DEBUTING AS AN ACTRESS CAME TRUE!
BUT...
sigh
...I HAVEN'T SEEN HER GET REALLY EXCITED, OR HEARD STORIES ABOUT THE SHOOTING...
I...
...SLAMMED MY JOY OF BEING ABLE TO ACT THE ROLE OF THE ANGEL INTO MOKO, RIGHT WHEN I WAS WALKING ON AIR.
And she scolded me.
Aaaaah mmmmo! I get it, so calm down!
Other-wise I'll hang up!
Yes...
I'm sorry...
thonk
And she came back down to earth.
HER FIRST JOB AS AN ACTRESS...
...IS TO BE HAPPY...
...WHY WON'T SHE TELL ME ANYTHING?

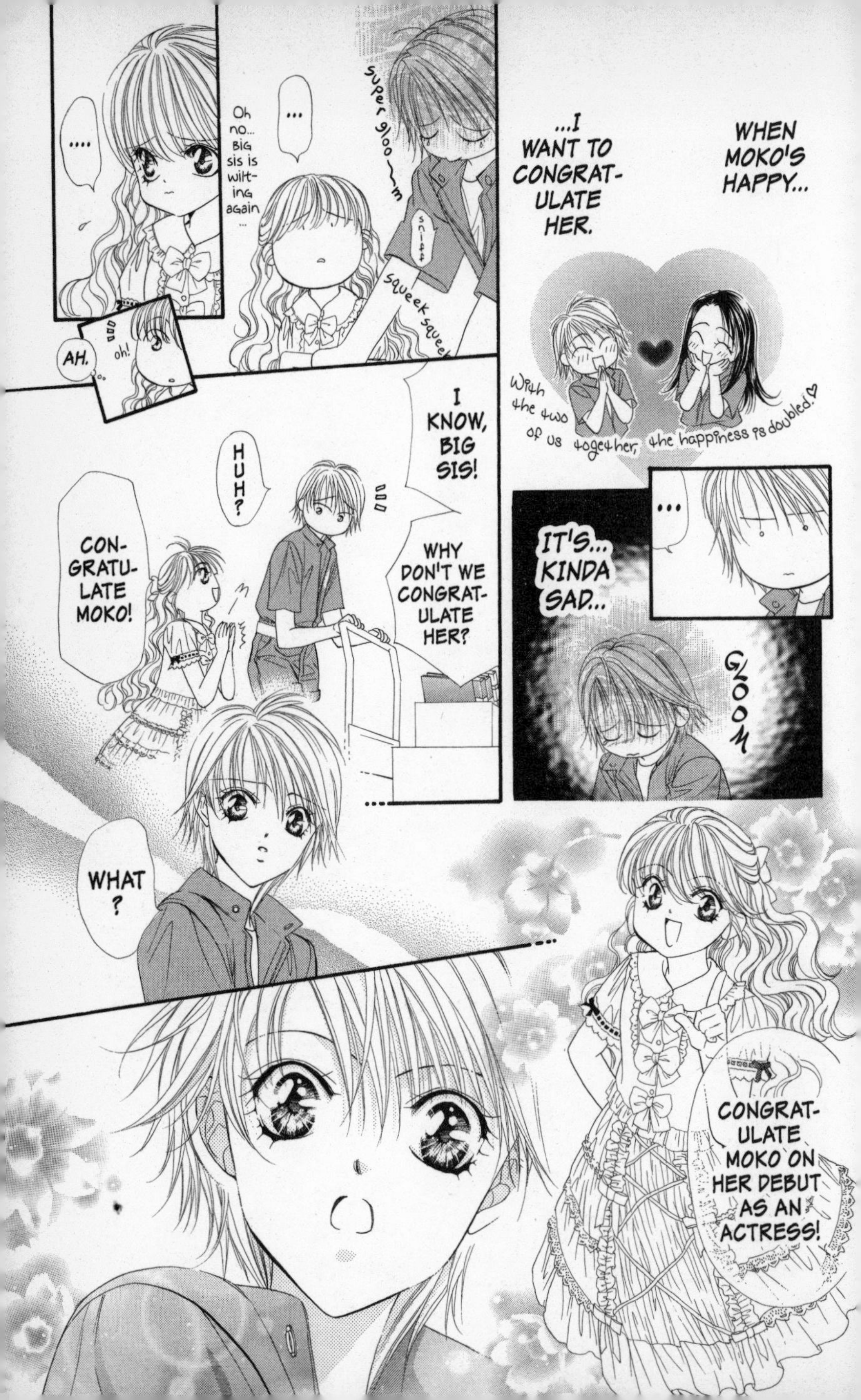
WHEN MOKO'S HAPPY...
...I WANT TO CONGRATULATE HER.
With the two of us together, the happiness is doubled.♡
...
IT'S... KINDA SAD...
GLOOM
super gloo~m
sniff
...
Oh no... big sis is wilting again...
....
squeek squeek
oh!
AH.
I KNOW, BIG SIS!
WHY DON'T WE CONGRATULATE HER?
HUH?
CONGRATULATE MOKO!
...
WHAT?
CONGRATULATE MOKO ON HER DEBUT AS AN ACTRESS!

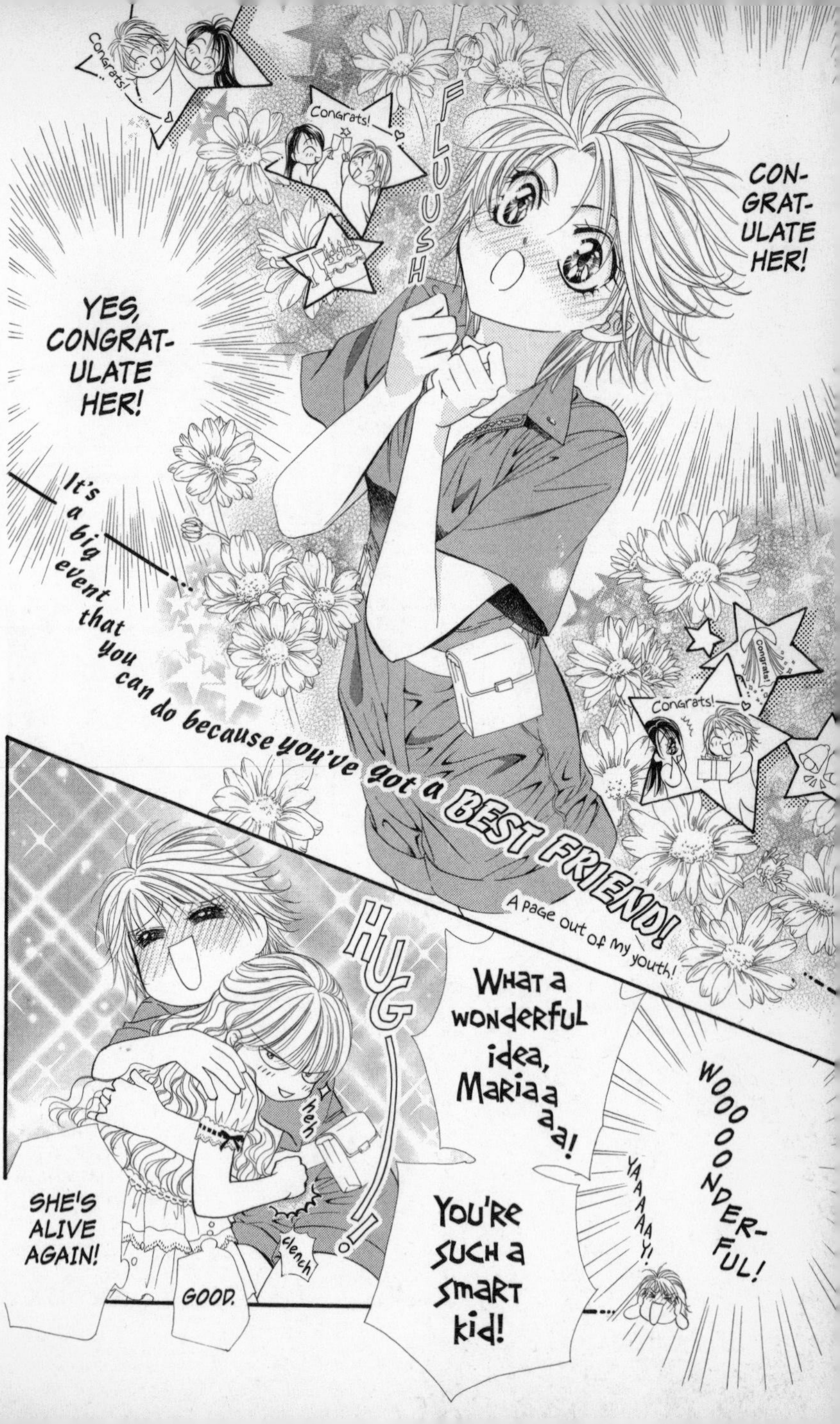
CON-GRAT-ULATE HER!
FLUUSH
Congrats!
Congrats!
Congrats!
YES, CONGRAT-ULATE HER!
It's a big event that you can do because you've got a BEST FRIEND!
A page out of my youth!
Congrats!
Congrats!
WOOOOONDER-FUL!
YAAAAAY!
What a wonderful idea, Mariaaaa!
You're such a smart kid!
HUG!
heh
clench
GOOD.
SHE'S ALIVE AGAIN!

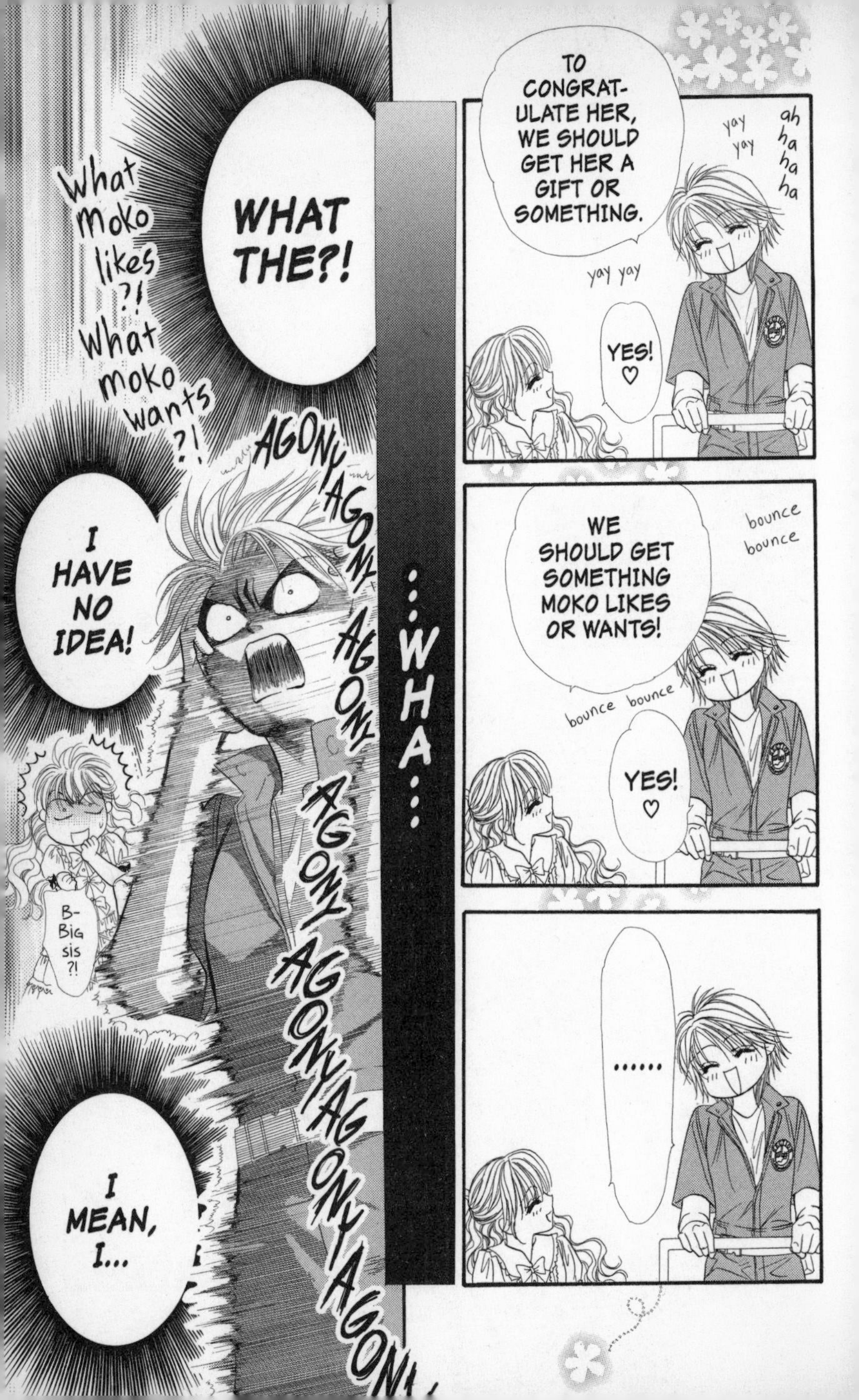
TO CONGRAT-ULATE HER, WE SHOULD GET HER A GIFT OR SOMETHING.
ah ha ha ha
yay yay
yay yay
YES! ♡
WE SHOULD GET SOMETHING MOKO LIKES OR WANTS!
bounce bounce
bounce bounce
YES! ♡
......
...WHA...
WHAT THE?!
What moko likes?! What moko wants?!
AGONY AGONY AGONY AGONY AGONY AGONY AGONY AGONY
I HAVE NO IDEA!
B-Big sis?!
I MEAN, I...

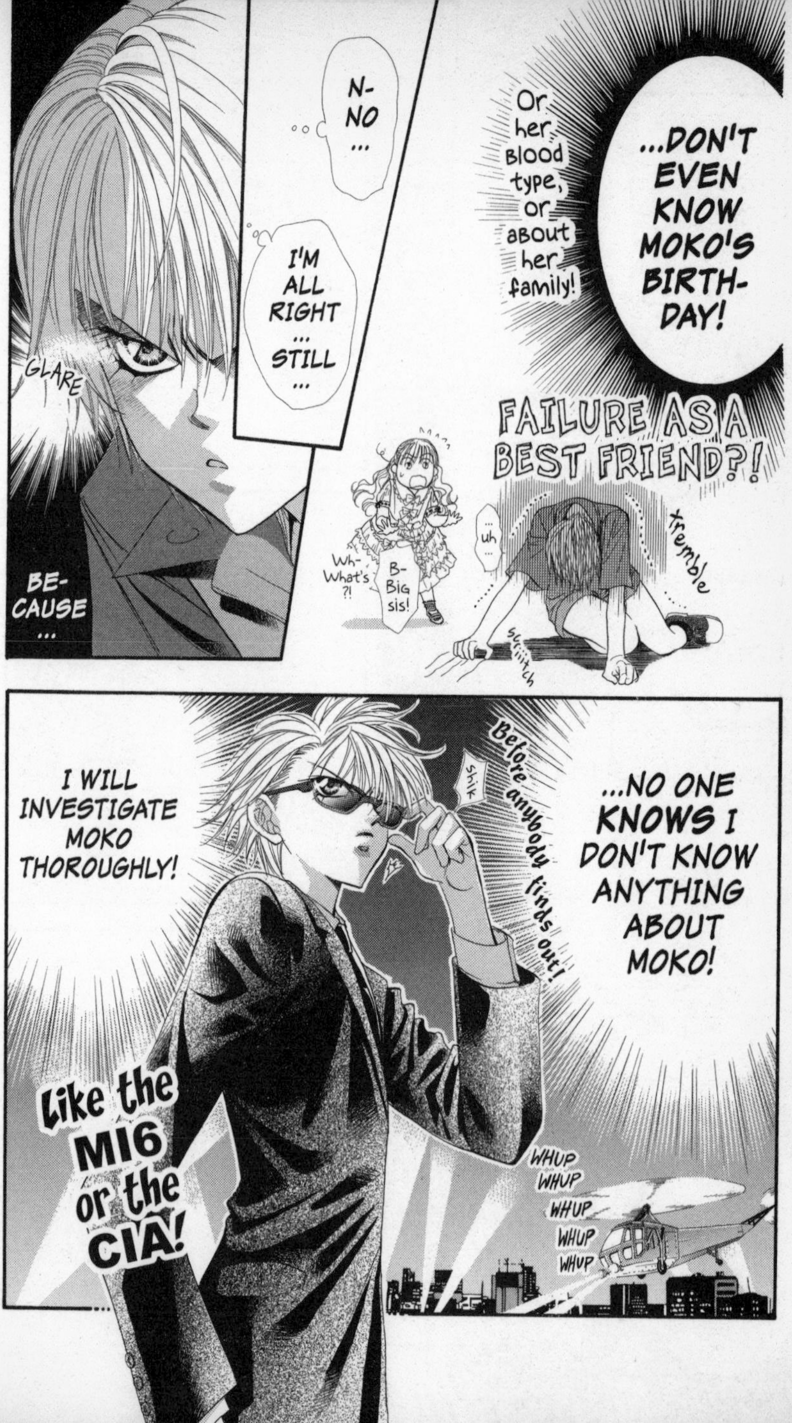
N-NO …
I'M ALL RIGHT … STILL …
GLARE
BE-CAUSE …
…DON'T EVEN KNOW MOKO'S BIRTH-DAY!
Or her blood type, or about her family!
FAILURE AS A BEST FRIEND?!
… uh …
tremble
scriiitch
B-Big sis!
Wh-What's ?!
…NO ONE KNOWS I DON'T KNOW ANYTHING ABOUT MOKO!
Before anybody finds out!
shik
I WILL INVESTIGATE MOKO THOROUGHLY!
Like the MI6 or the CIA!
WHUP WHUP WHUP WHUP WHUP
…

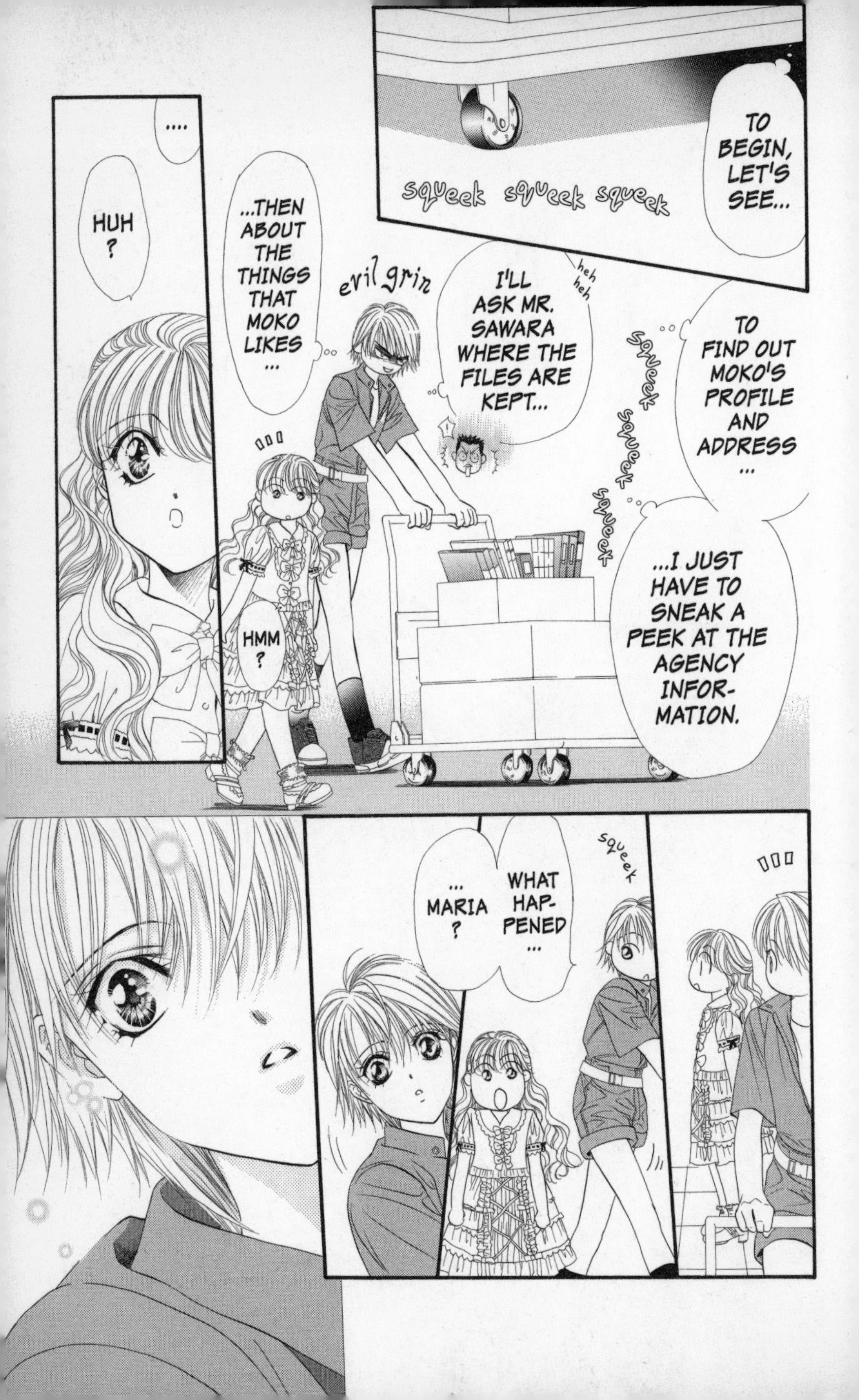
TO BEGIN, LET'S SEE...
squeek squeek squeek
TO FIND OUT MOKO'S PROFILE AND ADDRESS...
...I JUST HAVE TO SNEAK A PEEK AT THE AGENCY INFORMATION.
squeek squeek squeek
heh heh
I'LL ASK MR. SAWARA WHERE THE FILES ARE KEPT...
evil grin
...THEN ABOUT THE THINGS THAT MOKO LIKES...
HMM?
....
HUH?
squeek
WHAT HAPPENED...
...MARIA?

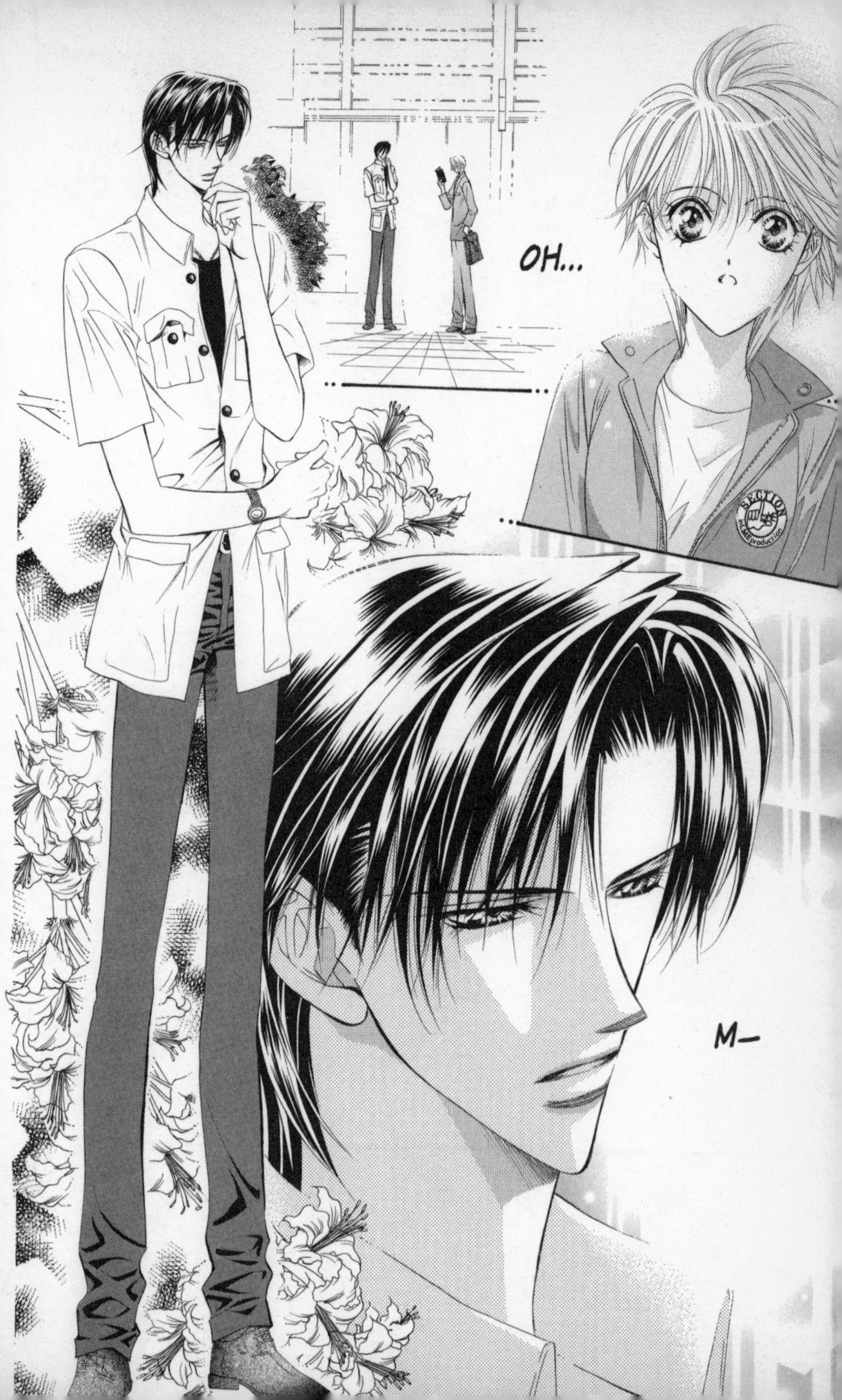
OH...
M—

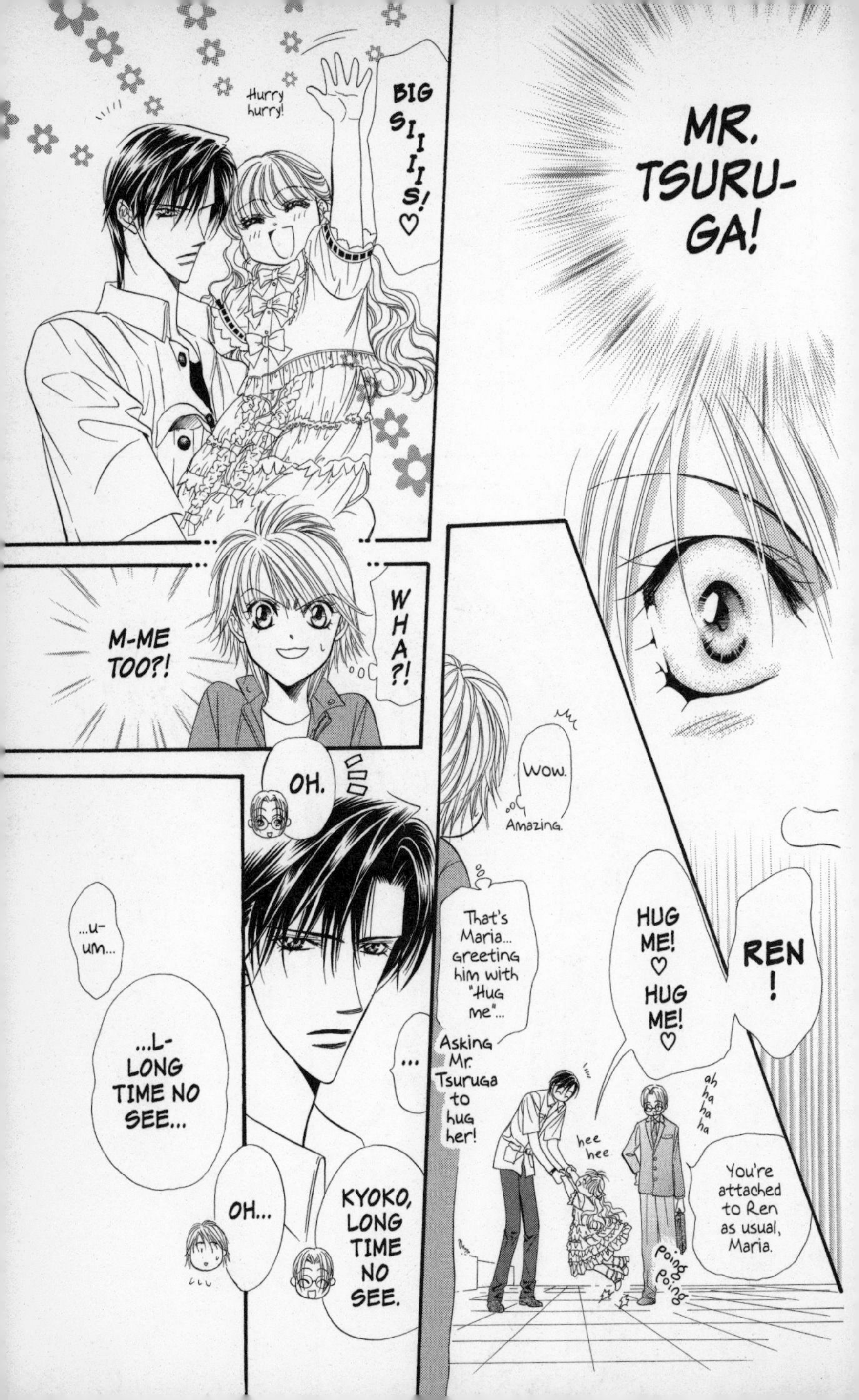
MR. TSURUGA!
BIG SIIIIS! ♡
Hurry hurry!
REN!
HUG ME! ♡ HUG ME! ♡
Wow.
Amazing.
That's Maria... greeting him with "Hug me"...
Asking Mr. Tsuruga to hug her!
ah ha ha ha
hee hee
You're attached to Ren as usual, Maria.
Poing Poing
WHA?!
M-ME TOO?!
OH.
...
KYOKO, LONG TIME NO SEE.
...u-um...
...L-LONG TIME NO SEE...
OH...

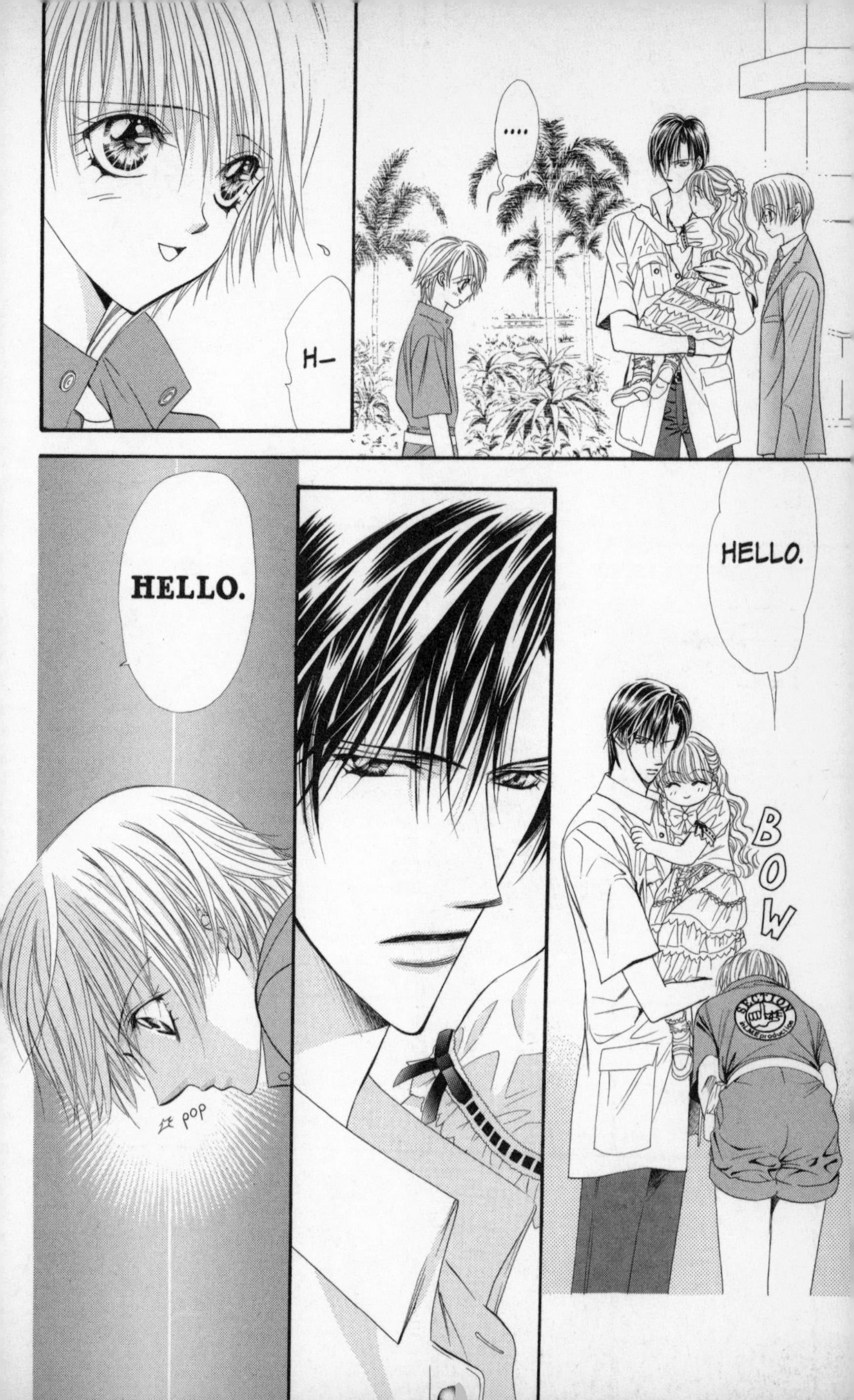
....
H—
HELLO.
BOW
SECTION
HELLO.
pop

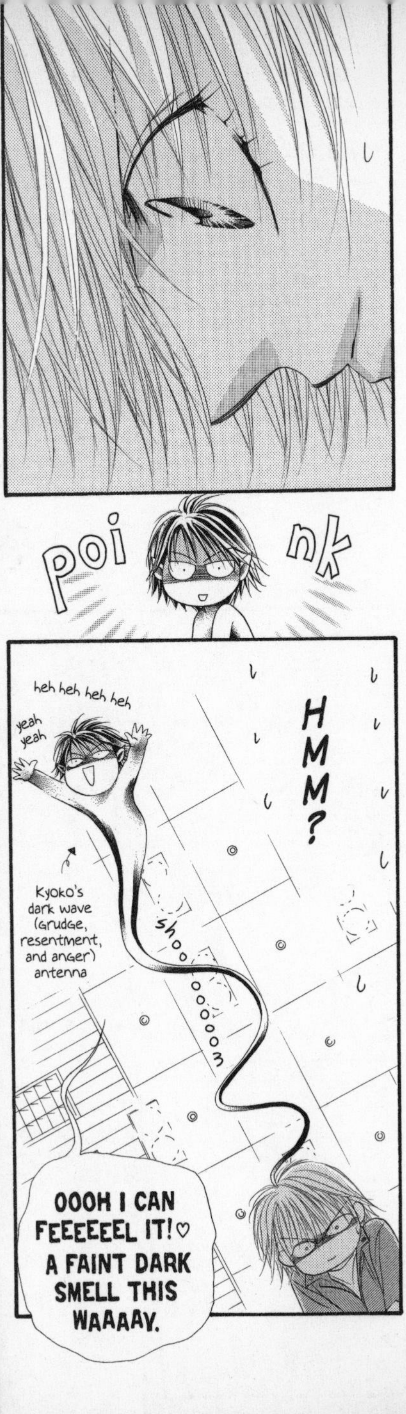
poi nk
HMM?
heh heh heh heh
yeah yeah
Kyoko's dark wave (grudge, resentment, and anger) antenna
shoooooooom
OOOH I CAN FEEEEEEL IT! ♡ A FAINT DARK SMELL THIS WAAAAY.

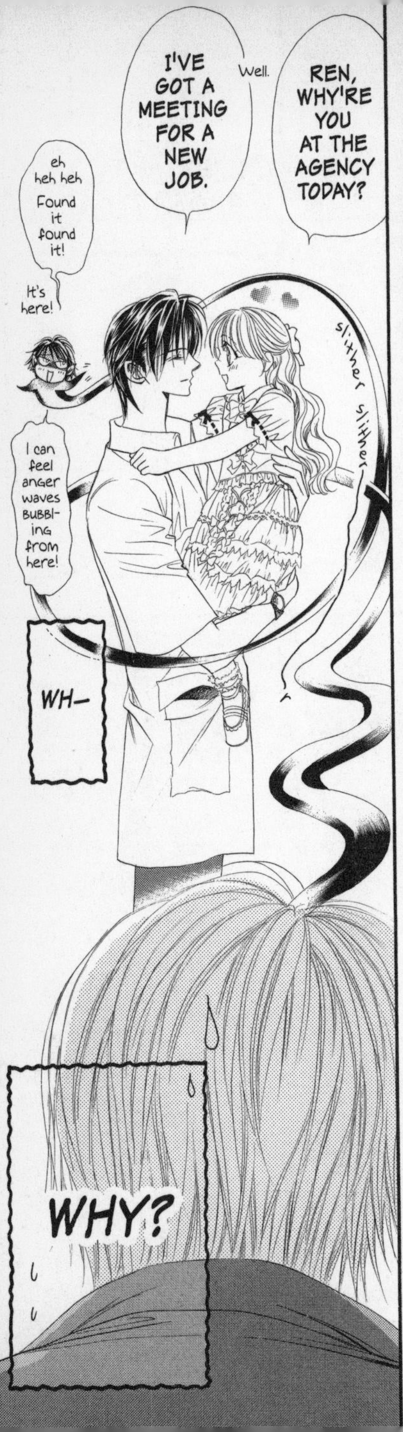
REN, WHY'RE YOU AT THE AGENCY TODAY?
Well.
I'VE GOT A MEETING FOR A NEW JOB.
eh heh heh Found it found it!
It's here!
slither slither
I can feel anger waves bubbling from here!
WH—
WHY?

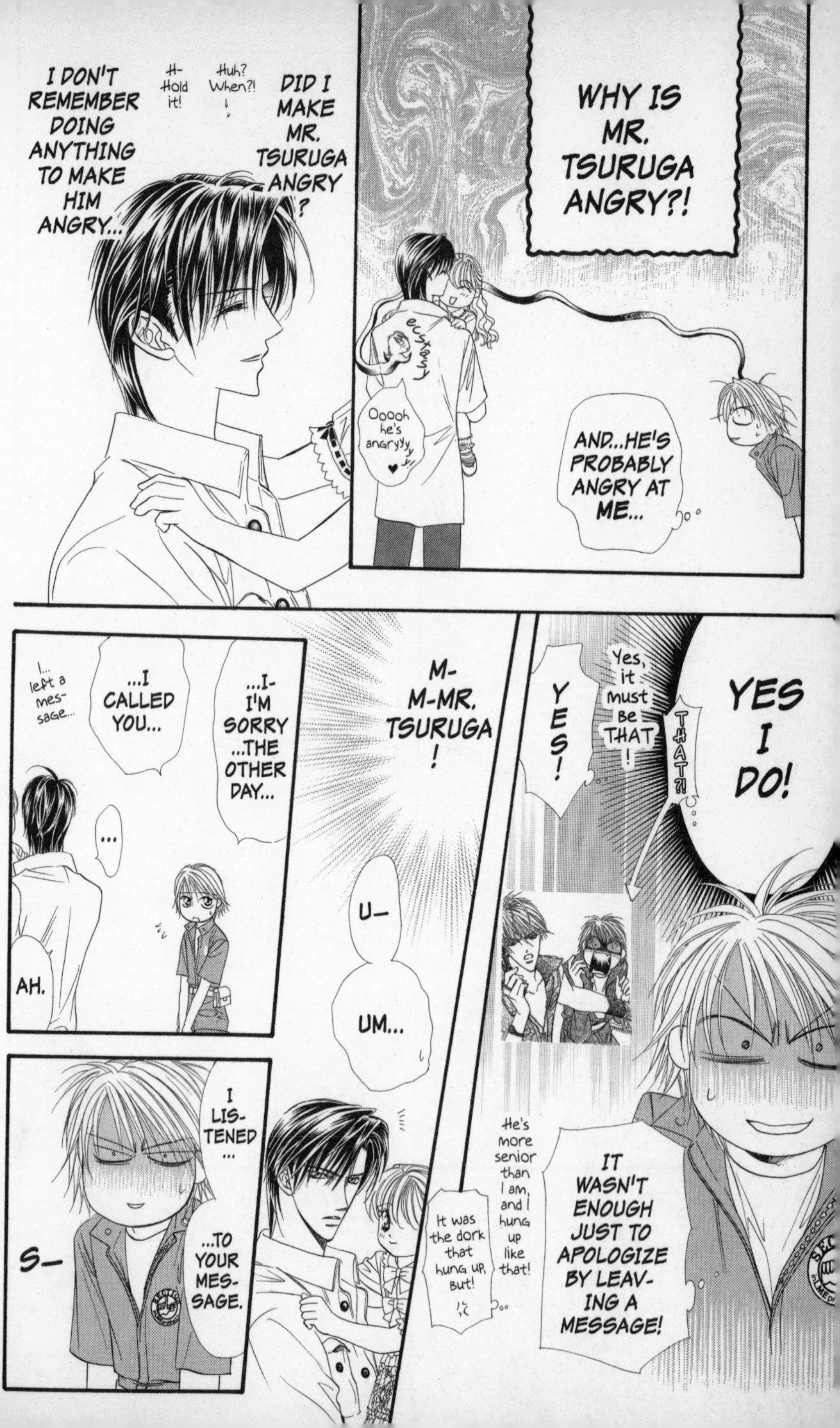
WHY IS MR. TSURUGA ANGRY?!
Ooooh he's angryyyy ♥
AND...HE'S PROBABLY ANGRY AT ME...
DID I MAKE MR. TSURUGA ANGRY?
Huh? When?!
H-Hold it!
I DON'T REMEMBER DOING ANYTHING TO MAKE HIM ANGRY...
YES I DO!
THAT?!
Yes, it must be THAT!
YES!
IT WASN'T ENOUGH JUST TO APOLOGIZE BY LEAVING A MESSAGE!
He's more senior than I am, and I hung up like that!
It was the dork that hung up, but!
M-M-MR. TSURUGA!
U—
UM...
...I-I'M SORRY ...THE OTHER DAY...
...I CALLED YOU...
I... left a message...
...
AH.
I LISTENED...
...TO YOUR MESSAGE.
S—

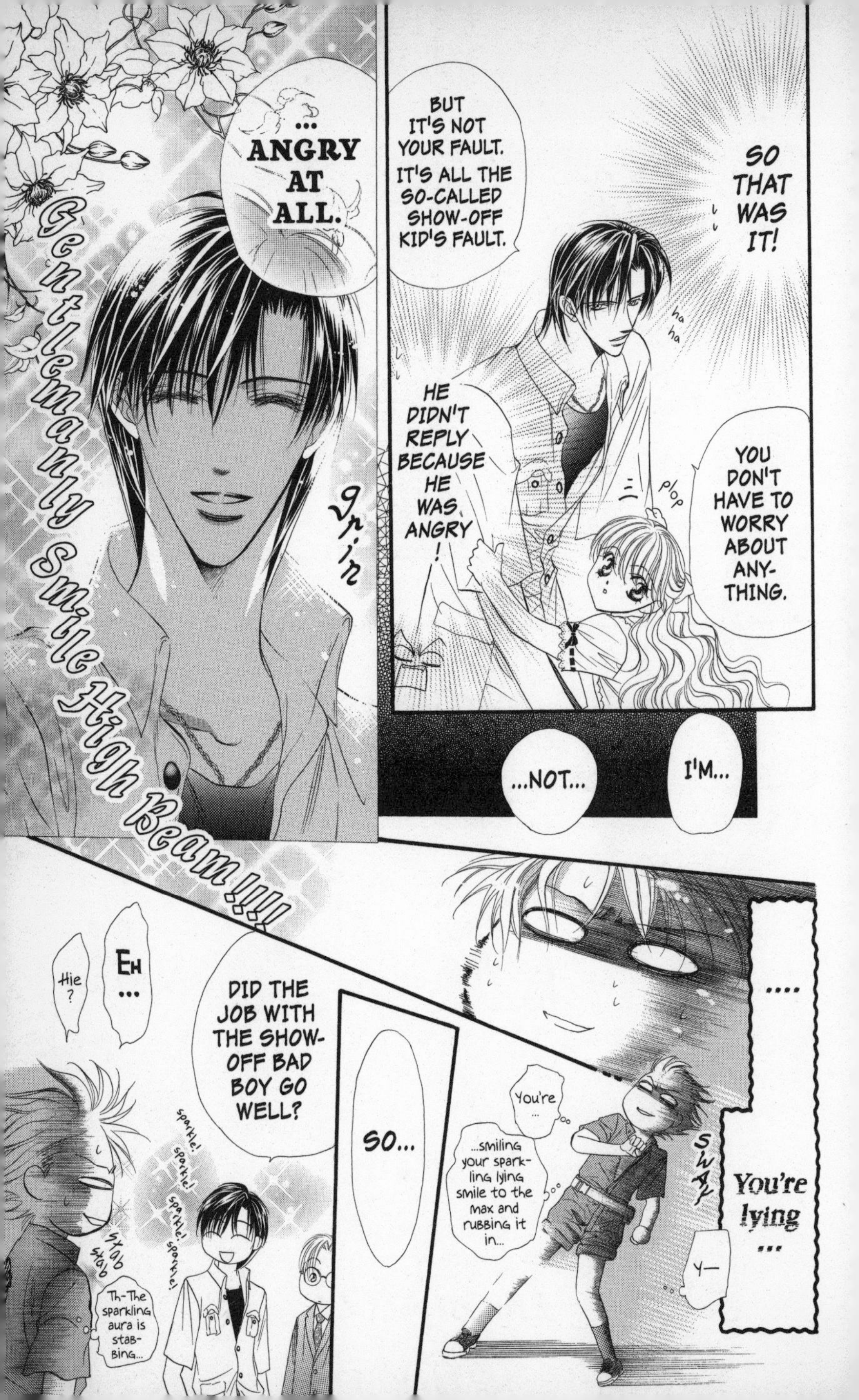
SO THAT WAS IT!
ha ha
BUT IT'S NOT YOUR FAULT. IT'S ALL THE SO-CALLED SHOW-OFF KID'S FAULT.
YOU DON'T HAVE TO WORRY ABOUT ANYTHING.
plop
HE DIDN'T REPLY BECAUSE HE WAS ANGRY!
I'M...
...NOT...
... ANGRY AT ALL.
grin
Gentlemanly Smile High Beam!!!!
....
You're lying ...
Y—
You're ...
...smiling your sparkling lying smile to the max and rubbing it in...
SWAY
SO...
DID THE JOB WITH THE SHOW-OFF BAD BOY GO WELL?
EH ...
Hie ?
sparkle! sparkle! sparkle! sparkle!
stab stab
Th-The sparkling aura is stabbing...

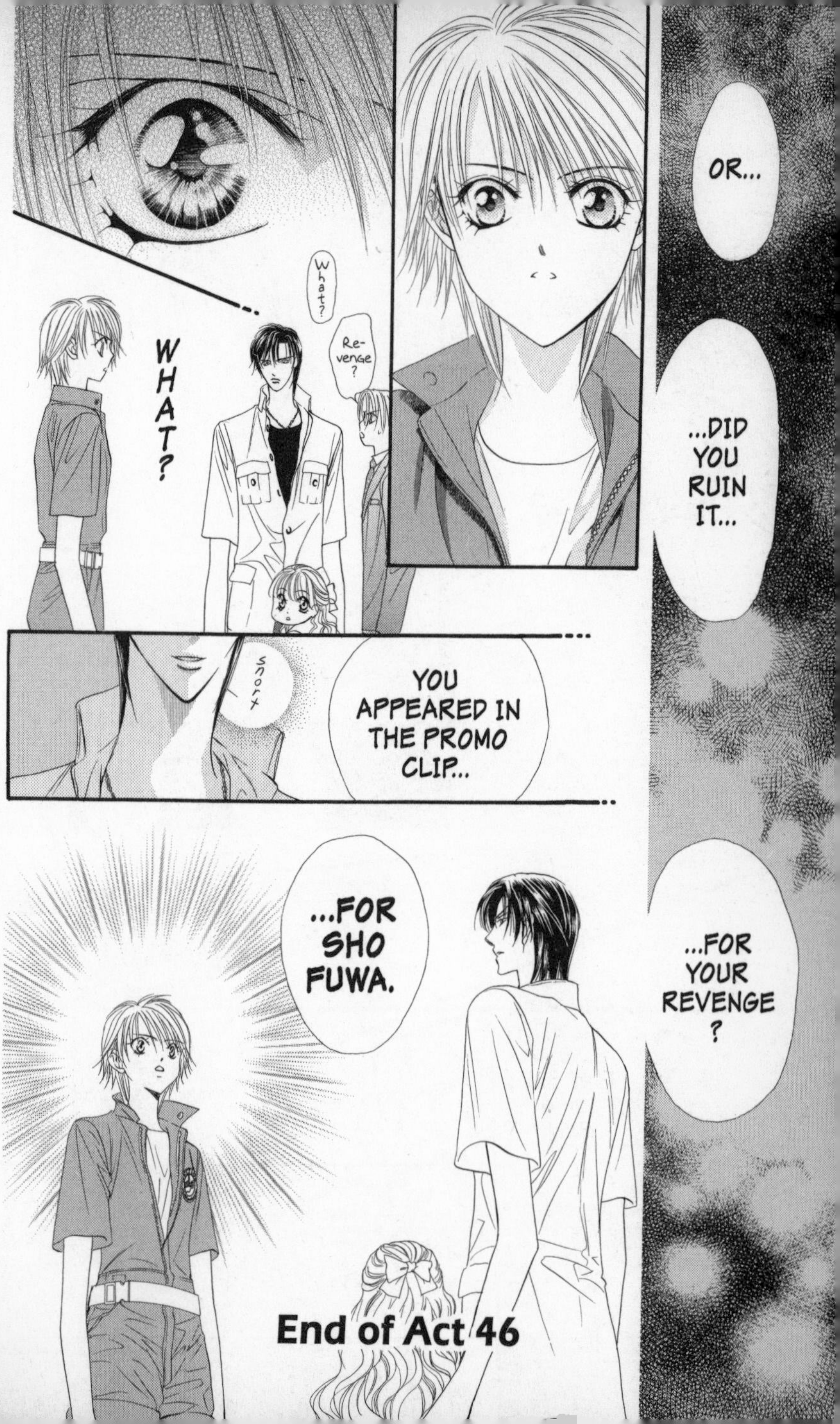
OR...
...DID YOU RUIN IT...
...FOR YOUR REVENGE?
What?
Re-venge?
WHAT?
YOU APPEARED IN THE PROMO CLIP...
snort
...FOR SHO FUWA.
End of Act 46

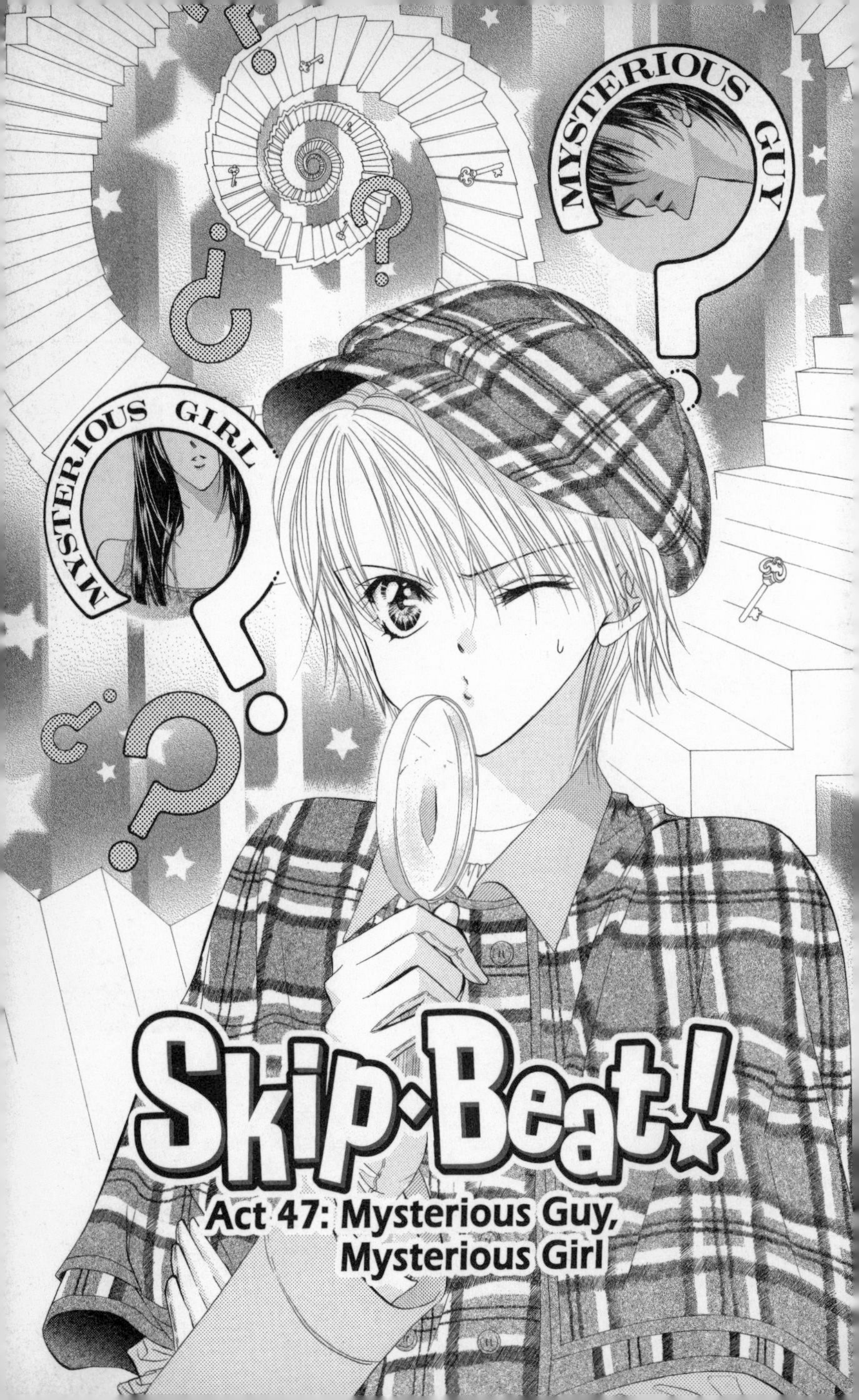
MYSTERIOUS GUY
MYSTERIOUS GIRL
Skip·Beat!
Act 47: Mysterious Guy, Mysterious Girl

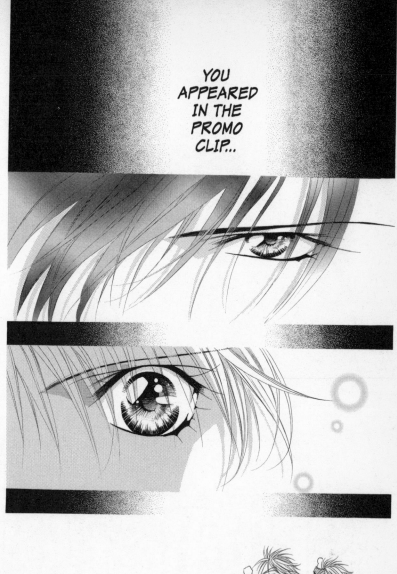

YOU
APPEARED
IN THE
PROMO
CLIP...

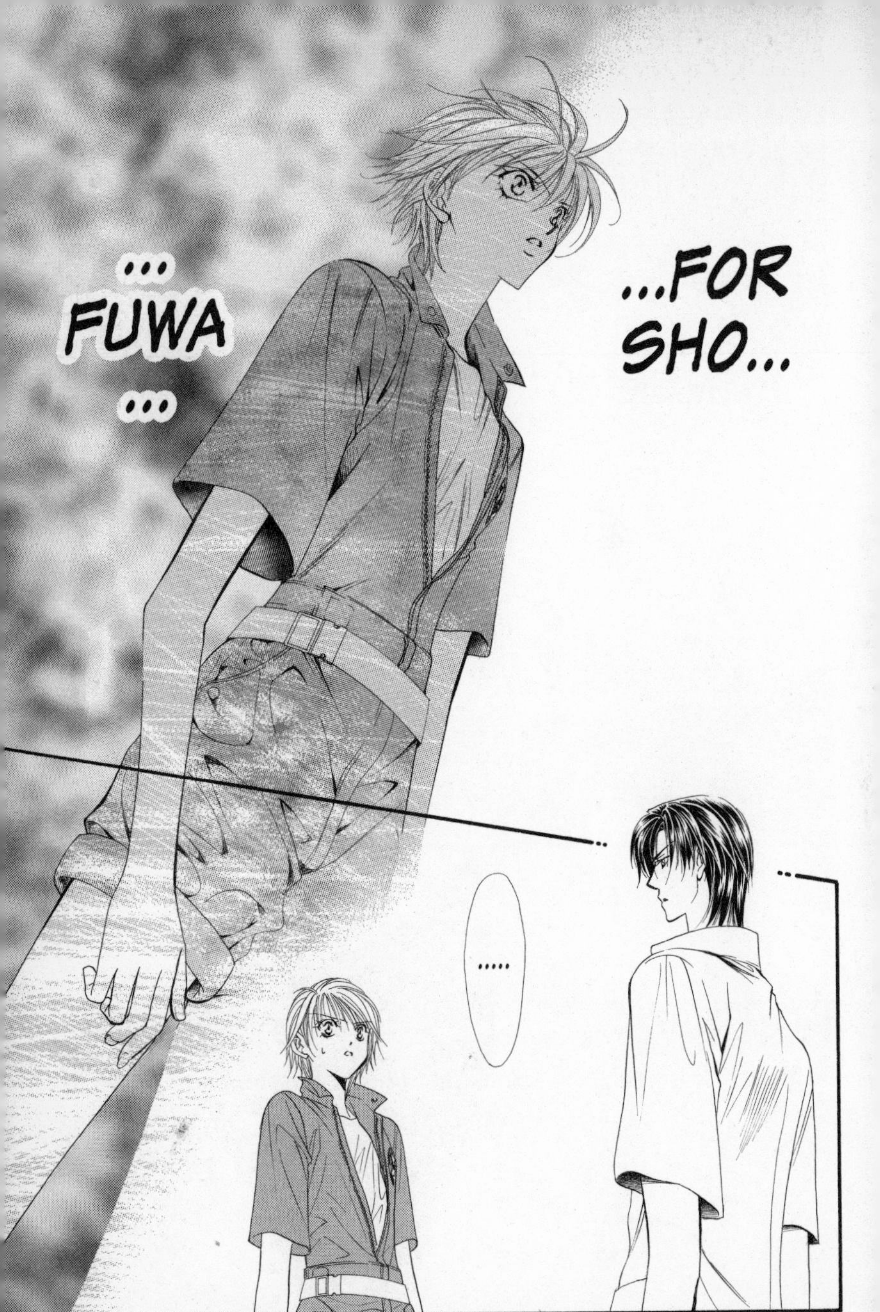
...FOR SHO...
... FUWA ...
.....

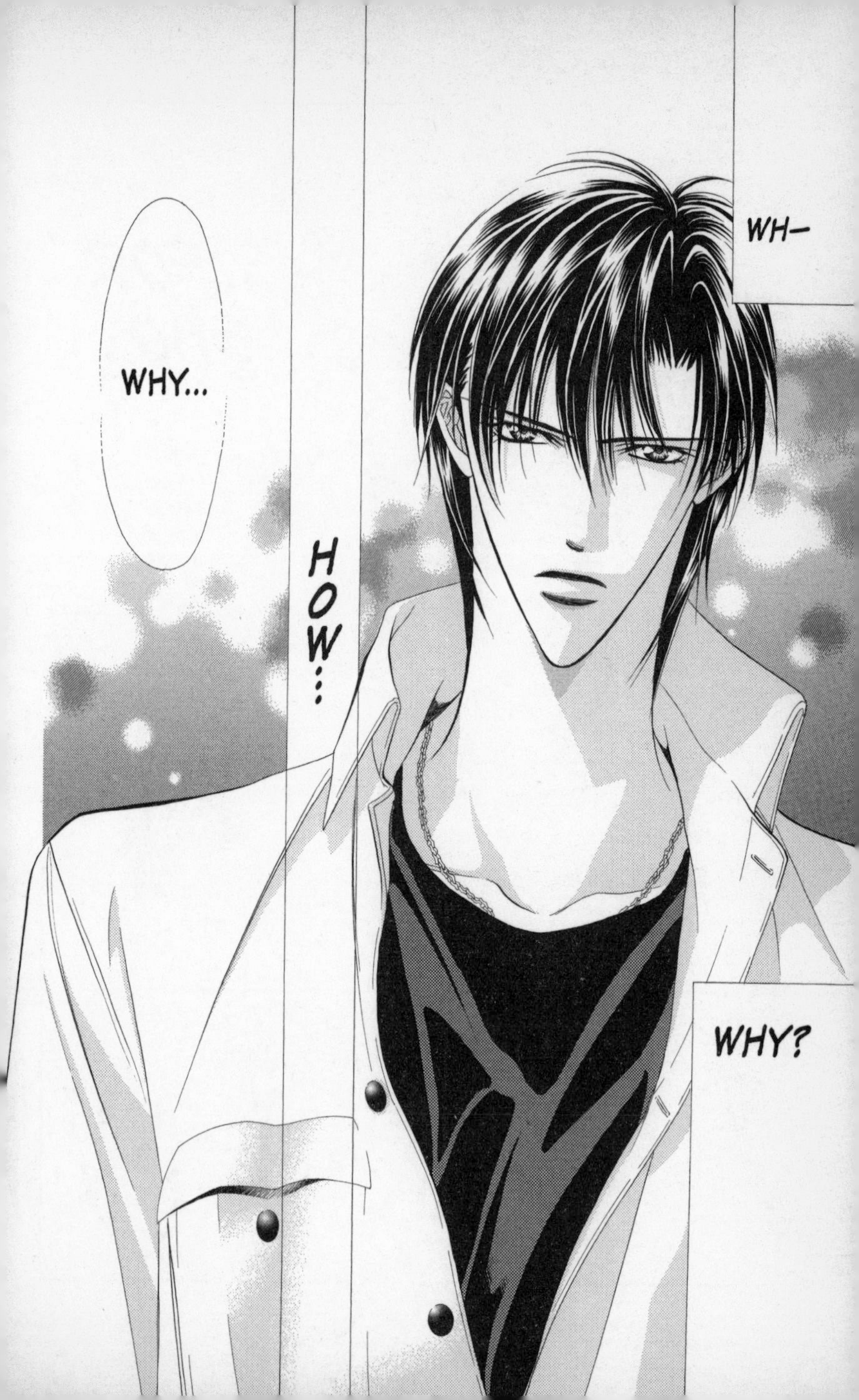
WH–
HOW...
WHY...
WHY?

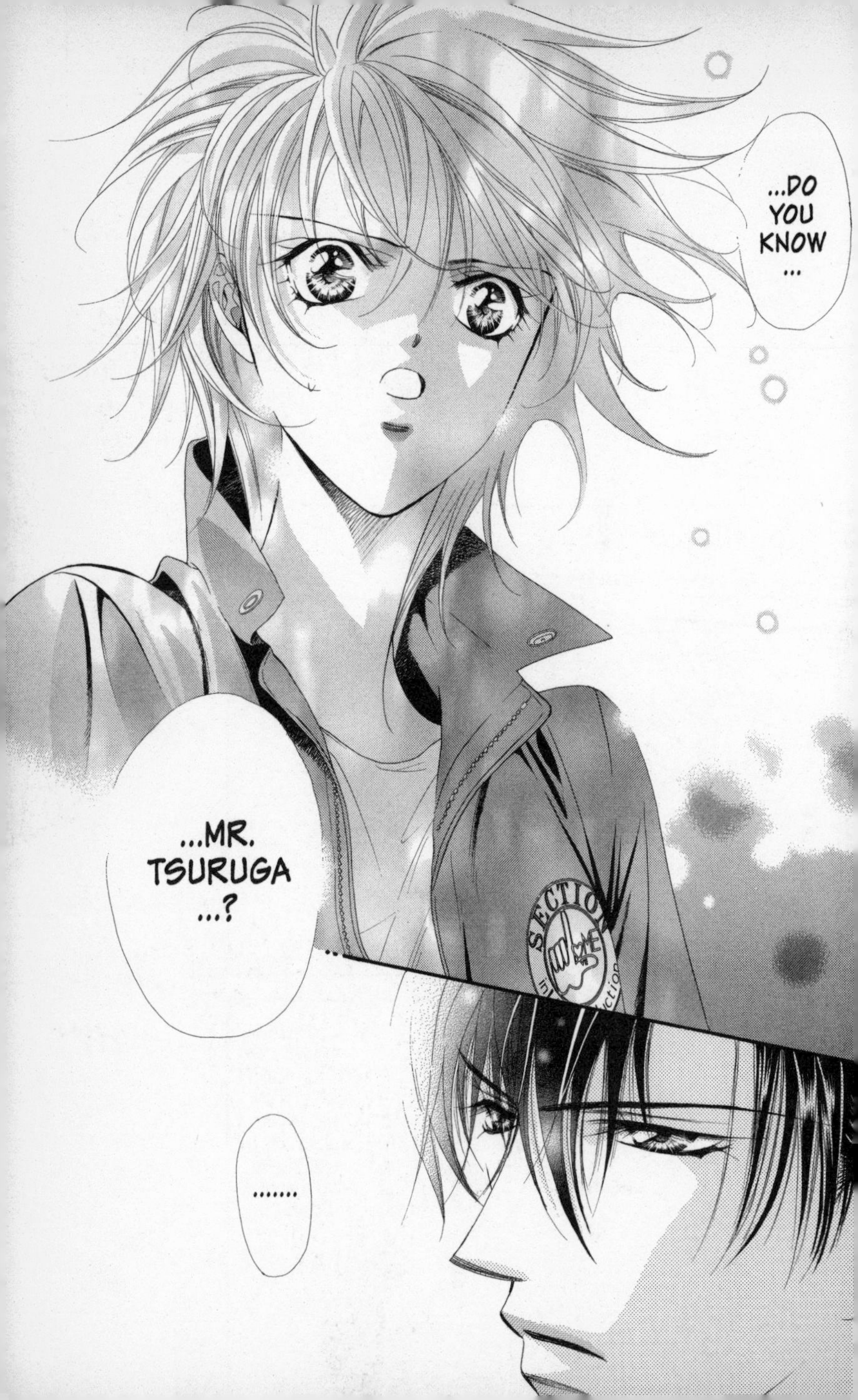
...DO YOU KNOW ...
...MR. TSURUGA ...?
.......
SECTION
ME

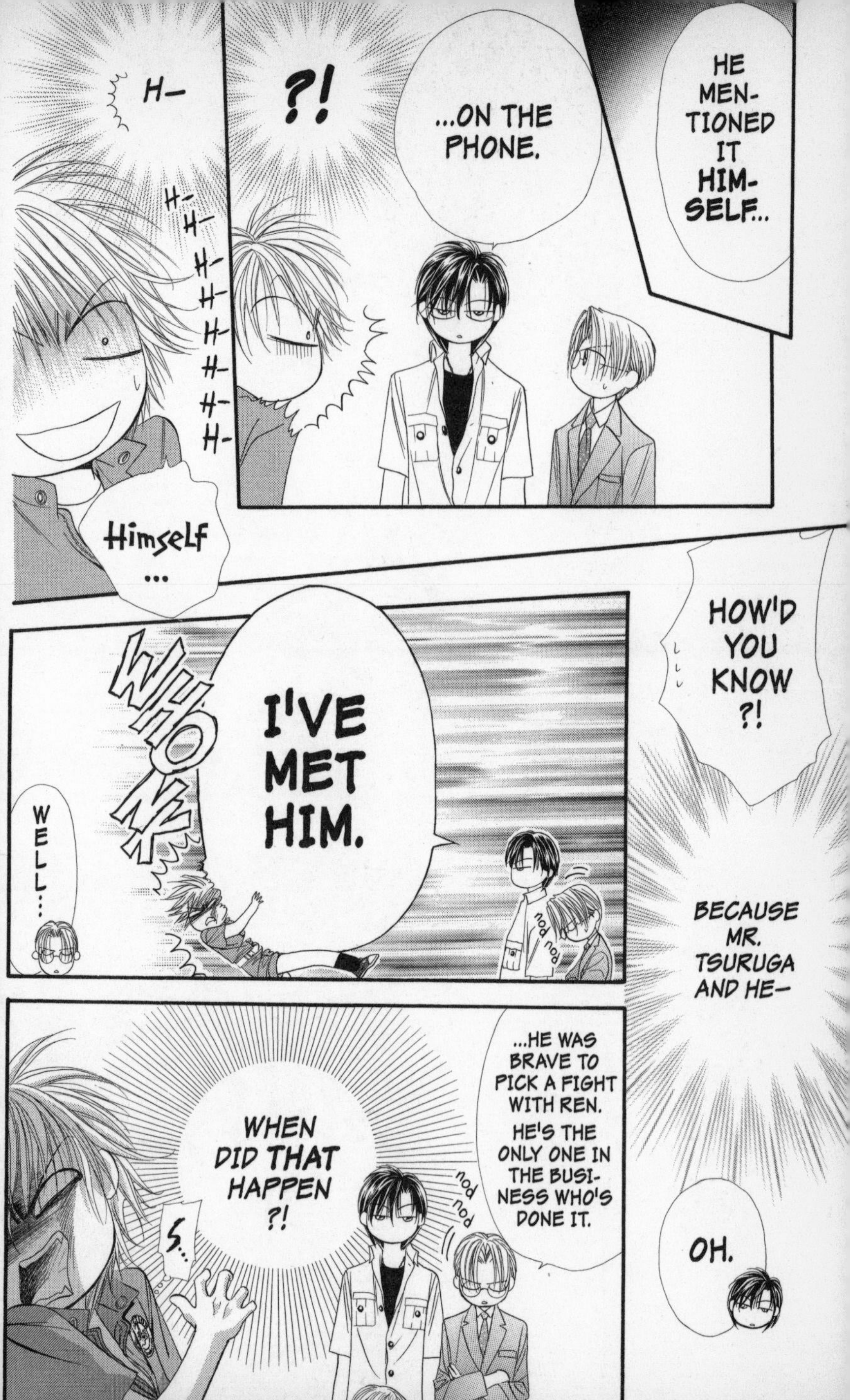
HE MENTIONED IT HIMSELF...
...ON THE PHONE.
?!
H—
H- H- H- H- H- H- H- H-
Himself ...
HOW'D YOU KNOW ?!
I'VE MET HIM.
WHOMP
nod nod
WELL...
BECAUSE MR. TSURUGA AND HE—
OH.
...HE WAS BRAVE TO PICK A FIGHT WITH REN.
HE'S THE ONLY ONE IN THE BUSINESS WHO'S DONE IT.
nod nod
WHEN DID THAT HAPPEN ?!
S...

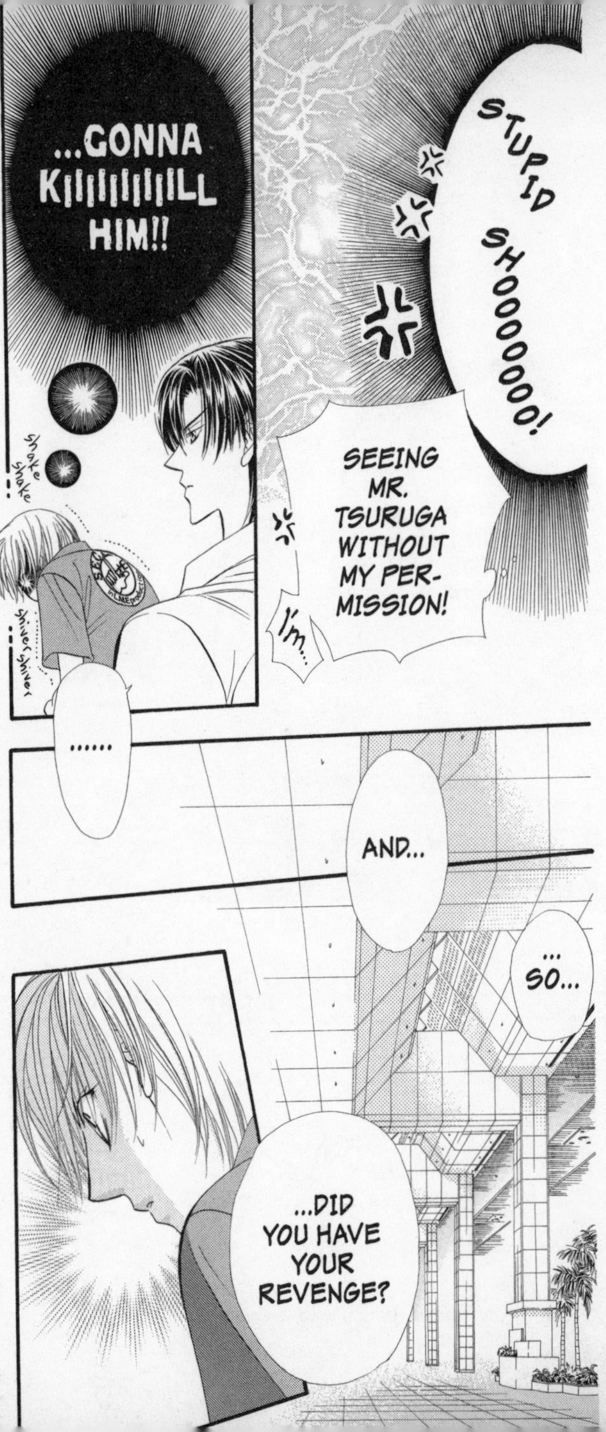
STUPID SHOOOOOOO!
SEEING MR. TSURUGA WITHOUT MY PERMISSION!
I'm...
...GONNA KIIIIIIIIILL HIM!!
shake shake
shiver shiver
......
AND...
...SO...
...DID YOU HAVE YOUR REVENGE?

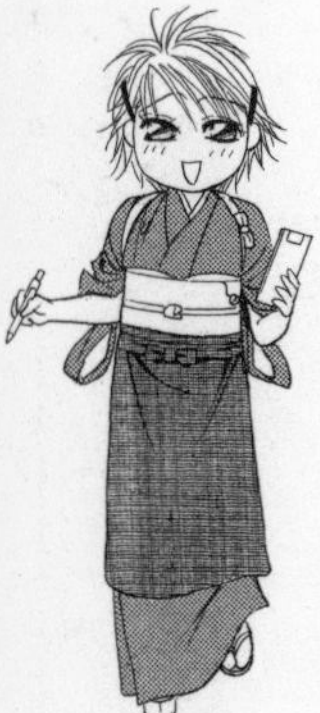

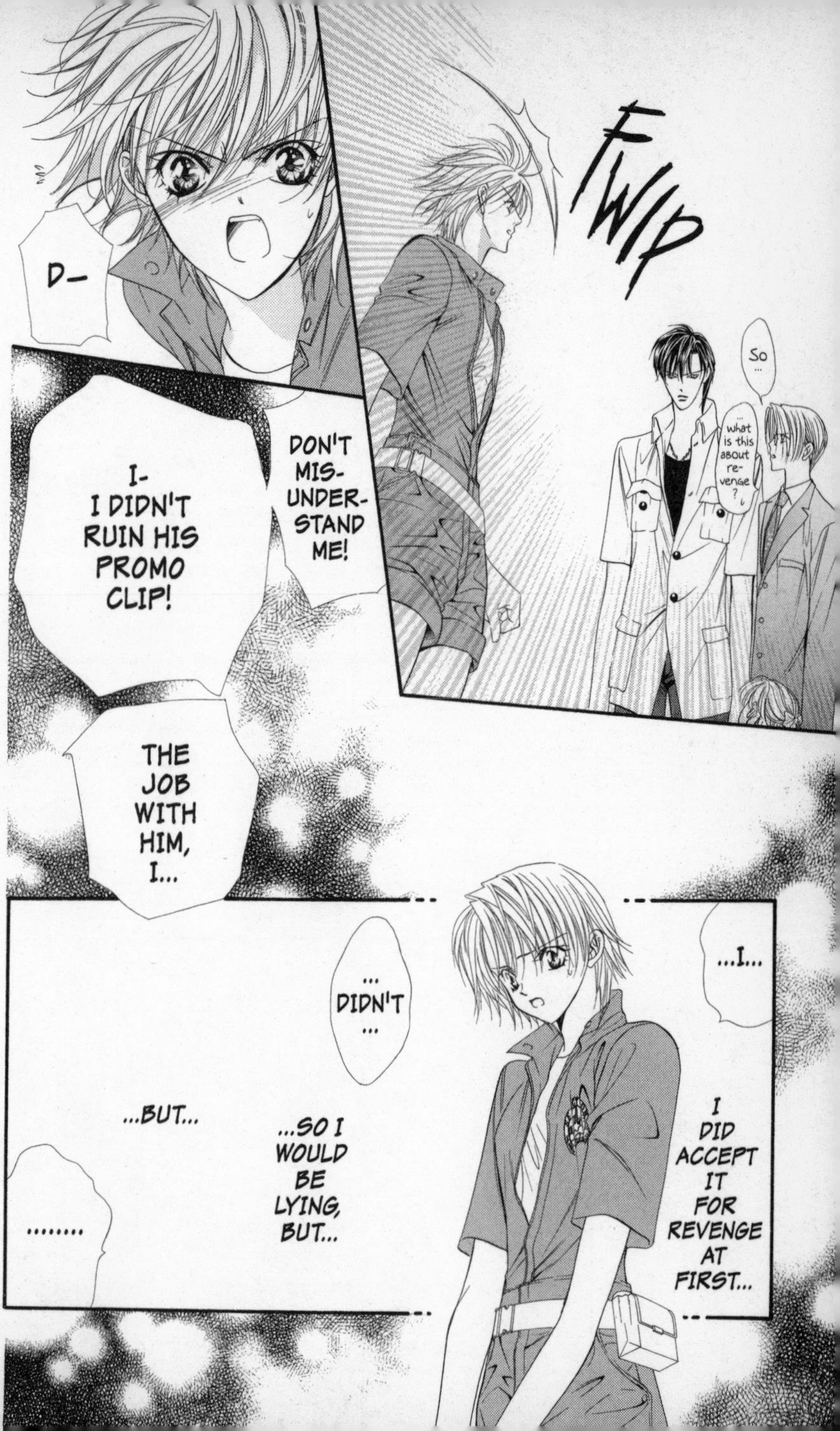
FWIP
So...
...what is this about revenge?¿
D—
DON'T MISUNDERSTAND ME!
I- I DIDN'T RUIN HIS PROMO CLIP!
THE JOB WITH HIM, I...
...I...
I DID ACCEPT IT FOR REVENGE AT FIRST...
...DIDN'T...
...SO I WOULD BE LYING, BUT...
...BUT...
........

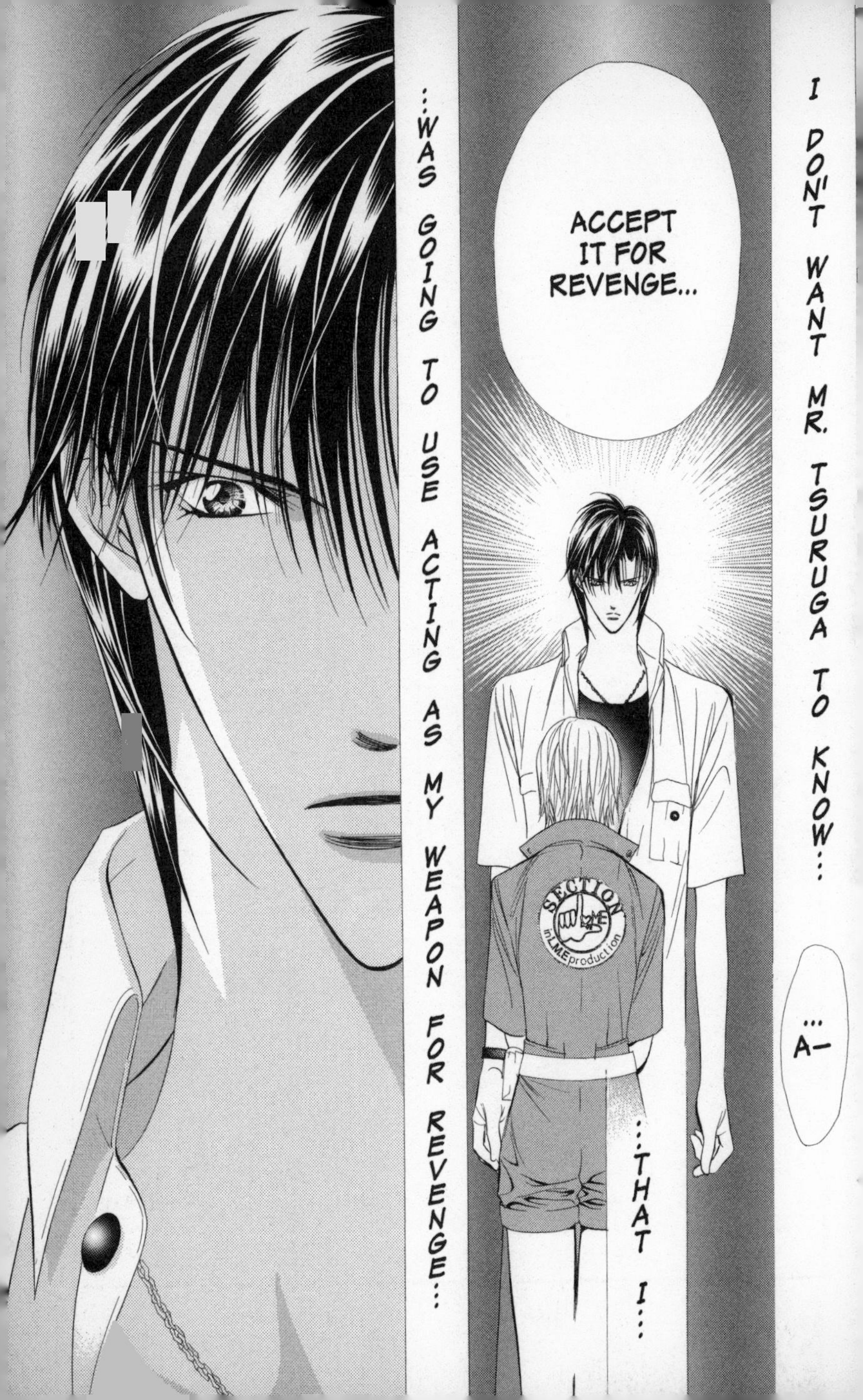
I DON'T WANT MR. TSURUGA TO KNOW...
...A—
ACCEPT IT FOR REVENGE...
...THAT I...
...WAS GOING TO USE ACTING AS MY WEAPON FOR REVENGE...

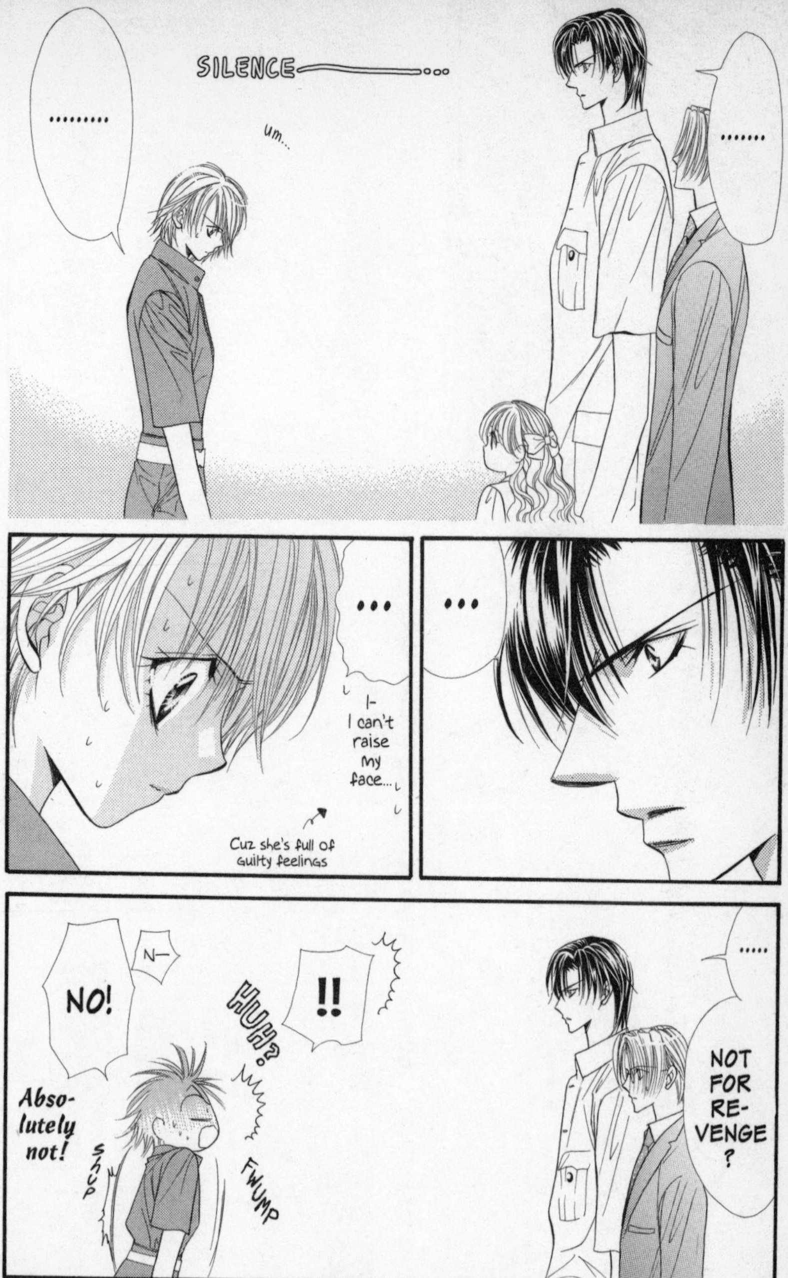
.......
SILENCE———...
um...
.........
...
...
I- I can't raise my face...
Cuz she's full of Guilty feelings
.....
NOT FOR RE-VENGE?
!!
HUH?
N—
NO!
Abso-lutely not!
FWUMP
SHUP

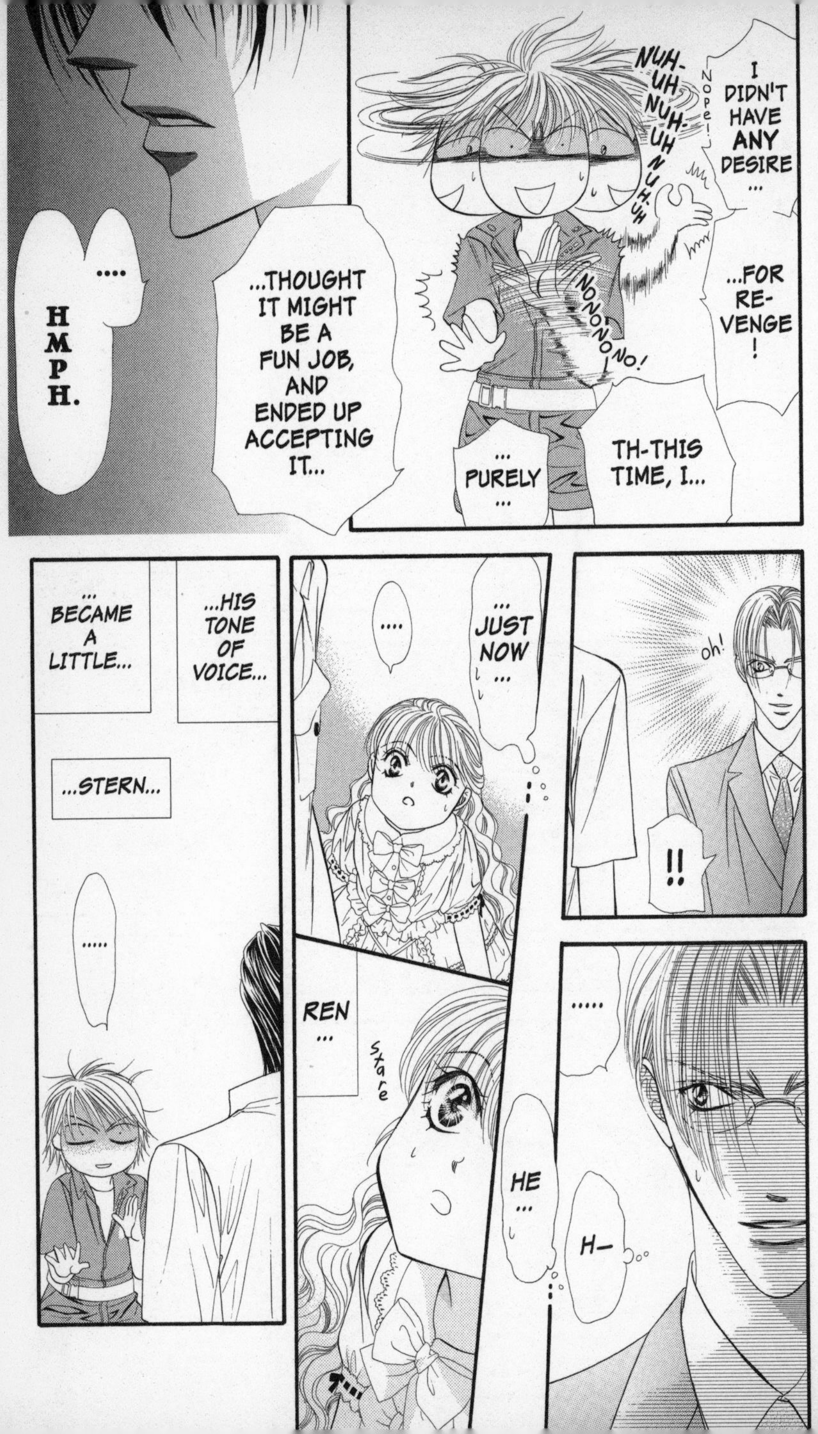

I DIDN'T HAVE ANY DESIRE...
Nope!
NUH-UH NUH-UH NUH-UH NUH-UH
...FOR RE-VENGE!
NONONONONO!
TH-THIS TIME, I...
...PURELY...
...THOUGHT IT MIGHT BE A FUN JOB, AND ENDED UP ACCEPTING IT...
....
HMPH.
oh!
!!
...JUST NOW...
....
...HIS TONE OF VOICE...
...BECAME A LITTLE...
...STERN...
.....
.....
H—
HE...
stare
REN...

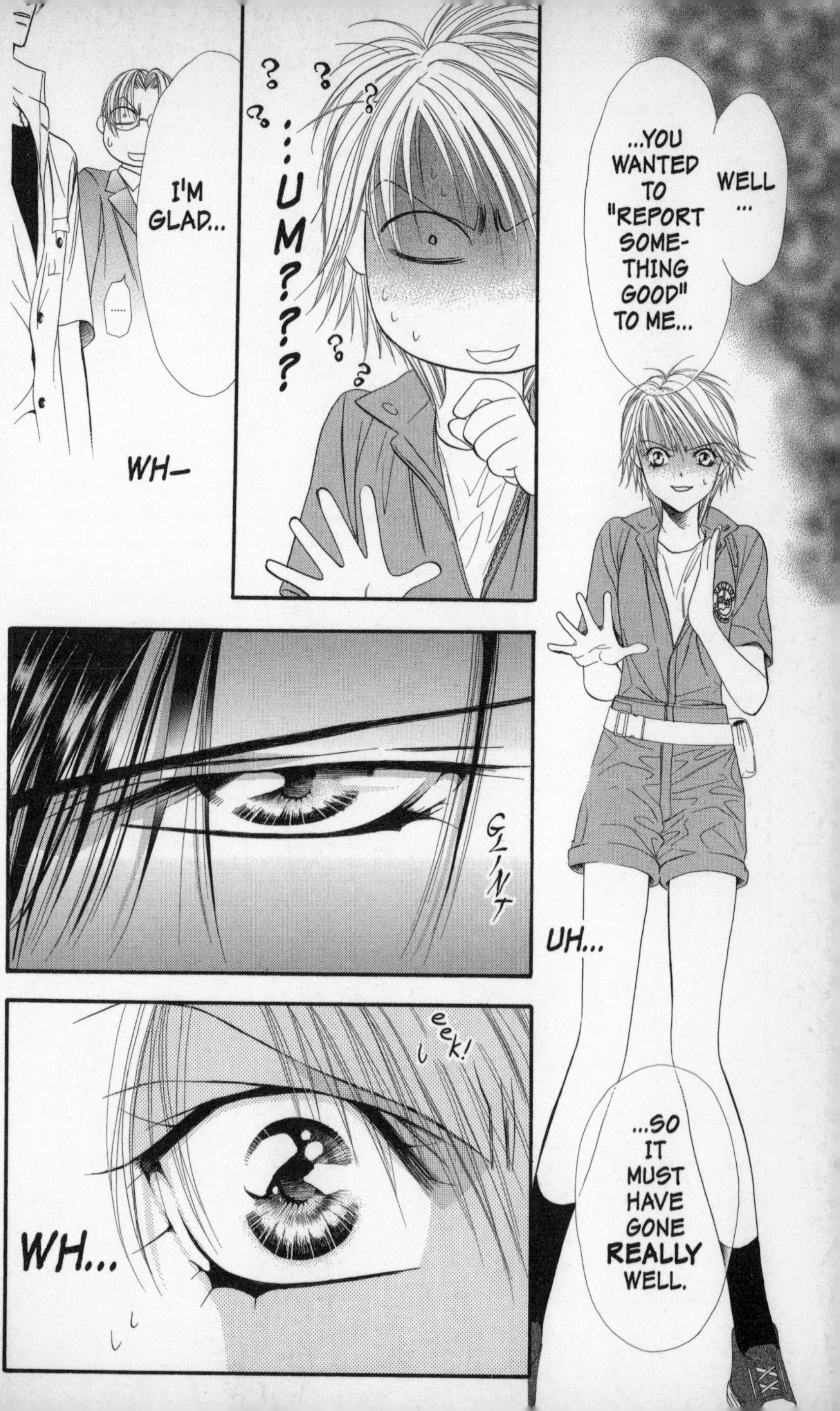
WELL...
...YOU WANTED TO "REPORT SOMETHING GOOD" TO ME...
UH...
...SO IT MUST HAVE GONE REALLY WELL.
...UM????
I'M GLAD...
.....
WH–
GLINT
eek!
WH...

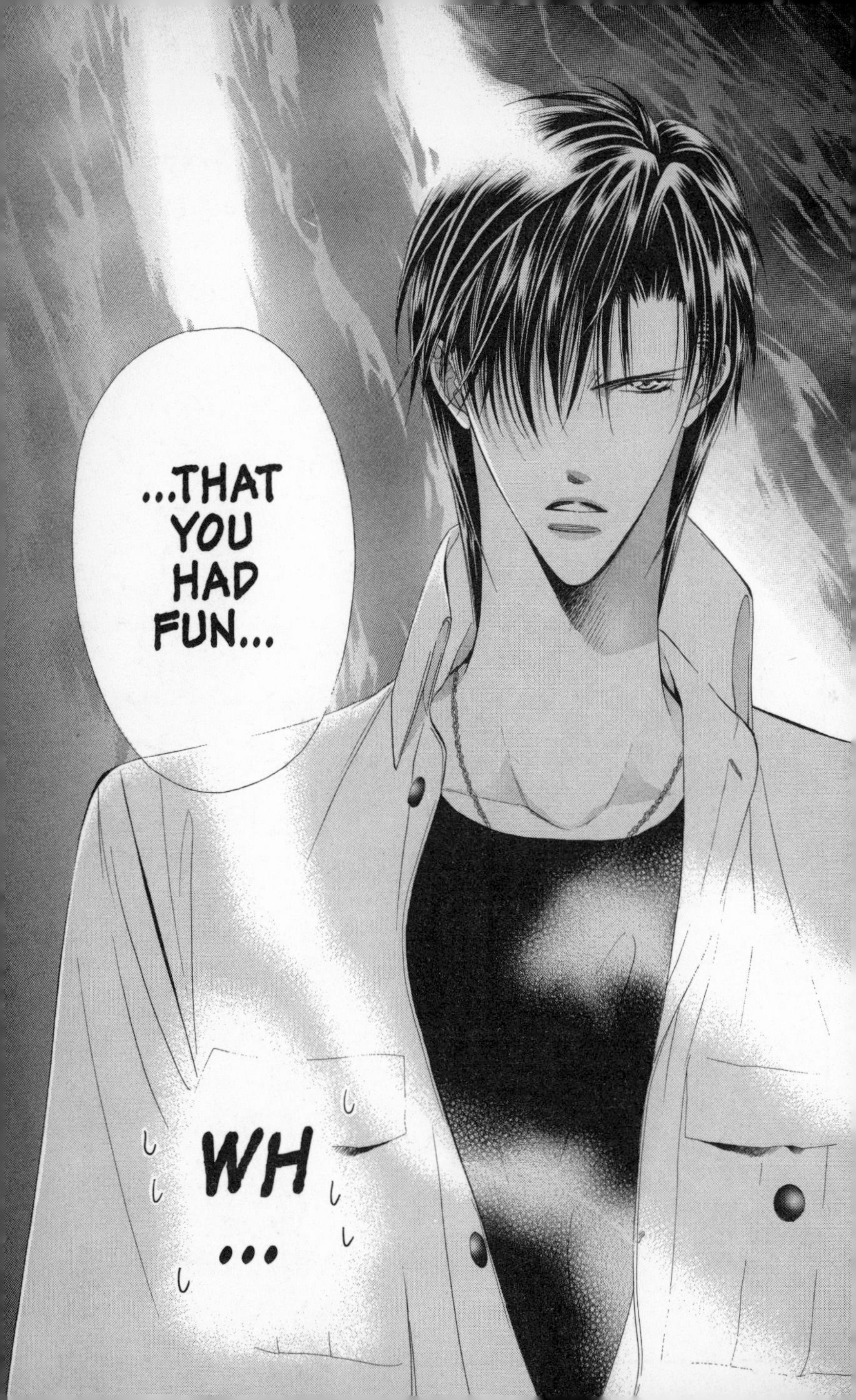
...THAT YOU HAD FUN...
WH ...

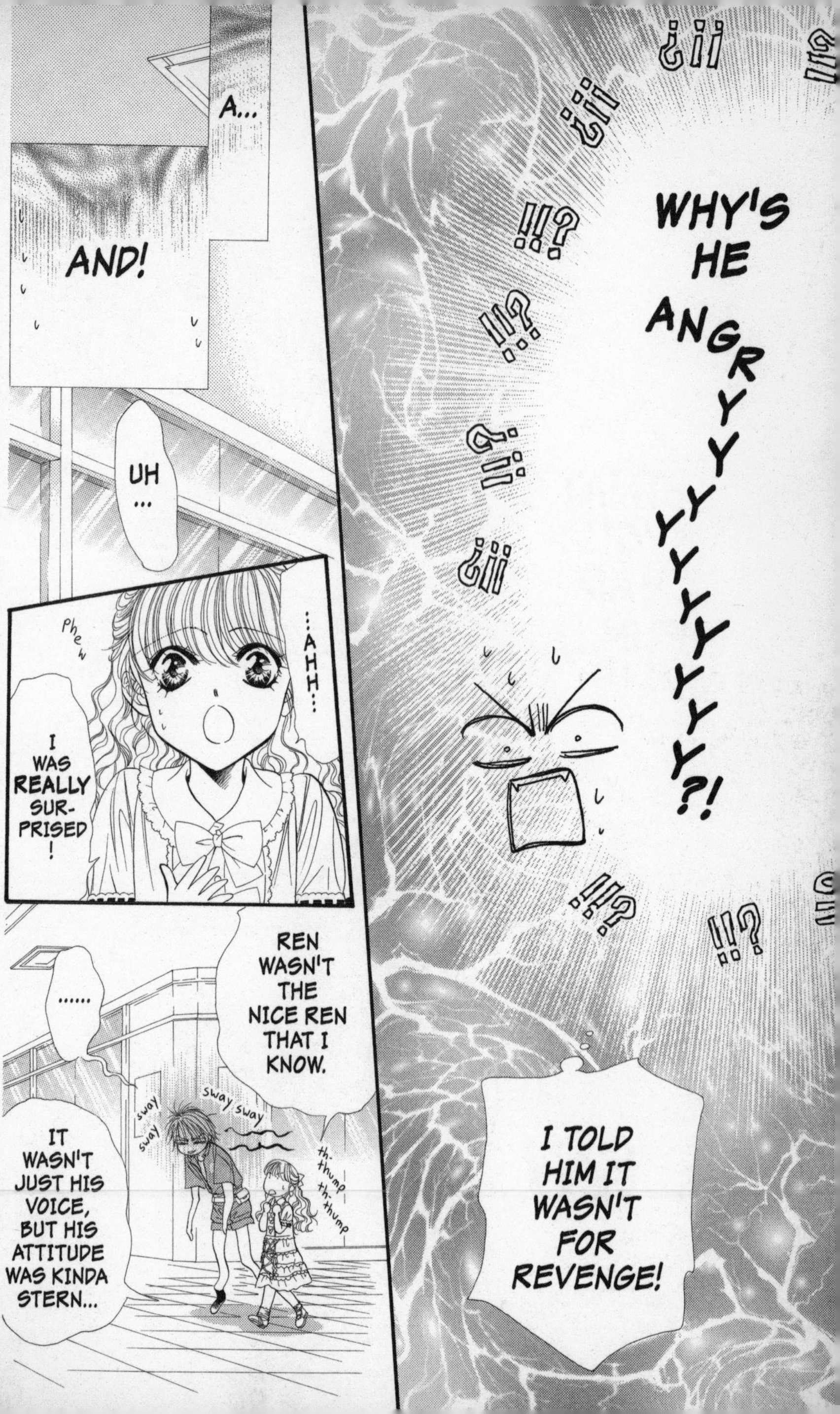
!!?
WHY'S HE ANGRYYYYYYYYYY?!
!!?
!!?
!!?
!!?
I TOLD HIM IT WASN'T FOR REVENGE!
A...
AND!
UH...
...AHH...
Phew
I WAS REALLY SURPRISED!
REN WASN'T THE NICE REN THAT I KNOW.
......
sway sway
sway sway
th-thump th-thump
IT WASN'T JUST HIS VOICE, BUT HIS ATTITUDE WAS KINDA STERN...

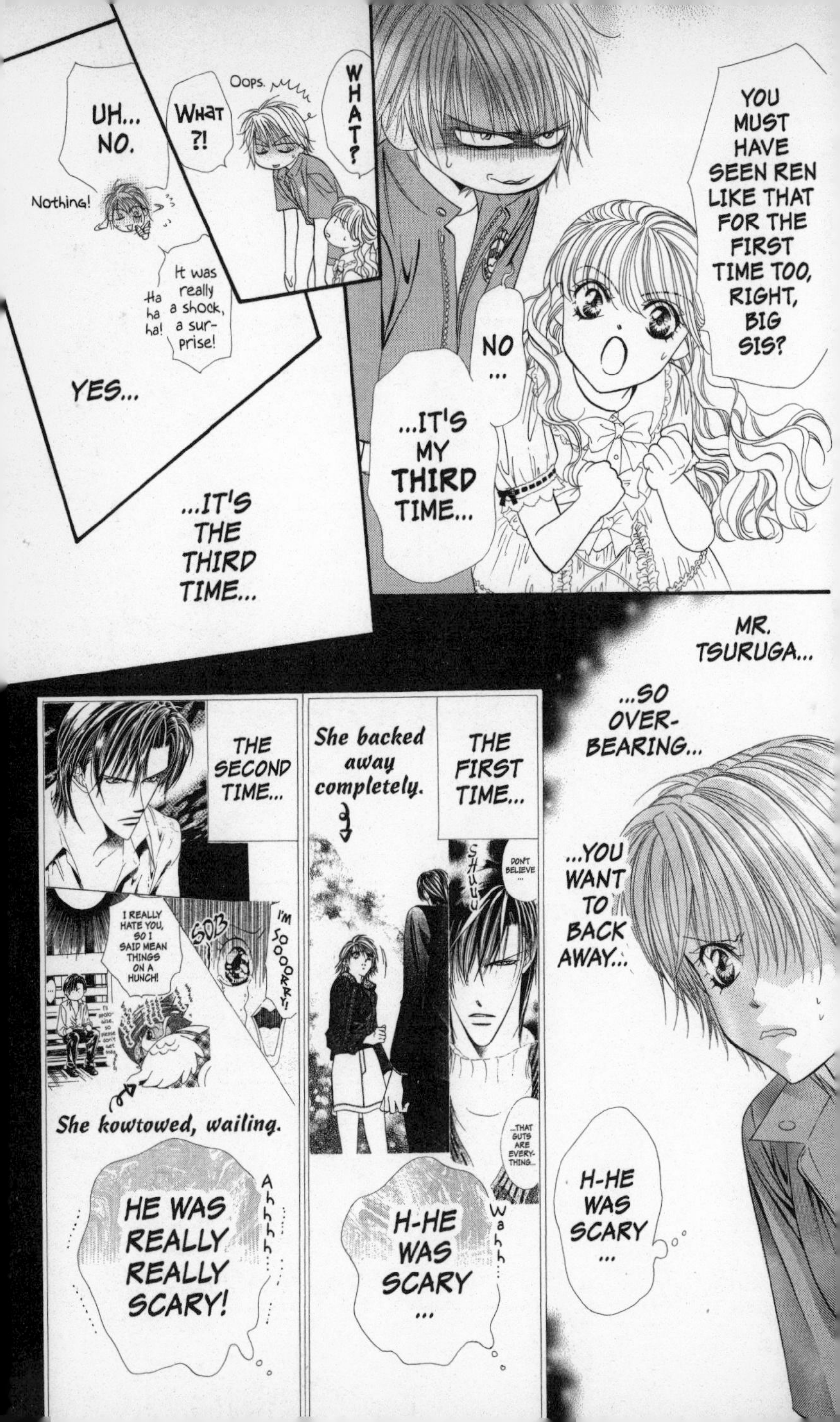
YOU MUST HAVE SEEN REN LIKE THAT FOR THE FIRST TIME TOO, RIGHT, BIG SIS?
NO...
...IT'S MY THIRD TIME...
WHAT?
Oops.
WHAT?!
UH... NO.
Nothing!
It was really a shock, a surprise!
Ha ha ha!
YES...
...IT'S THE THIRD TIME...
MR. TSURUGA...
...SO OVERBEARING...
...YOU WANT TO BACK AWAY...
H-HE WAS SCARY...
THE FIRST TIME...
SHUUU
DON'T BELIEVE...
She backed away completely.
...THAT GUTS ARE EVERYTHING...
H-HE WAS SCARY...
Wahh
THE SECOND TIME...
I'M SOOOORRY!!
SOB
I REALLY HATE YOU, SO I SAID MEAN THINGS ON A HUNCH!
She kowtowed, wailing.
HE WAS REALLY REALLY SCARY!
Ahhhh...

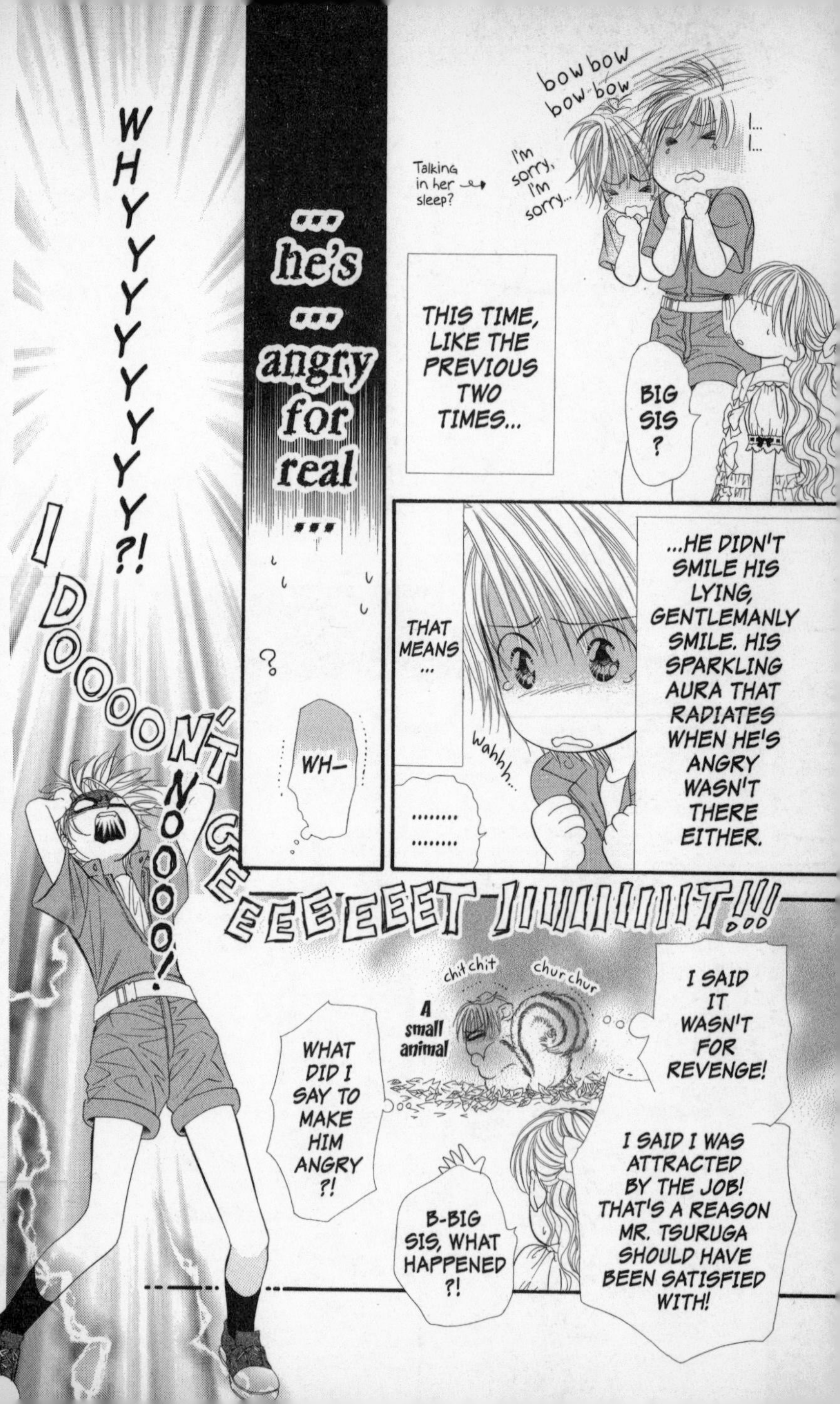
bow bow bow bow
I... I...
I'm sorry, I'm sorry...
Talking in her sleep?
BIG SIS?
THIS TIME, LIKE THE PREVIOUS TWO TIMES...
...HE DIDN'T SMILE HIS LYING, GENTLEMANLY SMILE. HIS SPARKLING AURA THAT RADIATES WHEN HE'S ANGRY WASN'T THERE EITHER.
THAT MEANS...
Wahhh...
........ ........
...he's ...angry for real...
?
WH-
I SAID IT WASN'T FOR REVENGE!
chur chur
chit chit
A small animal
WHAT DID I SAY TO MAKE HIM ANGRY?!
I SAID I WAS ATTRACTED BY THE JOB! THAT'S A REASON MR. TSURUGA SHOULD HAVE BEEN SATISFIED WITH!
B-BIG SIS, WHAT HAPPENED?!
WHYYYYYYYY?!
I DOOOON'T GEEEEEET IIIIIIIIIT!!!
NOOOOO!

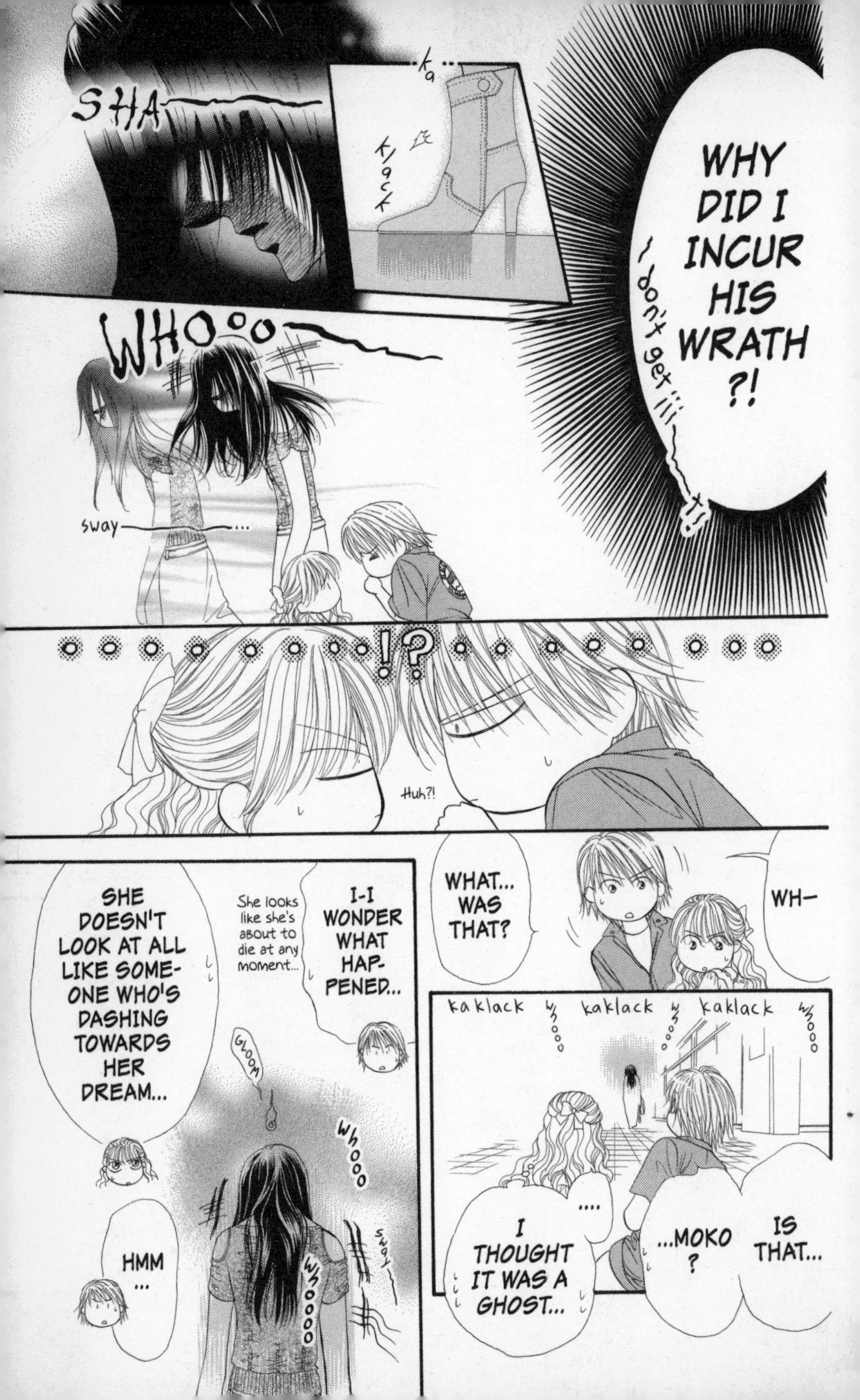
WHY DID I INCUR HIS WRATH?!
I don't get it!!!
ka... klack
SHA——
WHOoo——
sway——...
...!?...
Huh?!
WH—
WHAT... WAS THAT?
kaklack whooo kaklack whooo kaklack whooo
IS THAT... ...MOKO?
....
I THOUGHT IT WAS A GHOST...
I-I WONDER WHAT HAPPENED...
She looks like she's about to die at any moment...
SHE DOESN'T LOOK AT ALL LIKE SOME-ONE WHO'S DASHING TOWARDS HER DREAM...
GLOOM
whooo
sway
whoooo
HMM...

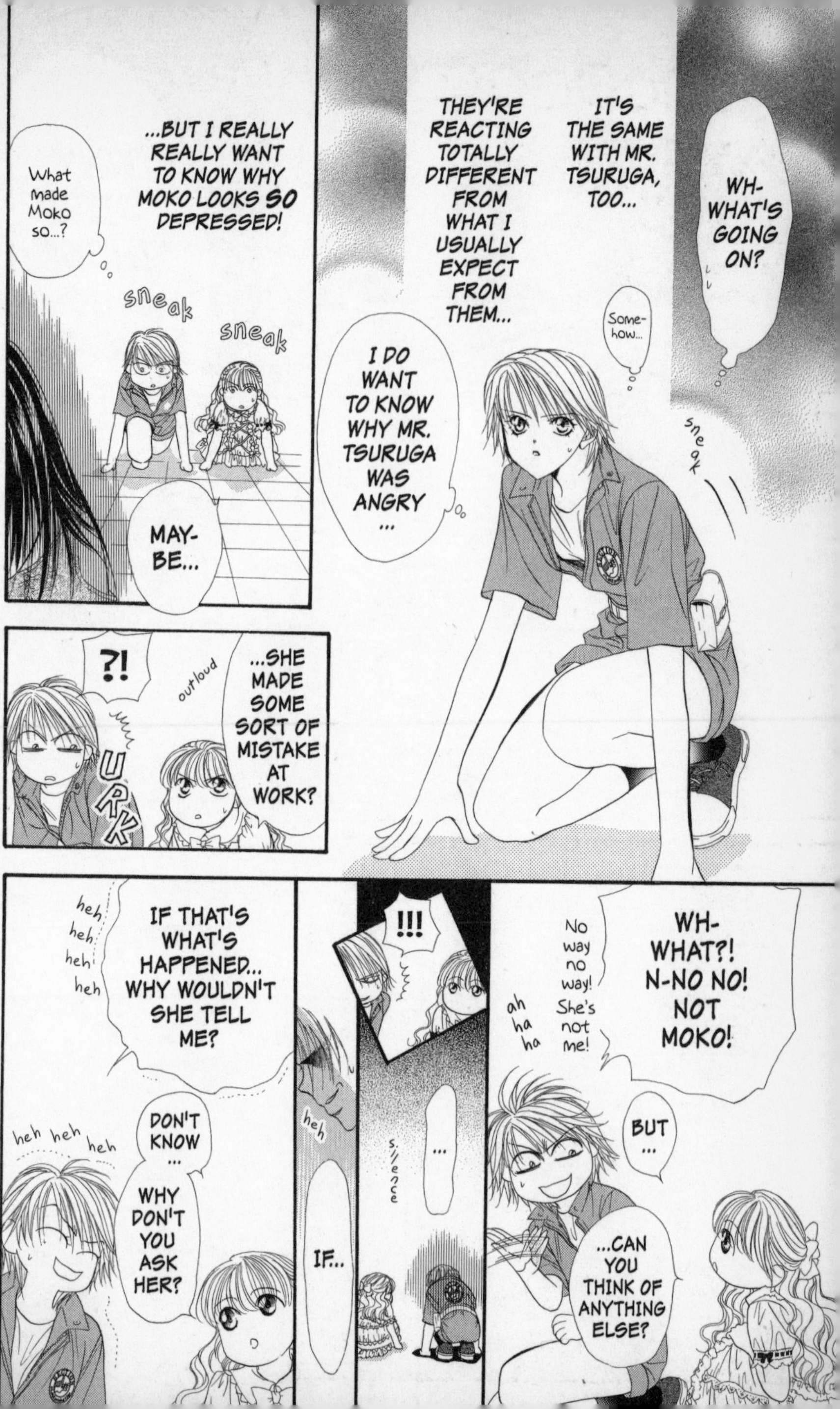
WH-WHAT'S GOING ON?
IT'S THE SAME WITH MR. TSURUGA, TOO...
THEY'RE REACTING TOTALLY DIFFERENT FROM WHAT I USUALLY EXPECT FROM THEM...
Some-how...
sneak
I DO WANT TO KNOW WHY MR. TSURUGA WAS ANGRY...
...BUT I REALLY REALLY WANT TO KNOW WHY MOKO LOOKS SO DEPRESSED!
What made Moko so...?
sneak
sneak
MAY-BE...
...SHE MADE SOME SORT OF MISTAKE AT WORK?
outloud
?!
URK
WH-WHAT?! N-NO NO! NOT MOKO!
No way no way! She's not me!
ah ha ha
BUT...
...CAN YOU THINK OF ANYTHING ELSE?
!!!
...
silence
heh
IF...
IF THAT'S WHAT'S HAPPENED... WHY WOULDN'T SHE TELL ME?
heh heh heh heh
DON'T KNOW... WHY DON'T YOU ASK HER?
heh heh heh

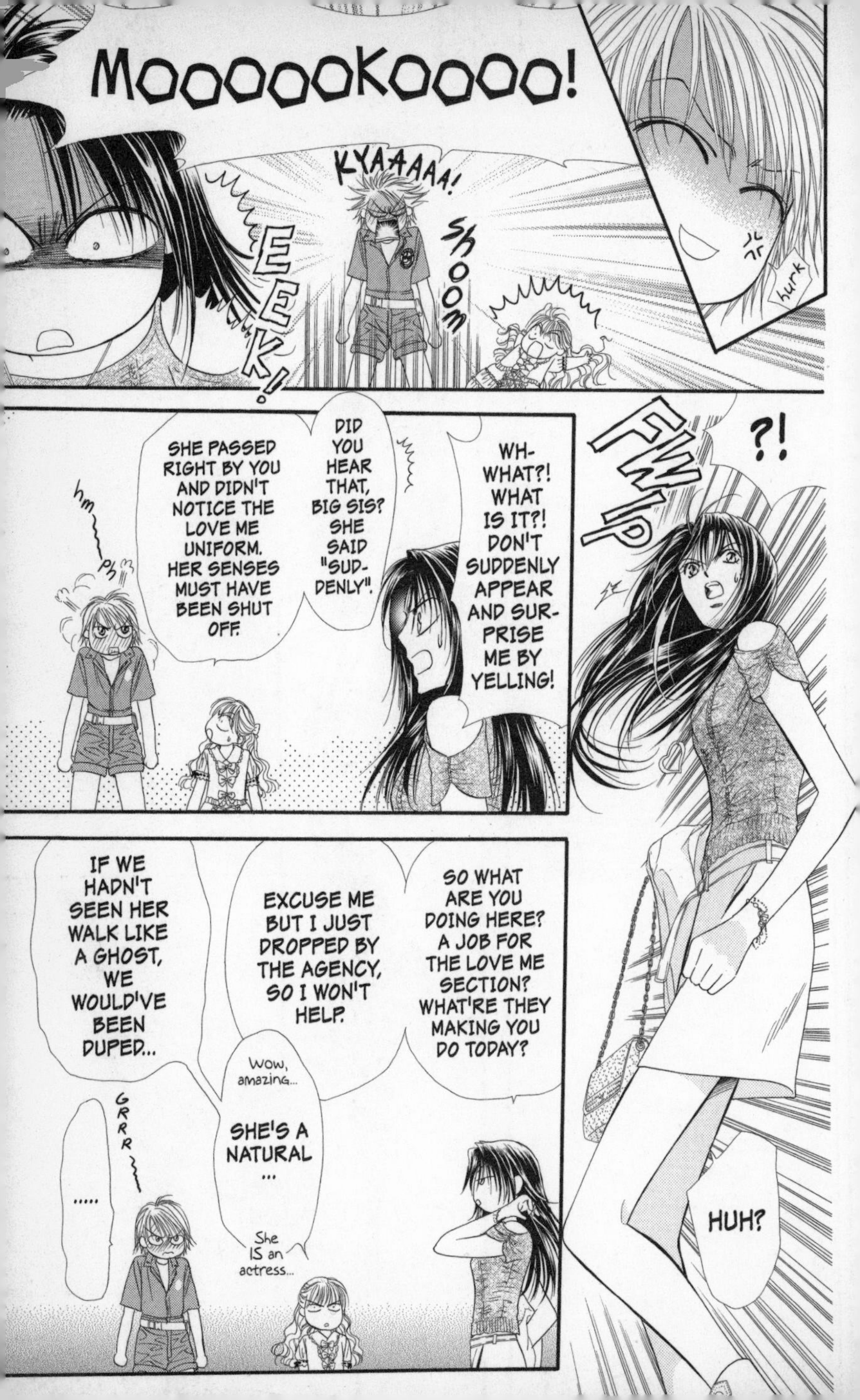
hurk
MOOOOOKOOOOO!
KYAAAAA!
SHOOOM
EEEK!
FWIP
?!
HUH?
WH-WHAT?! WHAT IS IT?! DON'T SUDDENLY APPEAR AND SURPRISE ME BY YELLING!
DID YOU HEAR THAT, BIG SIS? SHE SAID "SUDDENLY".
SHE PASSED RIGHT BY YOU AND DIDN'T NOTICE THE LOVE ME UNIFORM. HER SENSES MUST HAVE BEEN SHUT OFF.
hmph
SO WHAT ARE YOU DOING HERE? A JOB FOR THE LOVE ME SECTION? WHAT'RE THEY MAKING YOU DO TODAY?
EXCUSE ME BUT I JUST DROPPED BY THE AGENCY, SO I WON'T HELP.
IF WE HADN'T SEEN HER WALK LIKE A GHOST, WE WOULD'VE BEEN DUPED...
Wow, amazing...
SHE'S A NATURAL...
She IS an actress...
GRRR
......

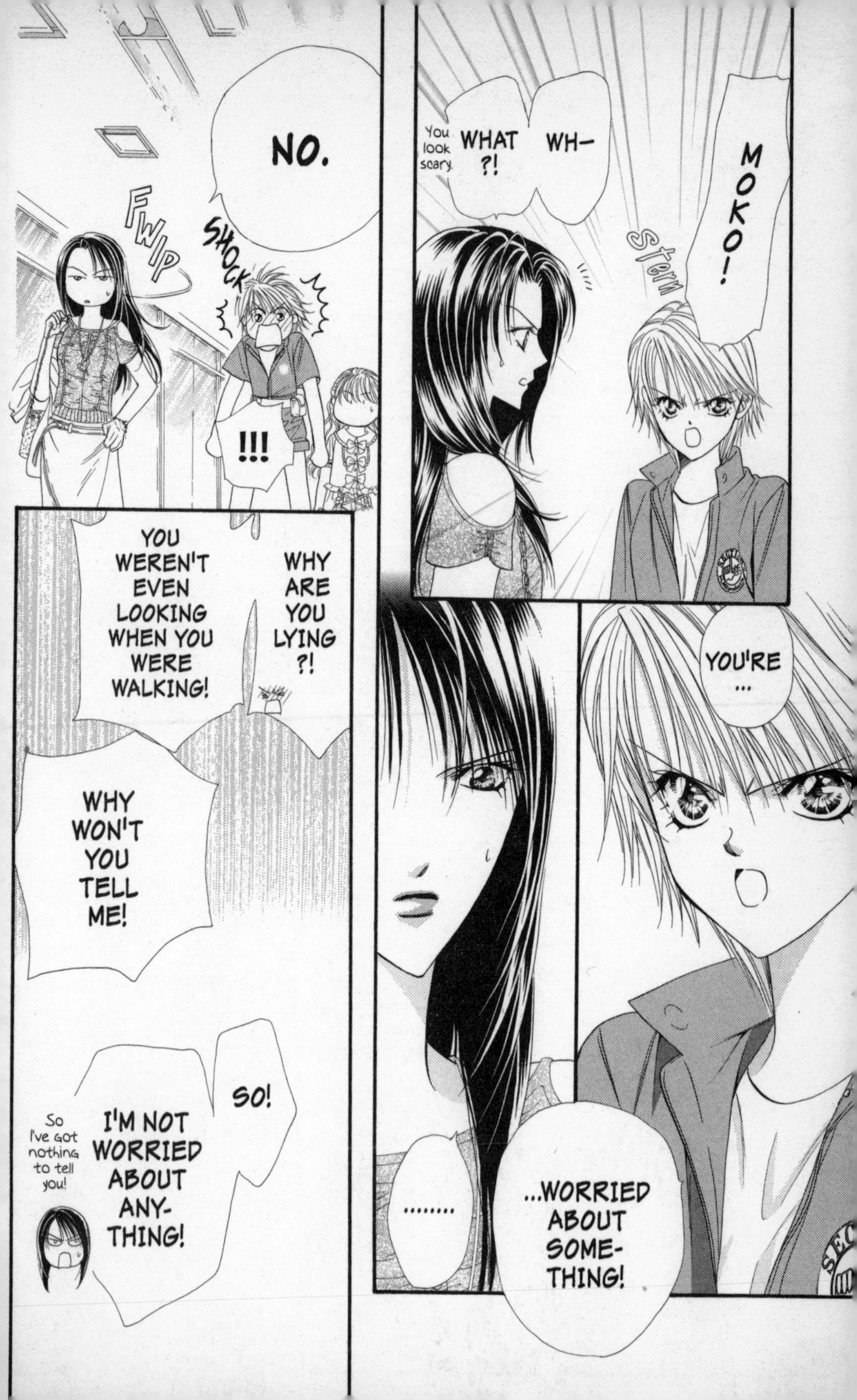
MOKO!
Stern
WH—
WHAT?!
You look scary.
YOU'RE ...
...WORRIED ABOUT SOMETHING!
........
NO.
FWIP
SHOCK
!!!
WHY ARE YOU LYING?!
YOU WEREN'T EVEN LOOKING WHEN YOU WERE WALKING!
WHY WON'T YOU TELL ME!
SO!
I'M NOT WORRIED ABOUT ANY-THING!
So I've got nothing to tell you!

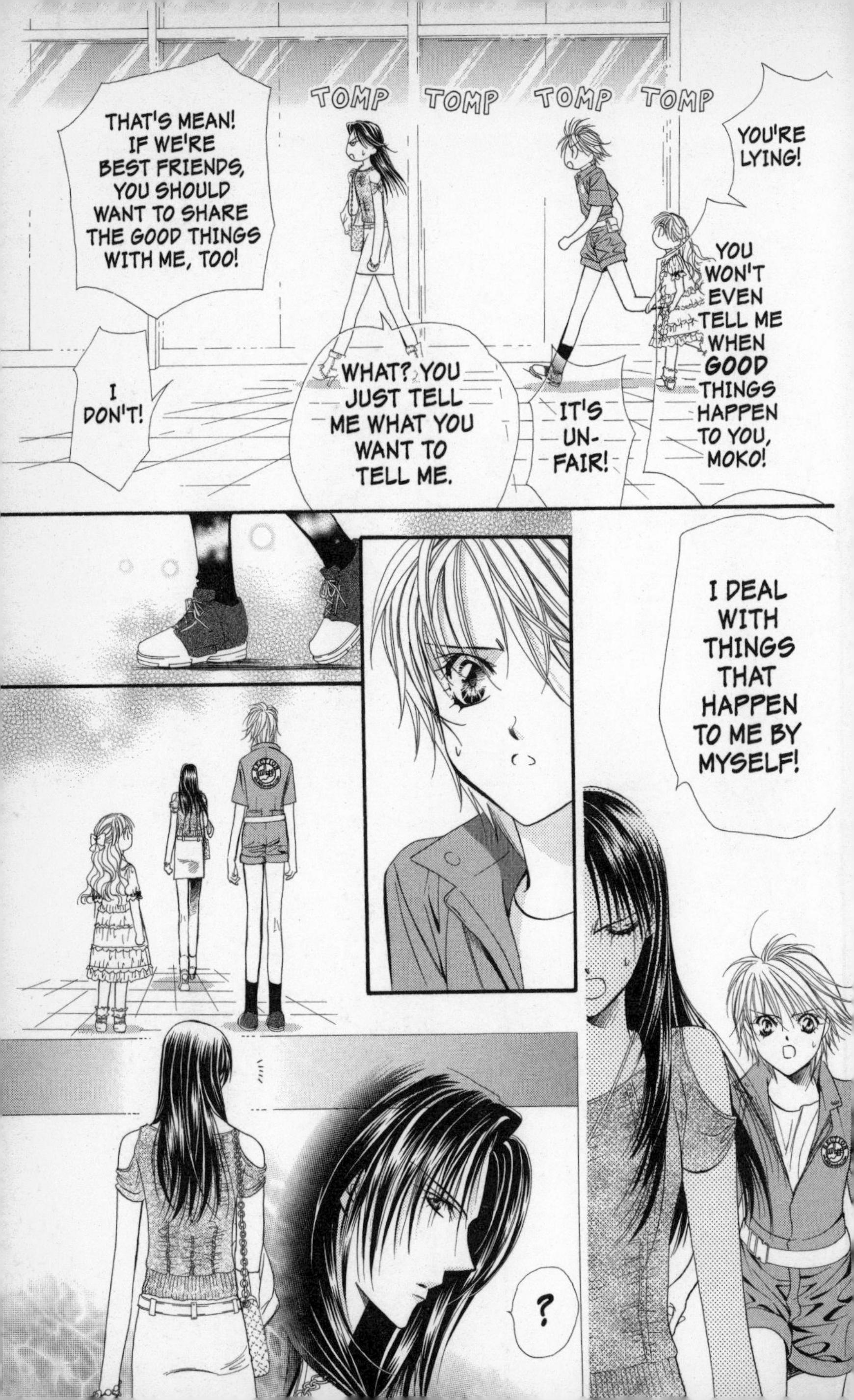
TOMP TOMP TOMP TOMP
YOU'RE LYING!
YOU WON'T EVEN TELL ME WHEN GOOD THINGS HAPPEN TO YOU, MOKO!
IT'S UN-FAIR!
WHAT? YOU JUST TELL ME WHAT YOU WANT TO TELL ME.
THAT'S MEAN! IF WE'RE BEST FRIENDS, YOU SHOULD WANT TO SHARE THE GOOD THINGS WITH ME, TOO!
I DON'T!
I DEAL WITH THINGS THAT HAPPEN TO ME BY MYSELF!
?

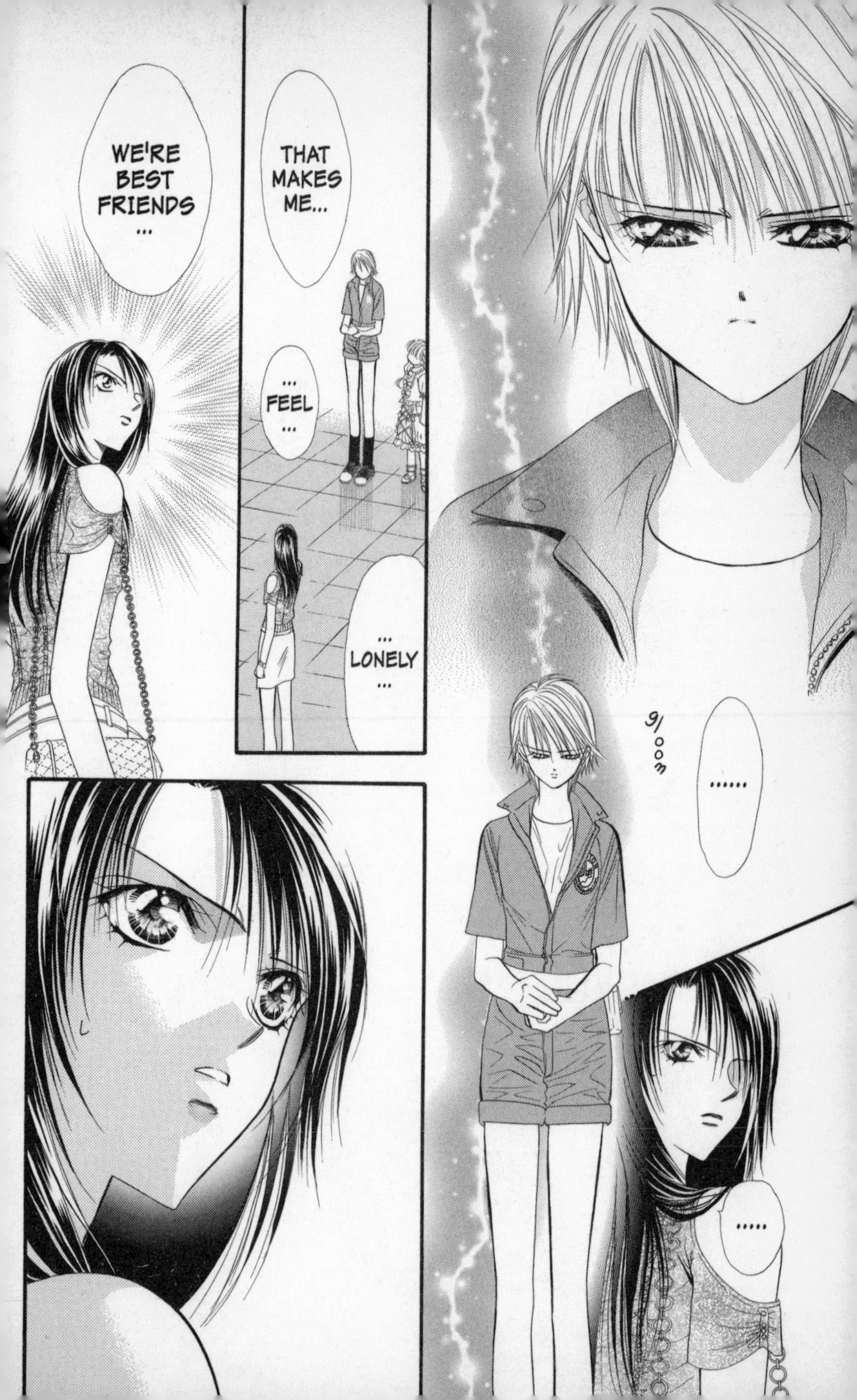
THAT MAKES ME...
... FEEL ...
... LONELY ...
WE'RE BEST FRIENDS ...
......
gloom
......

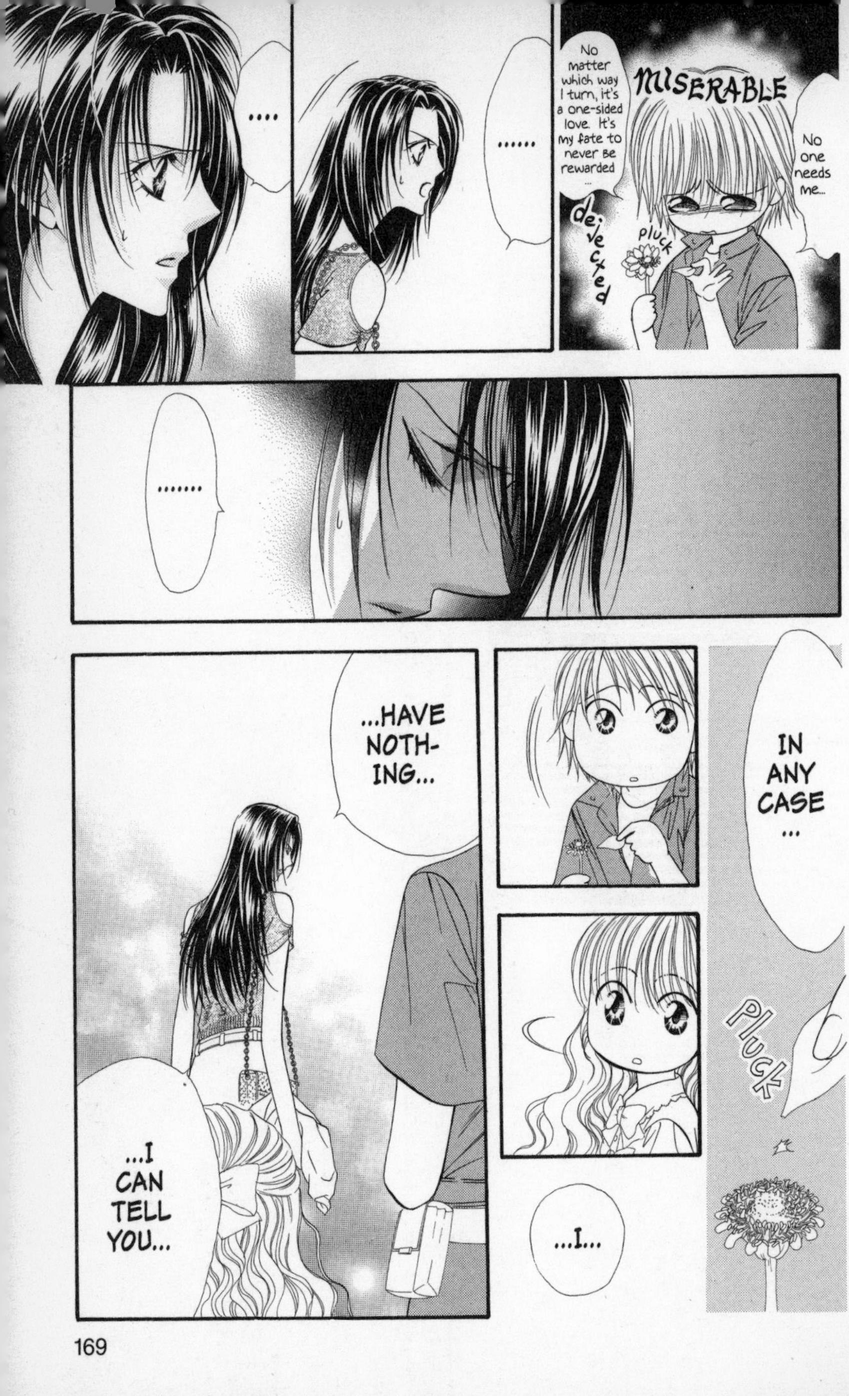
MISERABLE
No one needs me...
No matter which way I turn, it's a one-sided love. It's my fate to never be rewarded ...
pluck
dejected
......
....
........
IN ANY CASE ...
Pluck
...I...
...HAVE NOTHING...
...I CAN TELL YOU...

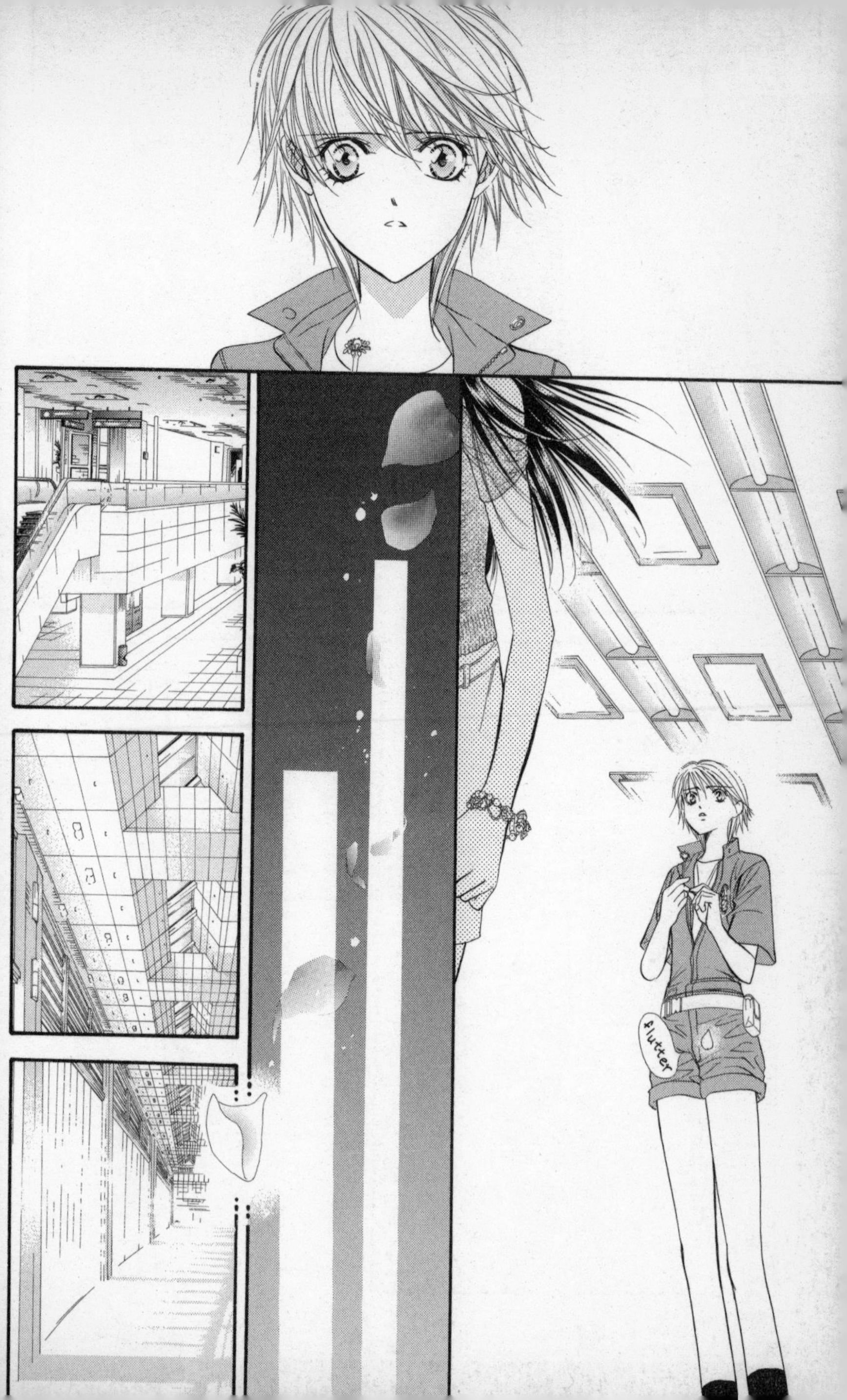
flutter

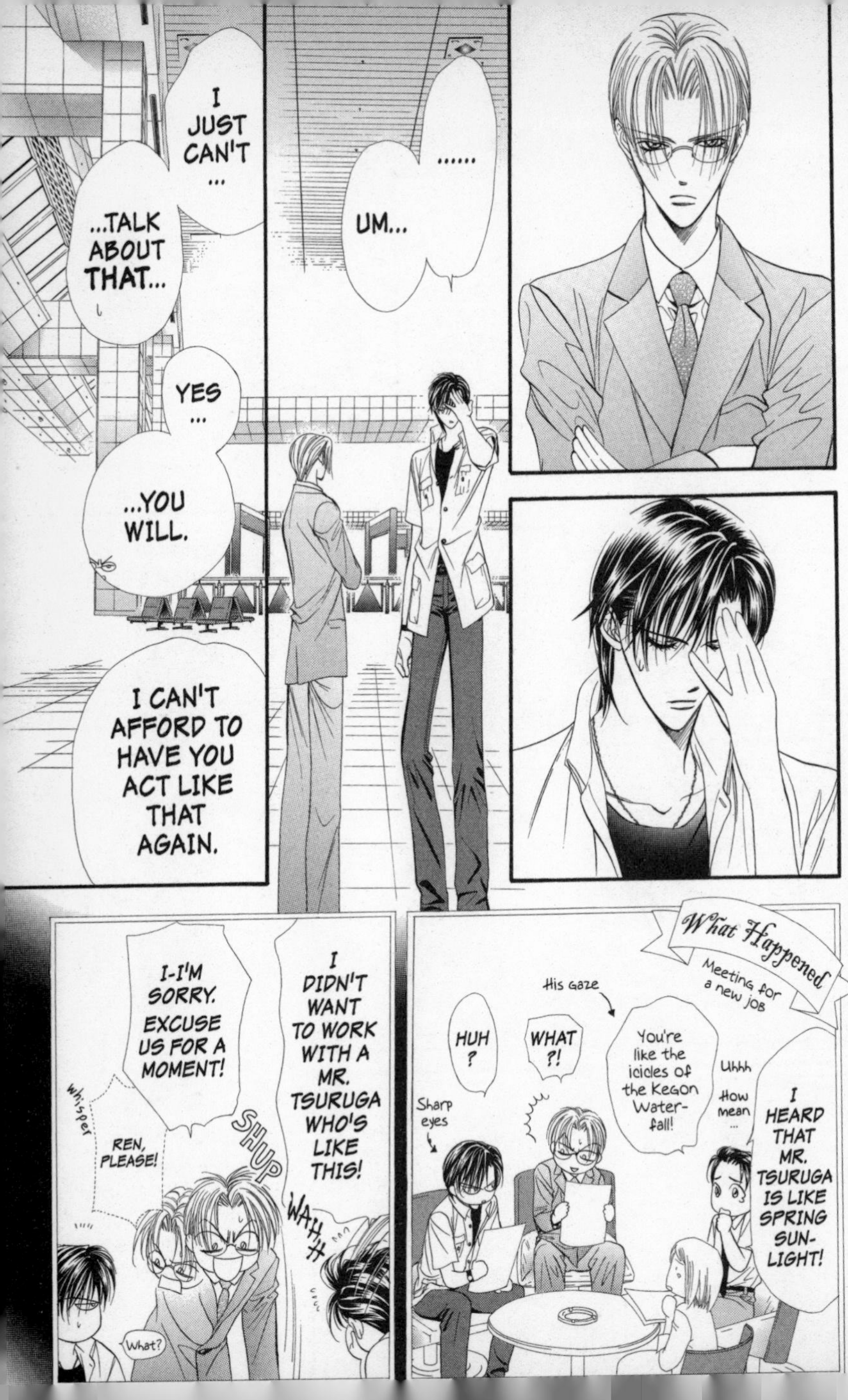
......
UM...
I JUST CAN'T ...
...TALK ABOUT THAT...
YES ...
...YOU WILL.
I CAN'T AFFORD TO HAVE YOU ACT LIKE THAT AGAIN.
What Happened
Meeting for a new job
I HEARD THAT MR. TSURUGA IS LIKE SPRING SUN-LIGHT!
Uhhh
How mean ...
You're like the icicles of the Kegon Water-fall!
His gaze
WHAT ?!
HUH ?
Sharp eyes
I DIDN'T WANT TO WORK WITH A MR. TSURUGA WHO'S LIKE THIS!
I-I'M SORRY. EXCUSE US FOR A MOMENT!
SHUP
WAH
whisper
REN, PLEASE!
What?

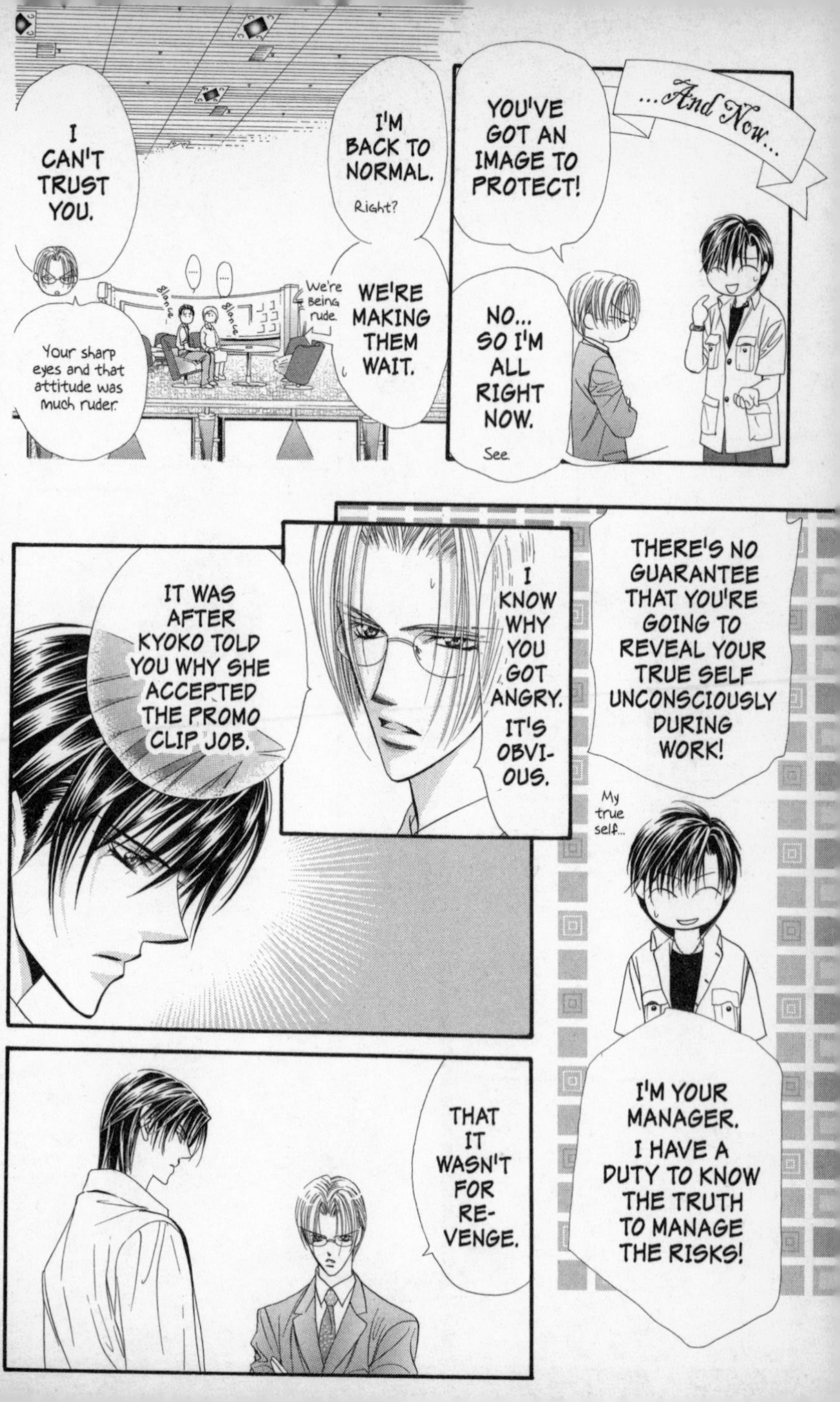
...And Now...
YOU'VE GOT AN IMAGE TO PROTECT!
NO... SO I'M ALL RIGHT NOW.
See.
I'M BACK TO NORMAL.
Right?
WE'RE MAKING THEM WAIT.
We're Being rude.
I CAN'T TRUST YOU.
Your sharp eyes and that attitude was much ruder.
THERE'S NO GUARANTEE THAT YOU'RE GOING TO REVEAL YOUR TRUE SELF UNCONSCIOUSLY DURING WORK!
My true self...
I'M YOUR MANAGER. I HAVE A DUTY TO KNOW THE TRUTH TO MANAGE THE RISKS!
I KNOW WHY YOU GOT ANGRY.
IT'S OBVIOUS.
IT WAS AFTER KYOKO TOLD YOU WHY SHE ACCEPTED THE PROMO CLIP JOB.
THAT IT WASN'T FOR REVENGE.

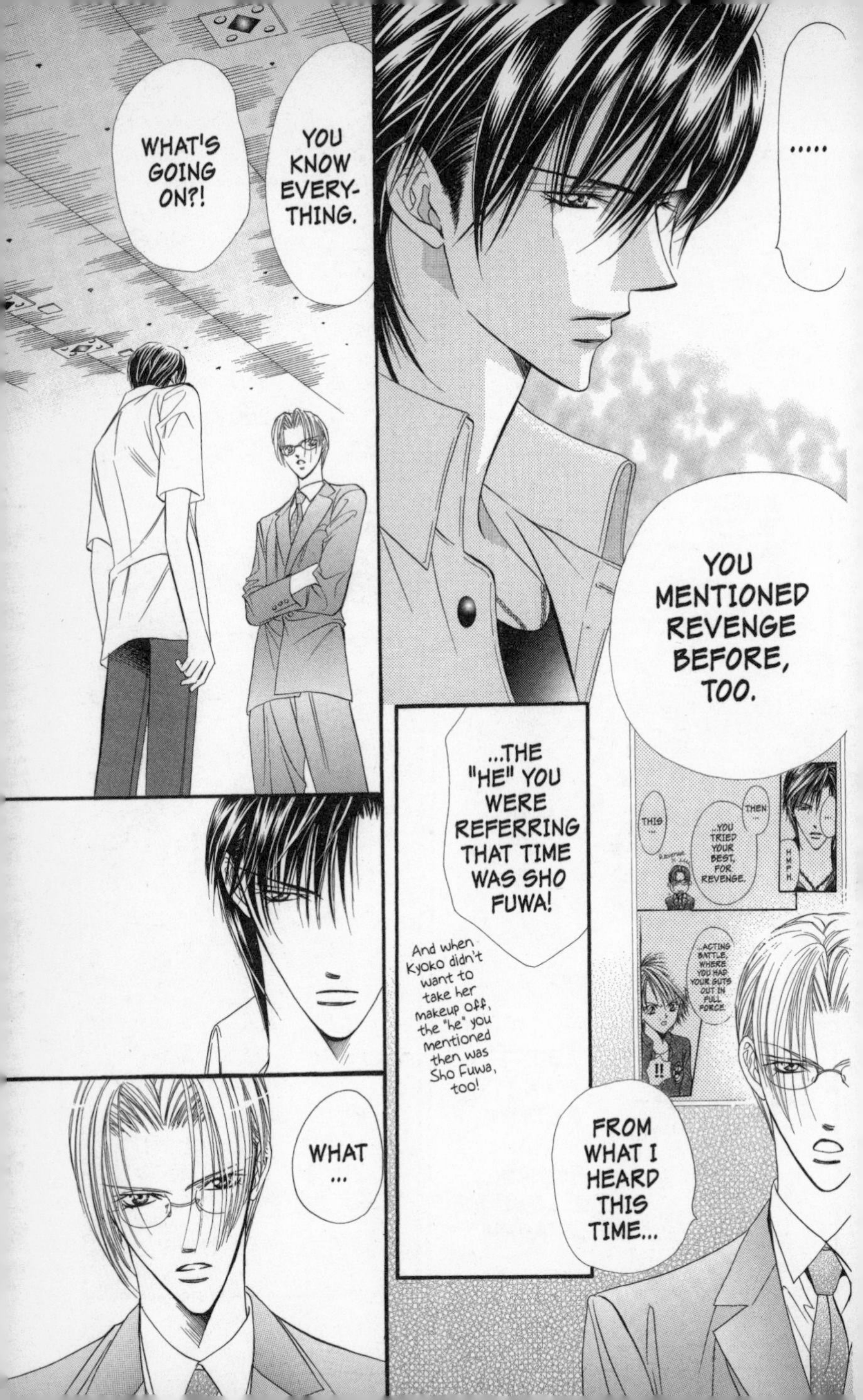
.....
YOU MENTIONED REVENGE BEFORE, TOO.
YOU KNOW EVERY-THING.
WHAT'S GOING ON?!
FROM WHAT I HEARD THIS TIME...
HMPH
THEN ...
...YOU TRIED YOUR BEST, FOR REVENGE.
THIS ...
...ACTING BATTLE, WHERE YOU HAD YOUR GUTS OUT IN FULL FORCE.
!!
...THE "HE" YOU WERE REFERRING THAT TIME WAS SHO FUWA!
And when Kyoko didn't want to take her makeup off, the "he" you mentioned then was Sho Fuwa, too!
WHAT ...

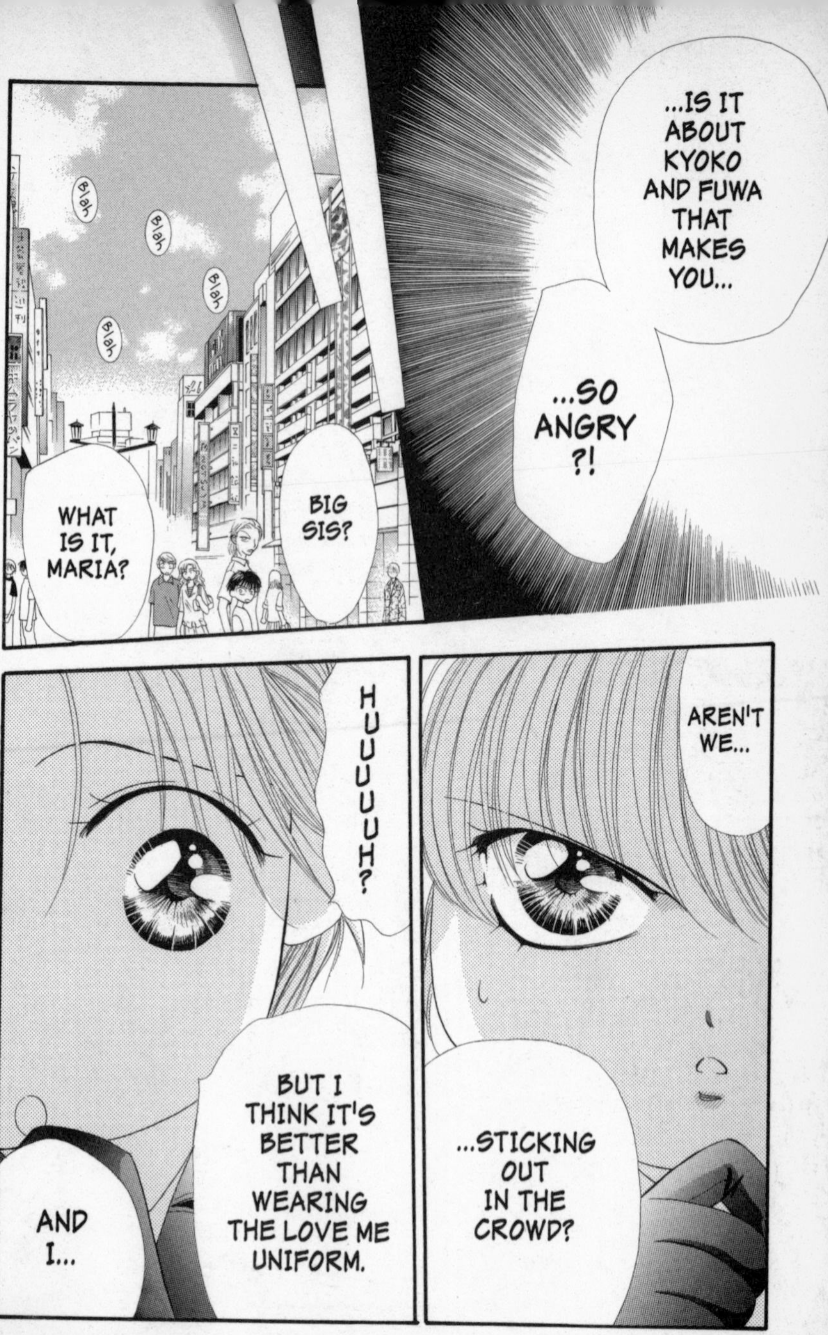
...IS IT ABOUT KYOKO AND FUWA THAT MAKES YOU...
...SO ANGRY?!
Blah
Blah
Blah
Blah
BIG SIS?
WHAT IS IT, MARIA?
AREN'T WE...
...STICKING OUT IN THE CROWD?
HUUUUUH?
BUT I THINK IT'S BETTER THAN WEARING THE LOVE ME UNIFORM.
AND I...

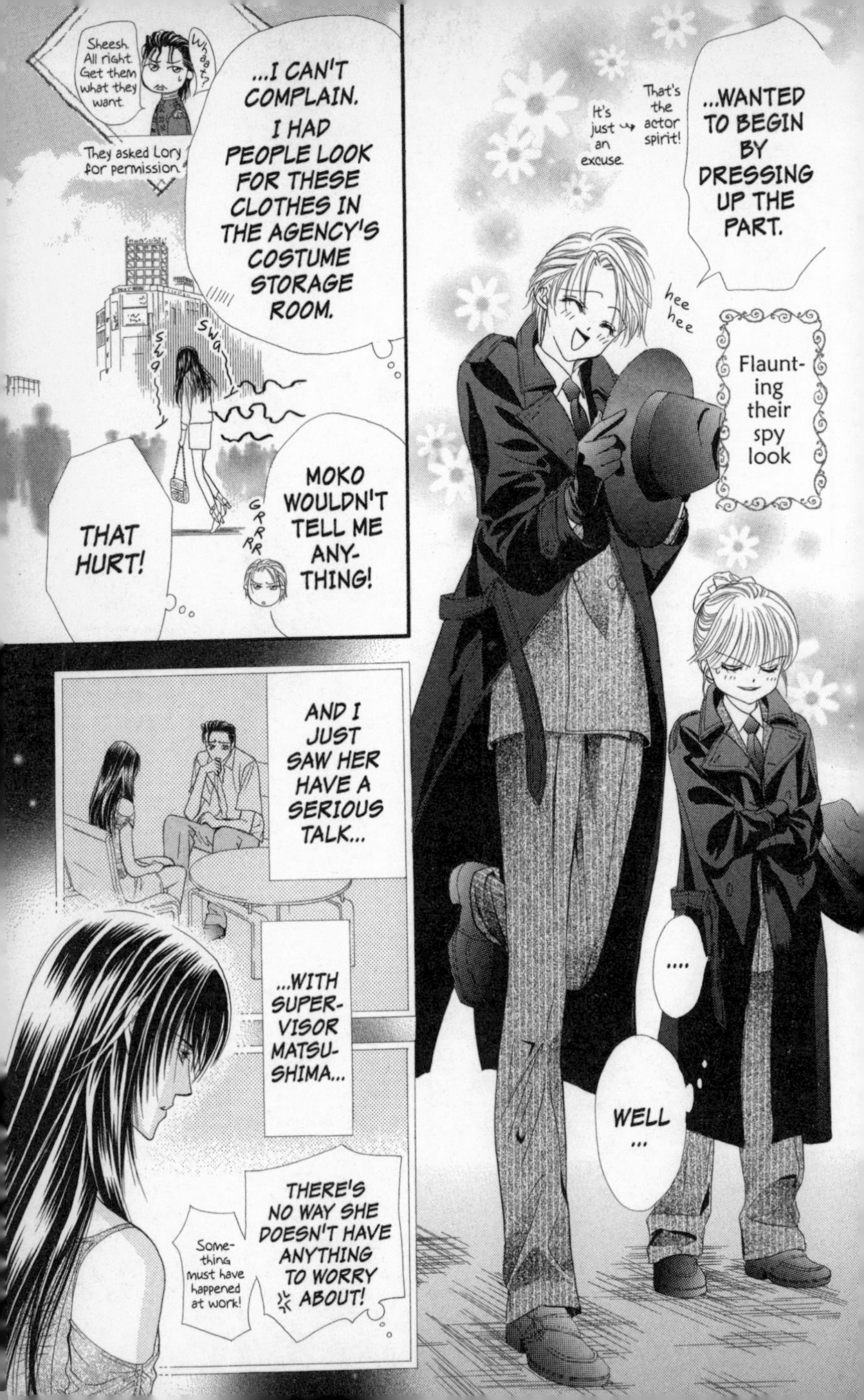
...WANTED TO BEGIN BY DRESSING UP THE PART.
That's the actor spirit!
It's just an excuse.
hee hee
Flaunt-ing their spy look
....
WELL...
...I CAN'T COMPLAIN. I HAD PEOPLE LOOK FOR THESE CLOTHES IN THE AGENCY'S COSTUME STORAGE ROOM.
Whaa?
Sheesh. All right. Get them what they want.
They asked Lory for permission.
MOKO WOULDN'T TELL ME ANY-THING!
GRRR
THAT HURT!
AND I JUST SAW HER HAVE A SERIOUS TALK...
...WITH SUPER-VISOR MATSU-SHIMA...
THERE'S NO WAY SHE DOESN'T HAVE ANYTHING TO WORRY ABOUT!
Some-thing must have happened at work!

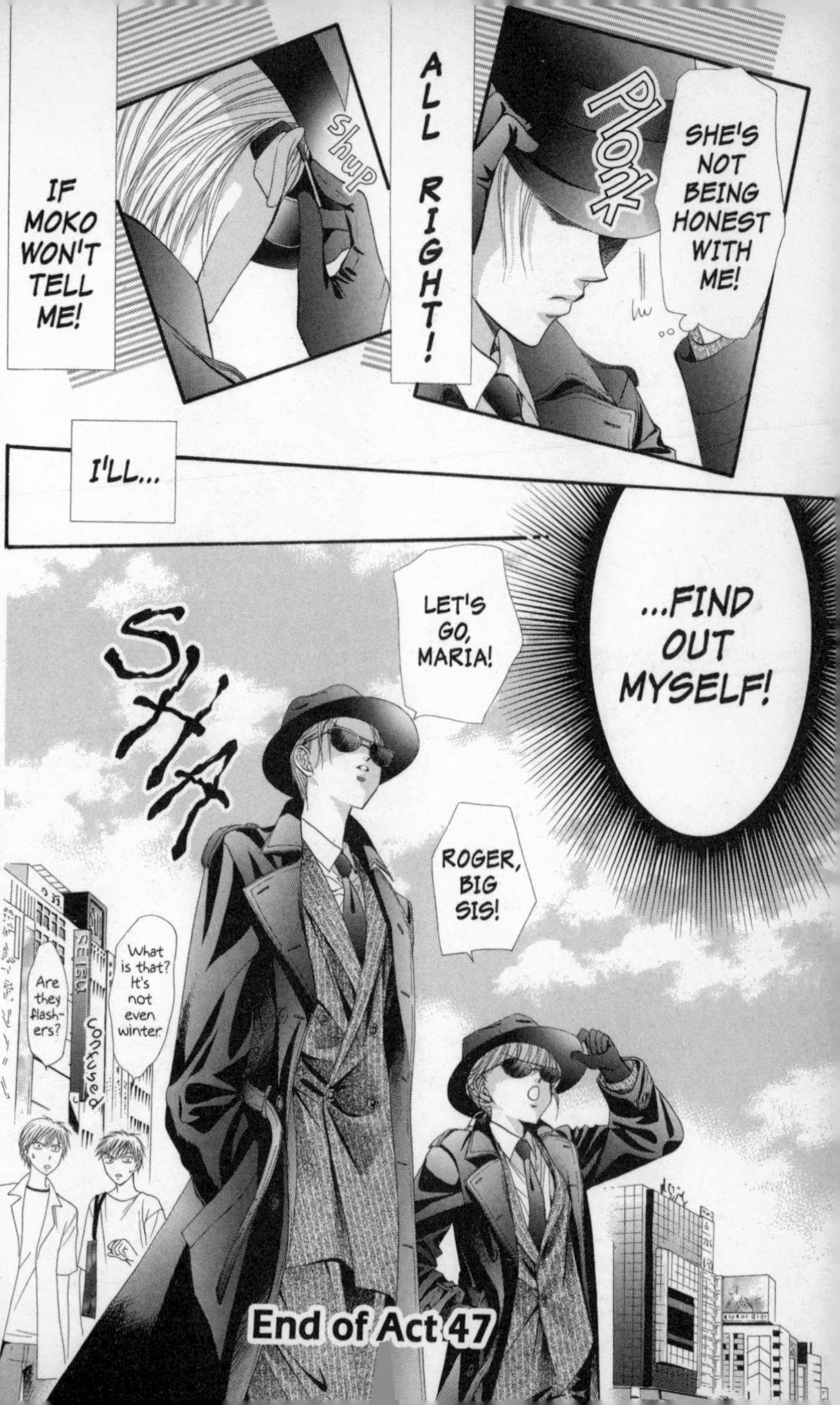
Plonk
SHE'S NOT BEING HONEST WITH ME!
ALL RIGHT!
shup
IF MOKO WON'T TELL ME!
I'LL...
...FIND OUT MYSELF!
LET'S GO, MARIA!
SHA
ROGER, BIG SIS!
What is that? It's not even winter.
Are they flashers?
confused
End of Act 47

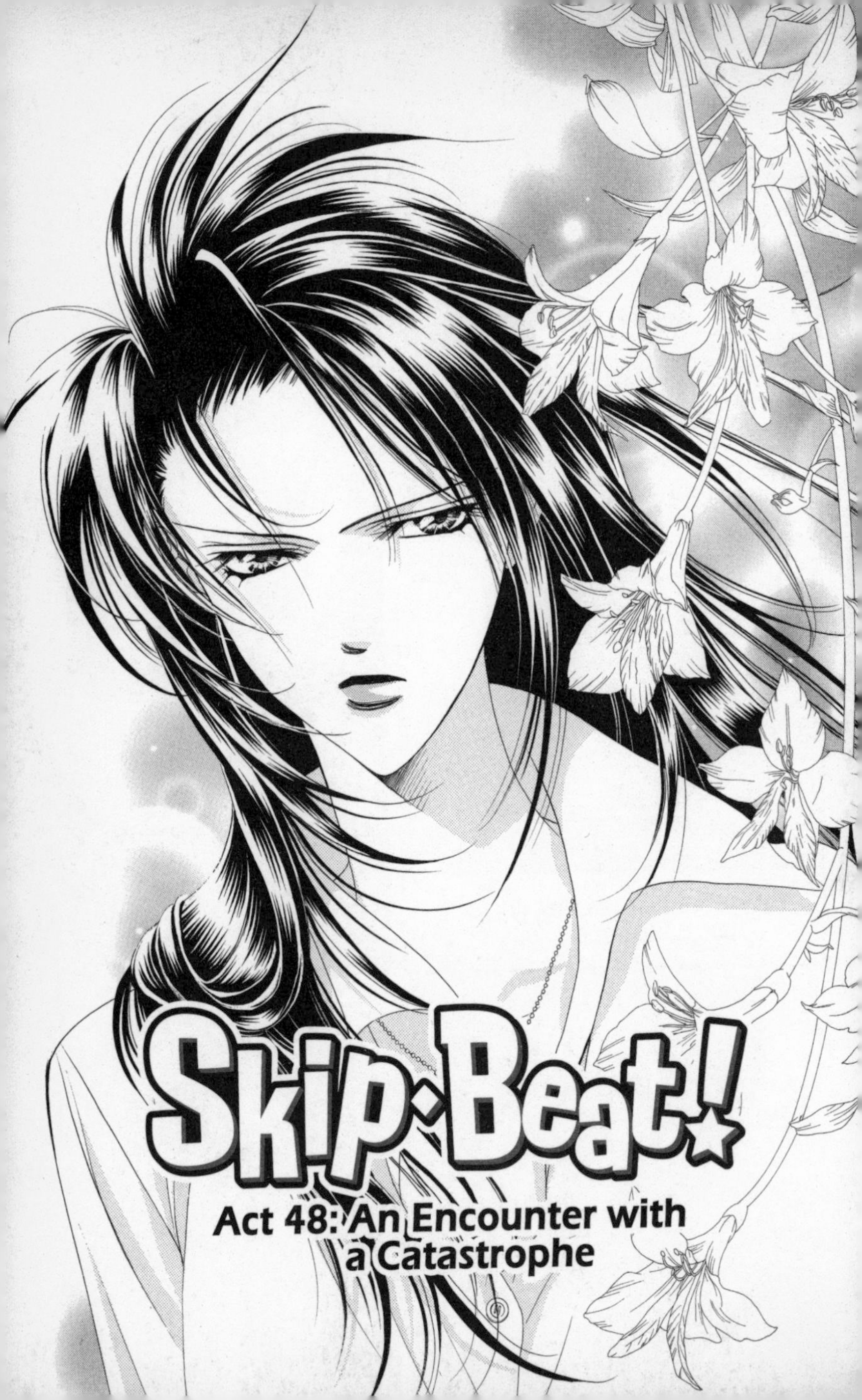
Skip·Beat!
Act 48: An Encounter with a Catastrophe

**Thin rubber gloves that doctors use during operations**

PUP

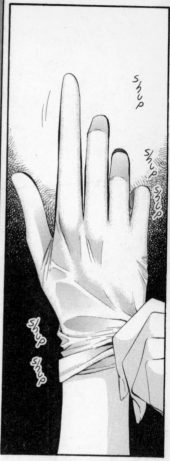

shup

shup shup

shup

shup

URK!

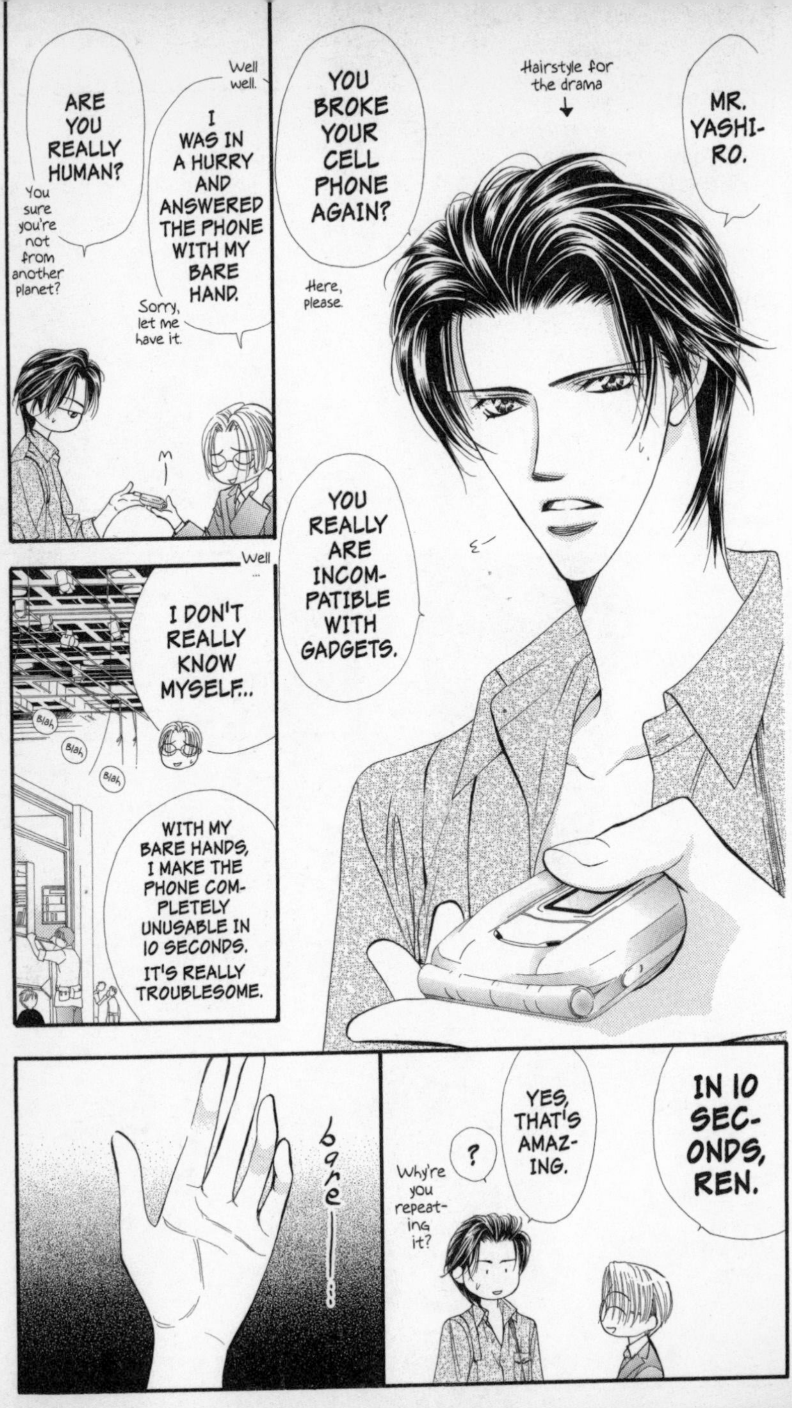
Hairstyle for the drama
MR. YASHIRO.
YOU BROKE YOUR CELL PHONE AGAIN?
Here, please.
YOU REALLY ARE INCOMPATIBLE WITH GADGETS.
Well well.
I WAS IN A HURRY AND ANSWERED THE PHONE WITH MY BARE HAND.
Sorry, let me have it.
ARE YOU REALLY HUMAN?
You sure you're not from another planet?
Well ...
I DON'T REALLY KNOW MYSELF...
Blah
Blah
Blah
WITH MY BARE HANDS, I MAKE THE PHONE COMPLETELY UNUSABLE IN 10 SECONDS.
IT'S REALLY TROUBLESOME.
IN 10 SECONDS, REN.
YES, THAT'S AMAZING.
?
Why're you repeating it?
bare

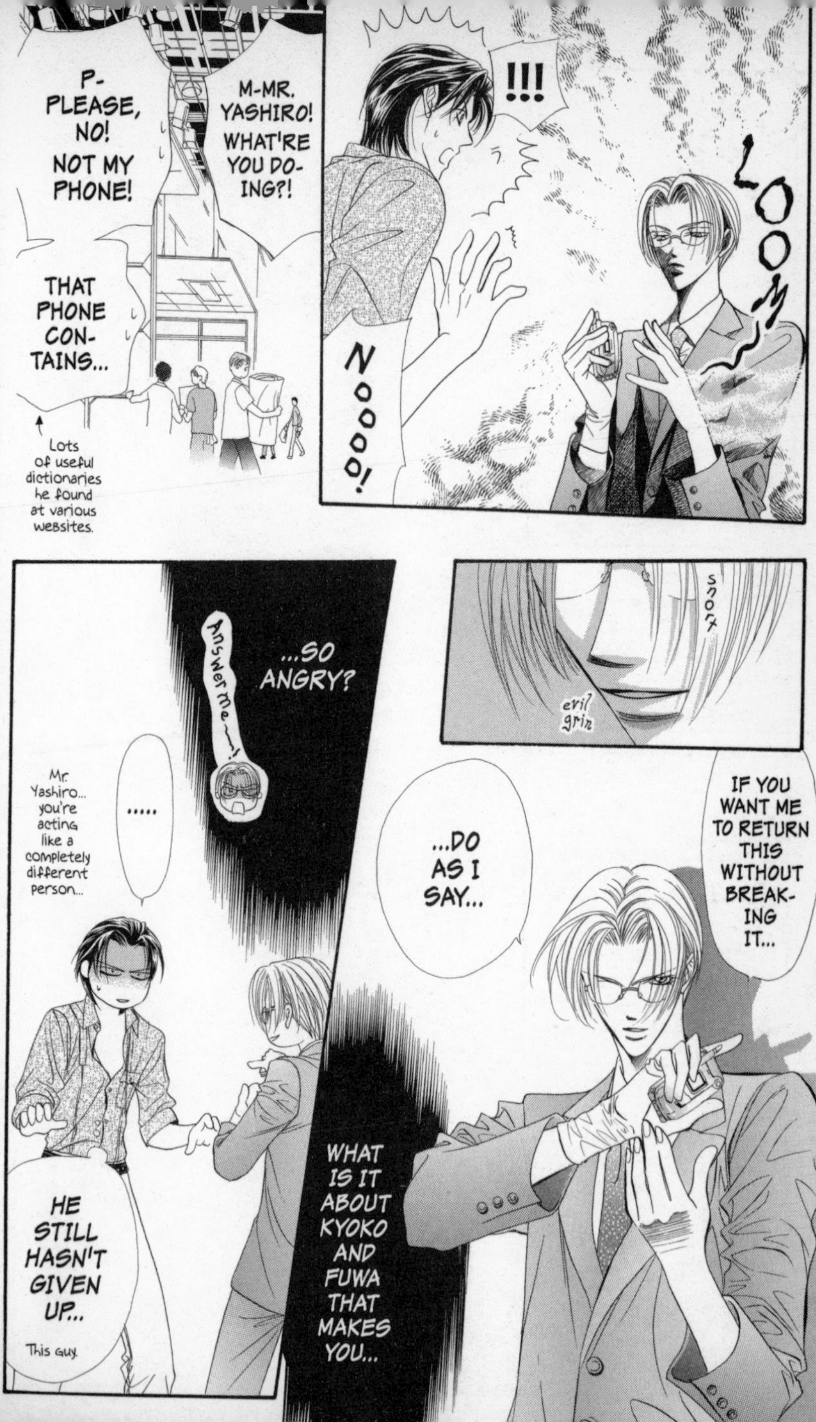
!!!
LOOM
NOOOO!
M-MR. YASHIRO! WHAT'RE YOU DO-ING?!
P-PLEASE, NO! NOT MY PHONE!
THAT PHONE CON-TAINS...
Lots of useful dictionaries he found at various websites.
snort
evil grin
IF YOU WANT ME TO RETURN THIS WITHOUT BREAK-ING IT...
...DO AS I SAY...
WHAT IS IT ABOUT KYOKO AND FUWA THAT MAKES YOU...
...SO ANGRY?
Answer me~!
.....
Mr. Yashiro... you're acting like a completely different person...
HE STILL HASN'T GIVEN UP...
This guy.

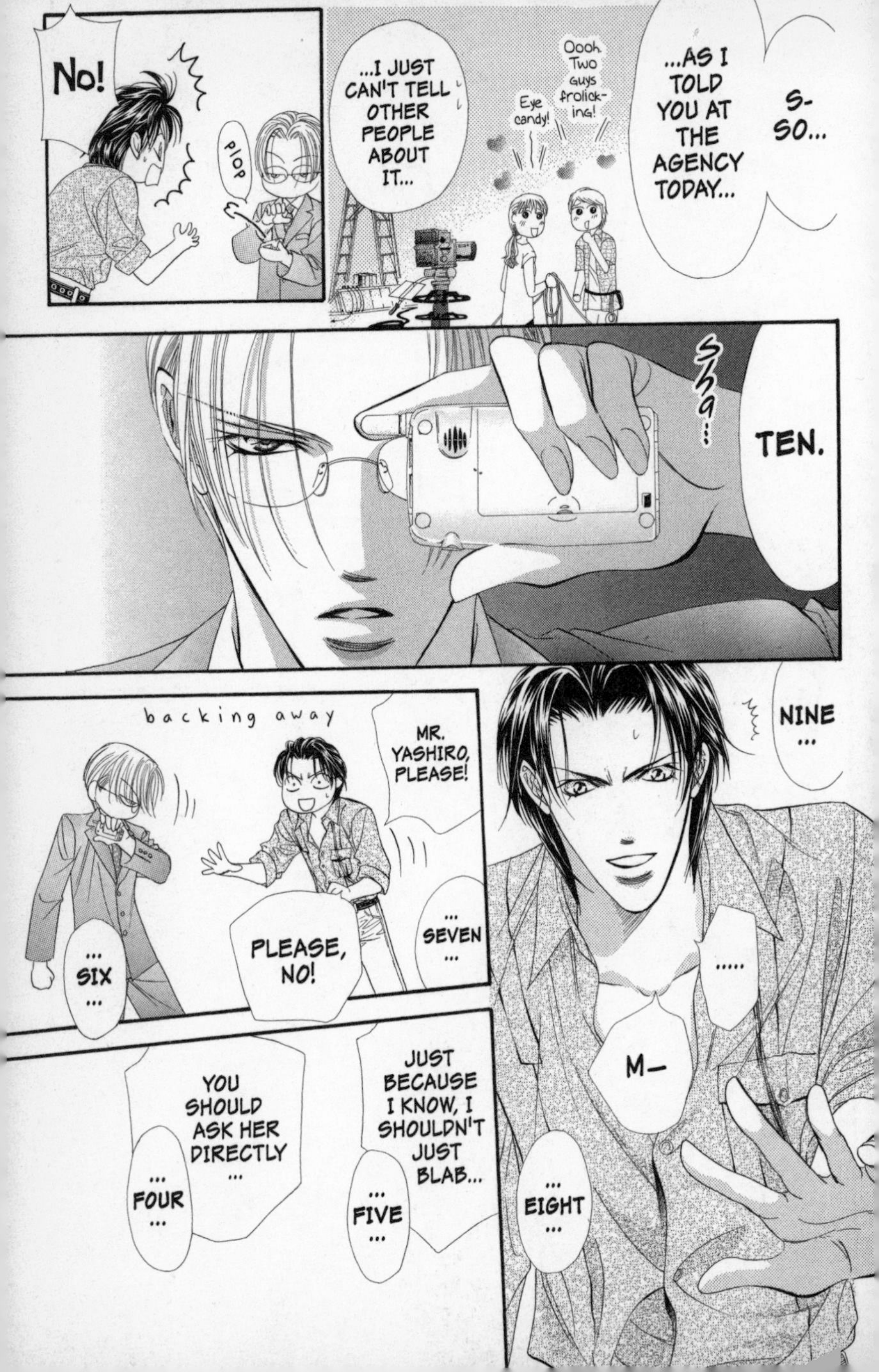
S-SO...
...AS I TOLD YOU AT THE AGENCY TODAY...
Oooh. Two guys frolicking!
Eye candy!
...I JUST CAN'T TELL OTHER PEOPLE ABOUT IT...
No!
PLOP
TEN.
Sha...
NINE ...
.....
M—
... EIGHT ...
backing away
MR. YASHIRO, PLEASE!
... SEVEN ...
PLEASE, NO!
... SIX ...
JUST BECAUSE I KNOW, I SHOULDN'T JUST BLAB...
... FIVE ...
YOU SHOULD ASK HER DIRECTLY ...
... FOUR ...

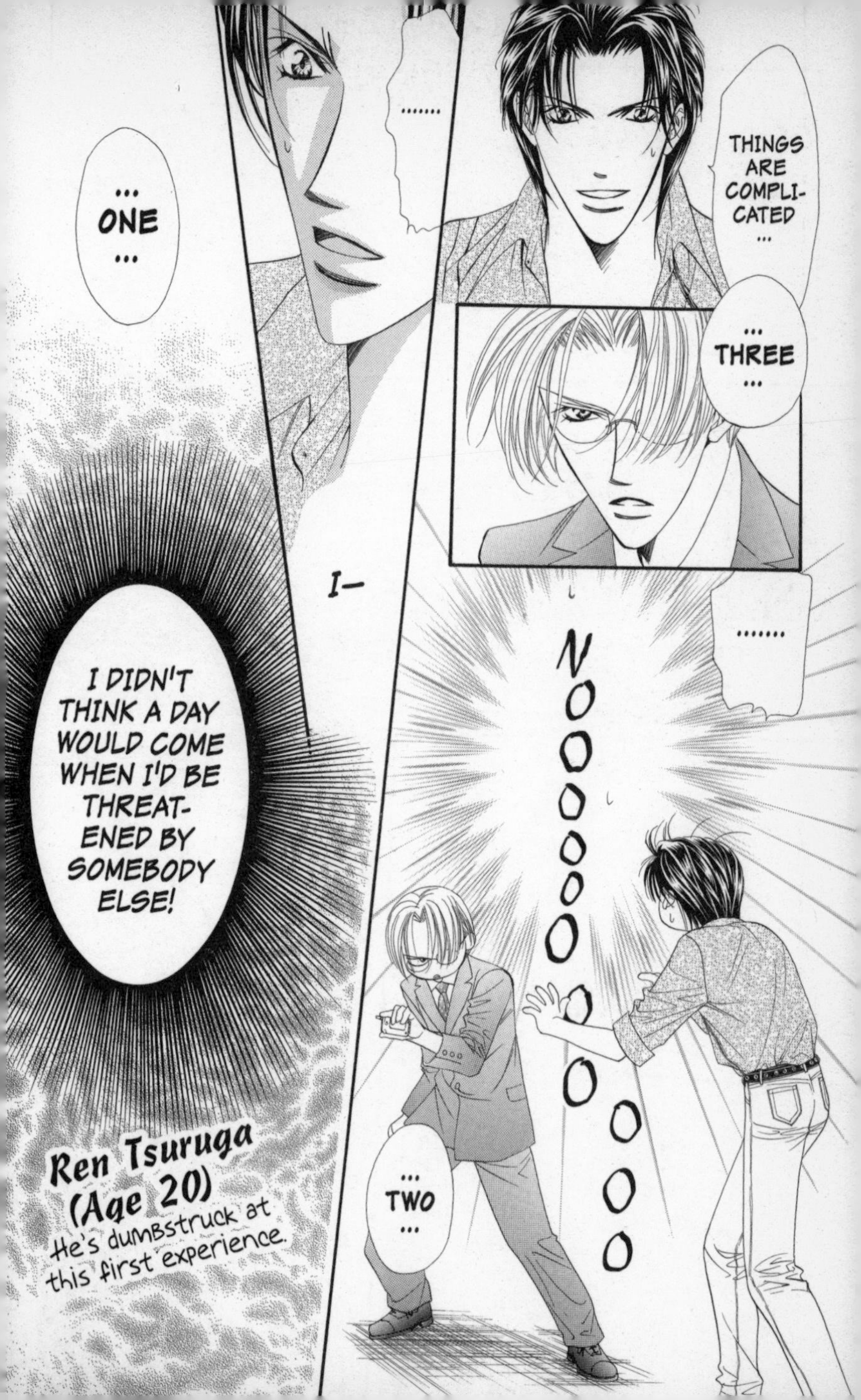
THINGS ARE COMPLICATED ...
.......
... THREE ...
.......
NOOOOOOOOOOOOO
... TWO ...
I—
... ONE ...
I DIDN'T THINK A DAY WOULD COME WHEN I'D BE THREATENED BY SOMEBODY ELSE!
Ren Tsuruga (Age 20)
He's dumbstruck at this first experience.

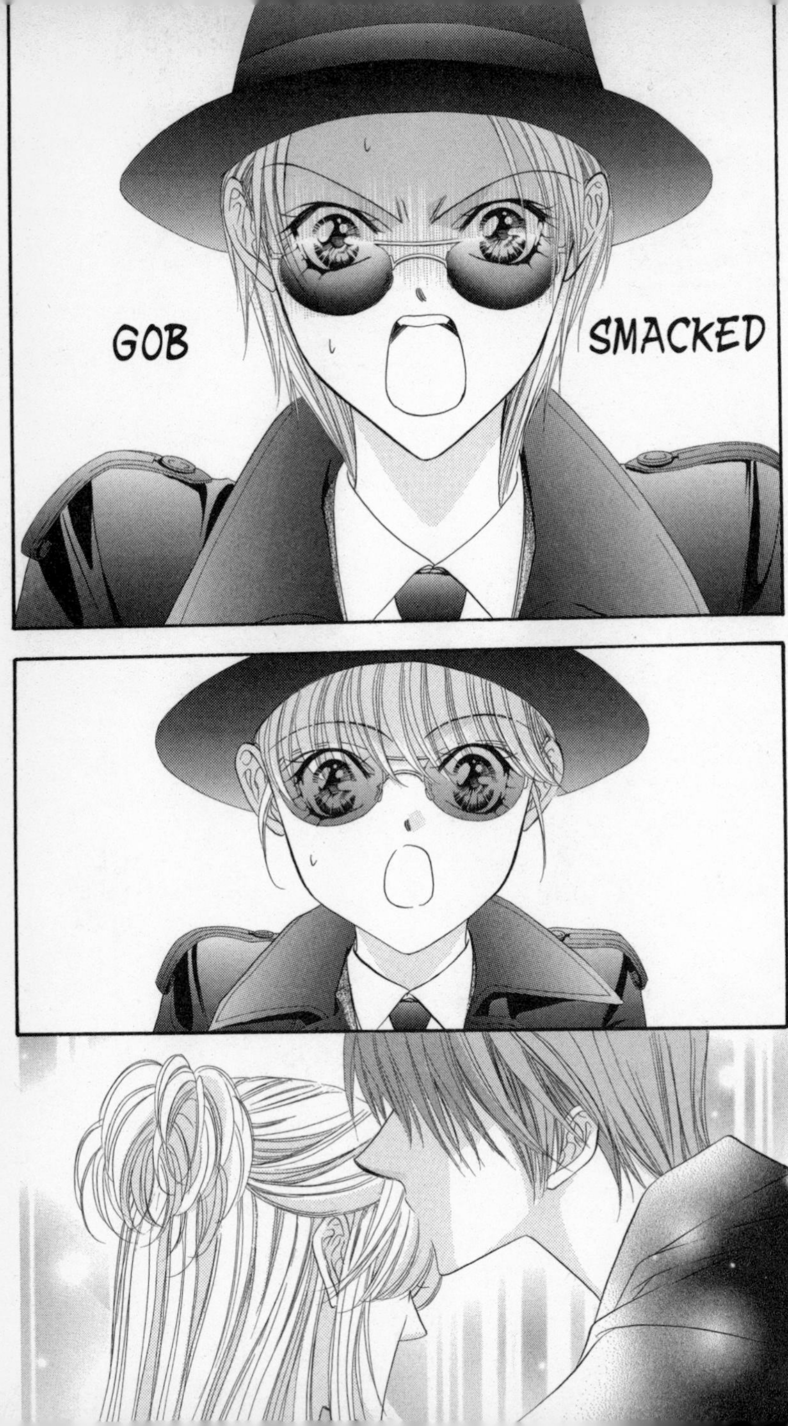
GOB
SMACKED

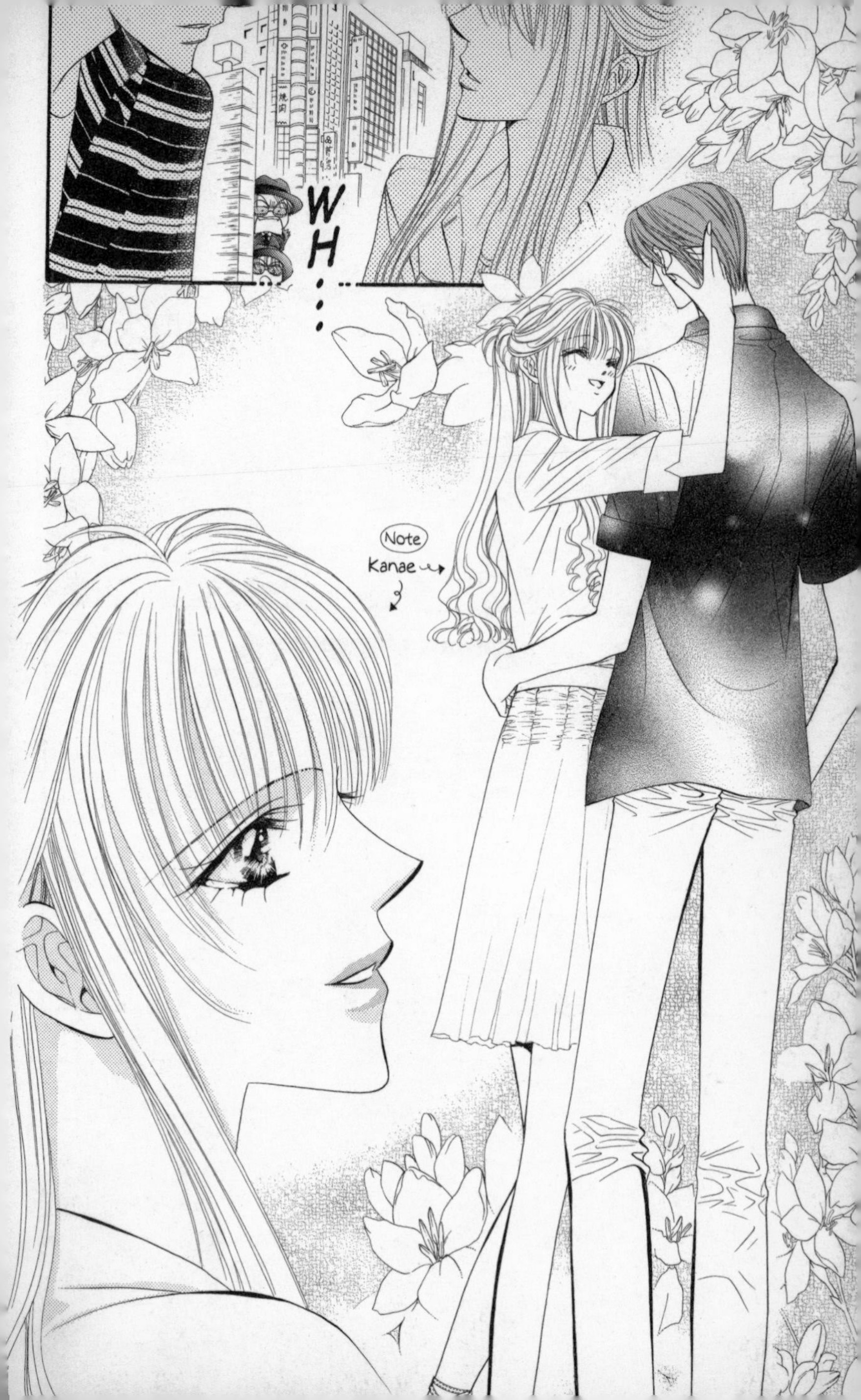
WH...
Note
Kanae

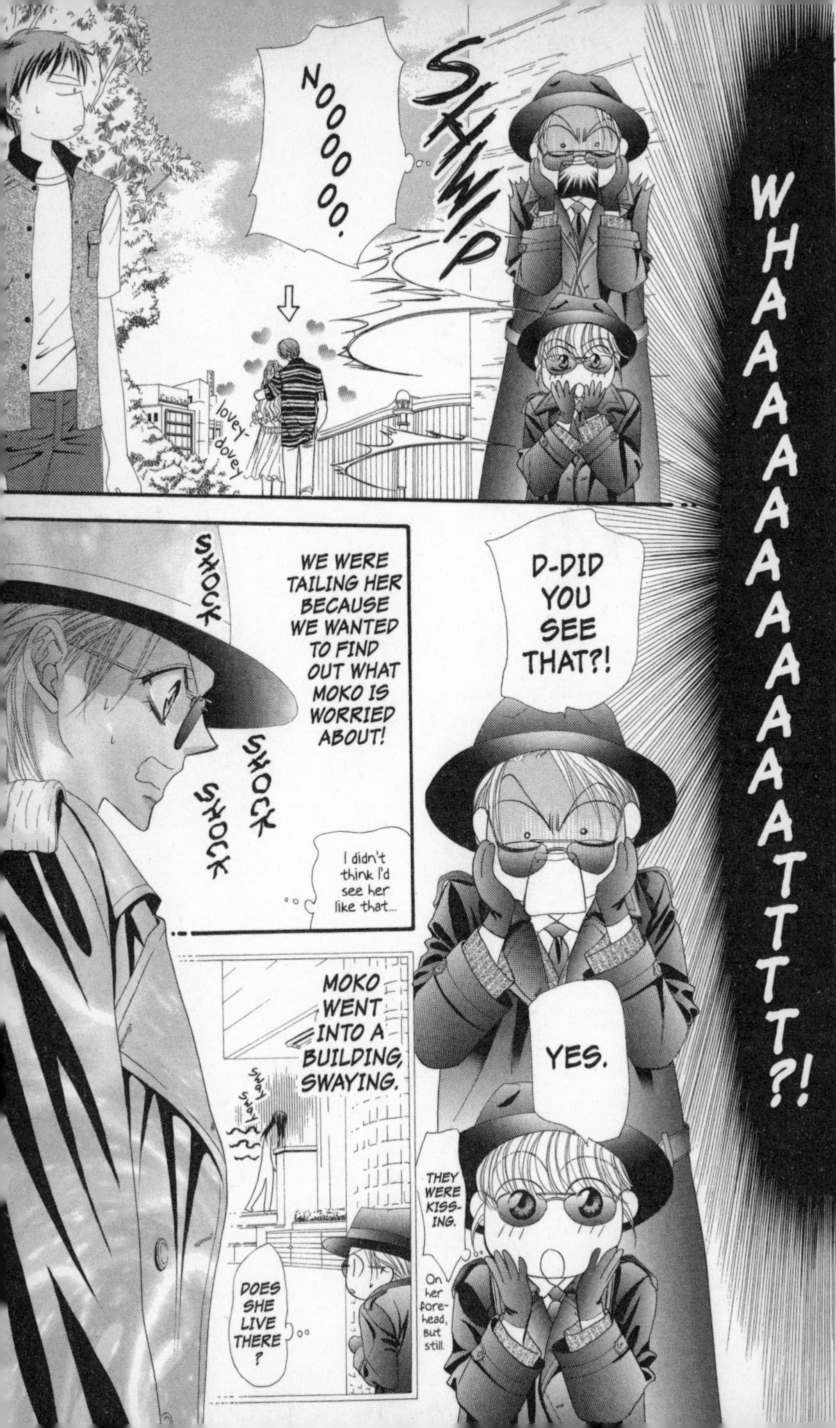
WHAAAAAAAAAAATTTTT?!
SHWIP
NOOOOOO.
lovey-dovey
D-DID YOU SEE THAT?!
YES.
THEY WERE KISS-ING.
On her forehead, but still.
WE WERE TAILING HER BECAUSE WE WANTED TO FIND OUT WHAT MOKO IS WORRIED ABOUT!
SHOCK
SHOCK
SHOCK
I didn't think I'd see her like that...
MOKO WENT INTO A BUILDING, SWAYING.
sway sway
DOES SHE LIVE THERE?

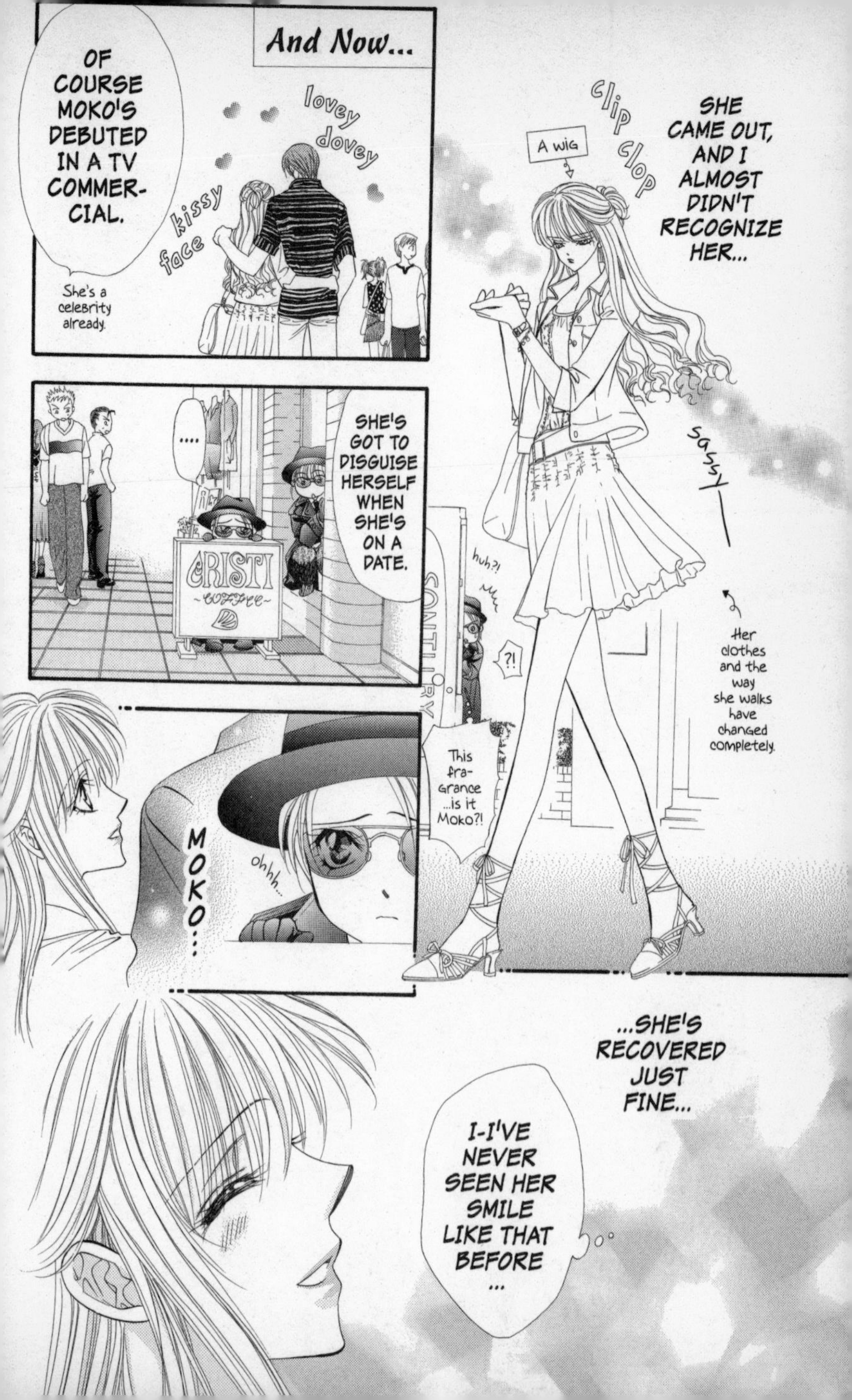
clip clop
SHE CAME OUT, AND I ALMOST DIDN'T RECOGNIZE HER...
A WIG
sassy
Her clothes and the way she walks have changed completely.
huh?!
?!
This fragrance ...is it Moko?!
And Now...
OF COURSE MOKO'S DEBUTED IN A TV COMMERCIAL.
lovey dovey
kissy face
She's a celebrity already.
SHE'S GOT TO DISGUISE HERSELF WHEN SHE'S ON A DATE.
....
ARISTI
~COFFEE~
MOKO...
ohhh...
...SHE'S RECOVERED JUST FINE...
I-I'VE NEVER SEEN HER SMILE LIKE THAT BEFORE...

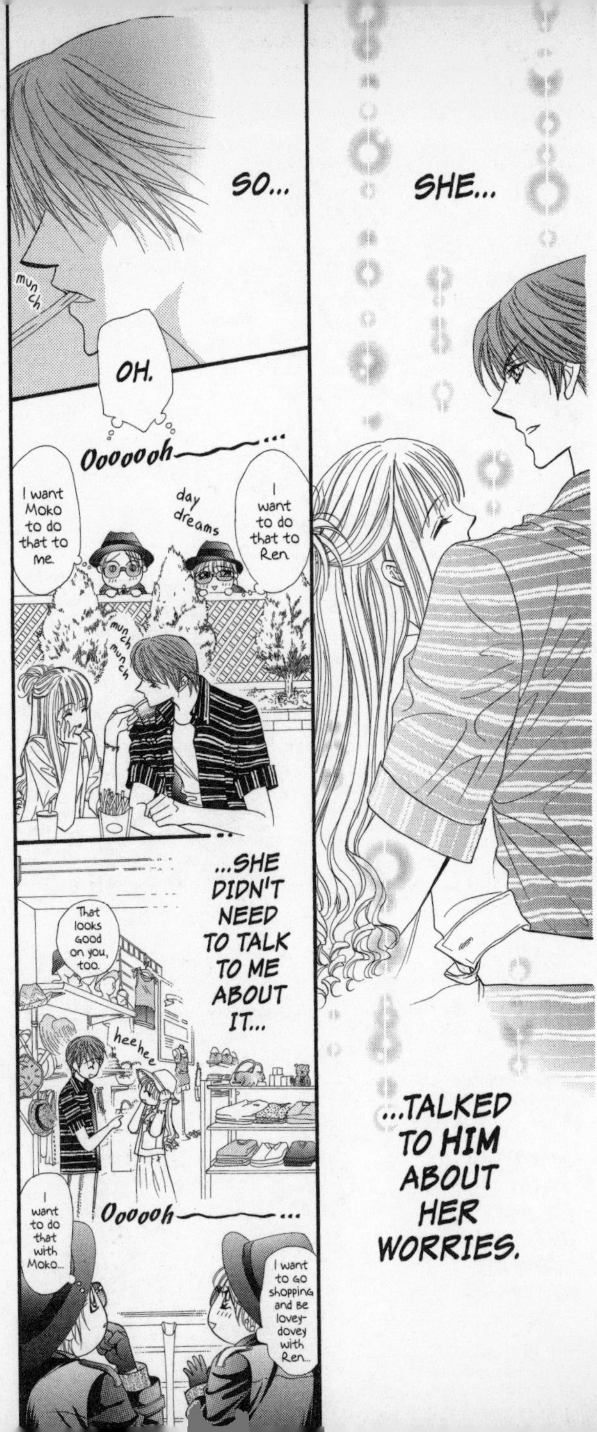
SHE...
...TALKED TO HIM ABOUT HER WORRIES.
SO...
munch
OH.
Ooooooh———...
I want to do that to Ren.
day dreams
I want Moko to do that to me.
munch munch
...SHE DIDN'T NEED TO TALK TO ME ABOUT IT...
That looks good on you, too.
heehee
Ooooh———...
I want to GO shopping and be lovey-dovey with Ren...
I want to do that with Moko...

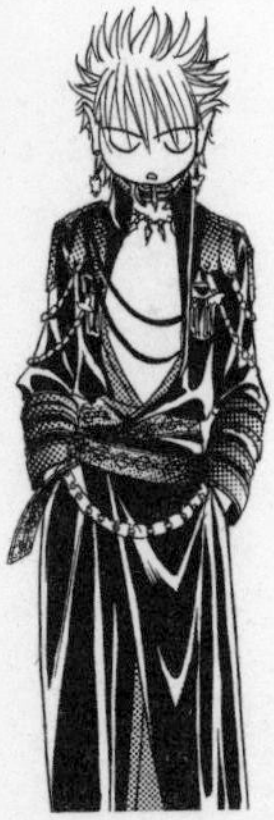

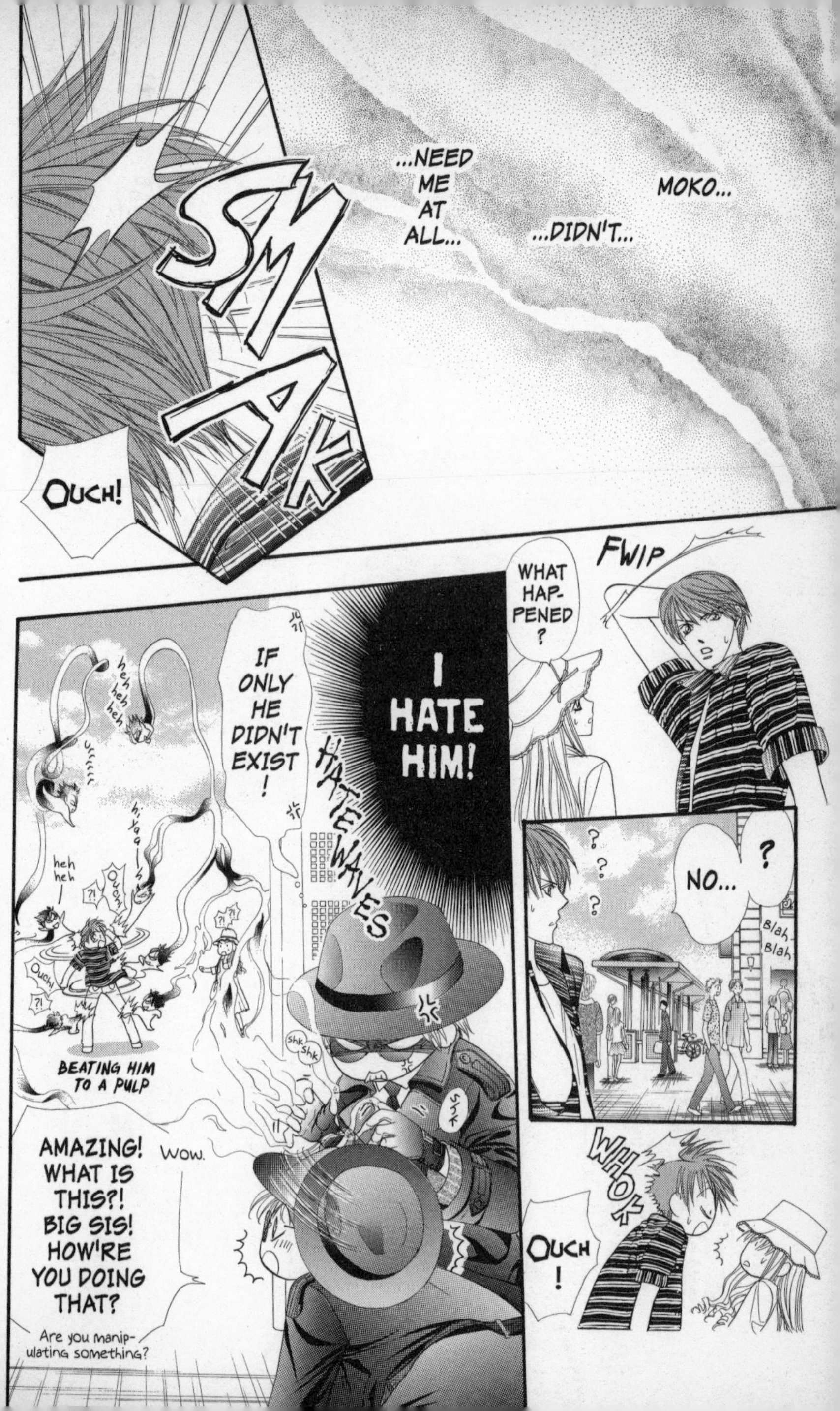
MOKO...
...DIDN'T...
...NEED ME AT ALL...
SMAK
OUCH!
FWIP
WHAT HAP-PENED?
?
NO...
? ? ?
Blah-Blah
WHOK
OUCH!
I HATE HIM!
IF ONLY HE DIDN'T EXIST!
HATE WAVES
heh heh heh
heh heh
Ouch
?!
Ouch!
?!
?!
shk shk
BEATING HIM TO A PULP
AMAZING! WHAT IS THIS?! BIG SIS! HOW'RE YOU DOING THAT?
WOW.
Are you manip-ulating something?

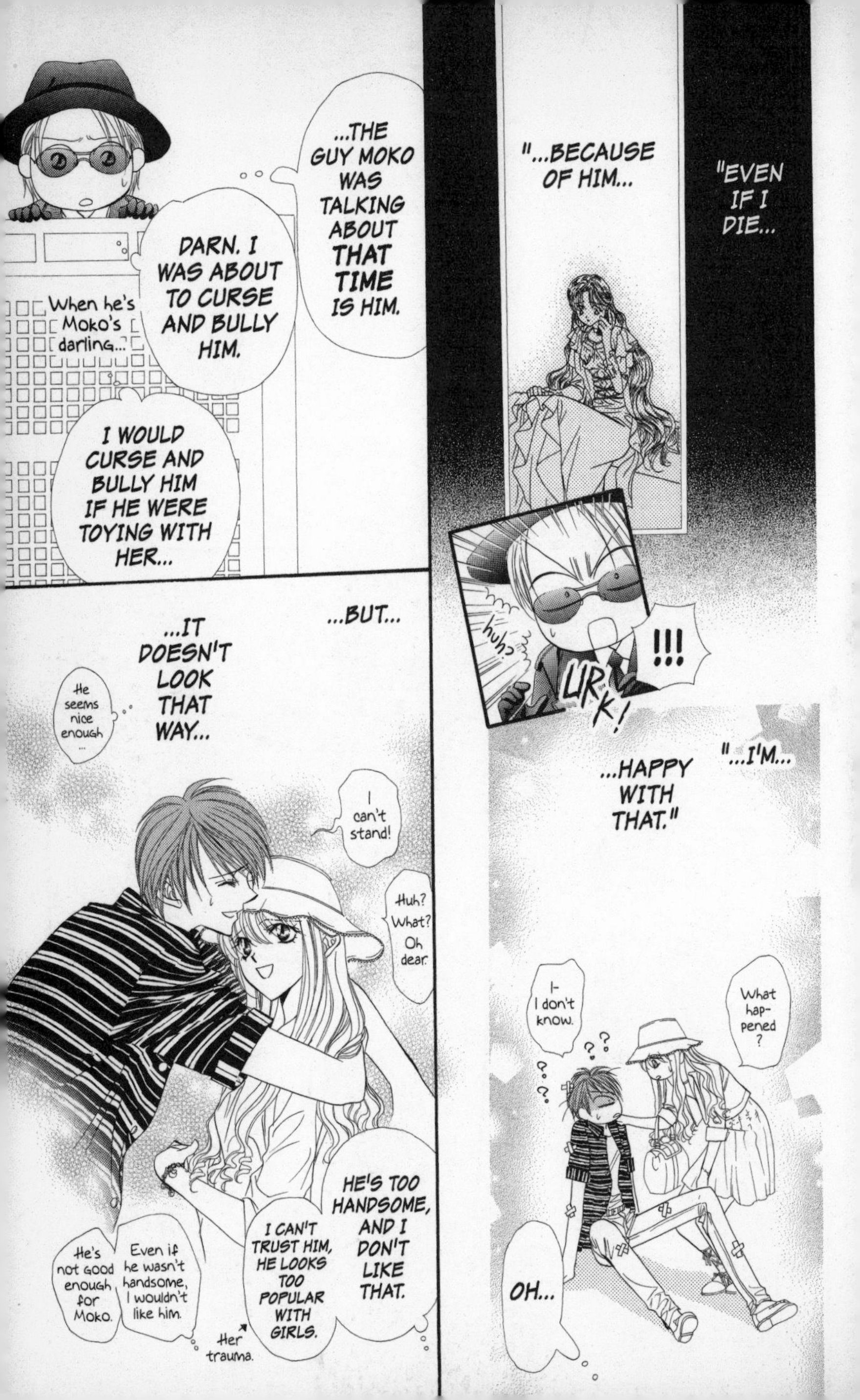
"EVEN IF I DIE...
"...BECAUSE OF HIM...
huh?
!!!
URK!
"...I'M...
...HAPPY WITH THAT."
What hap-pened?
I- I don't know.
OH...
...THE GUY MOKO WAS TALKING ABOUT THAT TIME IS HIM.
DARN. I WAS ABOUT TO CURSE AND BULLY HIM.
When he's Moko's darling...
I WOULD CURSE AND BULLY HIM IF HE WERE TOYING WITH HER...
...BUT...
...IT DOESN'T LOOK THAT WAY...
He seems nice enough...
I can't stand!
Huh? What? Oh dear.
HE'S TOO HANDSOME, AND I DON'T LIKE THAT.
I CAN'T TRUST HIM, HE LOOKS TOO POPULAR WITH GIRLS.
Her trauma.
Even if he wasn't handsome, I wouldn't like him.
He's not good enough for Moko.

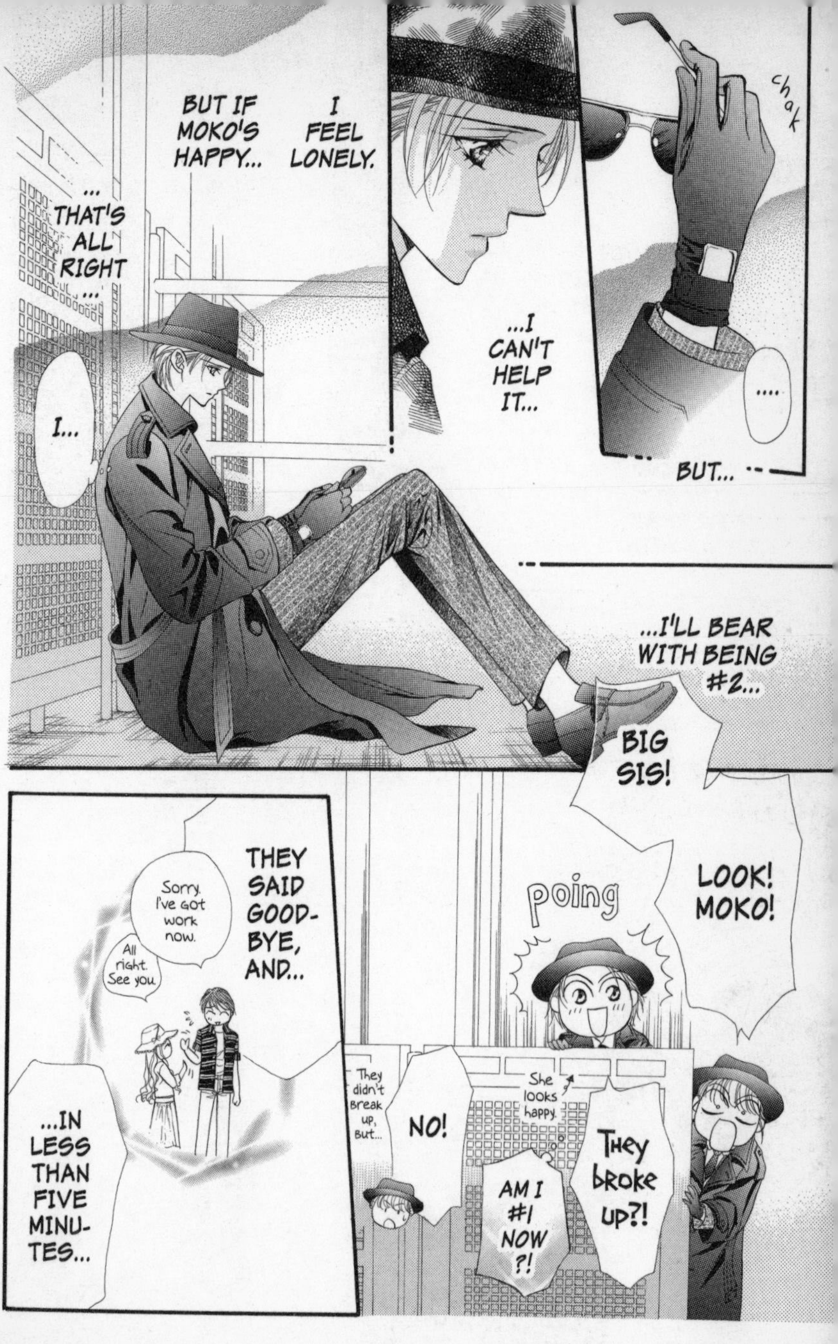
chak
....
BUT...
...I CAN'T HELP IT...
I FEEL LONELY.
BUT IF MOKO'S HAPPY...
...THAT'S ALL RIGHT...
I...
...I'LL BEAR WITH BEING #2...
BIG SIS!
LOOK! MOKO!
poing
They broke up?!
AM I #1 NOW?!
She looks happy.
NO!
They didn't break up, but...
THEY SAID GOODBYE, AND...
Sorry. I've got work now.
All right. See you.
...IN LESS THAN FIVE MINUTES...

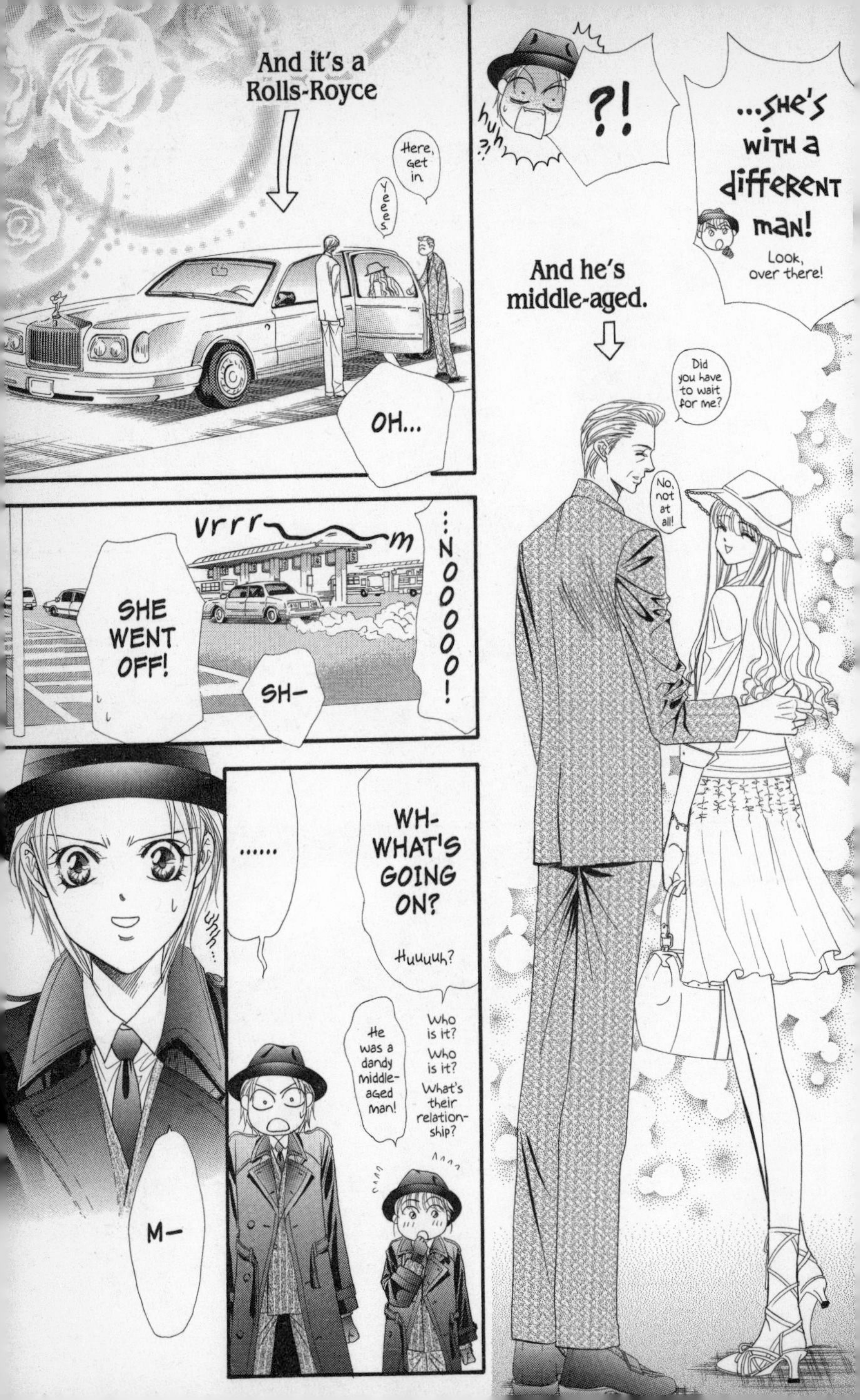
...SHE'S WITH A DIFFERENT MAN!
Look, over there!
?!
huh?!
And he's middle-aged.
Did you have to wait for me?
No, not at all!
And it's a Rolls-Royce
Here, get in.
Yeees.
OH...
Vrrr—m
...NOOOOOO!
SH—
SHE WENT OFF!
WH-WHAT'S GOING ON?
Huuuh?
......
Who is it? Who is it? What's their relationship?
He was a dandy middle-aged man!
uhh...
M—

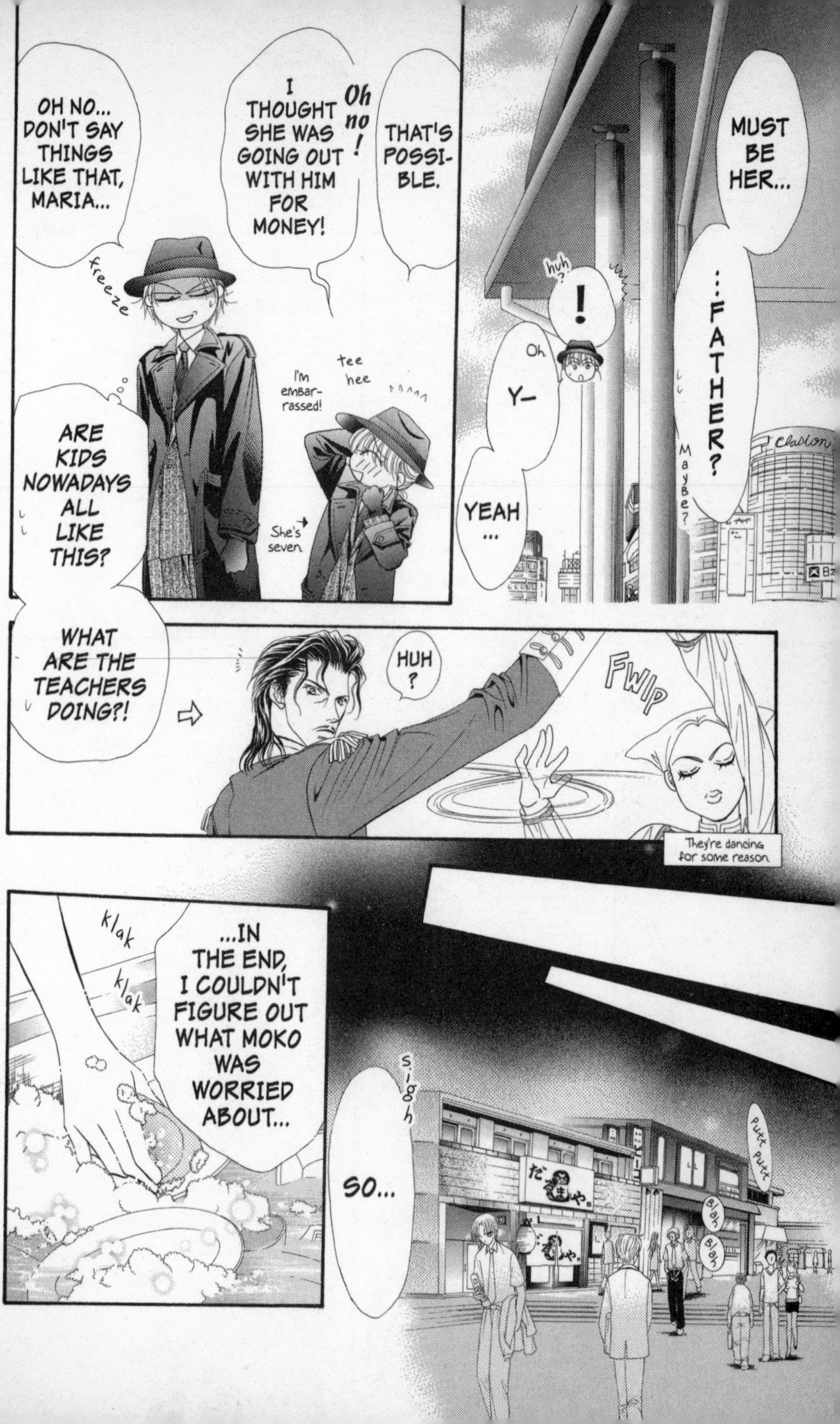
MUST BE HER...
...FATHER?
Maybe?
huh?
!
Oh.
Y–
YEAH...
THAT'S POSSIBLE.
Oh no!
I THOUGHT SHE WAS GOING OUT WITH HIM FOR MONEY!
OH NO... DON'T SAY THINGS LIKE THAT, MARIA...
freeze
tee hee
I'm embarrassed!
She's seven
ARE KIDS NOWADAYS ALL LIKE THIS?
WHAT ARE THE TEACHERS DOING?!
FWIP
HUH?
They're dancing for some reason.
putt putt
Blah
Blah
sigh
SO...
klak
klak
...IN THE END, I COULDN'T FIGURE OUT WHAT MOKO WAS WORRIED ABOUT...

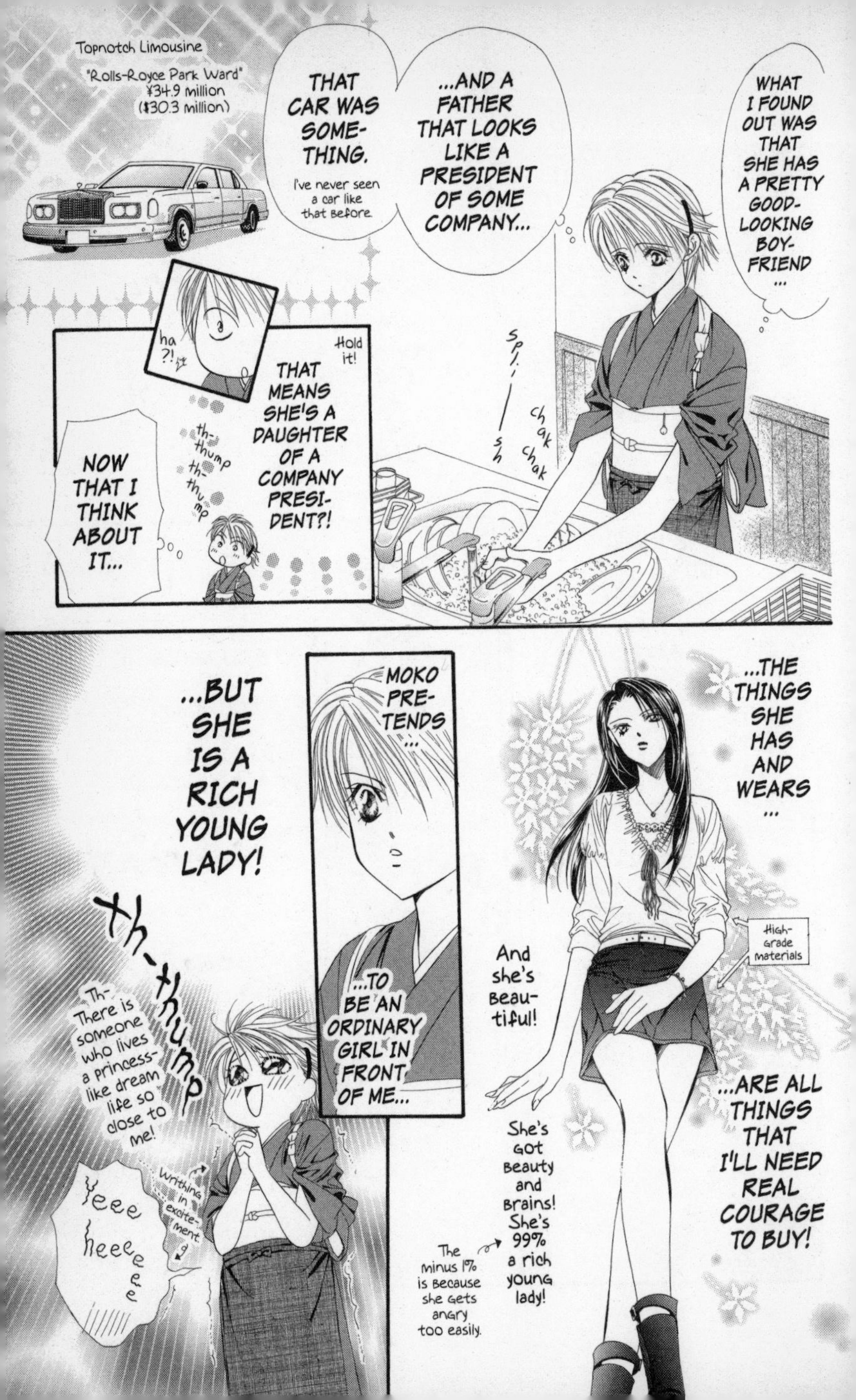
WHAT I FOUND OUT WAS THAT SHE HAS A PRETTY GOOD-LOOKING BOY-FRIEND...
...AND A FATHER THAT LOOKS LIKE A PRESIDENT OF SOME COMPANY...
THAT CAR WAS SOME-THING.
I've never seen a car like that before.
Topnotch Limousine
"Rolls-Royce Park Ward" ¥34.9 million ($30.3 million)
spl-sh
chak chak
Hold it!
THAT MEANS SHE'S A DAUGHTER OF A COMPANY PRESI-DENT?!
ha?!
th-thump th-thump
NOW THAT I THINK ABOUT IT...
...THE THINGS SHE HAS AND WEARS...
High-Grade materials
And she's Beau-tiful!
...ARE ALL THINGS THAT I'LL NEED REAL COURAGE TO BUY!
She's Got Beauty and Brains! She's 99% a rich young lady!
The minus 1% is Because she Gets angry too easily.
MOKO PRE-TENDS...
...TO BE AN ORDINARY GIRL IN FRONT OF ME...
...BUT SHE IS A RICH YOUNG LADY!
th-thump
Th-There is someone who lives a princess-like dream life so close to me!
Writhing in excite-ment
Yeeeheeeeee

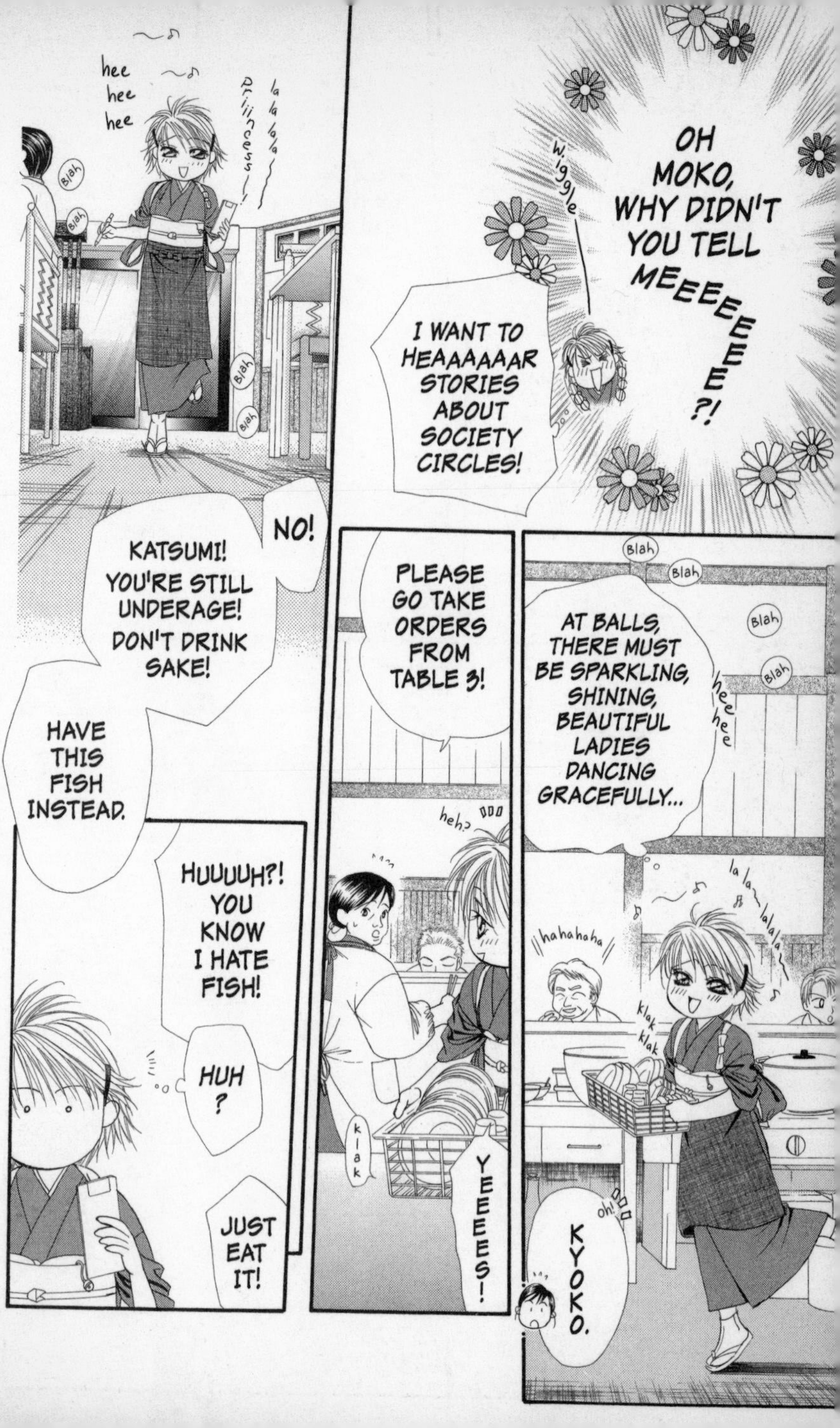
OH MOKO, WHY DIDN'T YOU TELL MEEEEEEEE?!
Wiggle
I WANT TO HEAAAAAR STORIES ABOUT SOCIETY CIRCLES!
Blah
Blah
AT BALLS, THERE MUST BE SPARKLING, SHINING, BEAUTIFUL LADIES DANCING GRACEFULLY...
Blah
Blah
hee hee
la la~ lalala~
hahahaha
klak klak
oh!
KYOKO.
PLEASE GO TAKE ORDERS FROM TABLE 3!
heh?
klak
YEEEES!
hee hee hee
la la la la Priiincess~!
Blah
Blah
Blah
Blah
NO!
KATSUMI! YOU'RE STILL UNDERAGE! DON'T DRINK SAKE!
HAVE THIS FISH INSTEAD.
HUUUUH?! YOU KNOW I HATE FISH!
HUH?
JUST EAT IT!

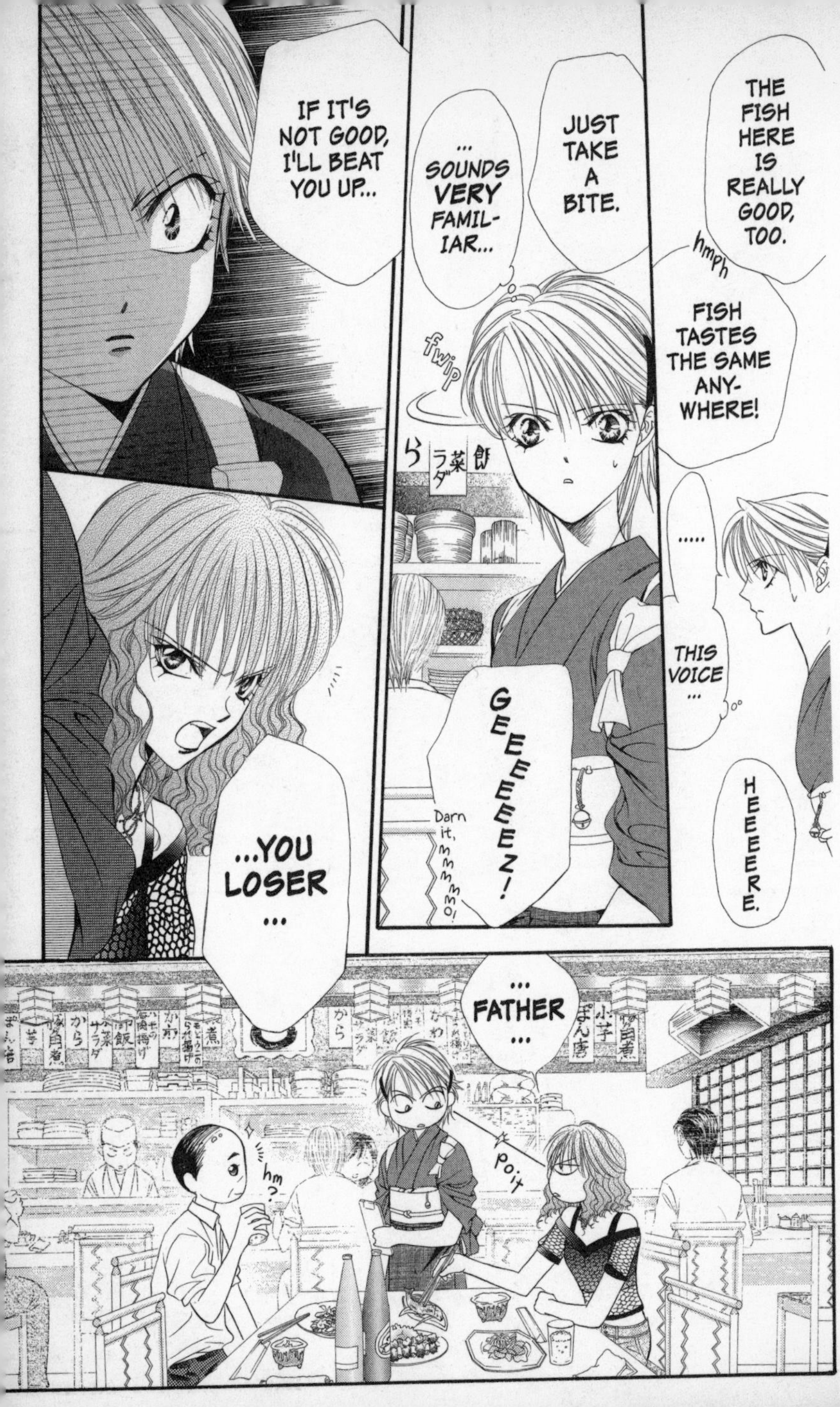
THE FISH HERE IS REALLY GOOD, TOO.
hmph
FISH TASTES THE SAME ANYWHERE!
.....
THIS VOICE...
HEEEERE.
JUST TAKE A BITE.
...SOUNDS VERY FAMILIAR...
fwip
GEEEEEZ!
Darn it, mmmmmo!
IF IT'S NOT GOOD, I'LL BEAT YOU UP...
...YOU LOSER...
...FATHER...
poit
hm?

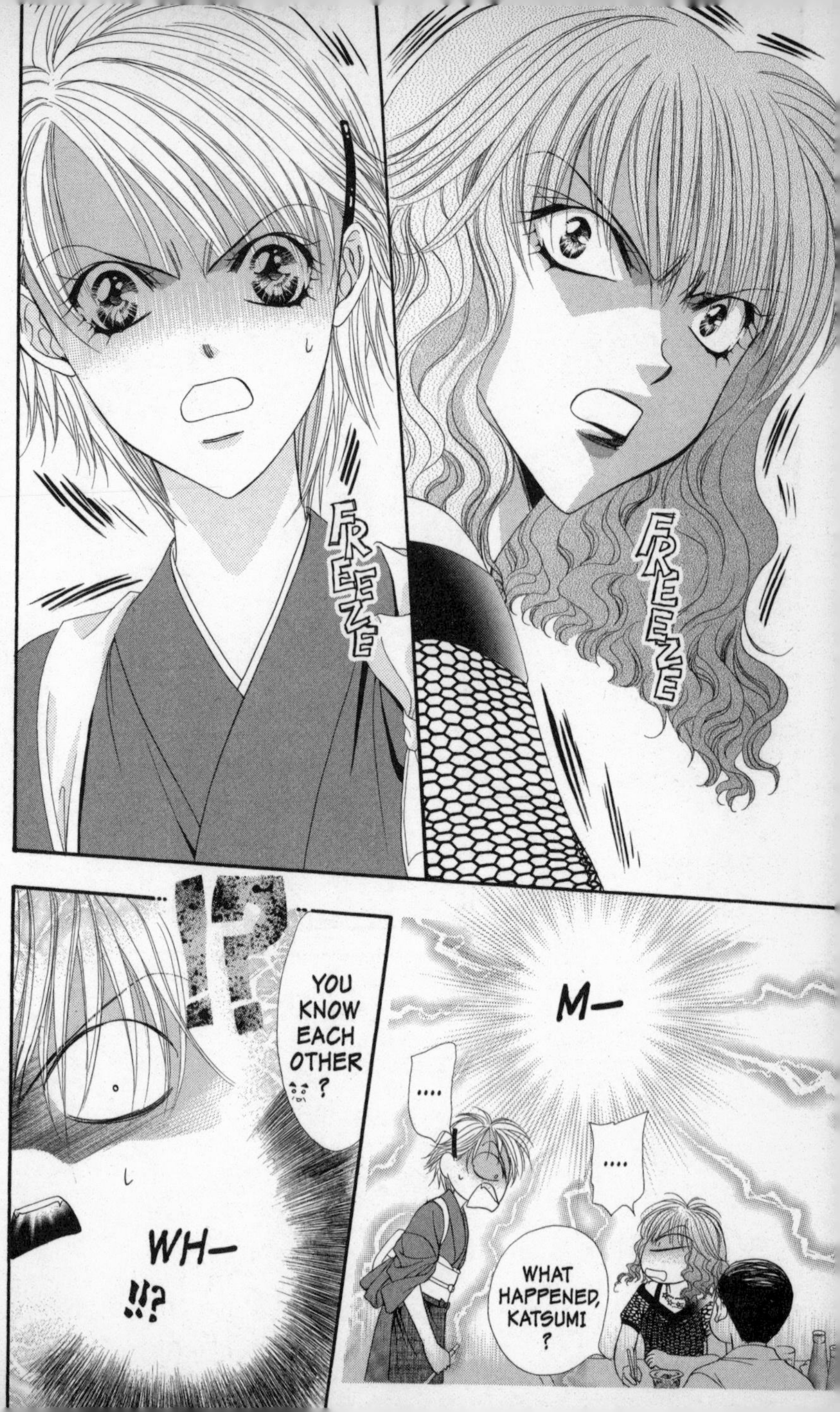
FREEZE
FREEZE
M—
....
....
WHAT HAPPENED, KATSUMI?
!?
YOU KNOW EACH OTHER?
WH— !!?

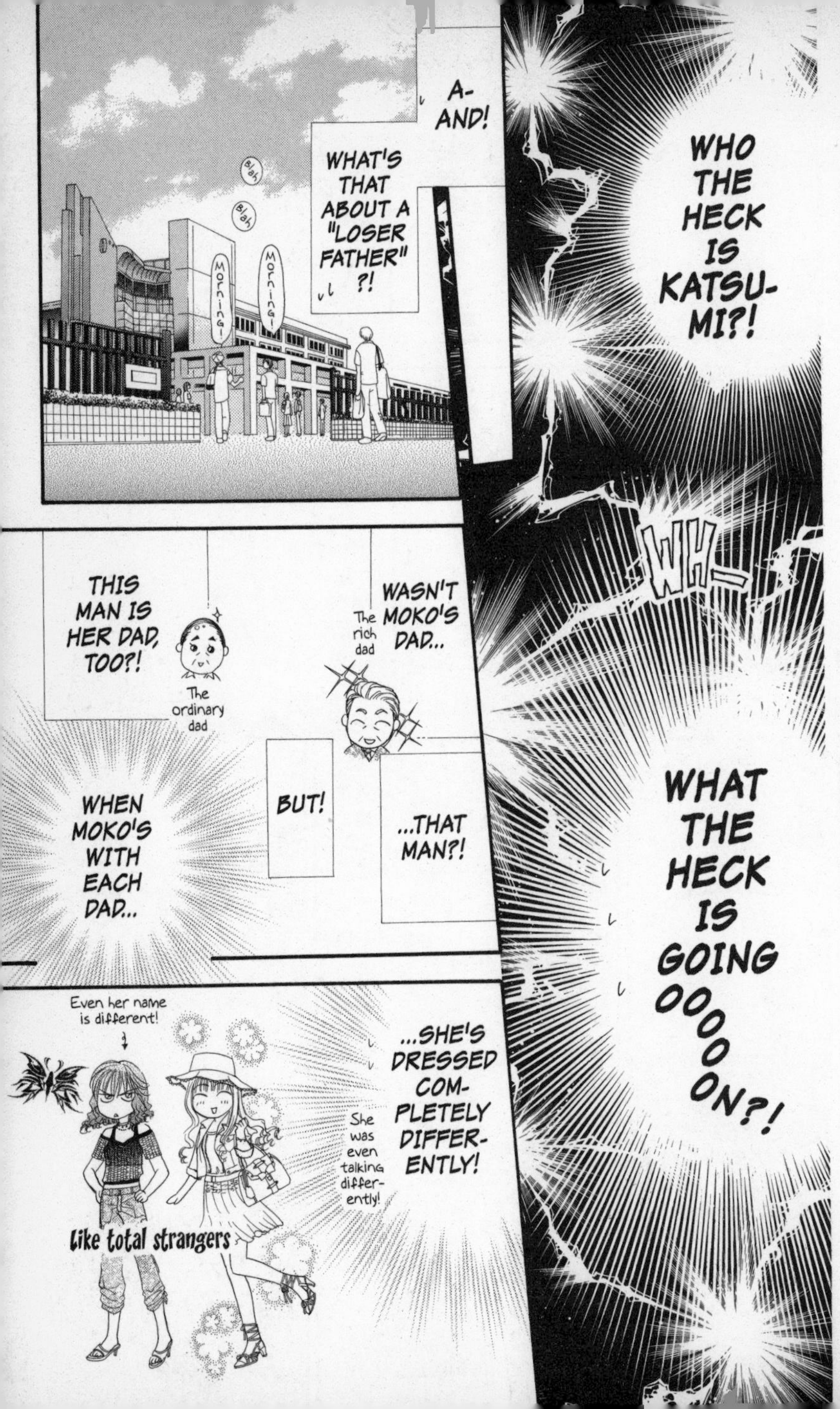
WHO THE HECK IS KATSUMI?!
WH-
WHAT THE HECK IS GOING OOOOOON?!
A-AND!
WHAT'S THAT ABOUT A "LOSER FATHER"?!
Blah
Blah
Morning!
Morning!
WASN'T MOKO'S DAD...
The rich dad
...THAT MAN?!
BUT!
THIS MAN IS HER DAD, TOO?!
The ordinary dad
WHEN MOKO'S WITH EACH DAD...
...SHE'S DRESSED COMPLETELY DIFFERENTLY!
She was even talking differently!
Even her name is different!
Like total strangers

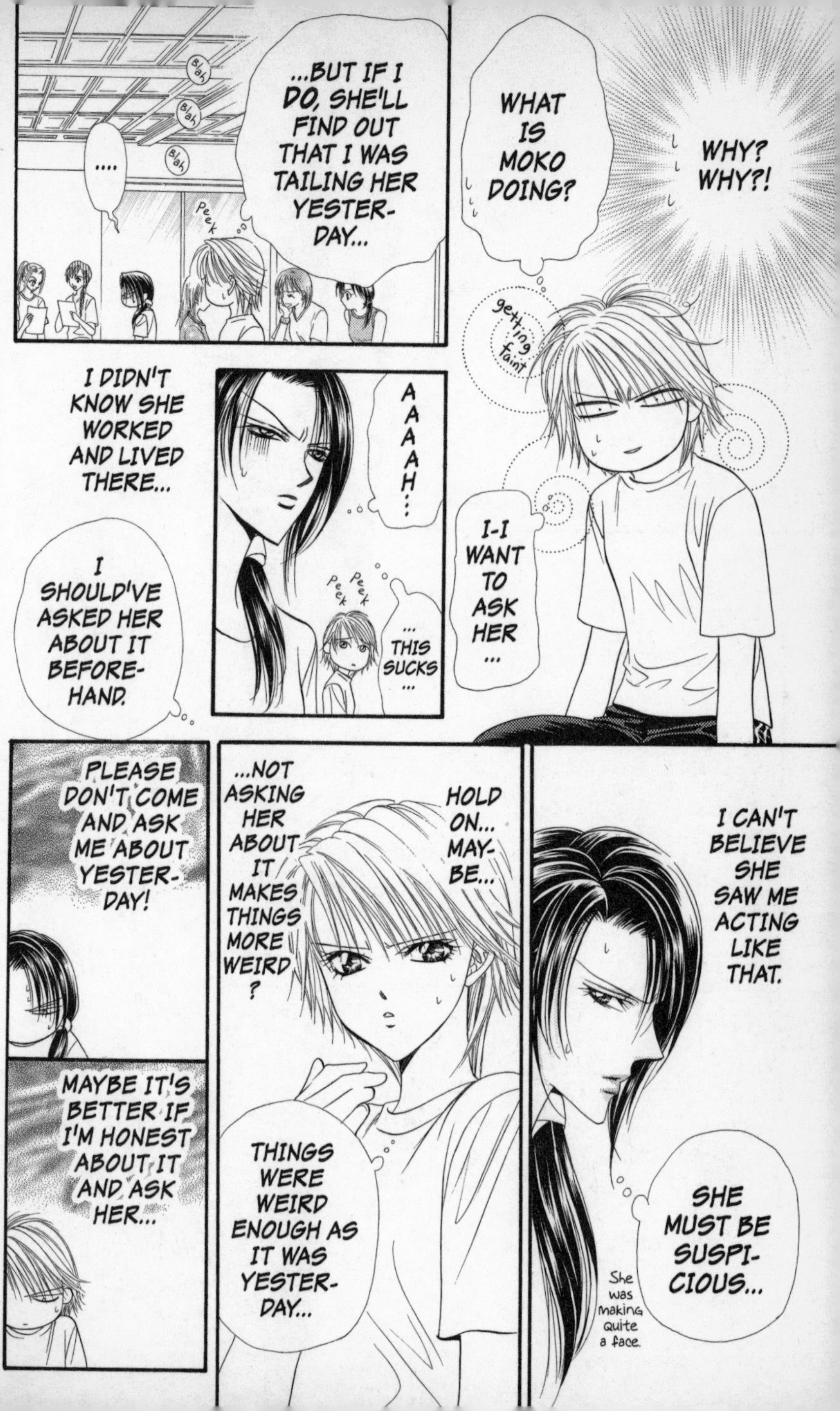
WHY? WHY?!
WHAT IS MOKO DOING?
getting faint
I-I WANT TO ASK HER...
...BUT IF I DO, SHE'LL FIND OUT THAT I WAS TAILING HER YESTERDAY...
Blah
Blah
Blah
Peek
....
AAAAH...
Peek Peek
...THIS SUCKS...
I DIDN'T KNOW SHE WORKED AND LIVED THERE...
I SHOULD'VE ASKED HER ABOUT IT BEFOREHAND.
I CAN'T BELIEVE SHE SAW ME ACTING LIKE THAT.
SHE MUST BE SUSPICIOUS...
She was making quite a face.
HOLD ON... MAYBE...
...NOT ASKING HER ABOUT IT MAKES THINGS MORE WEIRD?
THINGS WERE WEIRD ENOUGH AS IT WAS YESTERDAY...
PLEASE DON'T COME AND ASK ME ABOUT YESTERDAY!
MAYBE IT'S BETTER IF I'M HONEST ABOUT IT AND ASK HER...

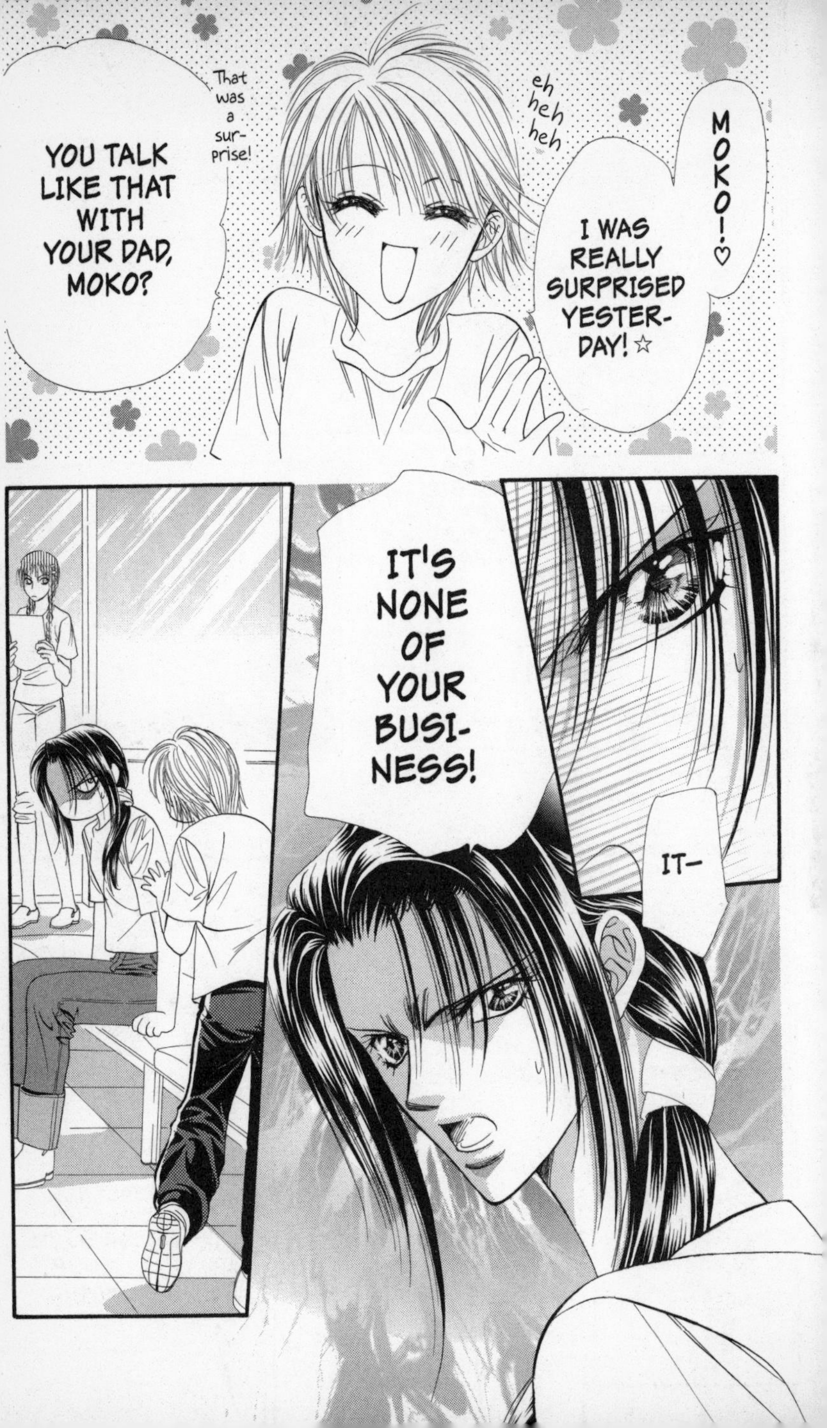
MOKO!♡
I WAS REALLY SURPRISED YESTERDAY!☆
eh heh heh
That was a surprise!
YOU TALK LIKE THAT WITH YOUR DAD, MOKO?
IT—
IT'S NONE OF YOUR BUSINESS!

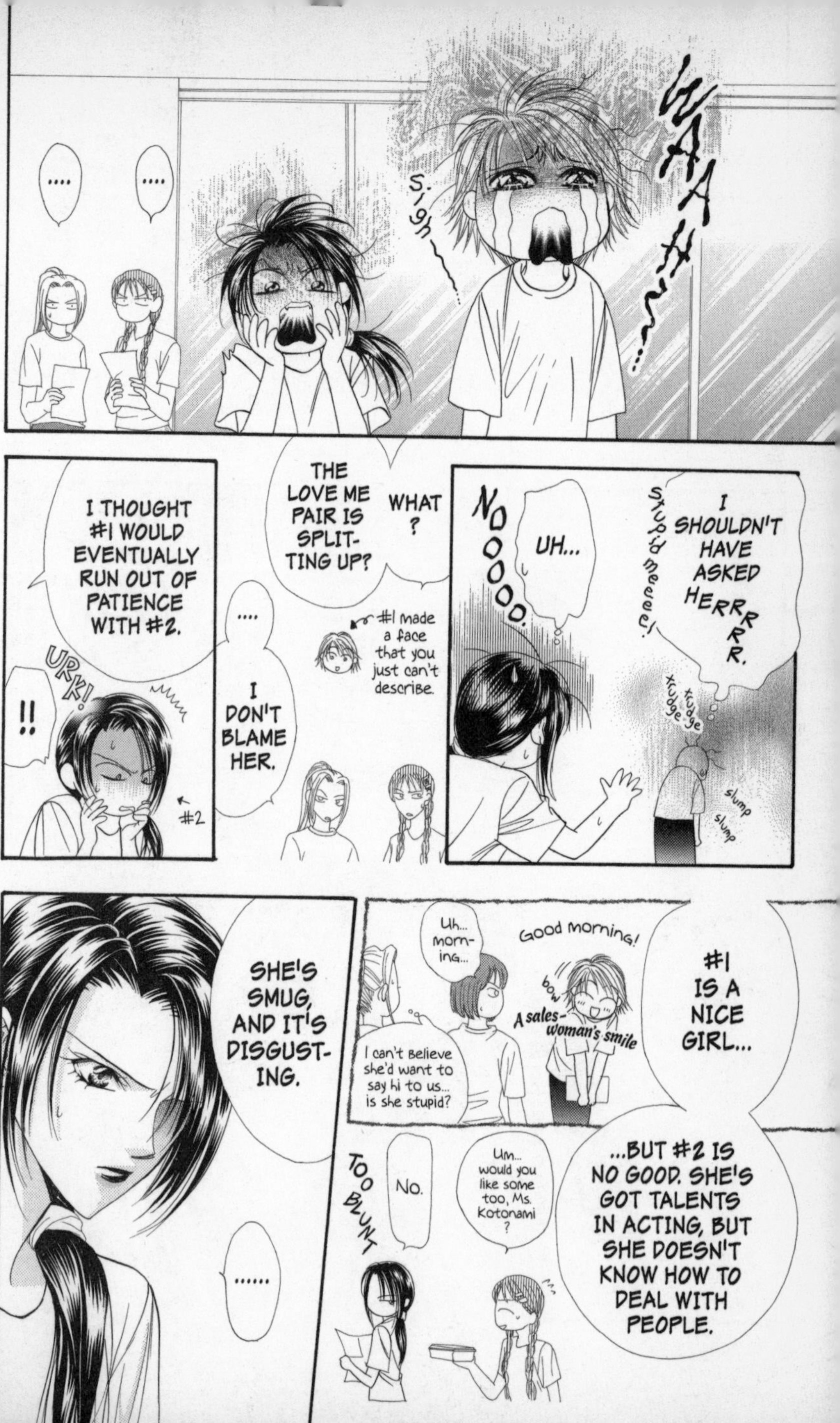
WAAHH~~...
Sigh~~...
....
....
I SHOULDN'T HAVE ASKED HERRRR.
stupid meeee!
NOOOOOO.
UH...
trudge trudge
slump slump
THE LOVE ME PAIR IS SPLITTING UP?
WHAT?
....
#1 made a face that you just can't describe.
I DON'T BLAME HER.
I THOUGHT #1 WOULD EVENTUALLY RUN OUT OF PATIENCE WITH #2.
URK!
!!
#2
#1 IS A NICE GIRL...
Good morning!
bow
A sales-woman's smile
Uh... morning...
I can't believe she'd want to say hi to us... is she stupid?
...BUT #2 IS NO GOOD. SHE'S GOT TALENTS IN ACTING, BUT SHE DOESN'T KNOW HOW TO DEAL WITH PEOPLE.
Um... would you like some too, Ms. Kotonami?
No.
TOO BLUNT
......
SHE'S SMUG, AND IT'S DISGUSTING.

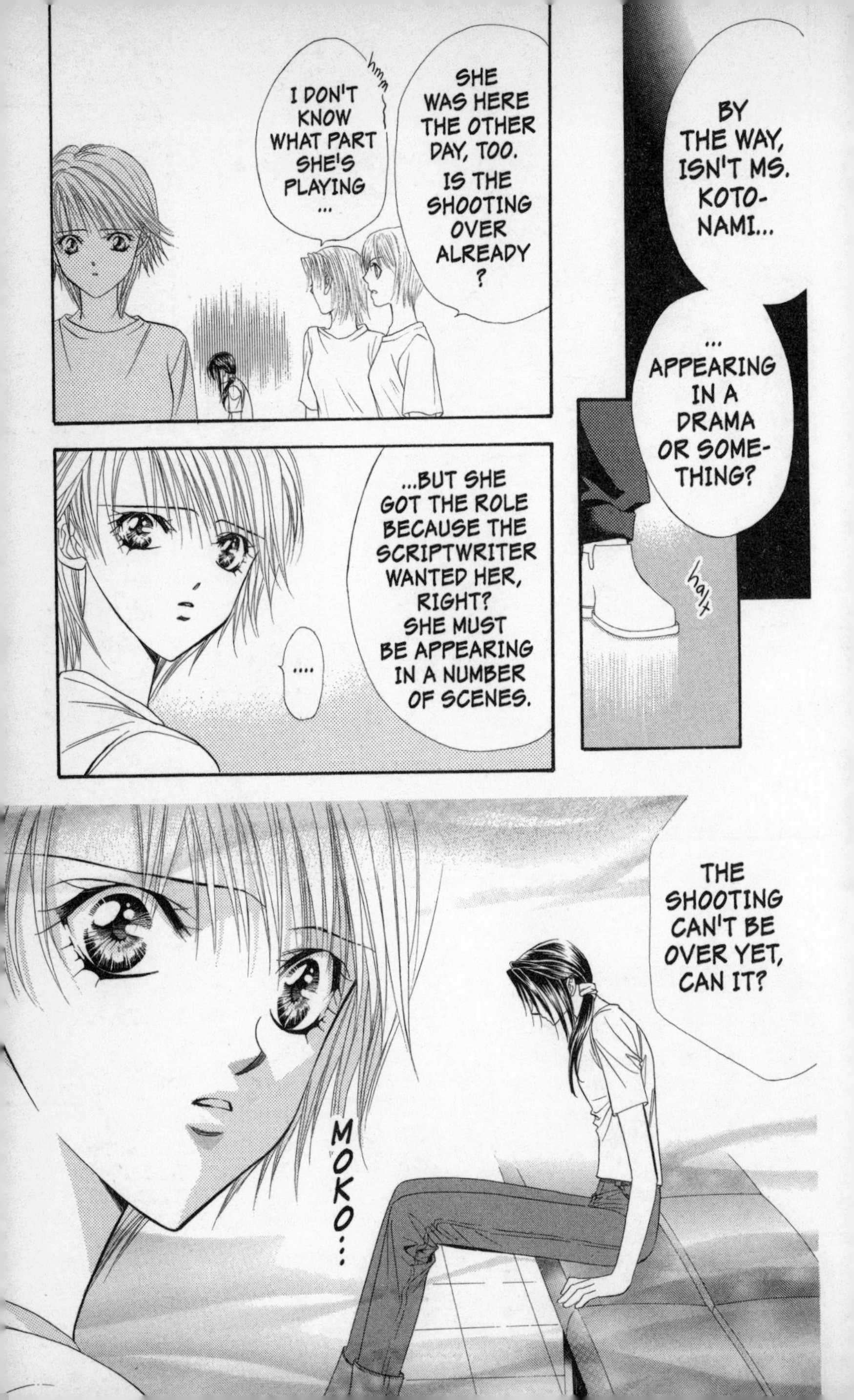
BY THE WAY, ISN'T MS. KOTO-NAMI...
...APPEARING IN A DRAMA OR SOME-THING?
halt
SHE WAS HERE THE OTHER DAY, TOO. IS THE SHOOTING OVER ALREADY?
hmm
I DON'T KNOW WHAT PART SHE'S PLAYING...
...BUT SHE GOT THE ROLE BECAUSE THE SCRIPTWRITER WANTED HER, RIGHT? SHE MUST BE APPEARING IN A NUMBER OF SCENES.
....
THE SHOOTING CAN'T BE OVER YET, CAN IT?
MOKO...

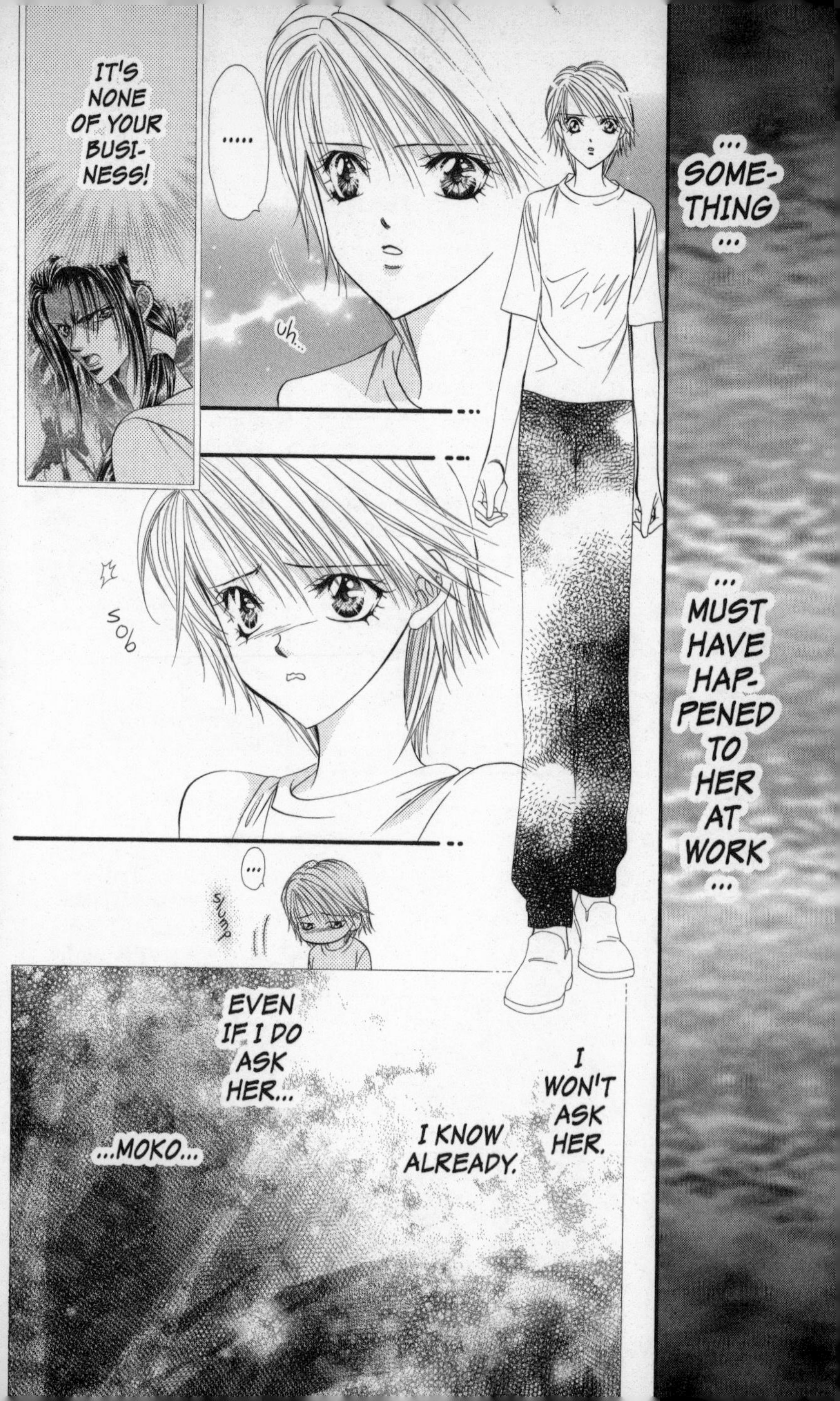
... SOMETHING ...
... MUST HAVE HAPPENED TO HER AT WORK ...
.....
uh...
IT'S NONE OF YOUR BUSINESS!
——...
——...
sob
——...
...
slump
I WON'T ASK HER.
I KNOW ALREADY.
EVEN IF I DO ASK HER...
...MOKO...

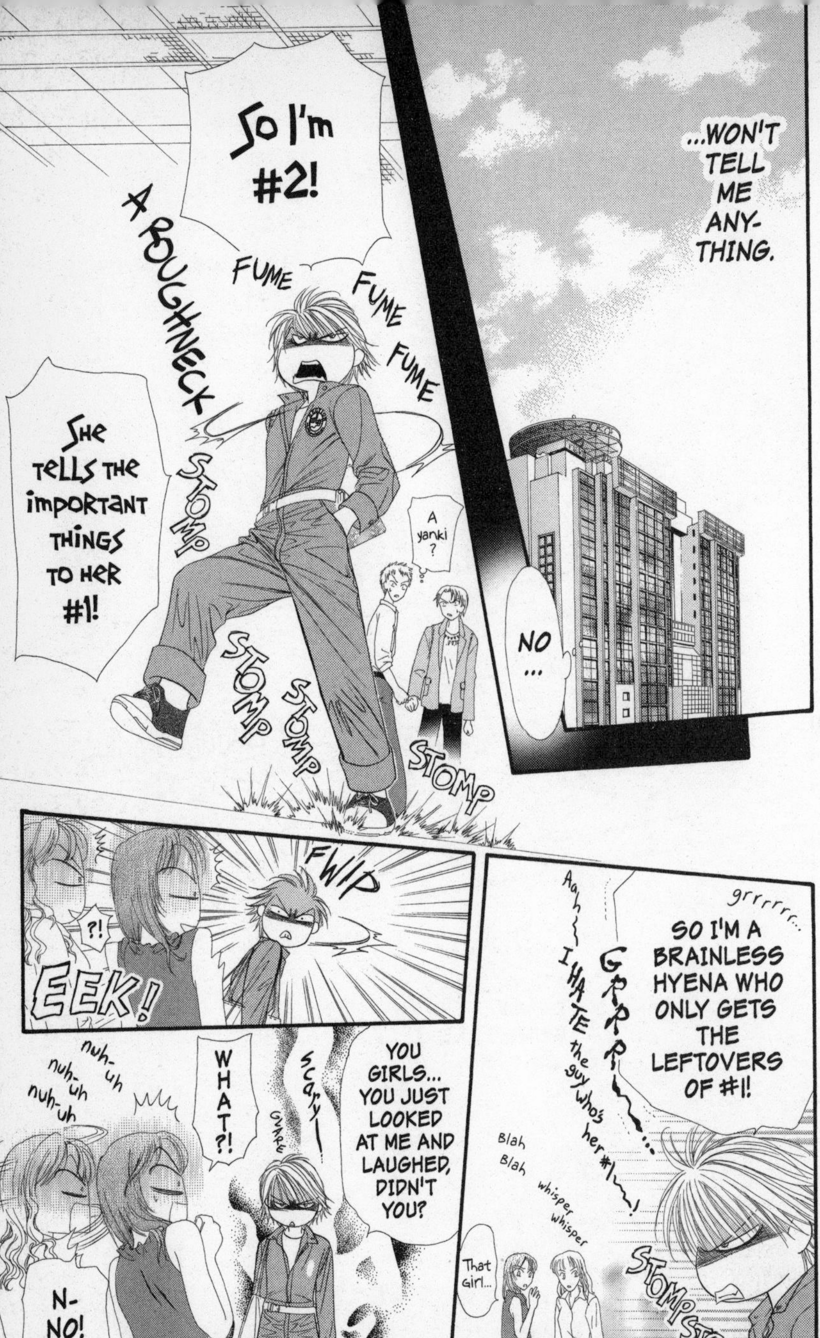
...WON'T TELL ME ANY-THING.
NO ...
So I'm #2!
A ROUGHNECK
FUME
FUME
FUME
She tells the important things to her #1!
STOMP
A yanki?
STOMP
STOMP
STOMP
grrrrrr...
SO I'M A BRAINLESS HYENA WHO ONLY GETS THE LEFTOVERS OF #1!
GRRR...
Aah~ I HATE the guy who's her #1~!
Blah Blah
whisper whisper
That girl...
STOMPSTOMP
FWIP
?!
EEK!
YOU GIRLS... YOU JUST LOOKED AT ME AND LAUGHED, DIDN'T YOU?
scary
GLARE
WHAT?!
nuh-uh nuh-uh nuh-uh
N-NO!

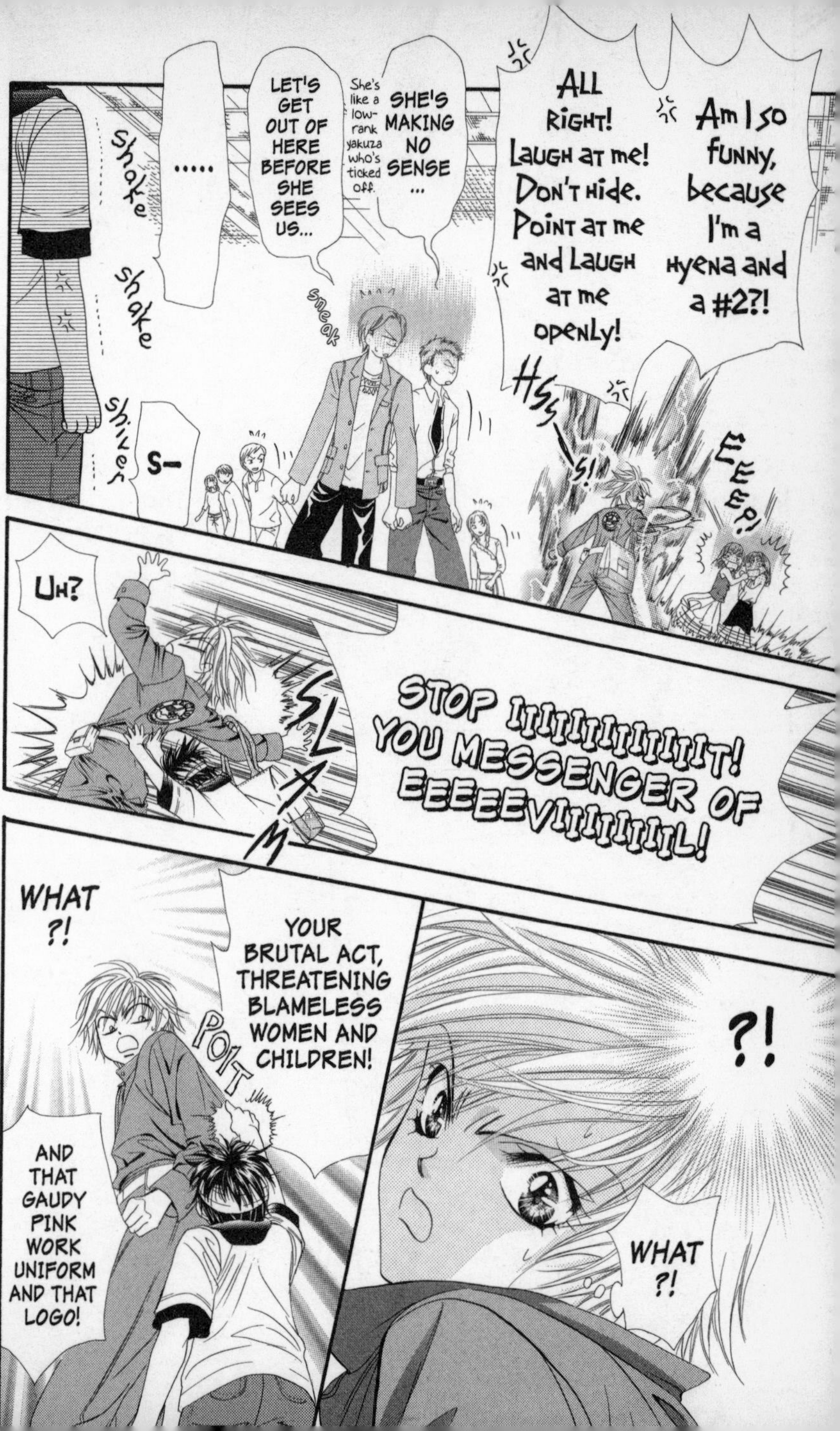
Am I so funny, because I'm a hyena and a #2?!
All right! Laugh at me! Don't hide. Point at me and laugh at me openly!
HSS-S!
EEEP?!
SHE'S MAKING NO SENSE...
She's like a low-rank yakuza who's ticked off.
sneak
LET'S GET OUT OF HERE BEFORE SHE SEES US...
......
shake
shake
shiver
S–
STOP IIIIIIIIIIIIT! YOU MESSENGER OF EEEEEVIIIIIIIL!
SLAM
UH?
?!
WHAT ?!
YOUR BRUTAL ACT, THREATENING BLAMELESS WOMEN AND CHILDREN!
POIT
WHAT ?!
AND THAT GAUDY PINK WORK UNIFORM AND THAT LOGO!

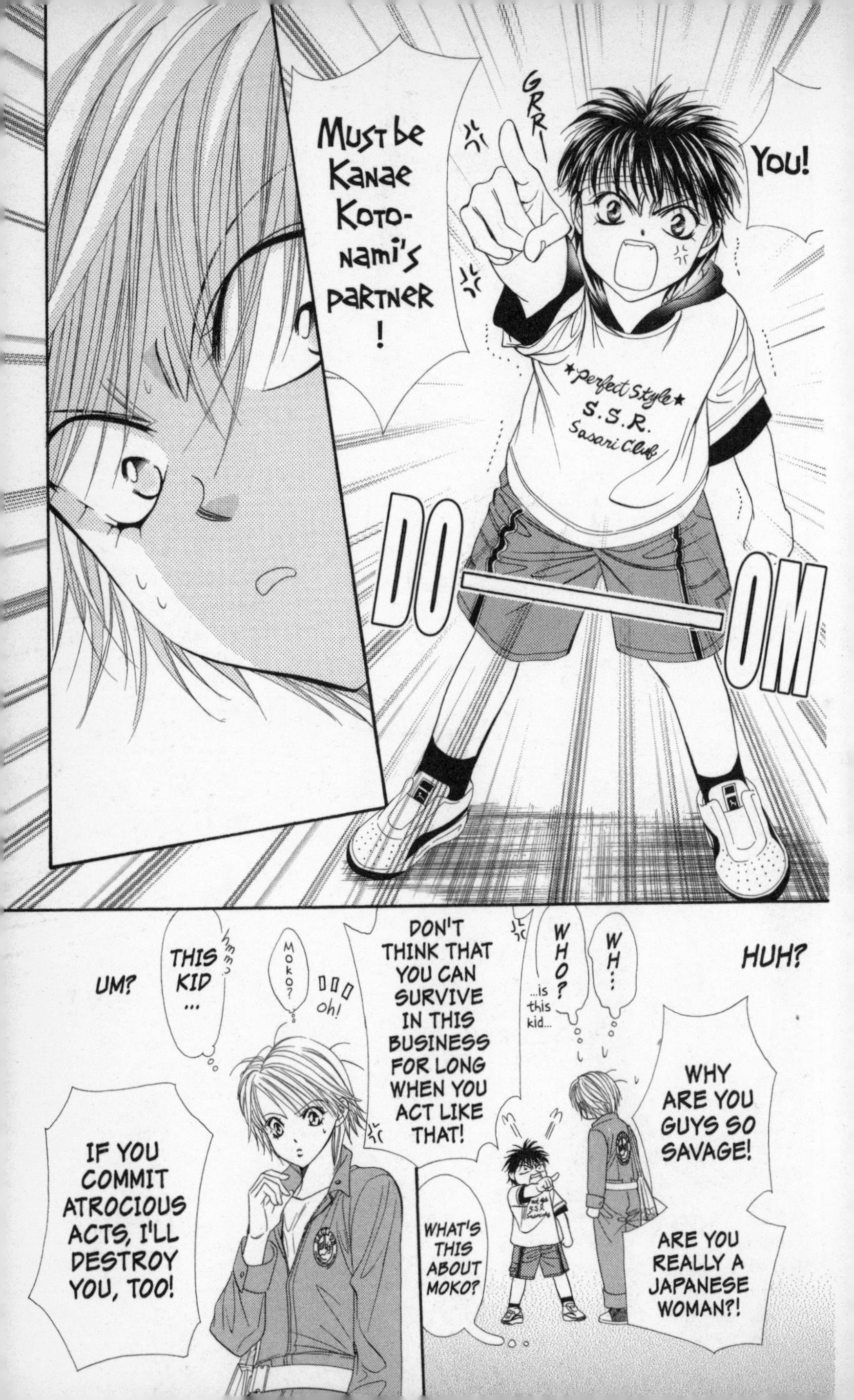
GRR
You!
Must be Kanae Koto-nami's partner!
DO-OM
HUH?
WH...
WHO?
...is this kid...
DON'T THINK THAT YOU CAN SURVIVE IN THIS BUSINESS FOR LONG WHEN YOU ACT LIKE THAT!
MOKO?
oh!
THIS KID ...
hmm?
UM?
WHY ARE YOU GUYS SO SAVAGE!
ARE YOU REALLY A JAPANESE WOMAN?!
WHAT'S THIS ABOUT MOKO?
IF YOU COMMIT ATROCIOUS ACTS, I'LL DESTROY YOU, TOO!

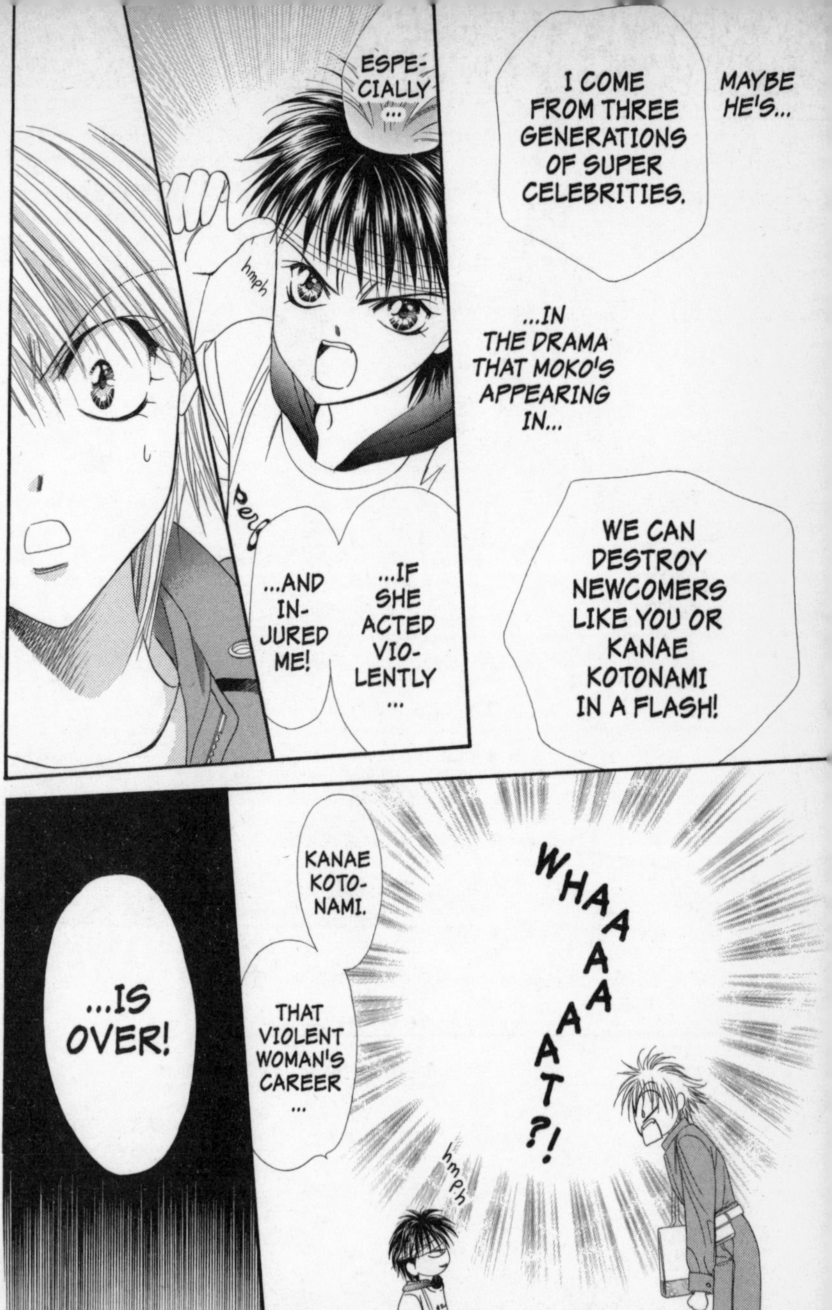
MAYBE HE'S...
I COME FROM THREE GENERATIONS OF SUPER CELEBRITIES.
WE CAN DESTROY NEWCOMERS LIKE YOU OR KANAE KOTONAMI IN A FLASH!
ESPE-CIALLY...
...IN THE DRAMA THAT MOKO'S APPEARING IN...
hmph
...IF SHE ACTED VIO-LENTLY...
...AND IN-JURED ME!
WHAAAAAAAT?!
KANAE KOTO-NAMI.
THAT VIOLENT WOMAN'S CAREER...
hmph
...IS OVER!

End of Act 48

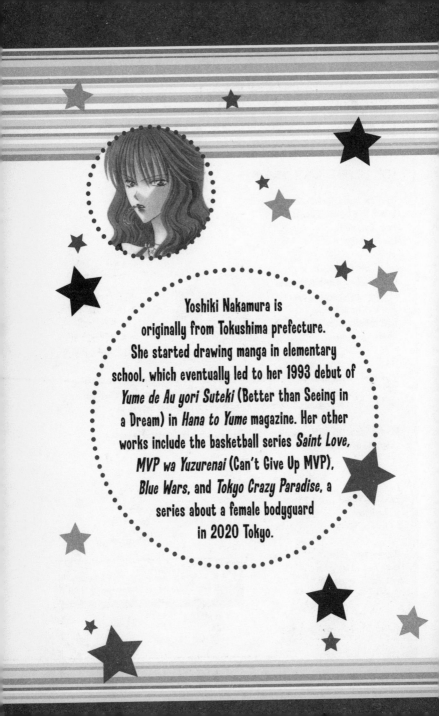

Yoshiki Nakamura is
originally from Tokushima prefecture.
She started drawing manga in elementary
school, which eventually led to her 1993 debut of
*Yume de Au yori Suteki* (Better than Seeing in
a Dream) in *Hana to Yume* magazine. Her other
works include the basketball series *Saint Love*,
*MVP wa Yuzurenai* (Can't Give Up MVP),
*Blue Wars*, and *Tokyo Crazy Paradise*, a
series about a female bodyguard
in 2020 Tokyo.

# SKIP·BEAT!
## Vol. 8
### The Shojo Beat Manga Edition

STORY AND ART BY YOSHIKI NAKAMURA

English Translation & Adaptation/Tomo Kimura
Touch-up Art & Lettering/Sabrina Heep
Design/Yukiko Whitley
Editor/Pancha Diaz

Editor in Chief, Books/Alvin Lu
Editor in Chief, Magazines/Marc Weidenbaum
VP of Publishing Licensing/Rika Inouye
VP of Sales/Gonzalo Ferreyra
Sr. VP of Marketing/Liza Coppola
Publisher/Hyoe Narita



Printed in Canada

Published by VIZ Media, LLC
P.O. Box 77010
San Francisco, CA 94107

store.viz.com

Shojo Beat Manga Edition
10 9 8 7 6 5 4 3 2
First printing, September 2007
Second printing, October 2007

RATED T FOR TEEN

**PARENTAL ADVISORY**
SKIP·BEAT! is rated T for Teen and is recommended for ages 13 and up. This volume contains suggestive themes.

ratings.viz.com

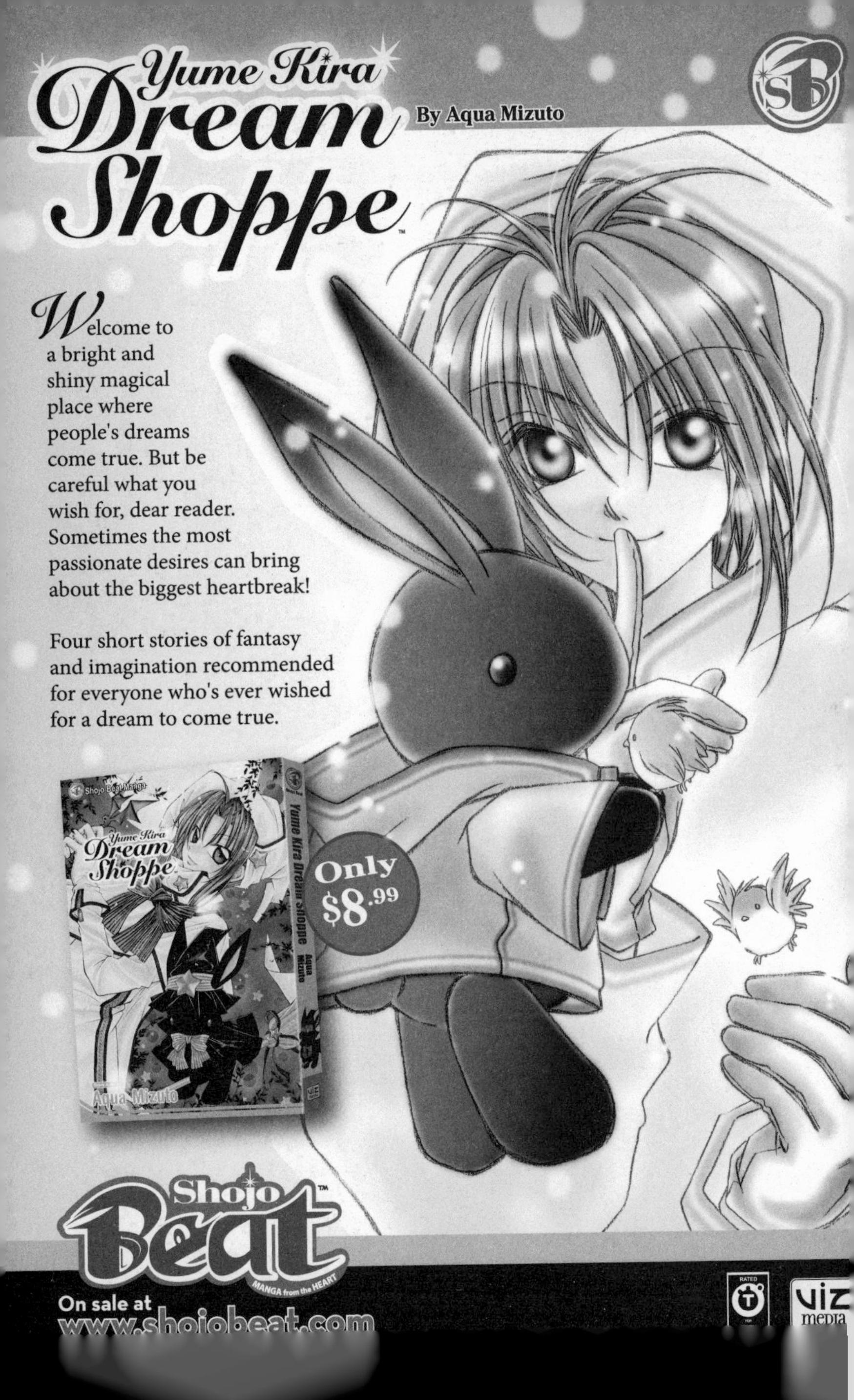
Yume Kira Dream Shoppe
By Aqua Mizuto
Welcome to a bright and shiny magical place where people's dreams come true. But be careful what you wish for, dear reader. Sometimes the most passionate desires can bring about the biggest heartbreak!
Four short stories of fantasy and imagination recommended for everyone who's ever wished for a dream to come true.
Shojo Beat Manga
Yume Kira Dream Shoppe
Aqua Mizuto
Only $8.99
Shojo Beat
MANGA from the HEART
On sale at
www.shojobeat.com
RATED T
VIZ media

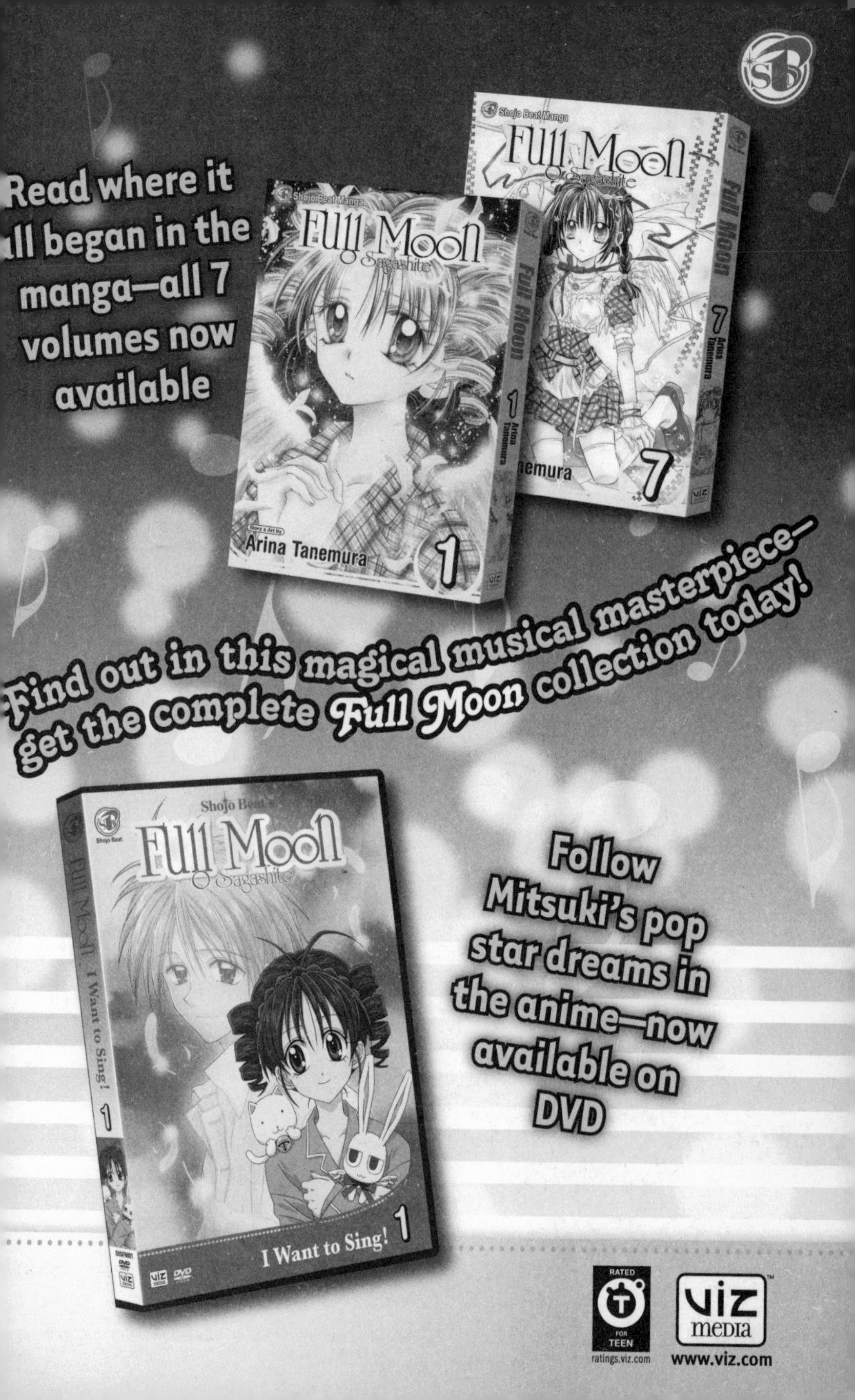
Read where it
ll began in the
manga—all 7
volumes now
available
Shojo Beat Manga
Full Moon
O Sagashite
Arina Tanemura
1
7
Find out in this magical musical masterpiece—
get the complete Full Moon collection today!
Shojo Beat's
Full Moon
O Sagashite
I Want to Sing! 1
Follow
Mitsuki's pop
star dreams in
the anime—now
available on
DVD
RATED T FOR TEEN
ratings.viz.com
VIZ media
www.viz.com

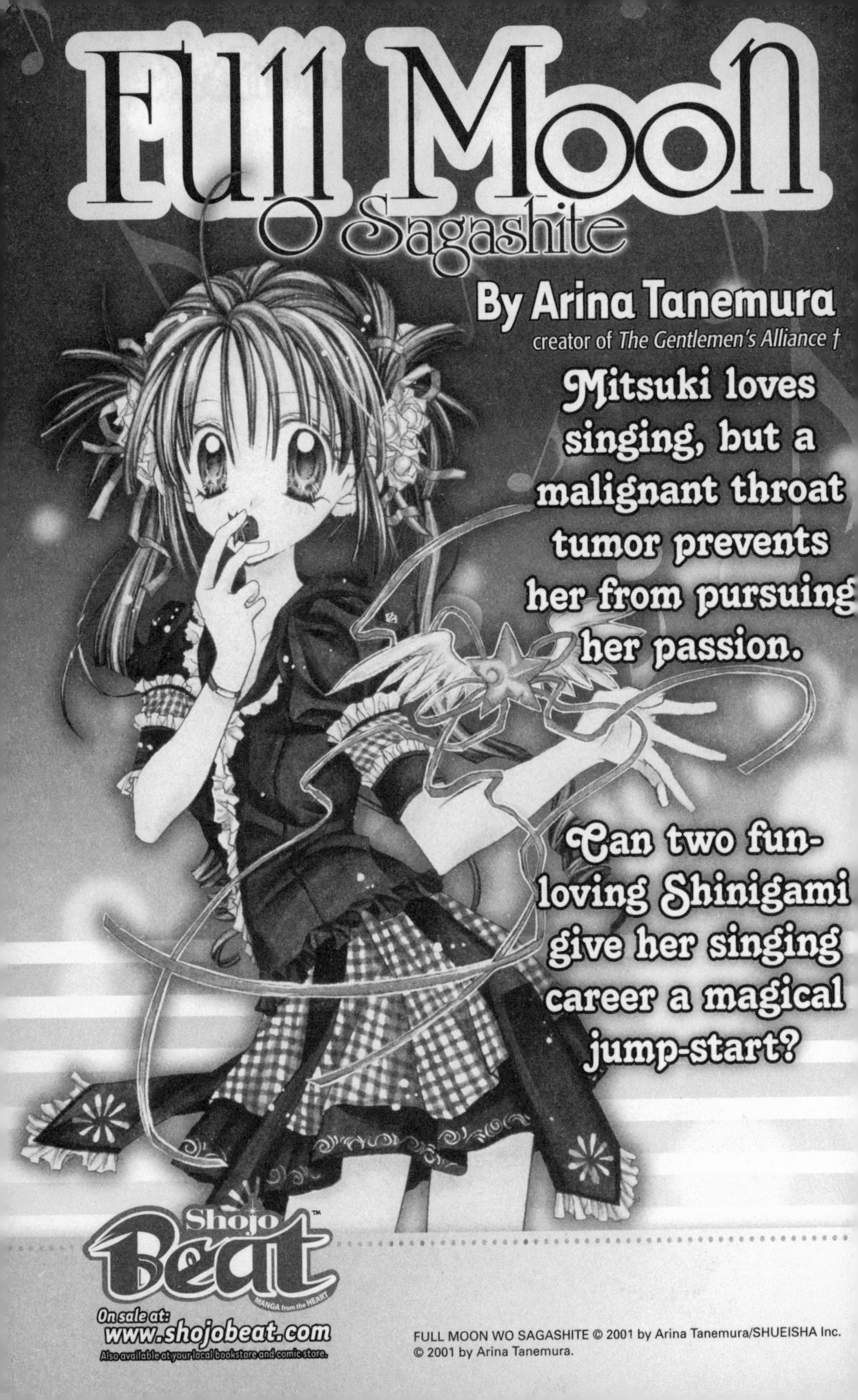
Full Moon
O Sagashite
By Arina Tanemura
creator of The Gentlemen's Alliance †
Mitsuki loves singing, but a malignant throat tumor prevents her from pursuing her passion.
Can two fun-loving Shinigami give her singing career a magical jump-start?
Shojo Beat™
MANGA from the HEART
On sale at:
www.shojobeat.com
Also available at your local bookstore and comic store.

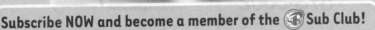